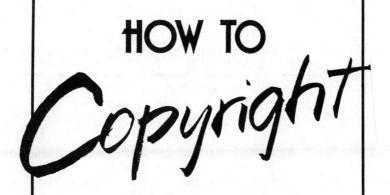

HOW TO
Copyright
SOFTWARE

By Attorney M.J. Salone
Legal Editor: Stephen Elias

Illustrations by Mari Stein

NOLO PRESS   950 Parker St., Berkeley, CA 94710

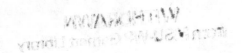

Printing History

Nolo Press is committed to keeping its books up-to-date. Each new printing, whether or not it is called a new edition, has been completely revised to reflect the latest law changes. This book was printed and updated on the last date indicated below. If this book is out-of-date, do not rely on the information without checking it in a newer edition.

First Edition   November 1984

PLEASE READ THIS: We have done our best to give you useful and accurate information concerning everything you need to know about copyright protection for your computer programs and output. But please be aware that laws and procedures are constantly changing and are subject to differing interpretations. You have the responsibility to check all material you read here before relying on it. Of necessity, neither Nolo Press nor the author makes any guarantees concerning the information in this book or the use to which it is put.

Mari Stein	Illustrations
Stephanie Harolde	Production & Copyediting
Sue Imperial	
Keija Kimura	Book Design & Layout
Toni Ihara	
Miriam Maxwell	Index

ISBN   0-917316-79-7
Library of Congress Card Catalog No.: 84-061587
© copyright 1984 by M.J. Salone

Acknowledgements

My heartfelt thanks to Dennis Everett and Larry Schultz of the United States Copyright Office. Both patiently answered many long and involved questions and contributed a number of suggestions that made this a better book. David Pressman, author of the Nolo Press book on doing your own patent, provided a number of helpful suggestions for Chapter 15. I would also like to acknowledge Stephen Hurst's help in the early stages of this project.

Many thanks also to Jake Warner, who conceived this book, allowed me to write it, and made numerous editorial contributions throughout. Thanks, too, to the people at Nolo Press, especially Stephanie Harolde, Toni Ihara and Keija Kimura, who all worked overtime and made personal sacrifices to turn my initial manuscript into a book.

Finally, my undying gratitude and appreciation to Stephen Elias of Nolo Press, who put his energy and creativity and hundreds of hours of his time into this project. Without Steve as my midwife, I would have not survived the labor of giving birth to this book. Now that it is in print, I think of Steve as its godfather.

This book is dedicated to my parents, Myrle and Joyce Hales, in appreciation for all the years of unfailing love and support.

UPDATE SERVICE

Our books are as current as we can make them, but sometimes the laws do change between editions. You can read about law changes which may affect this book in the NOLO NEWS, a 16-page newspaper which we publish quarterly.

In addition to the Update Service, each issue contains comprehensive articles, about the growing self-help law movement as well as areas of the law that are sure to affect you.

To receive the next 4 issues of the NOLO NEWS, please send us $2.00.

Name _____

Address _____

_____

Send to: NOLO PRESS, 950 Parker St., Berkeley, CA 94710

Recycle Your Out-of-Date Books & Get One Third off your next purchase!

Using an old edition can be dangerous if information in it is wrong. Unfortunately, laws and legal procedure change often. To help you keep up to date we extend this offer. If you cut out and deliver to us the title portion of the cover of any old Nolo book we'll give you a 33% discount off the retail price of any new Nolo book. For example, if you have a copy of TENANTS' RIGHTS, 4th edition and want to trade it for the latest CALIFORNIA MARRIAGE AND DIVORCE LAW, send us the TENANTS' RIGHTS cover and a check for the current price of MARRIAGE & DIVORCE, less a 33% discount. Information on current prices and editions are listed in the Nolo News (see above box). Generally speaking, any book more than two years old is of questionable value. Books more than four or five years old are a menace.

OUT OF DATE = DANGEROUS

This offer is to individuals only.

Table of Contents

Introduction

Here is a book which shows you how to legally protect software and computer output from the day it is first written to the time its commercial value is fully realized. Because we recognize that few readers have both a strong background in intellectual property law and computers, we carefully explain all relevant legal and computer concepts.

We focus on copyright law because, for the most part, it provides the best legal protection for the vast majority of software and computer output produced for distribution in the general marketplace. This is not the same thing as saying copyright law offers the only way to legally protect your computer work product. Indeed, in several specific contexts, the law of trademarks and trade secrets offers valuable supplementary, and sometimes even essential, legal protection. Patent law may also operate to protect computer-related work in certain very limited contexts. For these reasons, we pay close attention to how these other legal protective devices can best be used along with copyright law to protect your software.

From the perspective of the casual observer of the computer revolution, attempting to protect software and computer output from piracy may seem to be a hopeless proposition. After all, it only takes seconds to copy a disk, and it's almost a cliche to say no copy protect scheme exists that can't be beaten. Further, in the view of many, the expense and cumbersome nature of the legal system make the very term "legal protection" a contradiction in terms.

While these perceptions obviously contain an element of truth, the conclusion that software is impossible to legally protect is wrong. Why? In the same way that locks keep honest people honest, copyright protection works to protect an author's (or owner's) interest in most software or output most of the time. And, as prices for popular software have dropped, and major software publishers have acted to strictly enforce copyright laws, piracy at a commercial level has come to make little economic sense. In short, the illegal copying of software is becoming less of a problem as both market conditions and public perceptions change.

What about the phenomenon of the individual hacker sharing pirated software with countless others through bulletin boards and user groups? How can you stop this sort of conduct with a copyright? To a large extent, you can't, especially when it comes to computer addicts and 14-year-olds. But, as the number of business people and general users who see computers as tools--not playthings or quasi-religious instruments--increases, there is little reason to think they will spend the time and energy necessary to become software thieves. After all, most people buy or borrow copyrighted books rather than illegally photocopying them.

What about those situations where commercial piracy does occur? Isn't it just too costly to sue the pirates? Many of you will surely appreciate that going to court is expensive and probably unwise if you are chasing down a single hacker who has copied a couple of your programs. The important thing to know, however, is that this cost benefit analysis turns around quickly if your product is illegally copied in a commercial context. For example, if another company comes out with a word processing program, spread sheet or any other software that looks like yours, you will be delighted to know that going to court to stop this infringement and protect the value of your copyright can be both cost effective and efficient.

In a real sense, providing software and computer output with the maximum copyright protection is a type of reasonably-priced insurance. If your program is popular, it is well worth using every copyright law technique to protect it against potential commercial pirates. If it doesn't make it big, or you never need to invoke your copyright protection, you've lost very little by having established it. In short, only if you firmly believe your work will never have a commercial value in the marketplace should you assume that copyright protection is a waste of time.

When it comes to helping you accomplish the steps necessary to protect your work by copyright, our goal here is simple and direct. We start by telling you what a copyright is, how long protection lasts, how a copyright will protect your work. We also discuss copyright transfers, licenses, copyright protection for derivative work, upgrades, and much more. This material is designed to give you a thorough understanding of the copyright concept as it applies to gaining and maintaining maximum copyright protection in the real world of software development, licensing and sales.

Next, we deal with the nitty-gritty details of how to write a correct copyright notice, where to place it on your particular type of software, and how and why to register it. We do this with considerable care. To adopt a metaphor from the car repair business-- if we tell you to turn a certain bolt on the side of the transmission, we first explain what a wrench is, how to pick it up, and where to put your half-empty beer bottle while you're at it.

Fortunately, the great majority of readers can sensibly design and implement a good plan to protect their published software by use of copyright law doctrines without either memorizing several volumes of a legal encyclopedia or resorting to formal legal help. In other words, publishing your work with a correct copyright notice and registering your copyright is normally neither difficult nor fraught with hidden pitfalls.

Chapter 14 on international copyright law is a particularly valuable and unique part of this book. As you undoubtedly know, geographical boundaries mean little to the rapid, worldwide spread of intellectual property rights.

Whether it's a hot new accounting program, a wonderfully efficient operating system, or a database management program that can keep better track of all the Matsumotos in Tokyo and Joneses in London than anything on the market, software that is a big success in Japan one day is likely to be up and operating in San Francisco, London, Paris, and Sidney the next. This worldwide nature of trade in intellectual property means that everyone in the software business needs to know the basics of international copyright law. Fortunately, as a result of several international treaties covered here in detail, this is less difficult than you might imagine.

While we are discussing all the things this book will help you accomplish, it's only fair to tell you one big thing it won't do. When it comes to "how-to" information on fighting your own copyright infringement lawsuit, we stop short. Although our legal system should be organized so that an average citizen has reasonable access to our courts, this is manifestly not the case. It would take several volumes filled with lengthy explanations of pre-trial procedures, litigation rules, and courtroom etiquette to bring you up to speed on how to do your own lawsuit. Clearly, this is more than we can accomplish here. We do, however, give you an overview of how copyright infringement litigation works, including what you can expect if you end up in court. We also discuss how to approach the problem of hiring and working with an affordable computer-knowledgeable lawyer you can feel comfortable with.

Finally, we come to the pesky personal pronoun. We deal with gender sensibilities by using "he" and "she" more or less alternatively throughout this book. While this solution isn't perfect, it makes more sense than "she/he" or other cumbersome devices, such as writing "he and she" every time an abstract person must be identified.

CHAPTER 1

To Copyright Software
You Need to Know
How Computers Work

Those who have tried to communicate a clear view of what computers mean to our society have usually failed. Even the term computer is understood and defined differently by different experts. Although we could use this chapter to try and produce our own definition, the likely result would be a lot of weary, and probably confused, readers.

Fortunately, showing you how to protect your software and other computer-related products from competitors only requires a functional understanding of computers. Simply put, you don't need to stretch your mind to grasp what computers are as long as you know what they do. So, don't despair if your mind always goes blank at the first mention of binary code or microprocessors. The amount of technical material you must master to protect your legal rights is very manageable. We review the essential basics in this chapter. Indeed, this material is so elementary, those readers with strong computer backgrounds may wish to skip to Chapter 2.

Some of you who are new to the technical side of computers may find even our simple explanations hard to absorb. This is probably because you are dealing with this information in the abstract, not in a context that is meaningful to your life. It's a little like memorizing the countries of West Africa. Unless you go there, you are likely to forget what you learned. Once you do, the geographical relationship of Ghana to Togo will become second nature in a hurry. The point is this: if you have trouble with some of what follows, don't worry. As you need this information to effectively copyright your software, we will refer you back to it. In context, it should soon become familiar.

What, then, is a computer from a functional point of view? Let's begin with the terms "hardware" and "software." You would have to have been hiding in a closet since Eisenhower beat Stevenson the second time not to have at least heard these terms. Most simply, "hardware" is the general term used for the physical components of the computer, while "software" consists of the instructions which tell the computer what to do. However, it's important to realize that for copyright law purposes, hardware and software are most useful as general concepts, not absolute descriptions.

Indeed, sometimes deciding whether something is hardware or software presents a problem similar to that of deciding whether a particular illness is "mental" or "physical." In other words, the debate can be endless and the result clear only in the eye of the beholder. For example, sometimes instructions are contained in a physical component of the computer, in which case, that hardware tells the computer what to do. Terms such as "firmware," "microcode," and "embedded programs" have been coined to describe these hardware-software hybrids. We will discuss these many times as we proceed.

At this point you may be asking, why do we have to deal with the distinction between hardware and software at all? The answer is simple. Physical innovations are normally protectable through the legal doctrine of patent law, while innovative expressions are protected through copyright law. Thus, as a general rule, hardware innovations are patented, while software innovations are copyrighted. This generalization does not necessarily apply to the hybrid or mixed types of computer software, however. For example, software contained in a physical part of a computer (i.e., firmware, embedded programs, ROM's, etc.) is usually protected primarily by copyright law.

Another important computer term is "package." We will use it to describe a collection of software that includes one or more programs and all accompanying manuals and documentation used to accomplish a particular purpose. Thus, a word processing package is designed to help you write letters, a simple accounting package will balance your checkbook, and a specialized "transit" package operates the public transit

system. Each one of these packages may contain many programs, sometimes as many as one hundred or more, as well as manuals, training films, etc.

Now, let's take a closer look at hardware and software in terms of their computing functions.

A. Hardware

Here is where we focus on everything which is a physical part of the machine. Computers manipulate information (i.e., compute) in their "Central Processing Unit," or CPU. The CPU consists of a device known as a "processor" or "microprocessor" for microcomputers. This processor consists of one or more silicon chips containing a large number of permanent circuits enabling logical calculations to be performed at great speed. Essentially, all data manipulation occurs by means of such calculations. More about how this works later.

In addition to the CPU, all computers contain an area where the material being acted on by the processor is temporarily stored. This is usually referred to as "Internal Memory" or "Random Access Memory" (RAM). In essence, the RAM provides a type of "workspace" for the processor to do its work. The more RAM a machine has, the more data it is able to work on simultaneously. For our purposes, the important thing about RAM is that any data stored in it disappears when the machine is turned off or reset. For this reason, RAM memory is said to be "dynamic." Anyone who has lost data when their computer suddenly froze or the electricity failed knows all about "dynamic memory." To prevent this from happening, some computers are never turned off. Others have a separate power supply for a certain part of their RAM. This is especially true of "mainframes" (full-size computers).

In addition to the dynamic memory known as RAM, all computers are able to store information on a more permanent basis in an "external memory" or "peripheral storage" device. These are usually called "floppy disks," "hard disks," and "tapes." Once the processor is through acting on data in RAM, the operator can permanently store the result by instructing the computer to place the finished product on a disk, floppy disk, tape, or cassette, depending on the type of computer being used. Once information is placed in peripheral storage, the computer can be turned off without destroying that data.

This type of memory is said to be external because the medium used is physically separate from the CPU and RAM parts of the machine. Because of their external nature, the devices used for permanent storage are often considered to be "peripherals." In other words, they are outside or peripheral to the CPU and RAM.

Computers have a third type of memory which is very roughly analogous to the type of core memory every living being possesses. All living organisms contain DNA in the form of genes which contain the preprogammed information necessary to construct the cells that regulate the organism. When it comes to humans, this housekeeping system is often called the "autonomic nervous system" and takes care of such tasks as breathing, digestion and the growing of fingernails. In the case of computers, preprogrammed instructions necessary to the most basic computer functions are often placed in circuits which are embedded on silicon chips. These are called "Read Only Memory" or ROM chips. They perform such tasks as telling the computer what to do when the computer is turned on or a program is inserted.

The specific computer housekeeping functions that ROM chips perform in computers will be described in more detail in Section B(4) of this chapter. For the sake of thoroughness in our current review of computer hardware,

however, it's also important to know that there are variations of the ROM chip, called PROM's or "Programmable Read Only Memories" and EPROM's, or "Eraseable Programmable Read Only Memories." This type of memory involves specially constructed ROM's which can be altered by programmers.

HARDWARE-SOFTWARE HYBRID NOTE: We mentioned that the line between hard-ware and software can sometimes be fuzzy. ROM's and PROM's are prime examples of this, as the information contained in them is a physical part of the chip. However, under the Semi-conductor Chip Protection Act of 1983, the circuitry in semiconductor chips is now protectable by copyright. See Chapter 3, Section J, item 11. At one point, this "physical" aspect of the code in ROM's and PROM's did, in fact, contribute to the denial of copyright protection by some courts. However, the landmark court decision in Apple v. Franklin [714 F.2d 240 (1983)*] has, at least for now, settled this issue in favor of treating ROM's and PROM's as software for the purpose of the copyright laws.**

So far, we have seen that computer hardware consists of a processor, an internal or random access memory in which information is stored on a temporary or dynamic basis, and at least one of several types of peripheral permanent storage devices. In addition, as every reader surely knows, to be useful, a computer must have a means of receiving information and communicating with the outside world. Like storage devices, these pieces of communications hardware are also generically referred to as "peripherals."

There are two primary types of communications hardware. One is the terminal, or more specifically, the Video Data Terminal (VDT), also commonly called the "Cathode Ray Terminal"

---

* See also Stern Electronics, Inc. v. Kaufman, 669 F.2d 852.

** A truer hybrid is something known as "microcode." Microcode really is an integral part of the computer, but is found in soft (i.e., electrical) rather than physical form. Whether this type of code is subject to copyright protection has yet to be decided.

(CRT). As you probably know, terminals look like, and sometimes are, television screens with typewriters. Their principal function--one that used to be handled by keypunched cards and paper tape--is to put data into and take data out of the computer. The second principal type of communications hardware is the printer. Printers are another important way the computer talks back, or communicates, with you. Computers also have hardware that allows them to communicate their information directly to another machine. These are referred to as "modems," "acoustic couplers" and "communications hardware," depending on the type utilized.

It isn't necessary to know any more about computer hardware to understand this book. After all, legal protection through copyright law is relevant primarily to software programs and computer output generally, and not to how machines are engineered. However, to restate the obvious, computer technology has so blurred the difference between intellectual property (valuable information) and physical property (nuts and bolts), that some understanding of how computers function is essential to understanding the evolution of how copyright law is being applied to computers. Or, put another way, some things that traditionally were thought to be physical objects have, in computer application, transcended their physicality and become charged with so much information that we have begun to disregard "what they are" and look primarily to "what they do." This, for example, is what courts have done in allowing software on ROM chips to be copyrighted.

B. Software

Basically, everything having to do with computers that isn't hardware is classified as software. The term software is used to describe the instruc-

tions (programs) that make the computer work. It is also used, however, to include documentation such as flowcharts, instruction manuals, and other supportive materials that accompany the program. As noted above, when all of these materials relate to one operating scheme or system, they are called a package, or software package.

Perhaps the best way to understand what software is is to pay attention to the several important groupings that make it up. Again, our purpose here is not to give you precise technical explanations, but rather, a working definition sufficient for you to competently protect your software under copyright law.

1. Application Programs

Let's start with the best known form of software--application programs. Application programs are instructions specifically designed to carry out the specific task which lead a person to purchase the computer in the first place. They allow the computer to balance checkbooks, write letters, play games, and operate transit systems, under the direction of the user. In the rest of this book, when the word "program" is used, the reference will usually be to an application program.

The word "software," too, most commonly refers to applications programs and their attendant documentation, such as user's manuals.

Most of the programmers who use this book will be working with, and seeking to copyright, applications software. So too, those of you who need to understand the ins and outs of computer copyright rules because you are lawyers or people in computer-related businesses will most often want to use copyright law to protect an applications program. Accordingly, this book is designed to show you how to copyright this type of software and output, although all the legal concepts which we cover will apply to operating systems, databases and other types of software as well.

2. Operating Systems

The next most common type of software is described in computerese as "operating systems" or "system programs." At this point, some readers who don't have a computer background may want to zone out. It's important that you don't. Understanding this term is extremely important to understanding the law of computer copyright.

"Operating systems" or "system programs" essentially regulate the communications between the human operator and the different parts of the computer hardware. Operating systems for small computers (microcomputers) are very different from the system programs which regulate large machines (mainframes and minicomputers). For our purposes, however, they can all be lumped together under the term "operating system." Again, these are all the programs concerned with such machine functions as channeling information between the peripherals and the Central Processing Unit (CPU) and determining the exact location on a peripheral storage device where data is to be stored, etc.

Usually, operating systems are comprised of electronic instructions which are either fed (loaded) into the computer from an external source, or contained in Read Only Memory (ROM) chips. Common examples of operating systems include TurboDos, MS DOS, IMS, CP/M, OS/MVS, and Unix. In essence, operating systems are the traffic controllers, organizers, housekeepers and sometimes rulers of how the computer actually functions. For example, when a user tells her favorite word processing program (an applications program) to "save" a file (usually by pushing the save key), the operating system springs into operation and determines how the information is pulled out of RAM and put onto disk (or tape, or cassette, etc.) for permanent storage.

As you can probably guess from the previous example, application software has to be able to communicate with the operating system to work on a particular type of computer. If a particular application program is unable to communicate with the operating system, it just won't work, since the machine will be unable to respond to its instructions. Thus, the operating system is usually a major factor in determining whether microcomputers will "run" a particular application program and whether they are compatible with certain other microcomputers. In other words, computers with the same operating systems commonly are able to use the same general software.

3. Databases

Another type of software--the "database"--is becoming increasingly significant in our information-driven society. A database is actually raw information of any type organized in a manner which facilitates meaningful retrieval. The database (i.e., the collection of information) is really the output of an application program known as a "database manager system" (DBMS). Database managers tell the computer how to organize, store, and respond to user requests for the information in the database.

For example, suppose you need a mailing list for your business which keeps track of ten variables (such as name, zip code, status of account, goods ordered, etc.). In addition, you want to be able to extract partial lists of names from the master list according to combinations of variables (e.g., all customers with a particular zip code whose account is delinquent). You use a database program to accomplish this. It's up to you to supply (input) the basic ten kinds of information. It's up to the database manager to instruct the computer how and where to store the data so you can retrieve it in the way you desire. The actual information, and the way it is organized, together make up the database.

Under the copyright laws, the database management system (DBMS), possibly your instructions inputted to the DBMS, and the actual database itself may all be subject to copyright protection. Since the information in the database often consists of material previously protected by copyright (e.g., the full text of various articles and periodicals), sticky legal questions can sometimes arise. For example, suppose you decide to organize every issue of the Nolo News (a prominent self-help legal quarterly published by Nolo Press) by subject matter, and place the various articles in a computer database so that anyone seeking information on self-help law can retrieve the information by asking specific questions (e.g., What does the database have on "durable powers of attorney"?). Although Nolo Press owns the copyright to the individual issues of the Nolo News, you would own the copyright to your particular compilation of this information. How to determine who is entitled to protection in these situations (and when permission must be obtained) is discussed in detail in Chapter 4.

4. Firmware

These are programs which are so much a part of the hardware of the computer that it's sometimes difficult to remember that they have a separate and copyrightable existence. They include "hard-wired" programs, which are actually circuits wired into the computer itself and, more commonly these days, programs embedded on silicon chips known as ROM chips. The primary purpose of this type of software (commonly called "firmware" because of its hardware characteristics) has been to run the computer hardware on the most fundamental level.

As we discussed above, firmware is analogous to the autonomic nervous system in human beings, which takes care of such things as eye lubrication, heart action, and digestion, without any conscious intervention by the brain. You might even say our autonomic nervous system is "part of our wiring." In much the same way, ROM's often tell the machine what to do in such basic situations as when you turn on the machine, insert an applications program,* print out material and save or store it on a disk.

More recently, however, such diverse types of application software as computer games, word processing programs, and spreadsheets have also been placed on ROM's and sold as part of the computer. In short, ROM's are increasingly containing application programs as well as operating systems.

5. Forms of Software Expression — Languages

So far, we have identified three different types of software--operating systems, application programs, and

---

* In computerese, this is usually called "booting" or "loading" a program.

databases--and the hybrid type, firmware. While some readers may be wishing we would call a halt to this parade of jargon, there are several other crucial areas which you absolutely must understand before the copyright law materials included in the rest of this book will make sense. In this regard, it's particularly important to say a few words about computer languages. Obviously, without this most basic form of software, as well as the computer hardware with which it interacts, other software couldn't exist.

operating systems   firmware   application programs   databases

•A SOFTWARE NIGHTMARE•

Most of you will already have realized that language is a code designed for communication. At one time, humans used literally thousands of these codes to communicate with one another. Today, it's probably fair to say that the overwhelming percentage of all human communications takes place through the use of about two dozen codes. These codes vary in sophistication from English, Japanese and Russian, to Morse Code (dashes and dots, remember?), and Pig Latin. The computer hardware is only able to understand a very basic type of code, consisting of ones and zeros (i.e., binary numbers). Human beings, on the other hand, tend to communicate in one or more vastly more sophisticated languages. The big problem faced by computer programmers, therefore, is how to translate back and forth between machine and human languages so the two can communicate with

one another. Or, simply put, how can a bunch of zeros and ones be converted into the language of Shakespeare, Kawabata or Dostoyevesky, and vice versa?

The solution to this problem is as simple as it is ingenious. Special intermediary software has been developed to interpret and translate human language into machine language and vice versa. These programs are called "interpreters," "compilers" and "assemblers" (depending on their exact function in the translation process). In addition, specialized human level languages, often called "programming languages,"* have been developed for the sole purpose of communicating information in the kinds of logical relationships the computer's compilers, interpreters, and assemblers can efficiently use.

Now, let's put this information into a familiar context. John, a computer programmer, uses a human-style programming language when typing instructions into the computer. A compiler program, which is either contained in a ROM or on a disk or tape, then interprets this programming language and translates it into a form which the machine itself can then render into a string of zeros and ones. This process can be reversed so that information produced by the machine can be retrieved by the human operator in understandable form.

Just a few more words about computer languages. Application programs are usually originally written in what are referred to as "higher level" computer languages. Higher level computer languages are those which are close to what you and I speak. You have undoubtedly heard of, and perhaps worked with, a number of these, such as BASIC, COBOL, FORTRAN, FORTH, and PASCAL. The language you use depends on the type of application--scientific, accounting or word processing--and the size of the

---

* These "programming languages" are themselves classified into "higher level languages" and "lower level languages," depending on their syntax and the ability of individual words and phrases to control many machine functions.

machine. Larger machines can accommodate more complex languages.

Although we thoroughly cover the interesting question of copyright protection for computer languages later in Chapter 4, we want to tip our hand here. Basically, the electronic form of a computer language, as distributed by its creators, is protectable by copyright, whereas the use of the language in new programs is not (see Chapter 4, Section H).

6. Source Code and Object Code

When you first write a program using a higher level language, your program is in what computer people call "source code" form. This means it can be read by humans (e.g., its "source"). If you know the particular language, it can be read like a novel. However, as should now be clear, computers can neither read books nor understand programs in source code form. Why not? Because computers only understand information when it comes in binary code, a form represented as ones and zeros.

To remind you of ground we covered a few pages earlier, the compiler or translator program contained in the computer read the source code and translates it to a different form of the same program. This new form is usually called "object code." While object code is expressed in binary numeric form, it may still not be 100% ready to tell the computer to do its assigned task. The final bit of information that it takes to allow the computer to perform its given task is accomplished at the time the translated program is actually run on the computer. We'll discuss this in more detail shortly.

Needless to say, programs in object code don't make sense to people, as they are only a bunch of binary num-

bers. Just the same, as we will see, object code can be copyrighted. Several years ago, some courts debated the copyrightability of programs in object code form (especially when they are embedded on a chip), but all now agree, at least in the U.S., that object code is just another expression of a program, albeit in a different form.*

You should also know that sometimes the translation of source code to a machine-readable form is done by an interpreter without an intermediate object code step. This is called "machine code form." In many situations, this translated form of the source code cannot be saved, as it exists only while the computer is performing the assigned task. As we'll see in the next chapter, where you cannot physically save code, you cannot copyright it. This means that with some software, you can only copyright "source code," because there is functionally no object code. If this creates legal problems, and it sometimes does, you should know that it is usually possible to write a program directly in machine code (if you have the time, patience, and skill). If you do this, the program can be saved in object code (binary) form.

Why are the distinctions between source code and object code important? Because both levels of code, as long as they can be reproduced in a fixed medium, can be protected by copyright. As we later discuss in the chapters covering registration with the U.S. Copyright Office (Chapters 8 - 11) you may very well need to choose between source code and object code when deciding what type of code to deposit as part of your copyright registration. Depending on the fact situation you face, it is commonly more desirable to deposit one than the other. Change just a few facts, however, and you may well want to reverse your decision. To follow these discussions, you absolutely need to have a working understanding of object code and source code.

* Apple v. Franklin, 714 F.2d 240 (3rd cir. 1983); Apple v. Formula Computing (9th Cir. 1984); Stern Electronics v. Kaufman, 669 F.2d 852.

C. Computer Output

Computer output is the final result of your interaction with a computer. It may be the report you print, the video game you play, or graphics you create with a computer and display to your admiring public (or at least to very close friends and relatives). It can also be a database, music you create through a synthesizer program, or a laser light show, which will probably soon be more common for advertising outdoors events than searchlights sweeping the sky were 20 years ago.

Sometimes it will be important to copyright computer output separately from the program source code or object code. Why should this be true if the expression of your work in the form of the program is already copyrighted? We will go into more detail about this later, but at the risk of getting a little ahead of our story, it's often wise to copyright computer output for two reasons. First, output such as the popular characters or vehicles in a computer game can, and often do, take on independent value. And second, it is often easy to generate the same character or other valuable output by using a different program--that is, by writing different code. In other words, in some situations, such as might be the case if you program a world famous computer canary, your output may be much more expressive of your original idea than your underlying program. If this is true, it may be desirable to copyright your output independently. This is because whether copyrighting an applications program legally protects its output from people who would duplicate it by writing different code is an area of some legal doubt at the moment.

D. Summary

If you don't have a computer background, you may be a little muddled at this point. You probably wonder how much of this information you really need to understand to legally protect software by copyright. Relax. If you have grasped the following points, you are in good shape, at least for now. If one or more of them are still hazy, re-read the appropriate section.

■ Computer hardware is not generally subject to copyright protection;

■ Firmware (or microcode) is software which is made a physical part of a computer by imbedding it on a chip or handwiring it into the machine's circuitry;

■ Object code embedded in firmware (such as ROM's, PROM's or EPROM's) is subject to copyright protection;

■ Operating systems and system programs are subject to copyright protection;

■ Source code is the expression of a program as written (usually in a higher level language) by the programmer;

■ Source code is subject to copyright protection;

■ Object code is the expression of a program in a binary form understandable by the machine;

■ Object code is subject to copyright protection;

■ Application programs are those programs which instruct the computer to perform a specific task (e.g., word processing, spreadsheets, database manager).

■ Most application programs are written in source code (usually a higher level language) and distributed to users in object code form;

■ The same basic program (source code) can usually be written in different "higher level" languages (e.g., BASIC, FORTRAN, and FORTH).

■ Computer languages are subject to copyright protection in the form in which they are distributed to users. However, the language can be freely used to create other programs without violating the copyright;

■ Databases are compilations of information organized for the purpose of providing maximum differential access;

■ Databases (i.e., the particular compilation of information) are subject to copyright protection, assuming that permission is obtained from any persons who own copyrights in the data, or the data is in the public domain;

■ Databases are commonly created by using a separately protectable application program called a database manager system (DBMS);

■ Computer output is what is produced on the screen or printer or other output device as a result of a program being "run" by the computer;

■ Computer output is subject to independent copyright protection, although it may also be protected if the object code or source code necessary to generate it is copyrighted.

•CHAPTER 2•

Please Read This Chapter

This chapter is short but extremely important to the rest of the book. Because it covers several short unrelated subjects, we were unable to assign it a topical heading. Why should you read it, then?

First, we want you to meet the software developers who will help us illustrate numerous aspects of copyright law throughout the rest of this book. As with the classical Russian novel, it will save you much page flipping to become familiar with these characters at the beginning.

Second, we want to impress on you, here at the beginning, that good record keeping is almost as essential to protecting your software as is understanding and taking advantage of the legal protections afforded by copyright law. In this connection, we make several suggestions that should help make your record keeping tasks relatively easy.

Finally, we provide some suggestions as to how to find and work with a good copyright lawyer should that become necessary.

A. The Cast of Characters

Because we are going to rely heavily on the experience of three programmers, formal introductions are in order. Don't worry if the type of work each of them does, and the copyright problems they face, are somewhat different from yours. Each will encounter a positively bewildering array of programming and copyright adventures as we go along. Sooner or later, one or more of these is sure to be similar to your situation.

Mary Hales

Let's start by presenting Mary Hales. Mary was born and raised in a small town in southern Illinois. She attended the state university and graduated with a degree in computer science. Her first job was in a medium-sized city, working for Middle Bank, where she learned to program in COBOL. After a few years, Mary left Middle Bank and began writing more complex application programs for larger banks. She eventually found herself supervising computer applications at Big Bank, in New York.

After a few years, Mary found that working long, hard hours for medium compensation and the promise of an eventual gold watch was not fulfilling. Her feelings became stronger when she saw how much Big Bank paid outside vendors for certain application software packages which weren't very different from the ones she was helping develop in-house.

We join Mary soon after she has kissed the security of a regular paycheck goodbye and has launched her very own software business with a loan processing application package called LOANIT. Mary wrote LOANIT, which consists of 70 software programs, in the higher level language COBOL. While Mary prefers to sell the entire package for one nice, plump fee, she sometimes sells individual programs piece-meal.

Mary has created a training film which is included in the package she sells. It shows the employees of a purchasing bank how to interact with LOANIT to achieve optimum results. This includes everything from inputting data into the computer to interpreting the reports LOANIT produces. The LOAN-IT package also includes an instruction manual consisting of eight volumes (a four-volume user manual, a programmer reference, a computer operator manual, a manual of set-up procedures), and a subject index geared to helping users find information in the manuals efficiently.

Mary has also decided to capitalize on the microcomputer explosion. As part of preparing a microcomputer version of LOANIT, Mary realized that COBOL is not a suitable language for most micros, as it takes up more RAM to operate than most microcomputers can offer. Therefore, Mary translated LOANIT into PASCAL, a language more suitable to her new marketing strategy.

To save time, and in the spirit of not reinventing the wheel, Mary used several existing programs belonging to others to handle some of the LOANIT report generating and file creation functions. Specifically, Mary used WORDCRAZY, a word processing program, and DATABASECRAZY, a popular database manager program. Because these application programs were already subject to copyright, Mary had to make suitable arrangements with the copyright owners to license their use.

Carl Jones

Next, let's introduce Carl Jones. Carl has never had the benefit of any formal computer training. Indeed, Carl was a Volkswagen mechanic who was relatively content and well-adjusted to his work, until that fateful day when his sweetheart, Belinda Bonner (make that "ex-sweetheart"), gave him a microcomputer for his birthday. Quickly, Carl assumed several alarming (at least to Belinda) personality traits. He commonly stayed up all night, drank coffee by the gallon, and spoke civilly to humans only after what he considered to be a major programming breakthrough. In short, Carl became a developer of microcomputer software. Belinda put up with this for awhile before leaving Carl to marry an aerobic dance teacher.

By now, Carl has come to believe that there's more gold in them thar diskettes than in fixing VW's. Indeed, the only "bug" he'll work on is the high tech variety. Carl recently developed a video game called GOTTCHA. It has been a big success. So much so, that a full-length animated movie has just been made based on its plot. This cartoon version is called GOTTCHA COMIN' AND GOIN'.

Carl has also joined a computer user's group and writes for their newsletter, Rollin' On. He calls his column "Bughugs." In his spare time, he has developed a model car called CHIP-RACER by using a computer-generated graphics program. As if these activities were not enough, Carl also designed an auto parts database for Volkswagens, which he calls BUGBITS.

Encouraged to extremes by the fickle video game market (as evidenced by his last royalty check) and a fear that he may once again have to view the world from underneath an automobile, Carl has even tried his hand at computer-generated music. His composition, OFFKEY, has so far been politely ignored by the critics.

To distribute his software, Carl deals with several large computer software marketing companies, including Famegame, Silichip, and Video Publishing, Inc.

Kendra Salone

Kendra Salone, our last developer, is a bright-eyed seventeen-year-old who learned to program ten minutes after she learned to walk. Kendra, who has few starving artist fantasies, has a full-time job with BCA Graphics, although she isn't old enough to vote.

Kendra's specialty is writing computer programs that create works of graphic art. BCA retails these programs through its own stores and catalogue, and also sells them to wholesalers. Kendra's major product is a program which generates an unlimited number of different quilt designs in many different, and sometimes unusual, colors. This program is called QUILT-IT. As Kendra did this program while employed at BCA Graphics, they own it, and Kendra is one of the thousands of programmers who fall under the "work-made-for-hire" copyright rules.

So much for our cast of characters. You will encounter each many more times as we proceed.

B. Record Keeping

It should go almost without saying that it pays to run your affairs in a business-like way. In this connection, your first principle is as simple as it is straightforward. Agreements which aren't written down are likely to be either forgotten, misconstrued, or litigated. In some copyright law contexts, oral agreements may be legal. In most, they are not. In all cases, they are a bad idea.

Assuming you grasp this basic point and make sure all the important agreements you make with others regarding your copyright are in writing, you have made a good start towards protecting your copyright. You haven't accomplished the whole job, however. Lost or misplaced copyright forms, certificates, license contracts, or transfer documents can all have disturbing, if not disastrous, legal and practical consequences. Enough said. Here are some suggestions that should help you avoid trouble:

■ From the first time you fix any software in permanent form, include a copyright notice containing a © -- that is, the letter "c" contained within a circle, and your name. Do this routinely and you will avoid the common problem of software being accidentally cast adrift with no indication that someone is claiming a copyright in it. Later, if you publish your product, this notice will change to include a date of publication. Copyright notice is covered in detail in Chapter 6.

■ Set up a good filing system. Put each copyright certificate and application form (when returned by the Copyright Office) in a separate file, along with all documents that affect your ownership of that particular copyright, such as license, assignment or transfer contacts.

■ If you plan to apply for a number of copyrights, your next problem is where to keep the individual copyright files. One suggestion is a metal file cabinet, with each copyright file carefully marked as to name and copyright number.

IMPORTANT: Please set up your filing system now. We will refer to it often in the pages that follow and will regard it as a personal favor to us if you don't procrastinate.

C. Working with Attorneys

This book is not intended to replace the services of a qualified attorney, but to give you a general understanding of copyright law and show you how to perform most of the routine administrative copyright functions yourself. There are times when the services of an expert are a must. We identify these as we go along. But, while we have your attention, let's review several of the most important situations where it is wise to consult a lawyer.

1. When You Will Need an Attorney

We can't anticipate every situation in which you may need the assistance of a person with computer law experience, but here are some general guidelines which should help in making this decision:

■ As a general rule, if, after you have read the sections of this book which are pertinent to your situation, you have any doubts as to how to proceed, check with a lawyer.

■ If, after reading Chapter 10 on copyright deposits, you are still not sure what type of deposit to make along with your copyright application, and you feel your work is potentially of great value, see a knowledgeable attorney.

■ If you are involved in a serious dispute over whether a valuable copyright has been infringed, you should always check your understanding of the situation with a knowledgeable attorney. A good lawyer should help you resolve most of these disputes without going to court.

■ If you end up bringing, or defending, a copyright infringement law suit, definitely seek the assistance of a knowledgeable lawyer.

■ If you license a valuable copyright, a lawyer may be required to draft or review the agreement, especially if the terms of the license are complex. In straightforward cases, you can draft your own contract by referring to Legal Care For Your Software, by Daniel Remer (Nolo Press). Even if you do this work yourself, however, it is wise to have it checked by someone with experience in the field.

2. How to Work with an Attorney

It is rarely necessary to hire an attorney to handle all parts of the copyright or contracting process. Following the instructions in this book, and in Legal Care For Your Software, you can do a great deal of routine work yourself. One good approach is to find an attorney who is willing to answer specific questions as the need arises. Of course, your lawyer will need some background on how your business works so that her answers will be appropriate to your particular situation.

At a minimum, your attorney should also be available to review contracts, registration packages and other materials after you draft them, as well as to advise you, should you face any specific copyright infringement problems. The point is this: The lawyer should be ready and willing to help when her expertise is really necessary. In the meantime, she should primarily backstop your efforts to understand how the law impacts your business and help you do as many so-called legal tasks for yourself as possible.

3. What Is a Computer Attorney?

A genuine computer law attorney (as opposed to someone who began specializing in computer law yesterday) should be able to handle any legal problem relating to computers, from copyright and trade secret, to criminal and contract matters. Computer attorneys are sometimes computer professionals who later went to law school. Other good computer lawyers may not have a lot of hands-on computer experience. Instead, they may have gained their specialized knowledge in the legal department of a computer company or law firm which specializes in intellectual property law, or by simply applying themselves and mastering both fields.

Unfortunately, there are also a number of so-called "computer lawyers" who awarded themselves the title for no other reason than it looks like a hot field in which big bucks can be made in a hurry. For this reason, it is both appropriate and essential that you inquire into any potential lawyer's background. How much experience does she have? Where did she get it? How much of her practice is computer law related? Who are her other clients? If it is important to you that your lawyer have a specific understanding of how computers work, ask the appropriate questions.

You should also realize, however, that if you have a routine legal problem relating to copyrighting software or other computer output, you do not necessarily need a lawyer who is married to a mainframe. An attorney with a good background in general copyright law is probably more than adequate. Copyright attorneys practice copyright law as it relates to all types of expression. In the past, they primarily represented authors of books, or composers or musicians. However, as the law of copyright is quite similar whether you are copyrighting source code or a symphony, many of these lawyers have made the transition to software with little difficulty.

I READ A LOT OF BOOKS IN LAWSCHOOL - NO PROBLEM. A CONTRACT'S A CONTRACT. BY THE WAY, HOW LONG IS A COPYRIGHT THESE DAYS?

We should also say a few words about international attorneys. These lawyers specialize in contracts, finances and the many other kinds of transactions that commonly occur between countries. They may or may not understand computers or copyright law. They will, however, have a good knowledge of the ins and outs of doing business in other countries. Chances are you won't need the help of an international law expert unless you are doing a lot of business in other countries. Often your copyright or computer attorney can enlist the advice of an international specialist if that type of information is needed.

4. How to Establish a Relationship with an Attorney

Your first task is to find the right legal friend. If you are unsure of how to do this, network your problem to people you know and trust in the computer business. After you have several recommendations, we suggest you do the following:

■ Call each attorney. If the lawyer isn't there, leave a message. If he doesn't call back reasonably promptly, cross him off your list.

■ When you do talk to the attorney, make sure his so-called expertise in computer law extends to the areas with which you are most likely to need assistance. In this age of the "instant expert," all sorts of people are calling themselves computer lawyers who have trouble operating a push button phone.

■ Explain that while you are looking for a long-term relationship with a lawyer, and expect to pay for legal services promptly and fairly, you plan to do much of your own routine copyright work. You are looking for a lawyer who thinks this is an intelligent choice and isn't into a "me big expert, you ignorant client" approach to the practice of law.

■ Before making a final decision, arrange an appointment and discuss your needs in detail. Expect to pay for this appointment fairly. Ask yourself if you like the lawyer, and if the lawyer is someone you think you can work with over the long term, and determine if the lawyer has the expertise you need. If all goes well, you have found yourself the legal help you need.

5. Paying an Attorney

Experts don't come cheap. Most computer law specialists will charge at least $150 an hour, unless you have worked out a retainer agreement. Generally, charges are made in 15-minute intervals. If you anticipate needing a modest amount of continuing help, primarily to review the work you have done, paying for help as needed is probably your best approach.

However, if your business is large enough that you anticipate a steady need for help, you may wish to negotiate a retainer type agreement. Although this can take a number of forms, with a retainer you normally agree to pay the lawyer a fixed amount of money each month, or quarter, for an agreed-upon number of hours of help. In other words, you normally agree to pay for time whether you use it or not. Because of this guarantee, the lawyer will commonly agree to charge significantly less than his normal hourly rate.

Finally, if you find yourself faced with bringing (or defending) a copyright infringement court action, you will have to consider the whole fee issue anew. Unless you have extremely deep pockets and/or a very valuable product, any copyright infringement action is likely to cost more than you can afford. This leads to several possibilities:

■ If your copyright has been infringed by someone who can afford to pay damages, and your work has been registered in a timely fashion, as discussed in Chapter 8, an attorney may well take the case and agree to collect her fees from the infringer.

■ If your copyright has been infringed by someone who can afford to pay damages, and your work was not registered in a timely fashion so as to qualify you for attorney fees, you may still get an attorney to take the case in exchange for a percentage of any damages recovered. This is called a "contingency fee contract" and must usually be in writing.

■ If you are sued in a copyright infringement case and you are more or less guilty, paying an attorney out of your own pocket will probably only compound your problems. Your best bet is probably to try to settle the case.

D. Legal Research

We can't give you a comprehensive "how to" guide on legal research here. However, because we occasionally punctuate definitive legal statements with some strange looking "code" known as citations, it is essential that we at least tell you what they are and how to use them. This will allow those of you who are unfamiliar with legal indexing systems to access this information. Those of you with legal training can skip the rest of this chapter.

■ The United States Code (U.S.C.): When Congress passes laws known as statutes, they are placed in a series of books called the United States Code. These are divided into "titles," generally according to their subject matter. There are 50 titles in all. Each title is further divided by "section number." All statutes relating to copyrights can be found in Title 17 of the United States Code. Similarly, all statutes related to trademarks and servicemarks are contained by section number in Title 15. Laws applicable to patents are found in Title 35. Each subsection of these broad statutory groupings or schemes is further divided by number for easy access. Thus, Title 17 United States Code Section 101 contains the major definitions for terms used in the Copyright Act. If you desire to look these laws up for yourself, go to your nearest law library and locate either the United States Code Annotated (U.S.C.A.) or the United States Code Service Lawyers Edition (U.S.C.S.). Both of these publications contain not only the statutes, but also contain helpful references to court interpretations, and much additional explanatory information.

■ The Code of Federal Regulations (C.F.R.): Most regulations issued by a particular agency are gathered together and published by title in this series. So long as these regulations are valid, they have the force and effect of law. The title numbers in this series have no necessary relationship to the title numbers in the United States Code. For example, all copyright regulations are contained in Title 37 CFR, while all copyright statutes are, as we have seen, gathered in Title 17 USC. As with the USC, the broad subject matter of each area organized in each title is further broken down into sections. These are also numbered. Thus, Title 37 CFR 202.19 refers to section 202.19 of Title 37 of the Code of Federal Regulations. These specific regulations cover Copyright Office deposit rules. You will find this series of books in any law library. Most are open to the public.

■ Case Citations: Throughout the text you will see citations like this: Apple Computer, Inc. v. Franklin Computers Corp (1983) 714 F.2d 1240. This identifies a particular legal decision. It tells you where this decision may be found and read. This, and any other recent case decided by a federal court of appeals, is found in a series of books called the Federal Reporter (Second Series), or F.2d for short. Thus, to locate the Apple case, simply locate a law library which has the Federal Reporter, Second Series (almost all do); next locate volume 714. Finally, turn to page 1240.

Opinions by U.S. District Court judges are located in a series known as the Federal Supplement, or "F.Supp." for short. Cases decided by the U.S. Supreme Court are found in three publications: United States Reports (identified as "U.S."), the Supreme Court Reporter (identified as "S.Ct.") and the Supreme Court Reports, Lawyer's Edition (identified as "L.ed").

■ Treatises: In addition, an excellent looseleaf service published by Commerce Clearing House and called the "Copyright Law Reporter" can be found in many major law libraries. This will help you keep current on all we've covered in this book. You will also find Nimmer on Copyrights (a multivolume treatise on the general law of copyrights to be very helpful for answering specific questions. Finally, for general information on finding your way around the law library, and specific help on doing original legal research, we highly recommment Legal Research: How to Find and Understand the Law, Elias, Nolo Press.

CHAPTER 3

An Introduction to Copyright Law

A. The Roots of Copyright Protection

In the United States, copyright protection is legislated by Congress, but based on the U.S. Constitution. Article 1, Section 8 authorizes Congress "to promote the progress of science and the useful arts." Congress has done this by legislating mini-monopolies in favor of authors. The theory is that creative people will create more and better work if they have the opportunity to profit from their creations. In other countries, much the same result has been achieved through a number of legislative and constitutional theories.

Over the centuries, the U.S. Congress has provided a number of different schemes for copyright protection. Perhaps the best known was the Copyright Act of 1909, under which an author of a published work got protection for 28 years, and, upon timely application, an additional 28 years. This Act was replaced by a new Copyright Act,

effective January 1, 1978. [17 USC Section 101 et. seq.] Subsequent amendments pertaining to computer programs became effective in 1980. [17 USC Sections 101,117]

Because almost all computer programs now in use have been written since 1978, we do not discuss copyright rules prior to that time in any detail. Be warned, however, if you have a program published in 1977 or before, you are covered by the Copyright Act of 1909 and are subject to its renewal requirements. One excellent source of information about your rights and duties under that Act is Author Law & Strategies, by Brad Bunnin and Peter Beren (Nolo Press).

LAWYER NOTE: Many readers who have a strong intellectual property law background may wish to skim or skip this chapter, just as computer-wise people did not need to concentrate on Chapter 1. Our job here is to bring those readers with little background in copyright law principles up to speed. Once that is accomplished, we will all be ready to deal with the subtleties of copyrighting software.*

B. What a Copyright Does

A copyright provides its original owner (usually the author, or the employer in a work-for-hire context) with a number of exclusive rights in the copyrighted work. These rights can be summarized as the right to prevent others from exploiting the work for commercial purposes or for using it in a way that substantially prevents the author or developer from realizing expected profits. Assuming your copyrighted computer program has economic value, your exclusive right to make a copy of it and to market it can be of tremendous economic benefit. For works published by a U.S. citizen (or permanent resident), or works published for the first time in the U.S. by anyone, this economic benefit is extended to the over one-hundred countries which have signed the Universal Copyright Convention. We discuss international copyright rights in detail in Chapter 14.

Because the protection afforded the author by a copyright is personal in nature, it is both legal and possible for that person to keep her copyright entirely to herself. Thus, if an author only wishes to use a work on Christmas morning every other year in a closet, that's her business. Most people, however, will want to profit from their work and will, therefore, not want to literally interpret their exclusive right to make copies of their work. Rather, they will do all they can to authorize others to make copies and market their work, in exchange for fair compensation, of course.

EXAMPLE 1: Let's assume Mary Hales, who we introduced in some detail in Chapter 2, sells one copy of her copyrighted LOANIT loan processing package to Big Bank. It works so well, Big Bank wants to distribute LOANIT to each of its 900 branches. To do this, they must get Mary's permission and pay a fee (presumably a hefty one). The same is true of Mary's copyrighted LOANIT user's manual. In other words, just because Big Bank bought one copyrighted program or manual doesn't give them the right to knock out 900 more.

EXAMPLE 2: Carl Jones sends a copy of his copyrighted computer game GOTTCHA to Video Marketing, Inc., for evaluation. Video Marketing decides it wants to sell GOTTCHA through its chain of Gameland stores. They must either buy copies of GOTTCHA from Carl or his publisher, or contract with Carl to produce copies on their own.

EXAMPLE 3: Sew Right, Inc., a notions and fabric store, wants to sell a quilt pattern created by QUILTIT, the program Kendra Salone developed. As this program was done on a work-for-hire basis for BCA Graphics, and was copyrighted by them, it does not belong to Kendra. Sew Right must get BCA Graphics' permission to sell the pattern.

EXAMPLE 4: Able Hard designs a revolutionary new program to translate Swahili into Tagalog. For reasons of his own, he refuses to market this work or authorize others to do so. Indeed, he seems selfishly pleased to be the only person in the world who has access to this copyrighted translation system. This is his right under the copyright laws. Able doesn't legally have to sell copies of his program.

---

* As we will see, works are automatically protected by the copyright law from the time they are first created. But, there are additional steps which must be taken to maintain and enhance this protection. "Copyrighting" a work consists of taking these additional steps.

C. What Does a Copyright Protect?

1. Expressions Rather than Ideas

The fundamental principle of copyright law is that a copyright protects the expression of an idea rather than the idea itself. This seems simple enough until you think about it carefully. Then, if you're like many others, the distinction between an idea and its expression may seem less than clear. The question of whether a work for which copyright protection is sought is an expression or an idea has provided the basis for thousands of learned (and many not-so-learned) articles, books and court decisions.

This is not the place for an abstract philosophical debate over when an expression is an idea and vice versa. However, we will give you a good working approach to figuring out which is which for Copyright Act purposes. This is usually fairly easy. We will also alert you to the troublesome areas where you may need expert help. For now, understand that the Copyright Act protects the form which a program, book, manual, record, screen, script, etc. takes. It does not protect the ideas or concepts contained within it. Thus, you can't protect the idea of a story about a boy and his dog travelling around the world by balloon, but you can copyright your particular expression of that story.

EXAMPLE 1: Carl Jones' computer game, GOTTCHA, began with Carl's idea of having John Law Fuzz chase and capture Bad Guy Biker. The program, consisting of Carl's expression of the idea of John chasing and capturing Bad Guy, is protectible by copyright. But Carl's copyright will not protect him from someone else designing a game using the idea of a cop (or anyone else) chasing and capturing a criminal. In other words, another programmer is legally free to produce a similar cop and biker game, as long as he doesn't directly copy Carl's story (expression).

EXAMPLE 2: There are a number of loan processing packages on the market and there will be many more. Neither Mary Hales, who we introduced in Chapter 2 as the author of LOANIT, nor anyone else, can copyright the basic idea underlying a loan processing package. Similarly, the first children's book author to do a story about the adventures of a winged turtle cannot copyright that theme. Mary can, of course, copyright the expression of her idea (her loan package program), just as the author of SAMANTHA THE FLYING TURTLE can copyright her particular story.

----

2. Copyright — A Bundle of Rights

We mentioned earlier that a copyright is really a number of exclusive rights related to the commercial exploitation of a work of authorship. These rights are:

- The exclusive right to make copies of the work;

- The exclusive right to prepare derivative works (works based on the original work);

- The exclusive right to perform the work;

- The exclusive right to display the work in a commercial setting;

- The exclusive right to market or distribute the work.

Together, these rights give the owner of the copyright the exclusive authority to make money from the underlying product protected by the copyright. How these different rights can best be protected in the computer world is a re-occurring theme throughout this book. It's important to understand at the outset that these rights do not have to reside in one person or entity, and in fact are often separated as part of an overall marketing plan. The details on how to do this are covered in Chapter 12 on transfers.

D. Qualifying for a Copyright

1. Originality

To qualify as a "work of authorship," and thus be copyrightable, your software must be "original." The originality requirement is drawn from the constitutional language "to promote the progress of science and the useful arts," which, as we have seen, is the basis for the author's mini-monopoly established by the Copyright Act. The originality requirement is not difficult to meet. A first draft of a three-note cowboy song, a letter to your Aunt Ethel, and your database of all known facts about Polish goldfish all constitute original works of authorship and may be copyrighted. More to the point, most any original piece of computer code, whether source code, object code, or code embedded on a chip, is protectible through copyright. It need not be clever, artistic or marketable to qualify for copyright protection as an "original work of authorship." Indeed, it need not even be completely unique. One copyrighted program can be fairly similar to another as long as it originates with the author (programmer) and was not copied from the other program.

However, there is a flip side to this reasonably relaxed originality requirement. The less your program code is truly unique, the easier it is for another author to "independently" create the same program without running afoul of copyright law. In other words, copying won't normally be found

to exist unless two pieces of code are very similar.

EXAMPLE 1: Mary Hales, our LOANIT developer, attends a computer fair, where she spots a copyrighted program, HANDCALC. This program is designed to compute interest rates on loans, for use on small handheld computers. Impressed, Mary returns home and goes to work. She independently writes code that will, with the addition of several novel features, do much the same thing as HANDCALC. In addition, she takes pains to make her "finger count" program display look different from HAND-CALC. Mary can copyright her program and sell it without infringing the copyright rights of the owners of HAND-CALC. Why? Because you can only copyright the expression of an idea, not the idea itself. As long as Mary's expression is original, she has no copyright infringement problem as far as HANDCALC is concerned, and can copyright her own program.

2. Fixed In Tangible Medium of Expression

People who are trying to get a handle on what a copyright is and what it protects often ask, "When does a copyright start?" This is obviously an important question. The popular belief is that you have no copyright protection until you register with the government. Like so many other popular certainties, this one is wrong. A copyright exists from the moment a work is "fixed" on some tangible medium of expression. But, until it is fixed, you have nothing. You can take "fixed" almost literally to mean "settled" or "firm." The thoughts in your mind are not fixed, no matter how long they've been there or how inflexible you are when it comes time to change them. However, once you write or type them on paper, or program them in any retrievable form, they are fixed, and therefore protected by copyright law if they otherwise meet the requirements for copyrightable material. This is true even if you know your work is only in draft or outline form and will be reworked many times before it is marketed.

EXAMPLE: Carl Jones, our GOTTCHA developer, has a great idea for a new computer game. He talks it over with his friends, draws a picture for his wife on a napkin (which she promptly collects along with the dishes and silver when she clears the table, and tosses into the trash), and writes a "mock" program, which he doesn't bother to save either on disk or tape. When Carl turns the power to his computer off, his mock program disappears and can't be retrieved. Assuming the napkin has irretrievably journeyed to some friendly neighborhood landfill, Carl has not yet fixed his program and has nothing to copyright. The next morning, however, Carl gets up early and works on his idea again. This time he saves his draft program on a diskette. Even though he considers this work to be very preliminary, it is now fixed and therefore protected by copyright.

carl Jones

3. Summary of Copyright Ownership Rules

An item is only subject to copyright protection if:

■ It is original (i.e., independently developed);

■ It is a "work of authorship" (i.e., some type of symbolic expression). Computer programs, manuals and computer output all qualify;

■ It is fixed in a tangible medium of expression (i.e., reduced to some physical form which can be stored or saved over time).

E. What Is Not Subject to Copyright Protection?

Almost as important as knowing what kind of expression is subject to copyright protection is knowing what is not. Pay attention to this rule. A copyright does not offer legal protection for the unauthorized use of a floppy disk, computer tape, or chip as such. Rather, copyright only protects the exclusive rights which attach to "an original work of authorship." Put another way, it is the "expression" on the tape, disk or chip, rather than the medium itself, that is entitled to copyright protection.

Other items not subject to copyright protection include the titles carried by programs and manuals, company names, symbols, and abbreviations. Examples are names of programs, such as DATABASE-CRAZY, GOTTCHA, or LOANIT, and business names such as "Happiness Software, Inc." However, these may well be subject to legal protection as trademarks or tradenames, or in other ways. You will find an overview of these other protections in Chapter 15.

F. How to Profit from Your Copyright

Your exclusive copyright ownership means that one way or another, anyone who uses your work legally must receive your permission. Normally, this will involve payment. How the details of this payment are worked out will vary greatly depending on who you are, the type of work you produce or own, your marketing strategy, who wishes to use or market your work, and a dozen other considerations. But, before we continue, you should become familiar with one unavoidable piece of jargon in the intellectual property law area. Profiting from a copyright is generally called "exploiting" it. For example, you or your lawyer might prepare a copyright license agreement to commercially exploit your copyright in the United Kingdom.

---

1. Your Right to Divide Your Copyright

A copyright is not one right or entity, but a group or bundle of separate rights, each of which can be sold or licensed separately. In fact, a copyright is almost infinitely divisible. It is essential to your understanding of copyright law that you fully grasp this point. To take an extreme (and unlikely) example, you could provide 50 separate persons with exclusive licenses to distribute your copyrighted program to Panda computer owners in each of the 50 states. Or, more typically, you could separately sell one publisher the exclusive right to market your program in the U.S. for a particular computer, another publisher the right to market the same program in the U.S. for a different computer, and a third publisher the right to market the program in other major world markets, such as Great Britain and Japan. We thoroughly cover this subject in Chapter 12, but here is an anticipatory example.

EXAMPLE: Mary Hales sells the right to use her loan processing program, LOANIT, on all mainframe computers by licensing the exclusive marketing rights under her copyright to Financial Package Sell, a major mainframe software distributor. She then further divides her copyright by licensing a micro-computer version to Micromania. In exchange for letting Micromania and Financial Package Sell sell her program, Mary is to receive a percentage of the dollar amount these publishers receive for every program they sell (i.e., a royalty), in addition to a non-refundable advance upon signing the deal. Except for the specific copyright rights that Mary has sold (licensed, assigned, or transferred), she is still considered the owner of the LOANIT copyright. Accordingly, she can further divide it by licensing others to copy and sell LOANIT in other markets.

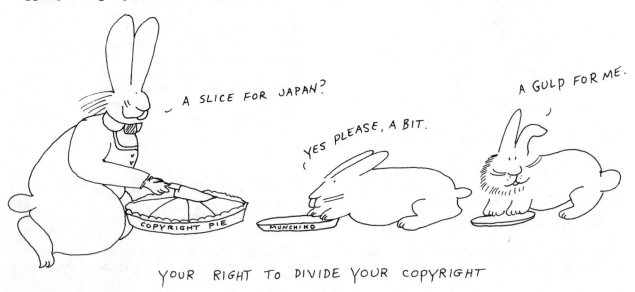

A SLICE FOR JAPAN?

YES PLEASE, A BIT.

A GULP FOR ME.

COPYRIGHT PIE

MUNCHIKO

YOUR RIGHT TO DIVIDE YOUR COPYRIGHT

2. Your Right to Exploit Derivative Works

As we mentioned, copyright ownership gives you the exclusive right to make derivative works. A derivative work is a subsequent work which is firmly based on an earlier work. To take a mundane example, the movie The World According to Garp is a derivative work of the book by the same name. Just what constitutes a derivative work in the computer world is explored in detail in the next chapter. However, for now you should understand that your exclusive right to make derivative works is vital to your ability to keep control over your original work. Why? Because this right gives you a legal basis to prevent anyone from marketing an altered version of your work.

EXAMPLE 1: Mary Hales first programmed her LOANIT package in COBOL. She then translated the package directly into PASCAL. This translation is a derivative work. Only Mary, or someone authorized by Mary, has the right to make such a translation of LOANIT.

EXAMPLE 2: Assume Carl Jones' computer game GOTTCHA becomes very popular. He authorizes BCA Graphics to make an animated television show, called GOTTCHA COMIN' AN GOIN', based on the characters in the game. The TV show is a derivative work. Only Carl, or someone authorized by Carl, such as BCA, has the right for commercial purposes to make a TV show based on GOTTCHA or otherwise exploit the GOTTCHA copyright for commercial purposes.

EXAMPLE 3: Kendra Salone wants to make a book cover design of a quilt pattern created by the QUILTIT program, which she wrote for BCA Graphics on a work-for-hire basis. Her book cover is to be an exact copy of the pattern. Since BCA Graphics owns the copyright to QUILTIT, and Kendra's book cover would be a derivative work, she must get BCA's permission to make and commercially exploit the painting.

SOURCE CODE AND OBJECT CODE NOTE: When we discuss the general subject of registering source and object code (Chapters 8 - 11), the question arises as to whether the object code can be copyrighted separately from source code as an independent creation. The answer is basically "No." This is because the Copyright Office currently considers object code as a copy of the source code and thus treats the source and object codes as one work of authorship. However, many other experts have long considered object code as a derivative of source code. We discuss this subject in detail in Chapter 4.

G. Who Owns a Copyright?

The basic rule is a copyright in a work is owned by the author of the work. However, there are several fact situations which routinely change this rule. The most important is that works made for hire are owned by the author's employer, or the person contracting for the work. Unfortunately, a poor understanding of copyright law and sloppy business practices often result in legal hassles over copyright ownership. This can occur when an author has made numerous, confusing, or overlapping grants of rights under his copyright. Another area of confusion over copyright ownership commonly develops as to whether a particular work is a legitimate work made for hire. There are, of course, all sorts of other potential problems regarding copyright ownership. Before we spend time on these, however, let's review the basic copyright ownership rules:

■ The copyright in any work which is authored by an independent contractor, writer, or developer is owned by that person;

■ The copyright in any work which is authored by an employee for her employer in the employment context is owned by the employer as an automatic work made for hire;

■ A work made under a written contract can result in the copyright belonging to the person contracting for it as a work made for hire if the written agreement so provides, and certain specific legal rules discussed in Part 4 of this section are met;

■ The copyright in any work made for hire, or work authored, or to be authored, by an independent developer, can be transferred or licensed to one or more other parties either before or after the work is completed (see Part 5 of this section, below).

Let's take a close look at the major categories of copyright ownership.

1. Work Done by Independent Developers

In most situations, if you develop or co-develop an original computer program or any other material subject to copyright protection while working for yourself, you automatically own a copyright in it from the moment your work is fixed in any tangible medium of expression. This is the same situation from a copyright law point of view as if you wrote a mystery novel. You do not have to register or complete any other act to be a copyright owner, although copyright formalities, such as placing a proper copyright notice on your work, are essential to preserve your copyright ownership if you publish your work (see Chapter 6).

Two big exceptions to the general rule that a copyright is owned by its independent developer involve works made for hire under an express contract and pre-development copyright transfers. These are discussed in Parts 4 and 5 of this Subsection, below.

2. Co-Authorship

When more than one person authors a work, they are considered joint copyright owners.

EXAMPLE 1: Mary Hales develops LOANIT, a loan processing system, on her own time. She is the owner of a copyright in LOANIT as soon as the code is saved on disk, paper, or other tangible medium.

EXAMPLE 2: Mary Hales and Robert Atkins work together on two programs that make up a portion of the total LOANIT package. Mary and Robert jointly own the copyright in these two programs. Mary alone owns the copyright in the other LOANIT programs.

When two or more people jointly "own" a copyright, the copyright laws provide protection to all owners equally, without regard to their share of ownership. This is true even though the copyright owners have divided ownership of their copyright between themselves in unequal shares. Incidentally, it is perfectly legal to do this by written contract. In other words, joint owners may divide copyright ownership as they see fit. Thus, suppose that Mary and Robert write a program together and agree that Mary owns 75% of the copyright, while Robert owns 25%. If Verminex Software Company infringes (violates) the copyright owned by Mary and Robert, either Mary or Robert may use the courts to obtain relief, despite the different percentages of their ownership interest.

3. Work for Hire in the Employment Context

The most common example of a work made for hire is a program written by a programmer for his employer within the scope of the employment. If your program is a work made for hire, the copyright is owned by the person or entity who hired you to write it.

EXAMPLE 1: Mary Hales is employed by Medium Bank as a programmer/analyst. She writes CHEQUEIT, a check processing program, at the request of her boss. Medium Bank, as Mary's employer, owns the CHEQUEIT copyright.

EXAMPLE 2: While employed at Medium Bank, Mary Hales writes a program to simplify loan processing. She writes this program in the evenings, at home, on her personal computer. The program is not directly related to the work Mary is doing for Medium Bank. Mary owns the copyright because CHEQUEIT was not written "within the scope of employment." This means it was not written under the direction of her employer, or on her employer's time, or using his resources. In addition, it is not connected with her work for Medium Bank.

NOTE: Doing work on your own time that is very similar to programming you do for your employer can raise nasty legal problems. In this situation, it's best to get a written release from your employer in advance. If you feel you are in a grey area, consult a lawyer.

4. Work for Hire under Express Contract

One of the major exceptions to the rules discussed above is big enough to sail the Queen Elizabeth II through, with enough room left over for a couple of tankers and the Love Boat. It involves the work-made-for-hire doctrine, but this time not in the context of employment. Independent developers may also legally be brought under the work-made-for-hire rule for certain types of works if they sign written agreements to that effect. Sadly, this is one of the principal legal means by which "independent" programmers end up losing the copyrights in the work they develop. If someone commissions or contracts with you as an independent contractor to do a specific programming job <u>and</u> there is an agreement in writing that the work is a work made for hire, that "someone" may own the copyright to your work instead of you. We say "may" because, to be a work made for hire, your work must also fall into one of six categories. We list these a little later in this discussion.

A work-for-hire contract in a non-employment context should state who is hiring who, that something of value ("consideration" in legalese) is being paid for the program, and that the work is done "for hire." In addition, the work to be done should be specified and defined in the contract as falling within one of the approved six categories of works made for hire by independent contractors. Of course, depending on the nature of the work and the agreement of the parties, it is also wise to set out normal contract terms, such as when the work is to be completed, when payments are to be made, etc. Here is a sample work-for-hire agreement. It is written in letter form without dozens of "wherefores," "therefores" and "parties of the first part." Hopefully, this makes it as intelligible as it is legal.

January 15, 198_

Mary Hales
123 Program Street
Anywhere, U.S.A. 12345

Dear Mary:

As we agreed on January 7, 198_, the purpose of this letter is to formally enter into an agreement with you for your services on a work-for-hire basis in developing our program #33, which will consist of loan pay-off calculations for our existing loan processing package called TOTAL and will meet the specifications sheet attached to this agreement as Exhibit 1. These specifications are hereby made part of this agreement.

It is agreed that your work will only constitute one part of the total loan processing package, which is owned by Big Bank.

For your services you will receive $4,000, half to be paid on signing this agreement and half when you deliver the completed pay-off calculation program which meets the terms of the specification sheet (Exhibit 1). The program must be delivered to us no later than July 15, 198_.

It is understood that your development of program #33 is to be a "work made for hire" within the meaning of 17 United States Code Section 101. All rights, including all copyright ownership rights, in program #33 will be the sole property of Big Bank. It is further understood that you hereby transfer any and all interests or rights that you may acquire in program #33, including, but not limited to, copyright rights and protections under 17 USC Section 106, to Big Bank.

It is further agreed that all aspects of the development of program #33 are to be held in strict confidence, as Big Bank considers this information to be a trade secret. This means you will not show your work on program #33 to, or discuss program #33 with, anyone without the written permission of Big Bank.

You understand that in rendering the above services, you shall be on a contract basis as an independent consultant and not as an employee of Big Bank. All services must be performed by you personally.

It is understood that you do not presently have any interest, and shall not acquire any interest, direct or indirect, financial or otherwise, which would conflict in any manner or degree with the performances of your services under this contract.

This letter is sent to you in duplicate. The specifications set out in Exhibit 1 are specifically made a part of it. If the terms set forth herein are acceptable to you, please indicate your approval by signing the original in the space provided below and return it to me. The copy is for your files.

Sincerely,

APPROVED AND ACCEPTED

_____
Jane Doe, Sr. V.P.
Big Bank

_____
Mary Hales

_____
Date

[EDITOR'S NOTE: We do not enclose the specification sheet here. It should contain the technical performance requirements for the program.]

As noted above, the fact that an independent contractor or developer has signed a work-for-hire agreement is not in itself sufficient to shift ownership of the work to the person paying for it. In addition, to qualify as a work for hire, the work in question must fall into one of the following groups:

■ The work is for use as part of a larger work;

EXAMPLE 1: In the above letter contract, Mary Hales is commissioned by Big Bank to write one of a hundred programs for a loan processing package that it plans to sell to other banks. This is clearly part of a larger work and qualifies as a work made for hire in a non-employment context. Were Mary an employee of Big Bank, it would make no difference whether she wrote one program or the entire package; the copyright in the entire work would belong to Big Bank.

EXAMPLE 2: Now assume Big Bank tries to hire Mary as an independent contractor to program the entire loan processing package. This would not be an effective work for hire in the independent contractor context and Mary would own the copyright in the resulting program.*

■ The work is a part of a motion picture or other audiovisual work;

EXAMPLE: Big Blue Motion Pictures contracts with BCA Graphics under a written work-made-for-hire agreement to do special effects for their upcoming film, HACKER AWAY.

■ The work is a translation of another work;

EXAMPLE: Mary Hales contracts with

---

* Realistically, however, Big Bank would probably prefer one of two alternatives. The first would be to hire Mary and ask her to program LOANIT within the scope of her employment. If this occurred, it would be a legitimate work made for hire (see Subsection 3, above). The second alternative involves ignoring the work-made-for-hire rule entirely and treating Mary as an independent author or developer, but insisting on a pre-development copyright transfer.

independent contractor Carl Jones to translate her COBOL programs into PASCAL. They sign a written work-for-hire contract.

■ The work is supplemental to another work;

EXAMPLE: Mary Hales decides that her user's manual is boring and hires Kendra Salone's wonderfully daffy uncle Brucie to add cartoons on a work-for-hire basis.

■ The work is part of a compilation of facts;

EXAMPLE: Carl Jones' auto parts database, BUGBITS, does not contain car parts from Korean or Russian cars. Carl commissions (contracts with) Red Page, a man he knows from his user's group, to add this information. They sign a written work-for-hire contract.

■ The work is an instructional text.

EXAMPLE: Mary Hales develops a complete training course to accompany her LOANIT package and signs a work-for-hire contract with Betty Figgins to write a textbook for the course.

If a work does not fall into one of these categories, and is not written within the scope of employment, it is not a work for hire, no matter how many agreements have been signed saying it is. If you are in doubt as to whether a work qualifies as a work for hire or not, you will probably want to get legal advice (see Chapter 2, Section C).

A little creativity at an early stage can usually eliminate any potential problems with the work-for-hire rule. For example, if Big Bank realizes that they cannot contract with Mary Hales as an independent contractor to develop an entire loan package as a work made for hire, they could offer to put her on the payroll, or hire her as an independent contractor, to create only part of the program, doing the rest in-house, or by contracting with other independent developers.

Realistically, however, there is also another, often easier, way to handle this problem. As we mentioned earlier, this is by use of a pre-development copyright transfer (discussed below).

CALIFORNIA WARNING: In California, for purposes of workers' compensation and unemployment insurance laws, persons performing works for hire are often considered as employees of the person paying for the work. This can have profound financial and tax effects on both the business commissioning the work and the independent developer. For this reason, be especially careful when signing work-made-for-hire contracts in California.

----

5. Pre-Development Transfers of Copyright

It is both legal and common for a software publisher, corporation, or anyone else, for that matter, to ask a developer, as part of the development contract, to transfer her copyright interest in a work not yet developed. This, of course, has long been common in the book business, where authors agree to assign their copyrights to a publisher prior to writing a word, in exchange for advance payment. Sometimes this payment is a one-time lump sum; more often it is an advance against future royalties. This means if the book sells enough copies so that the royalty per copy (say 8% of the cover price) adds up to more than the advance payment, the author eventually receives more money. Similar arrangements are common in the software business, although the royalty payments are more commonly computed as a percentage of the net price received by the publisher, rather than the sale price of the software.

For our purposes in understanding software copyright ownership, it's important to understand that if a person or company desires to purchase (or sell) all copyright rights to an entire program (or package) prior to its development, but are precluded from treating the arrangement as a work for hire because of the restrictions discussed in Subsection 4 above, an outright transfer of copyright ownership can accomplish the same result.

Obviously, work-made-for-hire agreements and pre-development transfers of a copyright provide alternative ways to structure contracts. However, this isn't the same as saying they will always achieve the same result. Work-made-for-hire agreements are usually used in a context where a specific programming or writing task is assigned and paid for on a piece-work basis (i.e., $3,000 for a database program listing all known popcorn recipes). When the work is done, the developer is paid and the copyright belongs to the person who paid for it.

Pre-development copyright transfers are normally much more complicated animals. As noted above, there is commonly a provision for continuing royalties, as well as advance payment. This isn't necessary, of course--the developer can sell out entirely if he wishes. If you are thinking of entering this sort of agreement, you will normally be faced with a document containing dozens of clauses, including how much is to be paid, when royalties are due, whose name will appear on the copyright notice (the developer or the transferee), what guarantees (warranties) the author makes that the material is original, and much more. Legal Care For Your Software, by Daniel Remer (Nolo Press), discusses this subject in detail and provides sample agreements.

Here is one short form example of a pre-development transfer-of-copyright agreement. This clearly tilts toward the simple end of the contract spectrum and will not prove adequate for developers who want to receive continuing royalties based on sales.

September 25, 198_

Mary Hales
123 Program St.
Anywhere, U.S.A. 12345

Dear Mary:

As we agreed, the purpose of this letter is to enter into a formal agreement under which you grant and assign all your rights in LOANIT (a loan processing package consisting of 70 programs and associated documentation to be developed by you) to Big Bank.

In exchange for this grant, you will receive $35,000, payable in ten equal installments, ten days after you submit each two programs and associated documentation.

As part of this agreement, you hereby transfer, grant and assign any and all interest or rights that you have, or may acquire, in and to the LOANIT loan processing programs, including worldwide copyright ownership, to Big Bank.

It is further agreed that all aspects of the development of the loan processing programs are to be held in strict confidence, as Big Bank considers this information to be a trade secret. You understand that in developing LOANIT you are neither an employee of Big Bank or doing "work made for hire," as that phrase is defined in the Copyright Act of 1976. All programming must be performed by you personally.

It is understood that you do not presently have any interest, and shall not acquire any interest, direct or indirect, financial or otherwise, which would conflict in any manner or degree with the performance of your services.

This letter is sent to you in duplicate. If the terms set forth herein are acceptable to you, please indicate your approval by signing the original in the space provided below and return it to me. The copy is for your files.

Sincerely,

APPROVED AND ACCEPTED

_____
Jane Doe, Sr. V.P.
Big Bank

_____
Mary Hales

_____
Date

LEGAL UNCERTAINTY NOTE: Our discussion here is based on the literal language of the Copyright Act as contained in the United States Code and court interpretations as of the date of publication of this book. Future court interpretations of this statute will undoubtedly shed further light on the entire work-for-hire question.

H. How Long Does a Copyright Last?

We provide a detailed discussion of copyright duration in Chapter 5. Our purpose here is only to give you an overview of how long copyright lasts. Except for copyrights on masks used to manufacture semiconductor chips, which last ten years, the duration of all copyrights established since 1978 depends on which of the following two categories the work fits.

Work Created by Identifiable Individuals

For works developed by an author working for herself--that is, everything but works made for hire--copyright protection lasts for the life of the author plus 50 years. If there is more than one author, the copyright lasts for 50 years from the death of the last surviving author. This is true even if the author sells (licenses) some or all of her copyright rights prior to development.

EXAMPLE: Let's return to Mary Hales and Carl Jones, two of our three developer friends, first introduced in Chapter 2. The copyrights in Mary's LOANIT and Carl's GOTTCHA last for 50 years after the death of each author. As with any other property, the copyrights can be left as part of their respective estates.

Work Made for Hire or by an Author Using a Fictitious Name or Choosing to be Anonymous

Works developed by an author working as a work for hire, either in the employment context or under a valid written work-for-hire contract, are copyrightable for 100 years from the time they are first fixed in tangible form, or 75 years from publication, whichever comes first.

Works which identify no natural person as the author are treated as anonymous works by the copyright law.

These are also copyrightable for 75 or 100 years.

I. How Do You Protect a Copyright?

We mentioned that you are protected by copyright automatically from the moment your work is fixed in any form (e.g., written on paper, recorded on tape or a floppy disk, embedded in a ROM, etc.). However, it's crucial to your economic health to realize that you will keep your copyright protection (at least in the U.S.) only if you take at least one affirmative step. This consists of putting a correct copyright notice on your work from the time it is first published.* A correct notice on a published work consists of ©, your name, and the date of first publication, or one of several other legal variations of the copyright symbol, such as the word "copyright" or "copr.," along with your name and the publication date. We discuss how to do this in detail in Chapter 6.

---

* Elsewhere, we recommend putting a notice without a publication date on any unpublished work which might have commercial value. We do this for practical reasons. The omission of such notice on unpublished work will not adversely affect your automatic copyright. Only when the work is published will the omission of a notice possibly cause you to lose your copyright.

In the United States, you can gain considerable additional copyright protection if you promptly register your copyright (see Chapters 8 - 11). In broad outline, registration gives you additional advantages if you end up in court suing an infringer. These include beneficial technical rules involved in the burden of proving your case, as well as the right to receive certain types of damages, court costs and attorney fees if you prevail. In short, while copyright registration is not nearly as essential to protect your copyright as is publishing your work with a correct copyright notice, it does provide you with a number of additional protections.

International copyright protection is covered by several international treaties. While copyright notice is not essential to protect work within some countries, it is essential to gain full international protection. Copyright registration is available in a few countries, but not in most others. Where it is available, it usually offers fewer additional protections than is the case in the U.S. See Chapter 14 for a full discussion of how to gain copyright protection around the world.

J. What Specific Types of Software, Computer Output and Computer-Related Materials Can Be Copyrighted?

Earlier, we provided a general description of the requirements for obtaining a copyright. To briefly review, we said that to be protected by copyright, a work of authorship must be an original work of authorship which is fixed in a tangible medium of expression. Obviously, these concepts are general in nature. The Copyright Office has divided "works of authorship"

into different categories, for their own internal record keeping and recording purposes. We cover this thoroughly in Chapter 8. For now, you need only understand that if your work is written on or for a computer, it can be protected by copyright. Works include:

1. Programs

All original programs, regardless of form or language (source, object, or assembler, COBOL or BASIC), or medium (tape, disk, ROM). This includes operating systems. See Chapter 1 for a discussion of these computer terms.

2. Documentation

Program documentation, no matter how mundane, is copyrightable as a literary work so long as it is expressed in words, numbers or other verbal or numerical symbols. This generally includes manuals, promotional and training materials (whether written, taped, or filmed), and computerized documentation. Again, remember that for copyright purposes a literary work does not have to even vaguely resemble the great American novel. However, it must contain sufficient text or content to "express" an idea or concept.

3. Data Dictionaries and Databases

All lists and compilations of material qualify for copyright protection if they are original and fixed in a tangible medium of expression. This includes both data dictionaries and data bases, whether in hard copy or electronic form.

4. Serials and Periodicals

All serialized, consecutively-numbered publications, such as magazines, newsletters and technical, scientific, or law reviews, are copyrightable. Personal computer magazines, user's group newsletters, update circulars, etc. that are published regularly, all qualify.

5. Still Life Graphic Works

Graphic, sculptural, and other types of still-life artistic works qualify for copyright protection. A large amount of computer output comes within this category and, as such, is subject to protection. This usually means selecting a different copyright form than is used for the underlying program. We describe how to do this in Chapter 8. The particular output needn't be acclaimed by critics as art, as long as it's a two- or three-dimensional picture on a display terminal. To reduce the screen image to the fixed or tangible form necessary for copyright protection, you can photograph or otherwise reproduce it.

6. Motion Pictures and Other Audio-Visual Works

All work that consists of "pictures in motion" can be copyrighted. This includes such types of computer output as video and computer games and other screens of a movie nature, including demonstration programs and the like.

7. Computer-Generated Movies

Computer-generated movies can also be copyrighted. Unlike regular movies, where individual picture sequences are fixed on film and displayed with the aid of a camera, computer-generated movies are created from scratch according to instructions fed to the computer through appropriate software. Images thus created can thereafter be shown on a computer screen while a program is executing, or they can be transferred to a reel of tape, like regular movies.

8. Charts

Visual works which present information rather than pictures, such as pie and bar charts, flow charts, pert and ghant charts and other "work horse" pictures, are all afforded copyright protection.

9. Phonorecords

Here we include all works where music or sound is the dominating expression. As soon as a song is recorded on some media, it is copyrightable. However, a song that is improvised and not recorded is not fixed and cannot be copyrighted.

10. Computer-Generated Sound Effects

Remember, before anything can be copyrighted, it must be fixed. When sound is involved, this usually means a tape or record. In the computer area, this often involves synthesized sound generated by computer. Computers can generate tones that are almost indistinguishable from real violins, pianos and a wide variety of other beeps and whistles. The human voice can be recognized and generated by computer as well. A tape or phonorecord, laser disk or other media must be used to fulfill the fixation requirement in this category. Once this happens, the result can be copyrighted.

NOTE: DUAL COPYRIGHT SCHEMES: In a few areas, you will want to copyright different forms of the same work. For example, it is often wise to copyright both a computer game program and its output screens. We will deal with the hows and whys of dual copyright schemes where appropriate.

11. Masks Used to Manufacture Semiconductor Chips

Effective January 1985, copyright protection will be extended to "masks" (a type of template used to create complex circuitry in semiconductor chips), "mask works" (three dimensional templates also used in the chip manufacturing process), and semiconductor chips which are produced from such masks and mask works. In short, the circuitry contained in computer chips and the devices used to create it will now be copyrightable.

NOTE ON SEMICONDUCTOR CHIP PROTECTION ACT: The Semiconductor Chip Protection Act of 1983 (Senate Bill 1201) was passed by Congress just as this book was going to print (October 1984) and was not yet signed by the President at the time of this writing, although his signature was expected. The Act provides definitions of "mask," "mask work" and "semiconductor chip product," extends copyright protection to these items, but limits it to ten years, and requires that compulsory licenses be granted to innocent purchasers of semiconductor chip products that have been made from a protected mask or mask work without authorization by the copyright owner. Because of our production schedule, we were unable to thoroughly analyze or integrate the Act into the book. Therefore, if you find statements which cast doubt on the copyrightability of chip masks or semiconductor chips, or which do not reflect the ten-year protection period, please disregard them.

K. Conclusion

In this chapter, we have discussed the fundamentals of copyright law. Hopefully, you now have an understanding of what copyrights are, what they do, who owns them, how long they last, how they can be exploited on a commercial basis and the kinds of computer-related works of expression which they protect. If any of this information seems murky, relax, take a deep breath and continue reading. These concepts will be reintroduced in succeeding chapters and explained in detail as part of showing you how to qualify your computer program or computer output for maximum legal protection.

—————————•CHAPTER 4•—————————

Derivative Works and Use of Pre-Existing Material

A. Introduction

In the world of software programming, a "new" program is commonly not completely original. Indeed, many new programs consist of a mix of new code, alterations to existing code, as well as some pre-existing routines which may have been taken from, or inspired by, a variety of sources.* For example, have you ever:

■ Created an innovative driver for your operating system?

■ Improved one of your earlier programs?

■ Borrowed several routines written and owned by somebody else and incorporated them into an otherwise new program?

■ Translated your (or somebody else's) program into a different computer language or adapted it to a different media (e.g., from a computer game to a video arcade game)?

---

* A "routine" is simply a subpart of a program which performs a specific limited task.

■ Created a database to organize existing material?

■ Substantially modified an existing language (say BASIC) into a new form ideally suited for your computer? or

■ Created any work which in any way uses, modifies, or builds on a pre-existing program, routine or piece of code?

If this sort of activity sounds familiar, this chapter is for you. On the other hand, if your work does not contain any pre-existing material (whether owned by you or somebody else), you can skip to the next chapter on the duration of copyrights. If later it turns out you do need the information presented here, you can always come back.

Understanding how to sort the original program wheat from the pre-existing program chaff is of vital importance in protecting computer software. This chapter will help you to do this. It's about recognizing and correctly labeling programs containing a mix of new and old material and how to legally protect the new material under the copyright law.

Let's start with the basics. If you use, or are inspired by, pre-existing work, your program falls into one of five categories:

1. A derivative work;

2. An original work which incorporates some pre-existing material, but which doesn't constitute a derivative work;

3. A compilation (a new arrangement or organization of existing works with very little or no new code);

4. A minor alteration to an existing work, with the result that, for copyright purposes, the work is considered to be a copy of the original, rather than a derivative work or a new work containing some pre-existing material; and

5. An original work.

The differences between these categories are important. They concern both the very nature of copyright law and the procedures which should be followed to provide maximum copyright protection. We will explain these distinctions in detail below, but first let's answer a preliminary question. Why, as a practical matter, do you need to know all of this? Well, did you ever wonder whether that special patch (alteration in code) you designed to make an application program hum on your brand of computer might be worth protecting under the copyright laws? Or, perhaps you have wanted to know if any additional copyright steps must be taken to protect a new or updated version of an already copyrighted work. Or, maybe you are concerned with who to get permission from to build on somebody else's work. Quite simply, the answers to these and literally dozens of similar questions depend on your having a working grasp of the five categories set out above.

It's easy to get your head in a spin when dealing with the copyright rules that pertain to derivative works, the use of pre-existing material and compilations, etc. For now at least, please relax and read the entire chapter. Then re-read the parts that are important to you. While it will take a little patience to put this all together, there is one helpful truth we want you to focus on right here at the beginning. Within limits, you have a fair amount of discretion in choosing both how to characterize a particular work and how best to protect it.

Before we begin, it's appropriate to remind you of what we mean when we talk about "copyrightability," "copyright protection" and "valid copyright." We use these terms to mean more than just the process by which you place a copyright notice on your work, and the process by which you register your copyright. Sure, these procedures are essential for attaining maximum copyright protection, but in the long run, they mean little unless the underlying work is eligible for protection. For example, if you put a copyright notice on someone else's work and register it, you gain no real protection. Why? Because when the real owner shows up and sues you, you will not only lose the right to profit further from the work, but may also face a damages judgment as well. So, as you read this chapter, please realize that when we refer to a valid copyright, or use a similar term, we mean not only that the proper copyright protection procedures have been followed, but that the person following them had a right to do so. This distinction is important because our job here is to teach you how to get the maximum legal copyright protection for a derivative work and how to use pre-existing copyrighted material, etc., not how to create lots of questionable copyrights that can be easily challenged later.

Let's start with four simple propositions:

■ If your work uses material subject to somebody else's copyright, you must obtain and presumably pay for their permission to use that material;

■ If you prepare a derivative work without the permission of the person who owns the copyright in the work from which yours was derived, your entire work is not subject to copyright protection;

■ The more you use the works of another without permission, the less copyright protection you will receive;

■ If you publish material belonging to someone else, you may well find yourself on the losing end of a copyright infringement suit (see Chapter 13).

B. Derivative Works Defined

The derivative work concept is central to understanding how to protect any work which uses all, or portions, of an earlier work. Congress has provided us with a very general definition of this term: "A derivative work is a work based upon one or more pre-existing works." [17 USC, Sec. 101]. For example, a motion picture version of a novel would be a derivative work, as would be an abridgement, condensation, sound recording, translation or any other form in which the novel was recast, transformed or adapted. Similarly, a work consisting of editorial revisions, annotations, elaborations or other modifications of an existing work qualifies as a derivative work. This is true even though the new material consists of original work.

Over the years, there have been numerous court fights over the question of whether a particular song, novel, play or story is derivative of another. Even after placing two printed works side by side, judges often have difficulty with this question. One reason for this difficulty, as with so many questions in the legal field, is that the answer to whether one work is derivative of another in a given dispute is found on a continuum. At one end of the continuum, a work so clearly relies on another that it is obviously derivative. An example would be a song with only a few notes changed from an already copyrighted one. At the other end of the continuum, a song with only a few minor similarities is clearly not derivative, but rather an original work of authorship entitled to copyright status on its own. In the middle of the continuum is a large gray area where the judgment as to whether one work is derivative of another is as likely to depend on what the judge had for breakfast as on any abstract legal principle or formula.

When it comes to computer software, the characteristic that is most likely to cause a court to conclude that one work is derivative of another is that the second work simply recasts the original program in some way, as is the case with a translation to a different computer language or operating system. A court is also likely to find the second work to be derivative if it uses so much code from an existing copyrighted program that the already existing material constitutes a substantial part of the new work.

1. Derivative Work: Altering an Original Work

Whenever you change an original work by altering the code, adding additional code or eliminating code, you have created a derivative work, unless you change it so much as to create an entirely new and independent work. The derivative work stands on its own and is entitled to a new copyright, assuming you own the underlying work. As you should grasp by now, however, if the earlier work is owned by somebody else, and their permission has not been obtained, you have violated their copyright, and your new work has no independent value if the original copyright owner challenges it in court.

EXAMPLE 1: Big Bank buys one copy of LOANIT from Mary Hales and then rewrites two program modules to improve the processing speed of LOANIT. This is a derivative work. So long as Big Bank uses this derivative work solely to improve the copies of LOANIT that it has legitimately purchased, no infringement of Mary's exclusive right to prepare derivative works has occurred.* However, if Big Bank distributes its derivative work to other banks without Mary's permission, Mary's copyright in the original work (which includes the exclusive right to make derivative works) has been infringed.

EXAMPLE 2: Mary Hales sells her LOAN-IT package to Big Bank and Small Bank. Small Bank then writes Mary, requesting significant revisions in the package, which will make LOANIT easier for any small bank to use. Mary makes the revisions requested by Small Bank, but does so in a way that leaves the program basically intact. She markets this new version to small banks under the name LOANIT-SMALL. LOANIT-SMALL is a derivative work based on the original LOANIT. Mary should place a copyright notice on it and register it.

EXAMPLE 3: Kendra Salone works at home to make a number of changes in her QUILTIT program which greatly improve it. She decides to call the old version, QUILTIT 1.0, and the new version QUILTIT 2.0. QUILTIT 2.0 is a derivative work. Because BCA Graphics owns the copyright to QUILTIT, they also own the copyright to QUILTIT 2.0. This means Kendra must obtain BCA's permission if she wants to sell QUILTIT 2.0 on her own. This is true even though Kendra wrote QUILTIT 2.0 on her own time.

EXAMPLE 4: A Big Bank programmer who has used LOANIT decides to write her own loan processing package. Although the new loan processing package accomplishes roughly the same tasks as LOANIT, and the programmer was inspired by some of Mary's ideas, it is fundamentally different and uses no LOANIT code. This is a new and original work and, assuming the employee did the programming at work, belongs to Big Bank as a work made for hire. The

fact that she was inspired to write the new package by using LOANIT is of no legal significance.

2. Derivative Work: Translations of Pre-Existing Material

Let's say you discover an obscure COBOL program which was written for the Buffalo Computer, an obsolete minicomputer. Although translating the program would take a lot of work, you believe that a PASCAL version for the up-to-date Unicorn Micro would sell like hot cakes. Are you free to do this? Not without the permission of whoever owns the exclusive right to make derivative works from the original COBOL version. Why? Because translations of a work are usually considered to be derivative works.*

3. Derivative Work: New Media

"Media" has a special meaning in the computer industry. It refers to whatever it is that physically holds or carries your code or output, such as the tape, disk, screen, printout and probably the ROM on which your program is housed. Thus, if the PacMan figure is reproduced on a t-shirt, the expression has changed from the screen medium to the t-shirt medium. Similarly, if the output of your computer game is changed to a laser disk setting, a media change has occurred. One traditional example of a media change

---

* This is because a purchaser has the legal right to do anything they want to the copy of the work they purchase, as long as they do it for their own use. 17 USC, Section 117. We discuss this concept in more detail in Section J of this chapter.

* This only applies to true translations from one language to another. When a program is "translated" to run on a different machine, however (e.g., the COBOL used on the Buffalo is modified to run on the Unicorn), it is normally considered to be the same as the original work for copyright purposes, unless the changes require original programming. For example, most popular application programs may be altered (patched) by the user to run on specific terminals and with specific printers. As these changes have normally been "pre-defined" by the software developers, they involve neither an original work of authorship, nor even the creation of a true derivative work. We come back to this subject in Chapter 11(C).

is when a book is made into a movie. The important thing to understand is that changing the media in which an original work is fixed normally creates a derivative work consisting of the expression as fixed in the new media. And, regardless of what new media is used, a copyright infringement occurs if you don't first obtain permission from the owner, unless of course you only use the derivative work for your personal use.

EXAMPLE 1: Carl Jones' computer game GOTTCHA is re-packaged as a handheld game module and a video arcade game. These new versions of GOTTCHA involve a change in media, but not in the basic program. They are, accordingly, derivative works. Only Carl, or someone authorized by him, has the authority to do this.

EXAMPLE 2: Carl Jones' cartoon, GOTTCHA COMIN' & GOIN', is a hit. Some enterprising person decides to create a t-shirt depicting the GOTTCHA characters. Since Carl copyrighted the pictures of these characters, as well as the program itself (see Chapter 8), the t-shirt maker must get Carl's permission for this derivative work.

I SEE MANY MEDIUMS IN YOUR FUTURE.

4. Derivative Work: New Organization of Existing Material

If you reorganize an existing program by reversing the order of the routines, or putting them in alternating order, or make similar changes, you have created a derivative work.

Because of the modularity of many programs (i.e., they are a collection of routines, subroutines and, in the case of operating systems, "drivers"), it is both possible and fairly routine to create a derivative work by reorganizing the components of an old one without changing virtually any code. Again, only the owner of the right to prepare derivative works (or someone who has obtained authorization from such owner) is authorized to do this.

EXAMPLE: Kendra Salone takes the routines she used in QUILTIT and reorganizes them into a new program which can determine the maker of a quilt by analyzing its design pattern. This new program would be a derivative work. Assuming the original QUILTIT copyright belongs to BCA Graphics, Kendra would be infringing that copyright unless she obtained BCA's permission, or the new program was solely for her own use.

C. Protecting Derivative Works Where You Own the Prior Works

When the author of a derivative work owns the copyright to the original work (or at least the right to prepare derivative works and make copies), the primary consideration is often what steps, if any, need to be taken to protect the new work? These are simple. The work should be published with the proper copyright notice (see Chapter 6). Assuming the original work was registered with the Copyright Office (see Chapter 8), you must decide whether the derivative work should also be registered. As a practical matter, your conclusion will probably depend on how you answer the following questions:

■ Is your new work almost the same as your previous one? If your answer is "Yes," your second work is probably protected adequately by the copyright registration for the first?

■ Is your new work different enough from your previous one to warrant considering the new work as being derivative of the prior one?

■ If your answer is "Yes," are the changes to your original work which create the derivative work valuable enough as a practical matter to warrant taking additional steps to protect them-- such as registering the derivative work? Remember, the original portion of the derivative work is already fully protected by your original copyright;

■ If your answer to this question is also "Yes," you should definitely register your derivative work. As a general rule, if your derivative work contains a substantial amount of new code, or it is very valuable (no matter how minor your changes), it should also be registered.

REGISTRATION NOTE: We discuss the benefits to be gained by registering copyright in detail in Chapter 8.

D. Protecting Derivative Works When Someone Else Owns the Prior Work

As we indicated, if the work you are borrowing from is covered by someone else's copyright, you cannot effectively protect your work unless you get permission to use the earlier work. Once such

permission is obtained, however, you can register your derivative work just as if the existing material were yours.

From whom do you get permission? Permission is obtained from the owner of the exclusive right to prepare derivative works. Usually this is the author or publisher but not always. In Chapter 12, we discuss the ins and outs of dividing copyright ownership and obtaining permission to use someone else's work. If you face a situation where one person owns the exclusive right to make copies and another person owns the exclusive right to prepare derivative works, you will need to know the difference between a derivative work and an original work with pre-existing material (i.e., a work which copies some of another person's already copyrighted work). In other words, you may need to know what kind of work you have created before you can figure out whom to get permission from. This subject is covered immediately below.

E. "Derivative Works" Distinguished from "Original Works with Pre-Existing Material"

If any part of your work consists of code covered by somebody else's copyright, ask this question: Is the pre-existing code significant enough a part of your program to make it a derivative work in the sense discussed in Section B of this chapter? If so, you will need to obtain permission from the owner of the exclusive right to make derivative works? However, if the significance of the pre-existing material you wish to use is not sufficiently great to make your work a derivative, you will need to get permission from the owner of the exclusive right to make copies of the original program. Again, in both situations, this is likely to be an author or a person or entity who has purchased all rights from the author. If so, you have no problem. However, if the bundle of copyright rights in an existing work has been divided, and you are only using a small part of that work, you need to be sure you are dealing with the person who has the right to make copies.

As we've seen, whether your use of already copyrighted material as part of a new work means the new work is a derivative of the original one depends upon the importance of the already copyrighted material to the new program. Up to a certain point, the pre-existing material is viewed as simply being a small part of a new original work. However, if you use a lot of pre-existing material, the new work is legally viewed as being based on, or derivative of, the earlier work. Unfortunately, deciding whether a work is derivative or not involves more than just comparing the volume of new code to pre-existing code. Thus, it might be possible to create a new (non-derivative) work by creatively combining a lot of pre-existing material taken from several different sources with a relatively small amount of new code to form a new program that is genuinely innovative. On the other hand, it is also possible to use less pre-existing code and still end up with a program so much like the one you borrowed from that it would be regarded as being a derivative work. Remember, although the difference between a derivative work and an original work with pre-existing material will only occasionally have practical importance, as detailed above, one thing is always true: If you create either type of work, you need to get permission from, and presumably pay, the original piper. This is especially true if the program you are using is a popular or well-known commercial product.

F. Ownership of New Code in Derivative Work

Now, let's look again at works that are created by adding additional code or programs to already existing works.

We've seen that the resulting work is derivative (or uses pre-existing material) and cannot legally be used without the appropriate copyright owner's permission (except as in Section J, below). But, what about the additional code itself, separated out from the original program? Assuming you wrote it and didn't copy it from anyone, doesn't the copyright on it belong to you? The best answer is "Maybe." Generally speaking:

■ If your new code is so interwoven with original code that it has little if any independent meaning, it is generally considered nonsense code and is not qualified for protection as an original work of authorship. If you own the original program, you need do nothing. If you don't own the original program, there is nothing that you can do.

■ If your code makes perfect sense when separated from the existing work, it may qualify as an independent work which you can copyright, even if you don't own the original program. This is particularly likely to be true if you treat it as an independent work. However, in some circumstances, it might still be a derivative work and thus not entitled to independent protection. This is because the Copyright Act says that one work is derivative of another if it is "based" on it. What the term "based on" means has been left to the courts to define, and they have done so case by case, without establishing any clear guidelines.

■ If your code constitutes its own separate program and accomplishes either a task not covered in the original program or changes some major part of the existing program entirely, it is probably subject to independent copyright protection. However, if it is marketed or used in connection with the pre-existing program, it may merge with that program. The result of this could be that you are right back to creating a derivative work.

■ If your changes are simply a minor modification of an existing program and don't fundamentally change it, you have probably created a copy, which means your work is covered by the original copy-

right. If you are the original copyright
owner, you don't need to re-register the
new work. If you don't own the copyright
in the original work, you don't own anything.

EXAMPLE: Big Bank needs a multi-bank
processing capability, since they just
purchased Little Bank and Middle Bank.
They add a program to Mary Hales' LOANIT
package (they purchased the copy from
her) to perform this task. The new program they write belongs to them as long
as it doesn't paraphrase or copy any of
Mary Hales' LOANIT code. As far as the
copyright law is concerned, they can even
market or sell their new module. They
can't, of course, sell LOANIT itself,
unless they get Mary's permission, since
Mary obviously owns the copyright in the
original work. If they try and sell
LOANIT with their new code without Mary's
permission, the new product will be
considered a derivative work and Mary
will prevail in any infringement lawsuit.

LAWYER NOTE: Obviously, making the
sorts of distinctions we discuss here is
tricky! As we have suggested earlier, if
you find yourself in a situation where
you don't honestly know whether your work
is "derivative" or "original," consult an
experienced attorney before marketing
your work.

G. Distinguishing Derivative Works from Compilations

Suppose you take routines from many
different copyrighted programs and
rearrange them into a new composite work
without producing any new code of your
own. If you only borrow a few routines
from any one program, your work will

probably be viewed as a compilation, not
a derivative work.

This type of work is usually considered a collective work and is entitled to
copyright protection independently from
the various works the code was taken
from. However, as is always true, you
may not gather routines belonging to
someone else and/or reorganize them for
commercial purposes without the permission of the appropriate copyright owners.

EXAMPLE: Mary Hales creates a program
for processing credit card payments by
taking her LOANIT routines and some other
credit card routines and putting them
together to form a credit card payment
program. Mary will have to obtain permission from the appropriate owners of
the non-LOANIT material unless the new
work is for her own personal use.

H. Using Languages Owned by Others as a Tool to Create New Works

What effect does the use of a language
compiler (i.e., a program which translates a higher level language into machine language or object code which the
computer can understand) have on the
resulting program? If you use one, is
your program somehow a derivative work,
or can you claim complete copyright ownership? In other words, to fully own
your program, do you need to get permission from the person who owns the copyright to the compiler? The simple answer
to these questions is that languages can
be used without obligation to create an
independent program. The new work is not
derivative. However, if it is necessary
to include the language compiler, or some
of the compiler routines, with your program when you distribute it, you will
need to obtain (and presumably pay for)
permission to do so.

To make sure that all of you fully understand this point, let's examine the relationship between languages and the products produced by their use. Programs are a series of commands (specific instructions to the computer) that make a computer perform tasks and produce usable output. Usually, the commands take the form of a source code. When you write this code, you use words developed by someone else. When combined, the words are called a "language."

The developers of languages do not own copyrights in the words or even the syntax. To allow them to do so would be like allowing someone to own French or Russian. Accordingly, you are free to use the words and syntax of any language, in any way you see fit, without worrying about copyright infringement. Practically, however, it will do you no good to use a language such as ADA or LISP to write your source code unless your computer is able to "understand" that language.

This brings us to the question of how a computer is able to understand the language of your source code and render it into the ones and zeros so near and dear to its processor. The answer, which we discussed in some detail in Chapter 1, is that your computer must already contain the translation capacity (program) to understand the language your source code is written in. To this end, most computer users receive at least one language as part of their computer purchase. This process of selling hardware and software together is often called "bundling." Some form of BASIC or PASCAL is common for microcomputers, whereas languages such as FORTH, FORTRAN AND COBOL must usually be purchased separately on a floppy disk. When you purchase (or receive free with a computer purchase) a particular programming language, you actually receive a language compiler (or interpreter or assembler, depending on the type of language and the sophistication of the machine). You might think of a compiler as a type of two-sided Rosetta stone. One side is compatible with the programming language used by humans, while the other communicates wonderfully in ones and zeros. The result is that communication between the human user and the computer is made possible.

Although the words and syntax of a computer language are not copyrightable, the actual translation program code (compiler, assembler, interpreter, etc.) is copyrightable as an original work of authorship. This means that while you can use the commands contained in the language without worrying about copyright ownership, you can't legally sell or copy the translation program necessary to make it intelligible to the computer. Think of it this way. The English language can be used by anyone. It's just the way English is organized into a novel, play, short story, etc. that can be protected. Similarly, a computer language can be used by anyone. It's just the particular program which tells the machine what to do with the language that is subject to the copyright laws.

Copyright problems commonly ensue when a developer or distributor of software cannot rely on the end user to already have all the routines (the translation program) necessary to run the particular operating program on her computer. To get around this problem, it may be necessary to include some routines from the translation program so the computer can use the operating system in question. If so, and the translation program is covered by copyright, as most are, the developer must get permission from, and presumably pay, the copyright owner of the right to make copies of her program. This is exactly the same process as we discussed above concerning new works using pre-existing material.

What about the fact that a great deal of software is distributed in object code form, with the subject code already compiled? Isn't it ready to run on the computer in this form? Probably not. Why? Because, many programs typically still require some additional compiling at the instant the code is "run." The programs permitting this last minute compiling are subroutines of the larger compiler program and are referred to as "run-time" compilers. Accordingly, you will need to either distribute a run-time compiler along with your object code program or depend on the end user to obtain one independently of your program. Copyrighted run-time compilers, like other pre-existing work, can only be used as a part of your otherwise original program with the copyright owner's permission.

EXAMPLE 1: Mary Hales converts LOANIT to PASCAL for use with a particular microcomputer. She has created a derivative work. Unfortunately, not everyone she plans to sell the PASCAL version to will have a PASCAL compiler. Although Mary plans to distribute her program in its object code form (i.e., already compiled), she still wants to include a PASCAL run-time compiler for those users who lack the full PASCAL compiler.* To do this, Mary would have to obtain the permission of, and presumably pay, the PASCAL com-

piler copyright owner before using it in connection with her new program.

EXAMPLE 2: As part of her LOANIT program, Mary Hales includes a program in the command language, DATABASE CRAZY. In order for end users to use her program, she could either:

■ Require everyone to already own DATABASE CRAZY; or

■ She could arrange for a DATABASE CRAZY run-time compiler as part of her program distributed in object code; or

■ She could include a copy of DATABASE CRAZY with each LOANIT package.

The last two alternatives would require permission of (and, presumably, payment to) the DATABASE CRAZY copyright owner, unless Mary owned it herself. This is because alternative 3 obviously involves a direct copy of DATABASE CRAZY, while the run-time compiler (alternative 2) is a derivative work of DATABASE CRAZY.

I. Using Database Manager Programs as a Tool to Create New Databases

Chances are that every reader has either created or worked with a database. A database is nothing more than information stored in a particular way designed to facilitate the user's access to specifically desired information. A "3 x 5" index card filing system counts as a database, as does an encyclopedia.

Due to the incredible ability of computers to quickly search through massive amounts of information to retrieve specific facts, the database concept has assumed great significance. In fact, almost every subject imaginable has been corraled into large centralized computer databases, many of which are accessible to microcomputer users through modems. At the microcomputer level, small busi-

---

* Some compiled PASCAL object code may not require run-time compilers. It depends on the particular translation program.

nesses and individuals routinely create smaller databases, many of which have potential value.

For computer databases to be constructed, the computer must be told (i.e., programmed) where the information placed in it is stored and how that information can be retrieved upon request. As databases become more complex, the computer must also be informed in advance, through programming, about the relationships between the various bits of data.

Although computer databases may often be constructed from scratch on a custom basis, application programs, generically called "Database Manager Systems" (DBMS's), are commonly used to create them, especially on microcomputers. These programs allow the end user to construct his own database without the need to use a programming language. Accordingly, when a database is actually constructed, it consists of:

■ The data; and

■ The unique set of instructions which defines the way the data is to be organized, stored, and retrieved.

Whether you construct a database by first designing a custom program, or by using a DBMS, the important thing to know is that you own a copyright to the entire database. In other words, the instructions you write are yours, as well as the particular expression (organization) of the data*. However, the copyright to the database management system (the custom program that allows the computer to organize data in the first place) is not yours. Rather, you have simply used the DBMS to create your product. Sound familiar? It should. It's the same concept

we just discussed when examining how a language is used to create a program. You own the program, but somebody else owns the copyright to the program (compiler) necessary to use it.

For example, remember Carl Jones' database of V.W. auto parts, called BUGBITS? The output of BUGBITS, consisting of the list of parts, constitutes Carl's original database expression (i.e., his information organized his way) and is entitled to copyright protection. However, if Carl wants to publish his database, he has a problem. He can either provide the underlying database manager program, or at least enough of it that users can access the information, or he can insist that all users of his program independently provide their own database manager program. Even if Carl only includes a run-time program with the database (i.e., just the code needed to run the database in the event it is distributed in compiled or object code form), he will have to get the permission of the run-time compiler copyright owner.

NOTE: GRAPHICS PROGRAMS AND SPREAD-SHEETS: For copyright purposes, graphics and spreadsheet programs are similar to database managers and language compilers. Whatever you create with them is yours, but the underlying programs allowing you to be creative belong to their authors (or owners).

EXAMPLE 1: Carl Jones buys WIZTALK, a popular spreadsheet program. He then creates a format ("template" in computerese) specifically designed for the needs of automobile dealers. Carl has no copyright problems if he sells his template with nothing but his own commands to allow it to input to the spreadsheet program. Of course, everyone who buys Carl's template must have WIZTALK, or there will be no communication between the user and the machine. However, if Carl adds any part of WIZTALK to his program, he must get permission of the WIZTALK copyright owner.

EXAMPLE 2: Carl Jones' design for the blueprint of the race car he uses in his

---

* These instructions may even be protected by copyright so long as you engage in some creative "programming" while using your DBMS. Sometimes, however, the instructions which you can input to build your database are well-defined in advance by the DBMS program. In that case, your program may not be copyrightable because only a very few different programs are possible to create the same database. Morrissey v. Proctor & Gamble, 379 F.2d 675.

program, CHIPRACER, was developed using a graphics program he purchased from Gameland. He doesn't need any of the graphic program itself as part of his work. He has no copyright problems.

EXAMPLE 3: Kendra Salone's QUILTIT program (owned by BCA Graphics, as she was their employee when she developed it) allows people to create original quilt designs. While the program itself is copyrightable, the quilt designs people create using it belong to them, not to BCA Graphics.

INDEPENDENT CREATION NOTE: Suppose BCA sells QUILTIT to Juggernaut Inc., a large corporation engaged in making packaging designs for advertising agencies. Now Juggernaut can make its own designs and obtain copyrights for them. If Juggernaut innocently develops the same design that someone else has already copyrighted (statistically unlikely, but possible), the second is neither a derivative nor a copy of the first, but is, instead, an original creation which may be subject to independent copyright protection. Why? Because theoretically, two identical works are entitled to copyright protection as long as they were both independently created.

Computer technology is creating the possibility that this unusual situation will become much more commonplace. Why? In the past, if two people expressed the same idea, the individuality of the authors virtually guaranteed different results. Or, put another way, consider the odds of another author independently writing exactly this book. Computers and their accompanying programs, however, are not quite so different. Thus, especially with examples like QUILTIT, where a program produces an artistic work, two people could coincidentally enter the same instruction in the same order and produce the identical result. As more and more "identical" works are independently produced through widespread use of computer

technology, the copyright law can be expected to change to account for this new phenomenon. The concept of "independent creation" is explored in more depth in Chapter 13 on copyright infringement. In the meantime, if you encounter this type of problem, see a copyright lawyer.

J. Derivative Works Can Be Legally Created for Personal Use Without Permission

Here we discuss a major exception to the rule that permission from the copyright owner is required in order to prepare a derivative work. When reading this section, keep in mind that ownership of a work itself is different than ownership of the copyright. Thus, you may own hundreds of programs, books, magazines, or films, but someone else probably owns the copyrights.

Under one part of the Copyright Act [17 USC, Section 109] the lawful owner of a work--that is anyone who has legally come into possession of a copy of the original work--can to do anything she wants with it, including giving or selling it to others, erasing it because she can't stand the label or pasting it on the wall of the patio and calling it "micro art."

Under another part of the Copyright Act [17 USC, Section 117], our lawful owner of a program can create her own derivative work so long as it is for her own personal use. Practically speaking, this right is often meaningless, since most programs are distributed in object code form and are therefore unchangeable for most purposes. However, if a purchaser reverse engineers the program code to its source code form, she is entitled to create a different program with the one she has lawfully purchased. She is completely within her legal rights, as long as she doesn't:

● Copy, distribute, display or perform the work itself for commercial purposes; or

● Sell the derivative copy or give it away.

It's also important to know that should a person no longer be entitled to the original work, she is also no longer entitled to any derivative she may have created.

Another right provided by Section 117 to the lawful owner of a program is the right to make a backup copy for personal use. If the original copy is transferred, however, the copy must either be transferred with it or destroyed. However, under no circumstances can you transfer a copy you have modified (a derivative work).

In sum, under Sections 109 and 117, ownership of software allows you to make a copy of, bend, fold, staple or mutilate the lawfully obtained copy to your heart's content, so long as it is for a purely personal and private purpose. Conversely, the minute you attempt to go public with your Frankenstein's monster or your copies, you will run afoul of the copyright owner's rights.

EXAMPLE: Big Bank buys Mary Hales' LOANIT package. It needs different loan interest algorithms and accordingly modifies the necessary computer code in Mary's programs. Big Bank doesn't need Mary's permission to do this for their own use. However, they may not exercise any right to sell or license these modified programs, as they are clearly derivative of Mary's program. If, later, Mary gets all rights to LOANIT back from Big Bank because Big Bank's license to use LOANIT expires, or for some other reason, Big Bank will also have to surrender any derivative copies prepared in the meantime.

K. Licenses and Warranties to Inhibit Modifications of Software

It is common for software developers and publishers to try and use contracts to limit the right of the purchaser of their work to change it. In other words, the copyright owner tries to take away the program owner's right to transfer the program or create a derivative work for personal use. For those of you who are wondering why they would do this, the answer is simple. The more a specific use of software is restricted, the greater control the software creator maintains over the product. This can not only mean better trade secret protection, but also can result in more users buying the program than would otherwise be the case. There are two common ways to restrict the use of software--license contracts and warranties. Let's look at both in more detail.

1. License Contracts

Much software is licensed for a specific period of time, for a specific use, rather than being sold outright. As part of doing this, a detailed contract covering all sorts of things, such as license fees, duration of the license, non-disclosure agreements, etc., is signed by the seller (the licensor) and the purchaser (the licensee). One common provision is to limit the use to which the program can be put. For example, the licensor might license a program designed to manipulate the arm of a robot to a robot manufacturing company for use in 100 robots and specify that the program must be used as is, with no changes. Assuming the license satisfies the basic principles of contract law (i.e., it represents a true bargained-for agreement on the part of the user, involves some benefits on both sides, and is not unduly oppressive), it is legal and binding according to its terms. See Chapter 12 for more on this.

Attempts are also made to use licenses to limit the use of over-the-counter software. Unlike licenses for expensive software to be run on mainframes and minicomputers, licenses for mass-distributed microcomputer software do not involve any legitimate negotiation. Instead, the terms of the license are commonly dictated to the user on the software package or an enclosed card. This lack of negotiation, the retail context in which such software is obtained, the ascendent position of the software developer (i.e., take my terms or leave the software) and several other factors, have led many experts to believe that so-called over-the-counter license contracts are invalid, and that the user retains the rights to modify the work for personal use granted by the Copyright Act.* Again, see Chapter 12 for more discussion on this point, and on licenses in general.

2. Warranties

Another way sellers of over-the-counter software try to restrict the purchaser's right to make modifications is through the use of warranties. Typically, the software producer refuses to stand behind (i.e., warrant) any program which has been modified in any way by the user. This means that if you engage in most types of software modification, even for your private use, you will breach the warranty contract, even though you have not violated the copyright law. The effect of this, in theory at least, is that if the software proves defective or needs upgrading, etc., the vendor no longer has any legal duty to help you. While this sort warranty restriction is probably legal up to a point, it is doubtful that courts will let software publishers use it as an excuse not to stand behind software that was clearly defective from the beginning.

---

* Louisiana has enacted a software license enforcement act which mandates that a consumer be bound by the specific terms of the manufacturer's license agreement if a software package is opened or used. It remains to be seen if other states will adopt similar laws.

L. Fair Use

One copyright rule which most of you already know about permits you to legally use a photocopying machine to copy all sorts of work protected by someone else's copyright. It also allows you to legally use portions of pre-existing copyrighted software as part of your work without getting permission or paying a fee. This is called the "fair use" doctrine and sets forth a number of situations in which a copyright owner's exclusive right to make copies does not operate. This includes using copyrighted material in works of criticism, for many educational purposes, as part of news stories and in a number of other contexts. As a general rule, questions regarding fair use almost always arise in the context of litigation where a person or business accused of infringing a copyright defends by saying, "No, I didn't infringe; my activity is protected by the fair use doctrine." Accordingly, we cover this subject in Chapter 13 on infringement.

M. Summary

We have just covered one of the knottiest of all copyright law areas. Even experts find it very difficult to make any one statement about derivative works without immediately throwing in a dozen qualifications. If you have a good overview of the issues involved, you are doing well. Just to be sure, check your knowledge against this review.

■ Any work which modifies, adapts or is based on one or more earlier works is a derivative of the earlier work if the end result is similar to the original work. Except for personal use, derivative works may not be used unless:

1. The developer owns the right to prepare derivatives from the original; or

2. Permission of the person who does own that right is obtained. If such permission is not obtained, the author of

the derivative work may be prevented from exploiting the entire program, including any new work it contains.

■ A new non-derivative work which uses pre-existing copyrighted material is subject to copyright protection as to the new material. But, you must obtain permission from the owner of the right to make copies of the pre-existing material if you wish to use it. If such permission is not obtained, you may be prevented from exploiting the new work unless you eliminate the pre-existing material from your program and republish the new material separately.

■ Compilations are collections of pre-existing material which do not contain much new code. They can be legally protected by copyright only if permission is obtained from the owners of all pre-existing material.

■ Databases, spreadsheets, graphics and programs may be developed through the use of other programs and language compilers without infringing the copyright in the underlying program. However, permission from the appropriate copyright owners must be obtained if any part of the compiler or database manager used to create the program or database is provided to the user along with the program or database.

■ New code added to an existing program which can't be separated out to form a coherent program or subroutine is generally considered to be nonsense code and is probably not copyrightable. However, stand-alone, newly-developed portions of already copyrighted work may be entitled to separate copyright protection, even though the copyright to the bulk of the work is owned by another, unless the code qualifies as a derivative work.

CHAPTER 5

Duration of Copyrights

A. Introduction

Now that you know what a copyright is and how it protects your work, you might want to know how long it lasts. Other than works made for hire, or anonymous works, a copyright lasts for the life of the author plus 50 years. In these other situations, the copyright lasts for between 75 and 100 years, depending on when the work is published.

The fact that your copyright survives you should be seen to illustrate an important truth. Your copyright is a type of property. As with other valuable property, such as land, society has devised ways to protect a copyright from theft, divide or transfer its ownership, borrow against it, leave it to the next generation, and so on. If your copyright came into being during your marriage, the copyright may also be subject to division by a court, should you later divorce, and when you die, your spouse may have a claim on at least a portion of it, even if you

don't approve. One important reason to understand that a copyright is property which, in the normal course of events, others may, and probably will, acquire an interest in, is to underline the point that the duration of your copyright is likely to be important to a number of people besides yourself.

If you own a copyright in a work published before 1978, you will eventually need to renew your copyright to retain your rights. Although this book is not designed for work copyrighted in 1977 or before, we discuss renewal briefly in Sections E and F of this chapter. Fortunately, if all your copyrighted work was published on or after January 1, 1978, you don't need to worry about renewal. Under the Copyright Act of 1976, your copyright is automatically good for the specific periods of time discussed in detail in the next section.

B. Duration of Copyrights (January 1, 1978 and after)

1. Single Author

Most copyrights in works published after January 1, 1978 are good for the life of the author plus 50 years. This time period applies to all computer works written by an individual on her own behalf, except if she remains anonymous or goes under a pseudonym.

EXAMPLE: Mary Hales is the sole author of her LOANIT loan processing package. Since we have a crystal ball, let's look into Mary's future. Ah ha! It appears that if she doesn't overdose on chocolate truffles (no small risk when Mary gets an attack of the munchies), she will live until 2050. This means her copyright on LOANIT will last for 50 years after her death, or until the year 2100. Since Mary wrote LOANIT in 1985, the effective length of her copyright is 117 years. This 117-year copyright is obviously more than adequate to protect LOANIT. Indeed, Mary will probably be lucky if LOANIT has a useful life of 15 years, considering how rapidly things become obsolete in the computer industry.

2. Joint Author Works

A joint work is simply a work authored by more than one person. Obviously, where you have more than one author, the general rule of basing the copyright on the life of a single author plus 50 years is impractical, unless you pick one author's life as the one to measure by. This is just what Congress decided to do. The next question the legislators had to deal with was whose life, or more accurately, whose death, should be used as the measuring standard? Fortunately, Congress decided the question in favor of the longer life. Thus, where joint authors are involved, a copyright lasts for the life of the last surviving author plus 50 years.

EXAMPLE: Mary Hales and Robert Atkins write LOANIT in 1985. If we take another look into our crystal ball, we learn that Mary will live until 2050, but Robert, who prefers carrots to truffles, will live until 2060. This means the LOANIT copyright will last until 2110, Robert's lifetime plus 50 years. Assuming the copyright still has value, Mary's heirs will receive the benefit of the extra 10 years of copyright protection. Put another way, any rights to LOANIT inherited by Mary's heirs will last for 60 years after her death, rather than 50 years, because Robert lived 10 years longer than Mary.

3. Works Made for Hire

Simply put, a work made for hire is either a work created within the scope of one's employment, or a work of a specific type (e.g., a translation, a compilation, a contribution to a collective work) which is commissioned by someone other than the person creating the work. Please refer to Chapter 3 for a discussion of the specific types of work that qualify for the strict legal definition of a work made for hire.

The copyright in a work made for hire lasts for a period of 75 years from its date of publication, or 100 years from the date of its creation, whichever comes first. This means that a 25-year delay in publication can result in a 100-year copyright. But, if the delay is only 5 years, then the copyright only lasts 80 years (75 years from publication plus 5 from creation equals 80). If creation and publication occur more or less simultaneously, as they usually do, the copyright lasts 75 years. See Chapter 6, Section C(1) for a discussion of publication, which usually means offering the work to the public with few or no restrictions.

EXAMPLE 1: Kendra Salone creates QUILTIT within the scope of her employment with BCA Graphics in 1985. If QUILTIT is never published, the copyright will expire in 2085. However, if QUILTIT is first published (i.e., sold to the public) in 1987, the copyright will expire in 2062, or 75 years from the publication date.

EXAMPLE 2: Big Bank commissions Mary Hales to write two very complex routines (subparts of a program) for their new credit evaluation package, called WORTHIT. As part of doing this, Mary signs a work-made-for-hire agreement with Big Bank. The work fits within one of the statutorily defined work-made-for-hire categories. Mary creates the programs in 1987, and Big Bank uses them for internal bank use only, never publishing them. In this situation, the copyright expires in 100 years, or 2087. Or, in other words, since WORTHIT is never published by Big Bank, the shorter 75-year time period doesn't apply. Instead, the copyright lasts 100 years from creation.

4. Anonymous and Pseudonymous Works

With an anonymous or pseudonymous work, there is no identified author with an interest in the copyright. Obviously, this makes it impractical to measure the duration of the copyright against the life of the author. For this reason, Congress decided to simply set the copyright term at 75 years from the year of first publication of the copyrighted work, or 100 years from the year of its creation, whichever comes first. Again, we discuss what constitutes publication in some detail in Chapter 6.

EXAMPLE 1: Carl Jones is worried about his privacy in the event GOTTCHA sells as well as he thinks it will. Accordingly, he registers his copyright under the pseudonym "Joy Stick." Although he created GOTTCHA in 1985, he waits until 1987 to sell it to the public. Since GOTTCHA is published under a pseudonym, Carl's copyright will end in 2062, which is 75 years from the date of publication.

EXAMPLE 2: Kendra Salone wrote PATERNHAPPY in 1985. Because the program was too sophisticated for current hardware, Kendra put it aside. Before long, she forgot about it. Again, let's look in our crystal ball to see that in 2010, Kendra rediscovers PATERNHAPPY (at the bottom of a trunk of quilts, of course) and markets it. Her copyright lasts until 2085 (75 years from publication, and not more than one-hundred years from the work's creation).

If the author of an anonymous or pseudonymous work becomes officially known to the Copyright Office before the 75 year term expires, the copyright term changes to the life of the author plus 50 years (i.e., the same as if the correct name had been on the copyright to begin with). Therefore, if you wish to publicize your interest in your anonymous or pseudonymous work, you should record a statement with the Copyright Office setting forth the following:

1. The name of the person filing the statement;

2. The nature of the person's interest in the copyright;

3. The name of the author;

4. The source of the information recorded;

5. The title of the particular work affected, and the copyright registration number if known.

This statement should be accompanied by a new copyright registration application plus the standard registration fee (see Chapter 11 for registration procedures).

EXAMPLE: Carl Jones decides that he can't bear to have his now world-famous game GOTTCHA registered under the pseudonym "Joy Stick." As part of coming out of his "software closet," he sends the following letter to the Copyright Office:

```
September 12, 198_

Register of Copyrights
Library of Congress
Washington, D.C. 20559

To Whom It May Concern:

    I am writing you regarding copyright
registration No. 1234567890, registered
on 1-18-8_ . This work is a computer
program registered under the title
GOTTCHA. It is registered under the
pseudonymous authorship of "Joy Stick."
This letter is to inform you that I,
Carl Jones, am the author and owner of
the copyright in this work. Enclosed
please find a new registration form
listing myself as the author.

Sincerely,


Carl Jones
```

5. Masks Used to Manufacture Semiconductor Chips

Effective January 1985, the circuitry contained in "mask works" is protected by copyright for ten years from the first authorized distribution, use in a commercial product, or manufacture in commercial quantities of semiconductor chips which have been manufactured with the use of such mask works. See Chapter 3, Section J, item 11 for information on the Semiconductor Chip Protection Act of 1983.

C. Calendar Year Rule

All copyright durations run until the end of the calendar year in which they would otherwise expire. In other words, whether your copyright in a work for hire is calculated to be 75 years

from April 17, 1985 or from September 2, 1985 makes no difference, as both expire on December 31, 2060. Similarly, you are the only author of a work, and you die on either March 7 or December 26, 1930, the result is the same. Your copyright would expire on December 31, 2080.

D. Notification of Death of the Author

If you have an interest in a copyright, but are not the author, you may notify the Copyright Office in the event of the author's death. What does having an interest in the copyright mean, and why would such a person want to notify the Copyright Office? As we've seen, because copyrights are property, they can be left by will or in a trust, or, in the absence of a will, can pass by the intestate succession rules of the state where the owner was living when she died.

The person who inherits a copyright clearly owns a property interest. This person should notify the Copyright Office of this interest. The notification is in the form of a statement to the Office setting forth the following:

1. The name of the person filing the statement;

2. The nature of the person's interest in the copyright;

3. The date of death of the author;

4. The source of the information recorded;

5. The title of the particular work affected and the copyright and copyright registration number if known.

EXAMPLE: Assume Mary Hales inherits the rights to a program which generates a telephone directory entitled NUMERO-

UNO from the author, a close personal friend. Mary wishes to update the copyright records showing that she is the new owner so that people wanting permission to use the work will know where to contact her. Accordingly, she sends the Copyright Office the following letter:

RE: Copyright Registration
     #098754321

To Whom It May Concern:

   This letter concerns copyright registration No. 0987654321. This work is a computer program registered under the title NUMEROUNO, by H.B. Lee, Jr., as author.

   This letter is to inform your office that Mr. Lee died 1/11/__. I, Mary Hales, received Mr. Lee's interest in this copyright through his will. Enclosed please find a copy of the death certificate and a copy of Mr. H.B. Lee, Jr.'s will.

   Please list me as the owner of this copyright.

Sincerely,

Mary Hales
123 Program St.
Anywhere, USA 12345
(222) 222-2222

   You need to include a copy of the will, signed by Mr. Lee. You also have to pay a fee to have your ownership document recorded. The will will be recorded by the Copyright Office in the same manner as any other document of transfer. These procedures are outlined in more detail in Chapter 12, on transfers.

E. The Presumption of Death Rule

   If the Copyright Office does not receive any notice of the death of an author of a work created after January 1, 1978, it will eventually presume it.

The presumed date of death is 75 years from the year of first publication, or 100 years from the year of creation, for an unpublished work, whichever occurs first. If an author lives longer than presumed date of death under this rule, a statement may be recorded with the Office, stating the author is still alive. This statement should contain:

■ The name of the person filing the statement;

■ The nature of the person's interest in the copyright;

■ The statement that the author is living;

■ The source of the information recorded;

■ The title of the particular work affected, and the copyright registration number if known.

DEAR COPYRIGHT OFFICER: I AM WRITING REGARDING...

   EXAMPLE: If Mary Hales published a work in 1980, she would be presumed dead in 75 years, or 2055. If this presumption turns out to be somewhat premature (she goes cold turkey on the truffles), and her work still has enough value to warrant the trouble, she could send the following letter:

```
Register of Copyrights
Library of Congress
Washington, D.C. 20559

RE:  Copyright #0987654321

To Whom It May Concern:

    I am writing you regarding copyright
registration No. 0987654321.  This work
is a computer program registered under
the title NUMEROUNO.  It is registered
under the name Mary Hales.

    This letter is to inform your office
that I, Mary Hales, am very much alive.
I will appreciate it if you do not spread
rumors of, or presume, my death.  Such
rumors are rather upsetting to a person
of my not-so-tender years.  I recently
confirmed my impression that I am alive
with my doctor, Philippa Philispont of
111 Pettigrew Place, Philadelphia, PA,
who insists that, while I ought to be
dead, I'm not.

Sincerely,


Mary Hales
```

F. Works Created but Not Published Prior to January 1, 1978

Works created any time prior to January 1, 1978, but neither published nor in the public domain on or before that date, are subject to the same basic copyright duration rules as those created after January 1, 1978. 17 USC 303 gives some extra rights to work created prior to Jan. 1, 1978 by providing that the copyright can't expire before 2002. We mention them in the interests of thoroughness only, as while these extra rights may have meaning for other types of copyrighted work, they don't have any practical meaning in the software field. This is because since virtually no software was created prior to the 1960's and very little before the mid-1970's, no copyrights would expire before 2002 anyway. This rule would help an author of a literary work created in 1890, however, if it wasn't published before Jan. 1,

1978, by extending her copyright until 2002. Otherwise, it would have run out 100 years from creation, or 1992.

EXAMPLE: Kendra Salone created LILTQUILT in 1975 as a work for hire for BCA Graphics, her employer. BCA didn't publish it until 1985. The copyright lasts for 75 years from date of publication. Because publication didn't occur until after January 1, 1978, the post-1978 rules apply.

G. Copyrights Registered Before January 1, 1978

If you own an interest in a copyright registered with the U.S. Copyright Office before January 1, 1978, you need more information than we provide here. You may want to consult a copyright lawyer. The term of these copyrights has been complicated by the Copyright Act of 1976. In many situations, you will need to renew your copyright to maintain your rights. It depends upon whether, under the definition of the former Copyright Act, your copyright was in its first 28-year term or had already been renewed on Jan. 1, 1978. Here is an overview of how this works, but if you have a valuable copyright dating from 1977 or before, consult an attorney.

1. Copyrights in Their First Term on January 1, 1978

Works that were copyrighted between January 1, 1950 and December 31, 1977 usually last 28 years from the date of publication. To obtain protection for a longer period of time, a renewal registration must be made within one year of the expiration date of the 28-year copyright term. This means works copyrighted in 1956 should be renewed in 1984. To accomplish this, Form RE must be filed with the Copyright Office and a fee paid. The renewed copyright is then usually good for another 47 years. This makes a total of 75 years. We don't provide this form because very few readers will need it. If you do, contact the Register of Copyrights, Library of Congress, Washington., D.C.

2. Copyrights in Their Renewal Term on January 1, 1978

Almost no software will have already been in its renewal term on January 1, 1978. However, in the interests of thoroughness, in this situation the copyright duration is to be calculated from the date the copyright was first secured, plus 75 years. Renewal terms under the former Act were not always 47 years, but nevertheless, the new Copyright Act, effective January 1, 1978, states that all works in any renewal term as of January 1, 1978 receive this copyright protection, i.e., 75 years from the date copyright protection was secured.

CHAPTER 6

Copyright Notice

A. Introduction

Copyright protection is initially automatic. It arises the instant your original work of authorship becomes fixed in a tangible medium of expression. Accordingly, if Sneaky Sarkus obtains a bootleg copy of your masterpiece right after it has been saved on disk, and immediately proceeds to copy and market it under his own name, he will have violated (infringed) your copyright. This is true even if you never realized you had a copyright.

However, although your work is automatically protected by copyright, peasant cunning dictates that you not rely solely on this "protection" any longer than is absolutely necessary. Why not? Two reasons. If you publish, distribute, or market your work without taking the additional protective step of affixing a valid copyright notice to it, your work is very likely to enter the dreaded legal realm known as the "public domain." If this happens, you lose all your exclusive rights in the work

forever. In other words, even though your work was originally protected by a copyright, anyone can now use, copy, and sell it without obtaining your permission.

The second reason is really an extension of the first. To ask a court to stop an infringement of your copyright, and/or award you money for any harm done, it is normally essential that you have placed a correct copyright notice on your work. Accordingly, in this chapter we provide you with step-by-step guidance as to the type of notice to place on your work and where to put it.

COPYRIGHT REGISTRATION NOTE: To fully protect your copyright, another extremely important action should be accomplished routinely. This involves registering your work with the U.S. Copyright Office. We thoroughly cover copyright registration and the advantages it can afford you in Chapters 8 - 11.

B. Copyright Notice Requirements

The function of a copyright notice is literally to put the public-at-large on notice as to three pieces of information:

■ That your work is protected by a copyright, as opposed to being in the public domain;

■ The date your work was first published; and,

■ Who owns the copyright in your work.

In this regard, the copyright notice on the back of the title page of this book-- © M.J. Salone 1985--tells anyone who sees it that:

■ M.J. Salone claims ownership of the exclusive rights associated with the copyright;

■ No one else can legally exercise any of these rights unless he or she gets permission (and presumably, pays for doing so); and

■ The book was first published in 1985.

When you think about it, a copyright notice packs a lot of information into a very compact space.

C. When Must a Copyright Announcement Be Made?

If you develop software, you need to know exactly when to begin including a copyright notice on your work. There is a lot of confusion in this area. Some people believe notice is desirable from the day they write the first line of code, others when they test the first module, and still others believe copyright notice is necessary only when they first market their software to the public. All of this confusion was put succinctly by a friend who called recently to ask, "Do I have to place a copyright notice on my work before I show the code to my mother, my publisher, or sell the first five hundred copies?" It will take about a page to completely answer this question--bear with us.

1. Published Work

At the moment a work becomes "published" (as that term is defined by the Copyright Act), a proper copyright notice is mandatory if your copyright is to be maintained. By contrast, notice on your work prior to publication is not legally necessary, although, as we will discuss below in more detail, it's a good idea to routinely include notice at a very early stage. "Publication," therefore, is the great watershed for copyright notice purposes and it is essential that anyone concerned with the copyright of software have a good gut-level understanding of what it means.

To publish a work means to make it generally available to the public without restriction. Selling copies to the public through retail outlets or by mail order, publishing code in a magazine, demonstrating a program at a widely attended computer show, and allowing a number of educational institutions to use your program without restriction are all examples of publication. By contrast, showing code privately to friends, publishers, financiers, or promoters does not constitute publication. Nor, in fact, does limited distribution of your software for commercial use, so long as you adequately restrict the recipients in how they can use your work and to whom it can be shown. This is generally accomplished through license contracts allowing use of your software under certain specified conditions, which include keeping it confidential, not making copies, and so on. We discuss these concepts in more detail in Chapters 12 on transfers, and Chapter 15 on other protections of intellectual property.

EXAMPLE 1: Carl Jones sells 10,000 copies of his game program, GOTTCHA, to Gameland for resale. This is publication! Copyright notice is required. If the program is sold without notice in this quantity, the program will enter the public domain, unless Carl takes certain immediate and urgent steps to correct his oversight and registers the copyright within five years (see Chapter 7 for how to correct copyright notice errors). If the work enters the public domain, anyone can copy it and not pay Carl for the privilege.

EXAMPLE 2: BCA Graphics displays many of Kendra Salone's computer art works in their lobby. Is this publication? Probably. Copyright notice must legally be included to maintain the copyright.

EXAMPLE 3: Mary Hales takes an ad in the trade magazine, Financial Institutions, advertising her loan processing package as being available, and giving some details of what it does. This probably constitutes publication of the program. From this time on, every copy of Mary's program (including sample copies, beta test copies, etc.) should contain a copyright notice. If Mary distributes copies of her program without copyright notice after the ad appears, she is in danger of losing her copyright.

EXAMPLE 4: Mary Hales goes to a financial software trade show and demonstrates part of her loan processing package. If she doesn't show the code or documentation, it's possible this is not publication, but the safer view is that it is. Copyright notice should always be included in this situation.

2. Unpublished Work

As we suggested, placing a copyright notice on an unpublished work is advisable, even though it is not legally required to maintain your copyright protection. Why do something that isn't legally required? Because it makes practical sense. Why? Because, if you include a copyright notice on your work from the beginning, you can afford to be a little more relaxed about what happens if your copyright is infringed. This is because when asked to protect copyrights and award damages against infringers, courts are much more responsive when the infringement is willful than when it is innocent. Willfulness, it turns out, is usually determined on the basis of whether the potential infringer actually knew of the existence of your copyright. Your copyright notice is the most effective way to establish this knowledge. We discuss this concept in more detail in Chapter 13.

At this point, the moral should be clear. Giving notice of your copyright to the world-at-large (for both published and unpublished works) greatly enhances your ability to protect it against all comers.

D. Form of Copyright Notice for Unpublished Work

Here is the form a copyright notice should take for unpublished work. (The correct notice for published work is discussed in the next section.)

© Copyright Robert Atkins
(This work is unpublished)

OR

© Copyright Robert Atkins
(Work in Progress)

Again, we recommend placing a copyright notice on all work in progress, even though you don't know when it will finally be finished, let alone published. Incidentally, if you are wondering why our suggested notices for unpublished works don't contain dates, it's because the date on a copyright notice denotes the date of publication. When you choose to consider your work as published, you will want to put a date on the notice; before that, it's better to leave it out.

NOTE: TRADE SECRET PROTECTION AND UNPUBLISHED WORKS: In Chapter 15 we discuss methods by which a copyrightable work can enjoy additional protection under trade secret laws. Briefly, a software author is permitted to maintain unpublished software, and, in a few situations, published software, as a trade secret. Trade secret protection means the underlying concepts inherent in your programming can be protected from use by others, as well as the literal expression of the program as represented in the program code and output, which is protected by copyright. To enjoy trade secret protection, work must be kept secret. In theory, if a trade secret became known to even one member of the public without proper confidentiality restrictions, the information can no longer be considered a trade secret.

Assume, for example, you have developed a fast, slick, information retrieval algorithm for your own use or for distribution under license to a few users. You don't intend to ever publish it, but instead plan to keep it a secret forever. If your plan succeeds, you will never have to rely on copyright protection. But, what happens if a copy of your algorithm is left on a plane, or at a computer fair, or a competitor ends up with one in some other way that doesn't involve illegal conduct? Well, unless it is also protected by copyright, your competitor is very likely free to use it. What does this mean in practice? Simply that it is always nice to maintain both trade secret and copyright status simultane-ously where possible. To this end, we strongly recommend that copyright notices (the unpublished variety) be placed on unpublished works, despite their trade secret status. If you wish to maintain your work as a trade secret, it is not wise to put a copyright notice on it that contains a date. Why? Because the date is the date of publication, and publication is not usually consistent with maintaining trade secret status.

At this point, let's check with our software developers for some examples of when notice is required and/or advisable. As you will remember, we introduced these people and their problems in Chapter 2.

EXAMPLE 1: While employed with Middle Bank, Mary Hales writes a special customer service program. This program will never be seen by anyone except the customer service project team within the bank, and maybe the electronic data processing (EDP) auditors. This program is not published. Accordingly, copyright notice is advisable, but not required. Why is notice advisable? Mary's unpublished program, or part of it, may be informally distributed, or even inadvertently published. In the former situation, the notice will prevent a pirate from claiming innocent infringer status. In the latter, it will prevent the work from entering the public domain.

EXAMPLE 2: Mary Hales agrees to sell her loan processing package, LOAN-IT, to a small number of financial institutions. Wishing to maintain LOANIT as a trade secret, Mary requires that each purchaser sign a license contract which contains a clause binding them not to show or disclose any of Mary's package to anyone else. This is not publishing according to the law. Just the same, under our better-safe-than-sorry approach, Mary would be wise to include a copyright notice (the unpublished variety, without a date). Again, remember that putting a date on the notice might actually conflict with the trade secret claim, since the date represents the date of "publication."

E. Copyright Notice for Published Work

It's easy to provide proper notice of your copyright ownership. Nevertheless, an amazing number of people screw it up. So please, pay attention to what follows. It is as important as it is simple.

To give you copyright protection in the United States, your copyright notice needs three elements. Let's look at each:

Requirement 1: The Copyright Symbol

The preferred copyright symbol is ©. As you can see, this is nothing more than the letter "c" inside a circle. This is also the symbol that is accepted internationally, under the Universal Copyright Convention, the treaty that governs reciprocal copyright protections between the U.S. and most other nations. The word "copyright," or the abbreviation "copr." are acceptable in the United States in lieu of the encircled ©, but not in all other countries. See Chapter 14 for a discussion of international copyright law. For now, all you really need to know is that this symbol-- © --is the best one to use.

WARNING! Some computer operating systems and/or printers cannot generate ©, but produce (c), instead. Although it is not possible to predict how the courts might treat this in the U.S., it is not, strictly speaking, a legally acceptable symbol according to the copyright law [17 USC, Section 401(b)(1)]. There is also considerable doubt about its legal effect in some other countries. For this reason, we suggest you routinely use both the symbol ©, and one of the legal alternatives in your notice. The one we prefer is the word "copyright." Then, if your © comes out (c), you are sure to be completely protected in the U.S.

The use of the word "copyright" will also enhance your legal protection status worldwide. However, you should still know that under several international treaties, only © is currently recognized, so if your work has particular international application, and you wish to be absolutely sure of your protection, be sure your circle really is one.*

Requirement 2: The Name of the Copyright Owner

The name of the copyright owner must be included in your copyright notice. The owner of a work is either:

1. The author(s);

2. The legal owner of a "work made for hire"; or

---

* In fact, many countries, such as France, England and Germany, don't require any copyright notice at all. Your published work will receive protection in these countries just by its existence as an original work of authorship. Others have different rules. The point to remember is that if the country you are concerned about is a member of the Universal Copyright Convention (U.C.C.)--and most are--it must recognize © in lieu of any local rule. See Chapter 14 for more details.

3. A person or entity to whom the entire copyright has been transferred (e.g., a publisher, hardware manufacturer, distributor).

In all situations, the owner can be an individual, partnership, or corporation. The name which is used can be either the owner's actual name, an abbreviation thereof by which the owner can be recognized, a false name (called a "pseudonymous name" by the Copyright Act), or an anonymous name (e.g., John Doe).* However, please remember that the point of a notice is to notify, so don't be cryptic or cute.

TRANSFER NOTE: In some copyright transfer situations, it is a little confusing as to what name to use on the copyright notice. As far as the law is concerned, you can always use the original author or owner's name if that person retains any copyright rights. In addition, where an author has retained some rights, but transferred the right to make copies to a publisher, the publisher's name can appear on the copyright notice. This is normally done by virtue of a clause found in the publisher-author contract assigning the publisher the right to put the copyright notice in its name. See Chapter 12 on transfers.

EXAMPLE: Mary Hales shows LOANIT to a software publisher while it's still in the development stage. The publisher likes it and enters into a contract with Mary, under which they agree to pay her royalties. The publisher asks for, and gets, the right to list the copyright notice in their name. It would be just as common, however, for the contract to provide that the copyright notice contain Mary's name, with the publisher receiving the right to publish and distribute the program for either the life of the copyright or some period of time established in the contract.

---

* Putting a pseudonymous or anonymous name on a copyright notice potentially shortens the period of the copyright. See Chapter 5 for a discussion of copyright duration.

Requirement 3: The Year of First Publication

Remember, to publish a work means to make it generally available to the public. If you publish your work in a certain year, list that year on your copyright notice. However, if you are placing your copyright notice on an unpublished work which you plan to work on for some indeterminate period of time, or may never publish, omit the year of publication. If the work is later published, the proper date should be made part of the notice.

As long as your work was not registered or published prior to 1978, the exact accuracy of the date on your copyright notice is not critical, as long as it is not more than one year after (i.e., in the future from) the actual publication date. If you do use a date which is more than one year after (i.e., in the future from) your actual publication date, your copyright notice may be invalid. This means, if Mary Hales puts a copyright date of 1978 on LOANIT, when it was really published in 1985, there is no problem. Nor does it create a legal problem if Mary puts 1986 on the notice of a program published in 1985. However, if Mary publishes in 1985 and puts 1987 or later on her notice, it is invalid. Accordingly, if you are uncertain about the date of publication, err on the side of listing an earlier rather than later date.

EARLY DATE NOTE: Some software authors deliberately put a falsely early date on their notice, hoping that if there is a conflict over whether their program was created before a similar competing one, the court will accept their made-up date as being accurate. Put simply, they won't. Not only is this sort of strategy dishonest, it is likely to be counter-productive. Why? Because the other party to an infringement lawsuit is sure to challenge your assertion, which you won't be able to back up. This will result in your being branded as a liar, an idiot, or both. It certainly won't win you an infringement suit.

Here are two correct U.S. copyright notices for published work. Again, we recommend the second version. It is valid in the U.S. and internationally (under the Universal Copyright Convention) and will survive circleless printers, at least in the United States:

© BCA Graphics 1985

© Copyright Kendra Salone 1985

Requirement 4: International Copyright Notices Only

There are several things to know about international copyright notices. The first, as we have mentioned, is that © is the international copyright notice standard under the Universal Copyright Convention (UCC), the most important international agreement. Used as part of a correct notice, it guarantees your copyright full protection in a large part of the world (see Chapter 14). Unfortunately, neither the word "copyright" nor the abbreviation "copr.," both of which are acceptable substitutes for © in the U.S., are generally acceptable worldwide.

Sometimes you will see the words "All Rights Reserved" at the end of a copyright notice. These words are not required in the United States or in the great majority of countries. However, in several Latin American nations, it is necessary to use this phrase to establish your copyright. We discuss the reasons for this in Chapter 14. However, all you really need to know is that if you think your software or computer output has any potential market in Latin America, include the words "All Rights Reserved" as part of your notice. Many programmers and publishers automatically do this on every

notice. Here is the correct way to accomplish this:

© Copyright Mary Hales 1985
All Rights Reserved

Requirement 5: Phonorecords or Other Sound Recordings

The copyright symbol for phonorecords and sound recordings is ℗. This is simply a "p" inside a circle. While you may never need this symbol, don't forget about it. Many programmers and publishers are finding ways to profit from the sound generated by computer and sound recordings which accompany programs for instructional or other purposes.

EXAMPLE: Carl Jones begins writing music with the aid of his computer. The program he writes to generate the tones is a literary work and should have a © in the notice. However, the phonograph records and audio cassettes Carl makes of his computer-generated compositions are protected by a separate copyright. To give proper notice of this copyright, Carl must use the ℗ symbol on all records and cassettes. His notice should look like this:

℗ 1985 by Carl Jones

F. Copyright Notice for Work Containing Previously Copyrighted Material

When your work includes routines (i.e., subparts of a larger program) or other work that was previously published by another owner, the Copyright

Act of 1976 [17 U.S.C., Sec. 401] specifies that your notice need not contain these earlier copyright dates unless this notice is required by the other copyright owner. In other words, your single copyright notice protects the work as a whole.* However, if the copyright owner of the earlier work you use wishes his copyright to be specifically noted, you would do it like this:

© Copyright Mary Hales 1985

© Copyright Prior Author 1980

Even if a formal notice reflecting the other person's copyright is not included along with your own, it is common practice to acknowledge your use of the work by a phrase such as "Original Code from the program Rackafrax Delight is included with permission of (The name of the copyright owner)."

G. Copyright Notice for Updated or Changed Work

If you update your work beyond minor editing changes (e.g., you create a new version or edition), or prepare a derivative work (e.g., a translation in a different language or an adaption to a different format), you should update your copyright notice as well. In other words, the new version, edition, or derivative work should include a notice with the date it was published. Under the Copyright Act, it need not contain the dates of the first or earlier publication. However, we recommend that you do so, as it serves an important function of telling the world the date you claim your copyright from. This can be important if there is ever an infringement suit.

EXAMPLE: Assume now that Mary Hales has created two new versions of her LOANIT package. LOANIT was originally published in 1983, the first new version in 1985, and the sound in 1986. Mary's notice on the latest version of LOANIT should ideally look like this:

© Copyright Mary Hales 1983, 1985, 1986.

However, if it just said: © Copyright Mary Hales 1986, it would be legally sufficient. For a detailed discussion of what constitutes new versions and derivative works, see Chapter 4.

You will get a better insight as to when to update your copyright notice when you read Chapters 8 - 11, on registration. This is because any time you are eligible to register your work as an updated work, you should also update your notice.

H. The Correct Placement of a Copyright Notice

Rules for placement of a copyright notice depend both on the type of work involved and how it's packaged. Let's look at the common situations faced in the computer business.

1. Programs

Programs are manifested in several ways. One is when they are listed on paper or printed in human readable form (usually source code), and another is when they perform their task in the computer. Copyright notice is required in both situations. In addition, certain programs have more than one mode or version when they are running or performing their task. For example, a video game has a "play" and an "attract" mode of operation. The attract mode occurs before you feed in your coin, when the game is trying to attract your attention. Play mode is when you are actually playing the game.

Other programs also commonly have more than one mode. For example, many complicated programs have a "training mode," separate from the program itself. Each mode should have a correct copyright notice. If it doesn't, that particular mode or version may not be protected. Of course, common sense will probably tell you that one mode is far more valuable than another, but don't let this lull you into only including copyright notice on the more valuable one. There is likely to be code in an attract or training mode that would be valuable to a competitor if left unprotected.

The Copyright Act says that for programs your notice must be placed as follows:

■ Copyright notice should be printed every time any output is converted, with or without the aid of machine or device, into a human perceivable form. Legally, the notice must be printed in or near the title of the program or at the end of the program;

OR

■ Displayed when the program is first activated;

OR

■ Displayed continuously while the program is being used;

OR

■ Affixed securely to the permanent container of the machine-readable copy.

Here is an example of source code which will instruct the computer to display the copyright notice on the screen:

```
tellem()                    /* outputs the diagnostic files */
{
int year,month,day,hour,minute;

printf("Interactive Design Language \n\n  by Arthur Abraham\n\n\n");
printf("(c) Copyright 1984 A-Squared Systems  All Rights Reserved")
getdate(&year,&month,&day);
gettime(&hour,&minute);
printf("Diagnostic File Dated: %u/%u/%u  %u:%u",
                   month,day,year-1900,hour,minute);
listflags();
listwords();
listmes();
listsize();
}           /* end tellem */


listflags()                 /* lists flags seen during run */
{int i;
```

OBJECT CODE NOTE: What happens when source code is translated into object code? Since only actual instructions are translated from source to object code, while comments accompanying the instructions are not (which is what a copyright notice is to the computer), no copyright notice would appear in the object code version. To solve this problem, Mary embeds a copyright notice in an unused data element of the source code. This means her copyright notice will be translated along with the rest of the program. In this way, if the object code were de-translated or reverse translated into source code from the object code, the copyright notice would appear.

EXAMPLE 1: Carl Jones puts a copyright notice in his game program, GOTT-CHA. He also affixes it to the ROM chip with a label and places a label with his copyright notice on the container. In addition, a notice is displayed on the screen for both "attract" and "play" modes of the game itself.

EXAMPLE 2: Mary Hales wants to protect her LOANIT loan processing package. To do this, she puts her copyright notices on the title page of every source code program in her package. She also embeds notice in an unused data element of the source code so that the copyright notice will be translated into object code with the rest of the program.

PLAY SAFE: Take our advice and display your copyright notice often and obviously. A good rule is to display it on the screen at the beginning and end of your program, as well as every time the program title is displayed. In addition, you should always include it prominently on any program pack-

aging. Remember, you are trying to give the world notice of your copyright claim, not hide it.

2. Program Documentation or Other Materials in Book or Pamphlet Form

Documentation includes everything that accompanies, explains, illustrates, or otherwise complements your program. Many manuals, such as user manuals, programmer reference manuals, and training manuals, look more or less like books. Short manuals or program documentation often take the form of a pamphlet. Rules for placing your copyright notice are the same for both, as long as the pamphlet consists of at least two pages. These are as follows. Legally, your notice must be printed on:

■ The title page;

OR

■ Page immediately following the title page;

OR

■ Either side of the front cover or front leaf, if there is no cover;

OR

■ Either side of the back cover or back leaf, if there is no cover;

OR

■ First or last page of the main body of text.

Be obvious! If your documentation resembles a book, putting your copyright notice on the back of the title page is sufficient. However, if it's a pamphlet, or staple bound sheets, it's wise to include it on the front page and then again several times on the next few pages.

3. Single Leaf Works

Single leaf works consist of one page. For copyright purposes, it makes no difference whether printed material appears on one side of the sheet, or both. As long as only one piece of paper is involved, the notice can be anywhere on the front or back of the page.

4. Audiovisual Works Such as Video Games or Training Films

Copyright notice must be embodied in all the copies of audiovisual work, whether this is done by a photomechanical or electronic process. The point is that it should appear prominently whenever the work is performed. Notice must be located either:

■ With or near the title;

OR

■ With the cast, credits, etc.;

OR

■ At or immediately following the introductory material;

OR

■ At or immediately preceding the end.

In addition to the above notice, the notice may also be on the film leader prior to the beginning of the work if the work is 60 seconds or less in duration. If the work is distributed for private, at-home use, notice should also be placed on the permanent container. For video arcade games, the notice should also be affixed to the cabinet.

5. Pictorial, Graphic and Sculptural Works

This category includes computer-generated art, charts, graphs, etc. Notice must be affixed directly or by label which is sewn, cemented or otherwise durably attached to two or three-dimensional copies. The notice must be attached to the front or back of copies, to any backing, mounting, base, matting, framing, or any permanent housing. Again, the idea is to give notice, not bury it, so be sure your notice can be seen easily.

EXAMPLE 1: Carl Jones designs a race car he calls CHIPRACER with the aid of his computer and a graphics design software package. Next, he has blueprints made from his computer designs. These blueprints fall into the Pictorial, Graphic and Sculptural Works category. Copyright notice should be affixed to them by glue or otherwise. The blueprints should have a copyright notice on each page.

EXAMPLE 2: BCA Graphics takes photographs of the quilt designs generated by Kendra Salone's QUILTIT program. These photos are pictorial works and fall under the Pictorial, Graphic and Sculptural Works category. Copyright notice should be attached to each prior to display.

6. Phonorecords and Sound Recordings

Copyright notice must be affixed to the phonorecord, or cassette, or the container which houses them. In practice, you should do both if you can. If the record or cassette has a label, include your copyright notice there. Also, include it on any container, jacket, plastic packaging, etc.

I. Conclusion

The information provided in this chapter is basic, yet profound. Simply put, the more notice the world has of your copyright claim, the better protection your work will receive. Including a proper copyright notice in your work is a lot like staking out a mining claim with markers or building a fence around your land. Just as good fences can make good neighbors, good copyright notices facilitate the relatively trouble-free utilization of an original work of authorship in the information age.

Of course, some people don't like fences and believe the land should be open to all. Others resent restrictions on the use of intellectual property, feeling it should be free to everyone. If this is your view, it makes little sense to learn more about copyright notices. But, if you're like most of us and believe developers of new software and computer output should be able to profit from their creative effort, you will want to be very sure you know how to write a correct copyright notice. And just in case you slip up, you will want to study the next chapter, which is devoted exclusively to correcting notice errors.

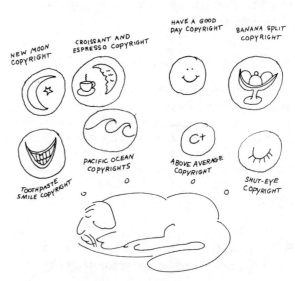

ANOTHER "NOT-GETTING-IT-RIGHT-COPYRIGHT-FRIGHT" NIGHT.

CHAPTER 7

Correcting A Defective Copyright Notice

A. Introduction

Murphy's First Law posits that "If anything can go wrong, it will." While this is often true in life, it seems to be close to a certainty in both the computer and legal fields. And when you put law and advanced technology together, watch out! Fortunately, however, when it comes to protecting your computer output through the use of a proper copyright notice, Congress has provided some help should your notice fall victim to Mr. Murphy's somewhat paranoid rule.

If you list an incorrect copyright notice in your work, or place it in the wrong position, or even omit it entirely, you can often correct the problem and save your copyright if you act promptly. What could go wrong with something as simple as a copyright notice, you ask? Our answer, based on considerable personal experience, is "anything and everything." Sometimes work is simply displayed or distributed without the proper notice from the beginning. At other times, a valid copyright notice which was originally included on a particular work, is omitted by a publisher, printer or manufacturer. And commonly, someone with not enough knowledge takes a stab at placing a copyright notice on their work, only to get it wrong. While we hope you don't have any copyright notice problems, a healthy respect for Murphy, and personal experience with several horror stories, convinces us that it's important to know how to cure a defective notice. Even if the problem is caused by someone else, it's up to you to protect your rights.

PUBLICATION NOTE: In Chapter 6, we said that publication was the great watershed of copyright notice law. Incorrect notices on unpublished works are not a problem. If you discover a mistake, simply fix it. Serious legal problems are reserved for copyright notice mistakes on published work, which is the subject of this chapter. Let's look at a couple of examples of common copyright notice screw-ups after publication.

EXAMPLE 1: Mary Hales grants Financial Package Sell (FPS) the right to sell
her LOANIT package in the Eastern U.S.
FPS reproduces and sells 30 copies of
LOANIT without any copyright notice.
Even though Mary had nothing to do with
the omission, these noticeless copies are
like 30 time bombs, waiting to explode.
What is the danger? Well, Mary will not
be able collect damages in an infringement action from anyone who makes copies
of these packages without knowing of her
copyright. And, even though Mary can sue
to prevent people from making more copies,
she can only do this if she can find them.
The grim reality is that once her material
is flashing around the world without a
proper copyright notice, Mary may never be
able to track it down and order the people
using the noticeless copies to cease selling or distributing them. If Mary fails
to take corrective action, and enough copies are distributed, LOANIT may even enter
the public domain, which means Mary loses
her copyright entirely. Of course, if
Mary loses her copyright, or loses sales
of her program, as a result of the negligence of FPS, she could sue them for damages. Unfortunately, this remedy involves
not only time and expense, but it will only
work as long as FPS is solvent.

EXAMPLE 2: Carl Jones contracts with
Silichip Manufacturing to embed his GOTT-
CHA program on ROM chips. The program
Carl supplies contains a correct copyright notice. During the embedding process, Silichip neglects to include the
date of first publication in the copyright notice. Failure to include the
date means the notice is fatally defective. Carl will be the first to suffer
the legal consequences, which could range
from loss of sales to loss of his copyright. Silichip, too, faces legal liability when Carl demands that they make good
the amount he lost as a result of their
negligence.

B. Effect of Total Omission of Copyright Notice

1. Works First Published Before January 1, 1978

If your work was published without a
copyright notice prior to January 1978,
you have quite simply lost your copyright
protection. This means that anyone can
copy your work or sell it or display it,
and you can't do anything but growl.
Clothed in legal lingo, your work has
entered the "public domain." The public-
at-large now has all of your formerly
exclusive rights.

2. Works Published on or after January 1, 1978

If your work was published on or after
January 1, 1978 (it does not matter when
it was created), then your exclusive
rights may not be lost even if you inadvertently omitted copyright notice or
included a defective notice.* This will
only be true, however, if you can satisfy
at least one of the following three legal
criteria:

■ CRITERION 1: Only a "relatively"
small number of copies of your work are
affected by your copyright omission. If
you fall within this category, you are
not legally required to take any affirmative action to maintain your copyright.
However, for the reasons discussed below,
you should do so anyway.

When Congress used the language "relatively small number" of copies, it was
deliberately vague. The idea was that

---

* If you omitted your copyright notice either because
you didn't know about copyright protection, or for
some reason you decided not to take advantage of it,
you will be deemed to have omitted it intentionally
and your situation may be different. The purpose of
most of what follows is to show you how to protect
your work in the event of an accidental error or negligence, not to recover material which you intentionally placed in the public domain. If you omitted
notice intentionally, see a lawyer.

the number would be decided on a case-by-case basis. It is probably safe to assume that either a few copies, in absolute terms, or a small proportion of a very large number of copies would meet their criterion. However, you can never be sure what a court will decide. For this reason, it's always wise to see if you can also comply with Criterion 2, discussed below.

HOW DOES IT FEEL TO BELONG TO THE WORLD?

PUBLIC DOMAIN

IT'S A GREAT FEELING F.D. IT'S TAKEN ME A LIFETIME PLUS FIFTY YEARS.

EXAMPLE 1: Silichip Manufacturing makes 50,000 ROM chips for Carl Jones' program, GOTTCHA, without any date in the copyright notice. Only 250 of these are shipped before the mistake is discovered. This would probably be considered a small number of copies, in which case Carl need take no steps to preserve his copyright. Yet, because one judge's "limited copies" might be another's "cornucopia," Carl should still follow the procedures outlined below in Criterion 2.

EXAMPLE 2: Financial Package Sell distributes 250 copies of Mary Hales' LOANIT package without any copyright notice. LOANIT is a fairly specialized loan processing package, and only 2,000 have been manufactured. Although the

same number of defective programs got out as in Example 1, proportionally many more defective LOANITS were sent out than GOTT-CHA chips, and Mary will probably not qualify in this category. In other words, it is essential that she take the specific corrective action specified in Criterion 2, just below.

■ CRITERION 2: In the event more than a few copies have been published without legally adequate copyright notice, you must take affirmative action. This involves two steps:

1. Registration: Your copyright must be registered (see Chapters 8 - 11) within five years of the first publication. This, of course, is a good idea anyway.

2. Practical Corrective Actions: All reasonable efforts must be taken to add your notice to the copies of your work already distributed without a copyright notice. How to do this is covered in Section D, below. If you are unable to make such efforts, you will not be able to satisfy this criterion and your copyright may be lost, unless the third criterion, listed below, applies.

Realistically, satisfaction of this second criterion depends on there only being a limited number of copies in circulation, or the publisher maintaining an accurate list of licensees. If thousands of copies have been sold without notice, and no track has been kept of the purchasers or licensees, you will not be able to catch up with your work and correct your error. This eventuality is likely to be the situation if your program is being widely sold by retailers. However, if you are handling distribution yourself, and use a context where each customer signs an individual license agreement, you may be able to track most of them down and notify them of your correct notice. We discuss the practical steps necessary to accomplish notification in Section D, below.

DAMAGES NOTE: You should realize that even though your copyright will not be lost if you meet the requirements of these first two criteria, you will not be able to recover any damages as a result of your noticeless program being sold, distributed or otherwise exploited by anyone who doesn't know of your copyright claim, unless you can demonstrate that they clearly should have known about it. This is because, in legal parlance, the infringers are "innocent" (without notice). In other words, assuming you qualify under one of the criteria listed here and you take corrective action to fix copyright notice, you will be able to legally stop infringers from capitalizing on your copyright in the future. However, if they didn't have actual knowledge of your copyright, all the money they have already made is probably theirs to keep. We discuss copyright infringement in Chapter 13.

EXAMPLE : Kendra Salone first developed her QUILTIT program for BCA Graphics in 1980, while she was employed by them for that purpose. Between then and 1983, BCA sold the program to ten designers, with no copyright notice. In 1983, BCA decided to market QUILTIT to the general public. BCA registered the copyright in 1983 and then went back to each of the ten designers and supplied them with a new program, complete with a copyright notice, and asked them to destroy the old programs. This was adequate to protect their copyright. However, if someone who legally got a hold of one of the original ten copies resold 500 copies of QUILTIT in the meantime, the proceeds might be theirs to keep unless they knew the program was protected by a copyright.

■ CRITERION 3: The omission of your correct copyright notice was caused by another party who you licensed or otherwise authorized to handle your work and who you required, in a written agreement, to place your notice on the material. Agreements in which software developers license publishers to produce and market their products are often quite complex documents, covering a variety of duties and rights on both sides. Among the many common clauses in such agreements is one requiring the publisher to take all steps necessary and proper to maintain the author's copyright.*

If you are in this situation, and discover that your notice has been omitted, you have a responsibility to take the corrective action outlined in Criterion 2, and set out in Section D, below, or get your publisher to do so. Again, you cannot collect damages from people who infringed your copyright without knowing they were doing so ("innocent" infringers). However, you can stop them from infringing in the future if you notify them of the existence of your copyright. Also, you can sue your publisher for any damages caused by their failure to perform their duty under the license agreement.

EXAMPLE: Carl Jones contracts with Silichip Manufacturing to distribute GOTTCHA. The contract requires Silichip to include Carl's copyright notice on each ROM chip. Silichip omits the notice on half of the chips they produce. Carl can save his copyright because he required Silichip to include the notice in writing and they failed to do so if he takes reasonable steps to correct the problem, such as registering the copyright and attempting to provide proper notice to the purchasers of GOTTCHA. However, Carl would not be able to recover from someone who infringed innocently because of the lack of notice. In addition, if Carl is slow or inefficient in correcting Silichip's mistake, or Silichip distributes too many copies without the correct notice to allow adequate correction, the work could enter the public domain. In short, Carl might conceivably lose his copyright should Silichip actually unload an unnoticed GOTTCHA on a mass distribution basis. However, Carl could hold Silichip liable for this.

---

* Here is a sample copyright notice clause that could be inserted in a license agreement if it doesn't already contain something similar: "Publisher agrees to place proper copyright notice on all copies of the work covered by this contract which are manufactured, sold, distributed, displayed or otherwise made available to any third party. Proper copyright notice is as follows: " c Copyright Carl Jones 1985." We discuss licenses in detail in Chapter 12.

WARNING! As the copyright owner, you are ultimately responsible to see that notices are placed on all copies which are distributed to the public. Accordingly, check up on your authorized agents. Whenever you sign an agreement to license anyone to sell or distribute your software, be sure they are obligated in writing to include the correct copyright notice.

C. Effect of Partial Copyright Omissions or Copyright Errors

Sometimes only part of a copyright notice is omitted, or only one of the required copyright elements or symbols is incorrect. This sort of error is sometimes harder to spot than total omission. But beware--don't treat any copyright notice error lightly. What may appear to you to be only a small mistake or omission may have the same legal effect as if your notice was entirely omitted. This is true even if the mistake was the result of a clerical error.

COPYRIGHT OFFICE NOTE: If you register your copyright, as we suggest in Chapter 8, the Copyright Office will send a letter if they detect a copyright notice problem. They will tell you that the notice should be corrected on all future copies. If your notice includes a symbol which is different than that required by the Copyright Act, but which the Copyright Office considers as an "acceptable variant," you will receive a different letter telling you that the notice is acceptable to them but that it may not do the job if a court decides differently. Our advice? Always use the legally correct notice.

Here is a review of the legal consequences of various types of copyright notice omissions.

1. Omitting the Copyright Symbol

If the correct copyright symbol has been omitted--that is, the notice does not have a circled ©, or "copr." or "copyright," (or a circled ℗ if you're dealing with a phonorecord), the result in the United States is the same as total copyright omission. In other words, at least one of these symbols must be present or your copyright notice is no good. This type of defect is cured in the same way you would cure a total copyright omission (see Section D, below).

2. Omitting the Owner's Name

Remember, for purposes of the copyright notice, the owner of a copyright is:

■ The author(s); or

■ The employer, or the person or entity who pays for a work made for hire performed under written contract; or

■ The person or entity who owns all of the exclusive copyright rights under one or more transfers of such rights by either of the above.

If the copyright owner's name is missing, it is the same as a total copyright omission unless the publisher's name appears as the result of a contractual assignment by the owner. However, if the name put in the notice is a "nomme de plume" (pseudonymous work), or simply "anonymous" (an anonymous work), the name requirement for the work is satisfied. See Chapter 6 for a discussion of which name should go on the notice. For the effect that placing an anonymous or pseudonymous name on a notice has on copyright duration, see Chapter 5, Section B(4).

3. Omitting the Copyright Date

If your copyright date is missing, it is the same as a total omission, if the work is published. To cure this defect, see Section D, below. Remember, the notice which goes on unpublished works does not usually have a date of publication. This means that when an unpublished work is first published, you will need to change the notice to contain the publication date.

4. Error in the Copyright Symbol

This could result if you put Ⓥ instead of Ⓒ , "kopyright" or "copyrite" instead of "copyright," or potentially, even from the use of (c). The result of an error in the copyright symbol is the same as if the symbol were missing. In other words, a wrong symbol has the same legal effect as if there was no symbol. However, if you include two copyright symbols and get only one wrong, your copyright notice is valid, at least in the U.S. Thus, Ⓥ Copr. Mary Hales 1985 is valid in the U.S. because "copr." is one of the acceptable alternative copyright symbols in the U.S. The result could well be different in other countries, however, unless you properly use a circled Ⓒ. This is because the word "copyright" and abbreviation "copr." are not generally accepted outside the U.S. (see Chapter 14). If you have a defective copyright symbol, see Section D of this chapter for instructions on how to cure it.

5. Error in the Copyright Owner's Name

An error in the name of the copyright owner does not affect the validity of the copyright. However, if the name used is completely different from the copyright author's or owner's name, it may not be adequate to provide good notice of your claim. Thus, if Carl Jones' copyright notice reads: Ⓒ Copyright Carl Janes 1985, his copyright is probably unaffect-

ed. This is because the name used on the copyright still reasonably identifies Carl Jones. If the name is very different, however, or the wrong name altogether, it doesn't identify Carl and should definitely be corrected. See Section D, below.

Let's look at two additional examples:

EXAMPLE 1: Let's assume Mary Hales marries just before completing her loan package program and adopts her husband's name (Spottswudde).* She forgets to put her new name, Spottswudde, on the copyright notice, which appears with Ⓒ Copyright Mary Hales 1985. There is no harm in this situation because a copyright notice only has to uniquely identify the person. Mary Spottswudde would have no trouble showing that she was also Mary Hales. What happens, however, if a third party, who has never met Mary, runs into another Mary Hales, who claims to own the program? In this situation, the innocent party would probably be protected and the other Mary Hales would be guilty of fraud and contributory copyright infringement. Suffice it to say that our friend Mary Hales can stop the other Mary Hales from benefiting from her lie, if she can catch up with her.

EXAMPLE 2: Now imagine Kendra Salone mistakenly puts her own name on a copyright notice on a phonorecording made at BCA Graphics as a work for hire while she was employed by them. The notice appears as follows: Ⓟ Kendra Salone 1985. XYZ, a new distributor for BCA Graphics,

---

* She wouldn't legally have to, of course, and could legally keep Hales for all purposes, or as her business name.

not realizing that Kendra did her work for hire, sends her royalty checks. Kendra cashes the checks and spends the money! What is the legal effect of her action? XYZ Distributor is protected when BCA Graphics sues them for royalties because they followed the notice correctly and didn't have independent knowledge that BCA owned the copyright. Kendra has cheated BCA Graphics out of their money and is obligated to repay them. She is probably in deep trouble.

EXAMPLE 3: Gameland obtains a non-exclusive right to sell GOTTCHA. They normally contract for the right to put their name on all copyright notices because they usually get exclusive rights to sell, display, modify and copy the games they sell. Forgetting their deal with Carl Jones is a non-exclusive right to sell GOTTCHA, and that Carl has retained the copyright, they follow their usual practice and put their name on the copyright notice. In this situation, anyone dealing with Gameland who procures rights under the copyright is protected from a suit by Carl for infringement until they are notified of Carl's ownership. This is true even though Gameland never owned the rights they sold in the first place. Gameland, of course, is responsible to Carl for all monies they receive.

6. Error in the Date

If you put a date on your software more than one year in the future (that is, after the actual date of your publication), it is treated by law in the same way as total omission of copyright notice. Of course, if you put a date on your works even 10 years in the future and don't publish until that time, no harm has been done. Remember, only if the notice is wrong on a published work are there legal ramifications. A date up to one year in the future is acceptable, however. If the date you list is for any year prior to publication, the date in the notice becomes the official (legal)

publication date for copyright duration purposes.*

For example, assume all of Kendra's works were first published in 1985. If so, © Copyright BCA Graphics 1987 is equivalent to total omission. If, on the other hand, the date is 1984, the 1984 date would be considered the date of first publication. The effect of copyright publication dates on the duration of the copyright is discussed in detail in Chapter 5.

REMINDER: We can't say often enough, check your copyright notice before publication. It's so much easier to correct it at that stage. If after publication, however, you have a serious problem that is not easy to correct, consult an attorney (see Chapter 2, Section C).

D. How to Cure a Copyright Omission

Okay, here is where the action begins. Assuming the number of copies of your published work which negligently escaped your clutches without a legally adequate notice was a "not small" number (see "Criterion 2," above), or your publisher forgot to put the notice on your work (as in "Criterion 3," above), you are required by law to take the following corrective action if you desire to maintain a copyright in your work. However, even if only a few copies of your published work are involved, so that you believe you are covered by Criterion 1, we recommend that you should still take affirmative corrective action. Why? Again, because even though failure to do so may not cause you to lose your copyright as a matter of law, your published works are loose in the world and can cause you practical copyright problems. Also, judges may

---

* If, in an infringement lawsuit, however, the question comes up as to who first created a work, listing an artificially early date won't help you. You will still have to prove the actual date of publication. If you claim a date earlier than the true date, you are guilty of perjury.

disagree on whether the number of unnoticed copies is small enough to escape the need for correction. Therefore, we recommend that you take the following steps to correct the omission of your copyright notice, no matter how many copies are published without it.

Step 1: Take All Reasonable Steps to Correct the Defect

Write a certified letter, return receipt requested, to everyone you know or even suspect has received a copy of your work without your proper notice on it, notifying them of your copyright (see the example, below). This insures that from the day they receive your letter, they can't be considered "innocent infringers." Work with distributors, wholesalers, users' groups, retailers and anyone else who can help you track down the noticeless copies. Ask the people you contact to help provide you with the names and addresses of anyone they may have re-sold copies to. Depending upon the circumstances, instruct them to return their old copies for replacement, or supply them with labels containing your proper copyright notice and instruct them to place the labels on their copies.

It is an excellent, practical idea to offer the holders of your unnoticed copies an appropriate incentive to exchange their copies and help you track down others. A free enhanced version of your program, or a good discount on another desirable product, can work wonders when it comes to getting cooperation. This will surely be worth what it costs if it results in your being able to place the proper notice on all copies with defective notices.

Here are two sample letters which you may want to adopt to your needs:

May 31, 198_

Gameland
64 Byte Alley
Computer City, U.S.A.

Dear Buyer,

It has come to my attention that your order #1234 was filled on January 27, 198__ with GOTTCHA games that did not contain the proper internal copyright notice and that Order #1235 was filled March 11, 198_ with GOTTCHA games without the proper external notice.

Please return all unsold copies from Order #1234 for cost free replacement. Please attach the enclosed labels to all copies from Order #1235. If there is any confusion, we will be happy to replace any and all copies of GOTTCHA. Please advise.

Please understand we must insist that you do not continue to sell these defectively noticed copies of GOTTCHA. We will follow up with a phone call shortly.

Sincerely,

Carl Jones

March 31, 198_

Gameland
64 Byte Alley
Computer City, U.S.A.

Dear Buyer,

It has come to our attention that your Order #9775 was filled April 11, 198_ with LOANIT training manuals that did not have the proper copyright notice on the back of the title page. Please rename the title page from all manuals you have in stock and insert the new loose leaf pages supplied herein. Please return all defective training manual title pages. We fervently hope you do this in a timely fashion.

We apologize for any inconvenience this may cause you and wish to extend you an additional 20% discount on all orders received in the next ninety (90) days. If you have already sold any LOANIT manuals from Order #9775 and know who you sold them to, please advise us of the names and addresses of the purchasers. We await your reply.

Sincerely,

Mary Hales

Step 2: Document Your Efforts at Correction

Keep detailed records of your efforts to track down all copies of your work which went out without the correct copyright notice. This includes copies of telegrams, telexes and correspondence, and should also involve a record of all of the work without proper notice that you succeeded in recalling or correcting. Document phone calls with a memo setting forth the time of the call, the person you talked to and the action agreed to. If you have sales reps who call on stores, have them follow up and document their efforts. You may need this paper trail later if the question ever arises as to whether you took reasonable steps to correct the defect. For this reason, it pays to be a little paranoid and keep your records as if you are going to show them to a judge. If things go badly, you may have to.

Step 3: Register Your Copyright

In addition to taking all reasonable measures to correct the defect, you must register your copyright within five years of the first date of publication. Just because you have up to five years, however, does not mean you should take your time about this. As we detail in Chapter 8, the earliest possible registration of a published work provides you with the greatest possible protection. If you face potential problems with your copyright notice, we believe early registration to be essential. Chapters 8 - 11 tell you when and how to do this.

E. Conclusion

The main point of Chapters 6 and 7 is to impress upon you the importance of a correct copyright notice. Without it, you can lose your copyright and your right to profit from it. In the next four chapters, we take you through the ins and outs of copyright registration. A timely registration of your work can mean the practical difference between being able to stop an infringement, on the one hand, and having to stand by while the infringer laughs all the way to the bank, on the other.

CHAPTER 8

Copyright Registration: Selection of Forms

A. What Good Is Copyright Registration?

1. Introduction

In this chapter, and the three that follow, we provide detailed instructions on how to register software and computer output with the U.S. Copyright Office. We begin here by showing you how to select the correct registration form. Chapter 9 deals with how to make second and supplementary registrations. Chapter 10 explains what to include in your required deposit. Finally, in Chapter 11, we bring all this information together and show you how to complete the appropriate copyright form.

Before we discuss registration details, we feel the need to first sell you on the very idea of copyright registration. This is because of a widespread misunderstanding that copyright registration is a legal formality of small importance which a copyright owner need only bother with if and when she decides to go to court. Put simply, this is not true. The benefits of registering your work at the earliest possible time are significant. This is because a timely copyright registration will often make it worthwhile to litigate an infringement claim (a claim that somebody else is exercising one of your rights under your copyright without your permission), whereas the lack of such registration can, as a practical matter, make your attempt at court relief an exercise in futility.

To make this point as forcefully as we can, let us emphasize the benefits of early copyright registration this way. The value of your copyright depends to a significant degree on your ability to obtain effective judicial action. This, in turn, will often depend on whether you registered your copyright in time. Do we have you hooked thoroughly enough that you are willing to learn some registration details?

2. Registration Makes Your Copyright a Public Record

When you register your copyright, it becomes a matter of official public record. In practical terms, this means:

■ You are the presumed owner of the copyright in the material deposited with the registration; and

■ The information contained in your copyright registration form is presumed to be true.

These legal presumptions contained in the Copyright Act are applied in favor of your registered work should you become involved in a dispute. Does this mean that if you register first you automatically win a copyright infringement case? No. Timely registration only causes the court to make these presumptions in the absence of proof to the contrary. In other words, should another author claim original authorship in a work which is identical or similar to yours, everything you state on your registration form, including the date you created your work, will be taken by the court as true, absent a contrary showing by the other author.*

REALITY NOTE: Don't worry if this information seems confusing. Presumptions are high among the legal devices that keep copyright lawyers in business. The only point you need understand is that early registration can be very helpful in any resulting lawsuit. We discuss the subject of copyright infringement suits in detail in Chapter 13.

3. Registration Provides Notice to Otherwise Innocent Infringers

Registering your copyright has another legal advantage. Once your registration

---

* In the event both of the works in dispute are registered when the case gets to court, the information on both registration forms will be presumed correct. In other words, if there is a conflict about a particular item, the presumptions will cancel out.

is a matter of public record, it has the legal effect of sending a message like the following to everyone in the United States:

"Hear ye, hear ye, know that the work of authorship described in this registration application and represented in the accompanying deposit is subject to copyright protection. Any of you who dare to infringe will be deemed guilty because of this notice."

"So what?" you may say. "Doesn't the copyright notice on my work do the same thing?" Yes, but as we mentioned in Chapter 6, it is not uncommon for work to be accidentally or negligently published or distributed without a proper copyright notice. It is here that registration helps. Why? Because, if a competitor "innocently" comes into possession of your work which, for reasons of neglect or inadvertence, does not have the proper copyright notice attached, you are only able to sue for damages or profits resulting from the competitor's use of the work if you have registered it, and only for use which comes after your registration. In other words, registration means that, as a matter of law, your competitor will be deemed to know of your copyright protection and cannot claim innocent infringer status (see Chapter 13).

LEGAL FICTION NOTE: Those of you with a practical bent will realize that, practically speaking, it's silly to assume an infringing party has knowledge of another's copyright solely on the basis of records buried in a Washington D.C. office. This is even more true when you understand that there is no systematic way to search the Copyright Office records for potentially infringing works, as there is in the patent and trademark areas. Nonetheless, by law, registration is considered adequate notice (called constructive notice) to turn an innocent author into a presumptively guilty copyright infringer.

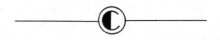

4. Registration Gives You the Right to Sue

You may not sue anyone who you believe has violated your copyright unless you have first filed your copyright registration form and paid the registration fee. It's as simple as that. You legally own a copyright, whether you register or not, but you may not use the legal process unless you have first followed the legal procedure for registration. This does not mean that infringers of unregistered copyrights can never be sued. In this situation, you can register your copyright and then sue.

This brings us back to the question we discussed in the second paragraph of this chapter. If you can register a copyright at any time, why not routinely wait to do so until you want to use the courts? In addition to the advantages of early registration which we just discussed (e.g., establishing the truth of your statements and giving constructive notice to otherwise innocent infringers), a delay in registration may, as a practical matter, destroy your chance of obtaining court relief to which you are legally entitled.

This is because you will not be eligible for certain types of damages and attorney fees unless you have registered in a timely manner.

B. Financial Advantages of Prompt Registration If You End Up in Court

If you register within the time specified by the Copyright Act of 1976, you are entitled to a number of benefits, in addition to those just discussed in Sections A(2) and A(3), in the event you prevail in a lawsuit. Before we discuss exactly what constitutes prompt registration in Section C of this chapter, let's preview the main advantages to early registration.

■ Your attorneys' fees and court costs may be ordered to be paid by the other side only if you have "promptly" registered;

■ You may elect to have the court award "statutory damages" without your having to establish what damage you actually suffered. If you do not register "promptly" within the meaning of the Copyright Act, you only collect your actual damages. In a number of situations, actual damages are very difficult to prove.

Again, the possibility of having the other side pay your attorneys' fees may often mean the difference between whether you are able to litigate in the first place. In many copyright infringement situations, the cost of an attorney will outweigh the potential benefits of winning the lawsuit. However, if your case is a strong one, the infringer has apparent ability to pay, and attorneys' fees can be collected because you promptly registered, a lawyer may well take your case for little or no money down and hope to collect from your opponent. In other words, from a real life standpoint, the possibility of recovering attorneys' fees often determines whether you can afford to file suit.

The ability to collect statutory damages is also a strong incentive for prompt copyright registration. The advantage to these damages is that to get them you do not need to prove the infringement caused you any monetary loss. As proving a specific monetary loss can often be far more difficult than establishing that infringement occurred, the right to receive statutory damages is important. Under the law, a judge may award a copyright owner from $250 to $50,000 in statutory damages, depending on the circumstances of the case. Typically, lower amounts are awarded in lawsuits involving innocent infringers, and more substantial amounts are awarded in situations of clearly purposeful infringement. Either way, the possibility of these fees is a real incentive to register early. Refer to Chapter 13 for more details.

COMMON SENSE NOTE: You may have observed that all the benefits of prompt registration relate to litigation. You are also probably aware that the overwhelming majority of copyrights are never involved in a lawsuit. Why, then, should you go to the trouble of registering, when the chances of it doing you any good are statistically marginal at best? The answer is that registration is a type of insurance. As with other forms of insurance, you pay for protection against fairly unlikely occurrences, but occurrences which are so potentially devastating that you are willing to plan in advance to cushion their impact.

Since registration is very easy to accomplish, only costs $10, and does provide significant added protection, we believe it to be one of the great insurance deals of all time, assuming, of course, that your work is valuable or potentially valuable. This is where your common sense comes in. No insurance, whether it consists of copyright registration or a more conventional variety, makes sense if what you are protecting has little or no value. Some published instruction materials, promotion copy and, occasionally even a program, may have no realistic value to anyone but you. In this situation, placing a copyright notice on the material and not bothering to register may be a wise choice. However, we strongly believe that in most situations, if your work is valuable enough to publish, it's valuable enough to register.

C. Best Time to Register Your Copyrights

To qualify for the benefits just discussed above in Section B of this chapter, you must register your copyright as follows:

■ Unpublished Works: Registration must occur any time before the infringement begins. Thus, if someone gets hold of your unpublished work and copies it before you register, and you then register and bring suit, you are not entitled to statutory damages, attorneys' fees, etc.

■ Published Works: Registration must occur any time before the infringement begins or must take place within three months of publication. In other words, unless you register within three months of publication, litigation over an infringement which starts before you register may result in your being awarded actual damages and injunctive relief, but not statutory damages or attorneys' fees. In the real world, because many infringements begin shortly after publication, getting your work registered within the three-month post-publication period is important.

EXAMPLE: Believing that the copyright notice is enough protection, Carl Jones publishes GOTTCHA. The great success of the program naturally stimulates others to create "highly similar" products (somehow Carl doesn't smile when ex-sweetheart Belinda says "imitation is the sincerest form of flattery"). One of these copies, HOTSHOT, hits the market two months after GOTTCHA is published and sells a ton. Although Carl believes that HOTSHOT has infringed his copyright, he doesn't like lawyers much and delays deciding whether to sue. Three months later, he finds an attorney he likes and decides to go to court. Accordingly, he registers his copyright and files his action. While Carl may recover actual damages and obtain injunctive relief against a future sale and distribution of HOTSHOT, he is not entitled to the additional litigation benefits available for early registrants. Why not? Since HOTSHOT was published before Carl registered his copyright, and because Carl failed to register his copyright within three months of GOTTCHA's publication, he simply doesn't qualify. If Carl had registered within the three-month period after publication, however, he would be entitled to the special benefits, even if this registration date came after HOTSHOT was published.

D. Potential Problems from Copyright Registration

Let's assume we've convinced you that early registration is wise and you've already started to obtain the necessary forms. Wait. There may be a down side to making your work a public record by registering it with the U.S. Copyright Office. Before you register, we want you to know about this.

Since your copyright application and at least some part of your work become available for public inspection when you register, others will have the opportunity to examine your work. They can view everything you send to the Copyright Office, although they cannot make copies. The right of the public to inspect at least a portion of your copyrighted material may be of real concern, depending on the nature of your work. In Chapter 10, we address this concern in detail and suggest several practical ways to alleviate it. Those readers who plan to maintain the trade secret status of their work will also want to read Chapter 15. At the risk of getting ahead of ourselves, our conclusion is that, in most situations, the danger that copyright registration will disclose your work is

usually more fanciful than real, assuming you take several routine self-protection steps. Again, if this area is particularly worrisome to you, why not jump ahead and read Chapter 10, Section D.

E. An Overview of Copyright Registration Process

Hopefully, we have convinced you of the reasons why you should register your copyright. Now we want to give you a glimpse of the entire registration process "forest" so you will have your bearings when we encounter the specific "trees" of the copyright registration process in the next several chapters. Fortunately, the registration process is simple. Most of the complexity and confusion which does exist is a reflection of the great diversity of types of copyrightable material. The Copyright Office itself is remarkably pleasant and professional in its dealings with the public.

First, the forms. The Copyright Office provides a number of different forms to be used for different types of work. Thus, there is one form for nondramatic literary works, another one for dramatic literary works, and so on. These forms are prepared by the U.S. Copyright Office and only their forms (no photocopies) may be used to register a copyright. Accordingly, you will need to send away for them.

Each of the forms is accompanied with a set of line-by-line instructions. Fortunately, these are much simpler and easier to understand than tax forms. Here is a copy of the TX form, the one most of you will use most of the time:

FORM TX
UNITED STATES COPYRIGHT OFFICE

REGISTRATION NUMBER

_____

| TX | TXU |

EFFECTIVE DATE OF REGISTRATION

_____

| Month | Day | Year |

DO NOT WRITE ABOVE THIS LINE. IF YOU NEED MORE SPACE, USE A SEPARATE CONTINUATION SHEET.

1

TITLE OF THIS WORK ▼

PREVIOUS OR ALTERNATIVE TITLES ▼

PUBLICATION AS A CONTRIBUTION If this work was published as a contribution to a periodical, serial, or collection, give information about the collective work in which the contribution appeared.   **Title of Collective Work ▼**

If published in a periodical or serial give: **Volume ▼**   **Number ▼**   **Issue Date ▼**   **On Pages ▼**

2

a

NAME OF AUTHOR ▼

DATES OF BIRTH AND DEATH
Year Born ▼   Year Died ▼

Was this contribution to the work a "work made for hire"?
☐ Yes
☐ No

AUTHOR'S NATIONALITY OR DOMICILE
Name of Country
OR { Citizen of ▶_____
Domiciled in ▶_____

WAS THIS AUTHOR'S CONTRIBUTION TO THE WORK
Anonymous?   ☐ Yes ☐ No
Pseudonymous?   ☐ Yes ☐ No

If the answer to either of these questions is "Yes," see detailed instructions

NATURE OF AUTHORSHIP Briefly describe nature of the material created by this author in which copyright is claimed. ▼

NOTE

Under the law, the "author" of a "work made for hire" is generally the employer, not the employee (see instructions). For any part of this work that was "made for hire" check "Yes" in the space provided, give the employer (or other person for whom the work was prepared) as "Author" of that part, and leave the space for dates of birth and death blank.

b

NAME OF AUTHOR ▼

DATES OF BIRTH AND DEATH
Year Born ▼   Year Died ▼

Was this contribution to the work a "work made for hire"?
☐ Yes
☐ No

AUTHOR'S NATIONALITY OR DOMICILE
Name of country
OR { Citizen of ▶_____
Domiciled in ▶_____

WAS THIS AUTHOR'S CONTRIBUTION TO THE WORK
Anonymous?   ☐ Yes ☐ No
Pseudonymous?   ☐ Yes ☐ No

If the answer to either of these questions is "Yes," see detailed instructions.

NATURE OF AUTHORSHIP Briefly describe nature of the material created by this author in which copyright is claimed. ▼

c

NAME OF AUTHOR ▼

DATES OF BIRTH AND DEATH
Year Born ▼   Year Died ▼

Was this contribution to the work a "work made for hire"?
☐ Yes
☐ No

AUTHOR'S NATIONALITY OR DOMICILE
Name of Country
OR { Citizen of ▶_____
Domiciled in ▶_____

WAS THIS AUTHOR'S CONTRIBUTION TO THE WORK
Anonymous?   ☐ Yes ☐ No
Pseudonymous?   ☐ Yes ☐ No

If the answer to either of these questions is "Yes," see detailed instructions

NATURE OF AUTHORSHIP Briefly describe nature of the material created by this author in which copyright is claimed. ▼

3

YEAR IN WHICH CREATION OF THIS WORK WAS COMPLETED This information must be given in all cases.
◀ Year

DATE AND NATION OF FIRST PUBLICATION OF THIS PARTICULAR WORK
Complete this information ONLY if this work has been published.   Month ▶ _____ Day ▶ _____ Year ▶ _____
◀ Nation

4

See instructions before completing this space.

COPYRIGHT CLAIMANT(S) Name and address must be given even if the claimant is the same as the author given in space 2.▼

TRANSFER If the claimant(s) named here in space 4 are different from the author(s) named in space 2, give a brief statement of how the claimant(s) obtained ownership of the copyright.▼

APPLICATION RECEIVED

ONE DEPOSIT RECEIVED

TWO DEPOSITS RECEIVED

REMITTANCE NUMBER AND DATE

DO NOT WRITE HERE OFFICE USE ONLY

MORE ON BACK ▶   • Complete all applicable spaces (numbers 5-11) on the reverse side of this page.
• See detailed instructions.   • Sign the form at line 10.

DO NOT WRITE HERE
Page 1 of _____ pages

DO NOT WRITE ABOVE THIS LINE. IF YOU NEED MORE SPACE, USE A SEPARATE CONTINUATION SHEET.

PREVIOUS REGISTRATION Has registration for this work, or for an earlier version of this work, already been made in the Copyright Office?

☐ Yes ☐ No If your answer is "Yes," why is another registration being sought? (Check appropriate box) ▼

☐ This is the first published edition of a work previously registered in unpublished form.

☐ This is the first application submitted by this author as copyright claimant.

☐ This is a changed version of the work, as shown by space 6 on this application.

If your answer is "Yes," give: **Previous Registration Number ▼**   **Year of Registration ▼**

5

DERIVATIVE WORK OR COMPILATION Complete both space 6a & 6b for a derivative work; complete only 6b for a compilation.

a. Preexisting Material Identify any preexisting work or works that this work is based on or incorporates. ▼

b. Material Added to This Work Give a brief, general statement of the material that has been added to this work and in which copyright is claimed. ▼

6

See instructions
before completing
this space.

MANUFACTURERS AND LOCATIONS If this is a published work consisting preponderantly of nondramatic literary material in English, the law may require that the copies be manufactured in the United States or Canada for full protection. If so, the names of the manufacturers who performed certain processes, and the places where these processes were performed **must** be given. See instructions for details.

Names of Manufacturers ▼   **Places of Manufacture ▼**

7

REPRODUCTION FOR USE OF BLIND OR PHYSICALLY HANDICAPPED INDIVIDUALS A signature on this form at space 10, and a check in one of the boxes here in space 8, constitutes a non-exclusive grant of permission to the Library of Congress to reproduce and distribute solely for the blind and physically handicapped and under the conditions and limitations prescribed by the regulations of the Copyright Office: (1) copies of the work identified in space 1 of this application in Braille (or similar tactile symbols); or (2) phonorecords embodying a fixation of a reading of that work; or (3) both.

a ☐ Copies and Phonorecords   **b** ☐ Copies Only   **c** ☐ Phonorecords Only

8

See instructions

DEPOSIT ACCOUNT If the registration fee is to be charged to a Deposit Account established in the Copyright Office, give name and number of Account.

Name ▼   **Account Number ▼**

9

CORRESPONDENCE Give name and address to which correspondence about this application should be sent. Name/Address/Apt/City/State/Zip ▼

Area Code & Telephone Number ▶

Be sure to
give your
daytime phone
◀ number.

CERTIFICATION* I, the undersigned, hereby certify that I am the

Check one ▶

☐ author
☐ other copyright claimant
☐ owner of exclusive right(s)
☐ authorized agent of _____

Name of author or other copyright claimant, or owner of exclusive right(s) ▲

of the work identified in this application and that the statements made by me in this application are correct to the best of my knowledge.

10

Typed or printed **name and date ▼** If this is a published work, this date must be the same as or later than the date of publication given in space 3.

     date ▶

Handwritten signature (X) ▼

**MAIL
CERTIFI-
CATE TO**

Name ▼

Number/Street/Apartment Number ▼

City/State/ZIP ▼

**Certificate
will be
mailed in
window
envelope**

Have you:
• Completed all necessary spaces?
• Signed your application in space 10?
• Enclosed check or money order for $10 payable to *Register of Copyrights*?
• Enclosed your deposit material with the application and fee?

MAIL TO: Register of Copyrights. Library of Congress. Washington. D.C. 20559.

11

To accomplish your registration, you must complete the following four steps:

Step 1: Select and Obtain Appropriate Copyright Application Form(s)

Refer to the chart and discussion in Section F of this chapter to determine which registration form is appropriate for your work. Once you determine the correct registration form or forms, you will need multiple copies of each. Copyright forms are free. Again, please pay attention to the rule that photocopies are not acceptable.

To obtain forms, write to:

Information and Publication
  Section LM-455
Copyright Office
Library of Congress
Washington, DC 20559

Or, call: (202) 287-9100

You can call 24 hours a day. Leave your name, mailing address, the type of forms you need, as well as how many of each you require. The maximum order for each type is 25.

To get more information:

If you have trouble selecting the correct form from the chart set out below, you can get advice from the Copyright Office by calling (202) 287-8700. This number is available from 8:30 a.m. until 5:00 p.m. eastern time, Monday through Friday.

Step 2: Fill Out Your Copyright Form(s)

We provide a detailed discussion of how to fill out your copyright form in Chapter 11.

Step 3: Pay Copyright Registration Fee

Each registration form submitted to the U.S. Copyright Office requires a $10 fee. Make your check or money order payable to: Register of Copyrights. Your registration fee is nonrefundable. This means that should the Copyright Office reject your application for any reason, they keep your money. However, in most cases you will be given additional opportunities to correct deficiencies in your application without paying a new fee. If you follow the instructions in this book, and those which accompany the registration form, however, you shouldn't have this problem.

Step 4: Include a Deposit of Your Work

You must include either your entire work or a representative sample with your copyright application. This is called a "deposit." Deposit rules can be a little complicated, and there can be considerable strategy involved in what and how much you should deposit. For this reason, we discuss deposits in detail in Chapter 10.

Step 5: Mail Your Material to the Copyright Office

Send your application with the correct deposit of your work, and the fee, in a single envelope to:

Register of Copyrights
Library of Congress
Washington, DC 20559

We discuss this in more detail in Chapter 11.

NOTE: Due to the absence of Copyright Office guidelines, we are unable to provide advice regarding registration of semiconductor masks under the Semiconductor Chip Protection Act of 1983. See Chapter 3, Section J, item 11.

F. Choosing the Correct Copyright Form

Now, let's backtrack to Step 1 of the copyright application process. This involves choosing the correct form for your type of work. Here is a list:

TYPE OF WORK	FORM TO USE
Program, source code	TX
Program, object code	TX
Output screens	PA
Training film	PA
Training manual	TX
Flowchart	TX/VA
Graphs	VA
Articles	TX
Newsletters, Journals	SE
Computer-generated art	VA
Computer-generated music	SR
Database (not program)	TX

Now let's examine each of these forms in more detail, using the three developers--Kendra Salone, Mary Hales and Carl Jones--we introduced you to in Chapter 2, as examples.

1. Form TX: Nondramatic Literary Works

a. Programs

Form TX should be used for all published and unpublished nondramatic literary works. This includes computer programs (whether in object code or source code form), books, databases, operating systems drivers, compilers, assemblers, interpreters, database management systems, code embedded in ROMS and virtually every other form of organized code. It also includes associated documentation, such as manuals, instruction sheets dictionaries and flow charts of a textual nature. One TX form can be used for each program (and its associated documentation). However, this is expensive if you're registering a complete system (such as Mary Hales' LOANIT loan processing package) with anywhere from 5 to 100 or more programs. Having to part with $10 and prepare a separate deposit of your work to copyright each program certainly qualifies as a substantial pain in the pocketbook, as well as in the neck.

b. Multi-Program Works

Fortunately, there is another legal way to approach a large system registration like the LOANIT package. This is to think of the whole package as a book and the individual programs as chapters. When LOANIT is viewed this way, for example, Mary Hales would need only one TX form and one fee to register all of her programs. However, by adopting this approach, Mary treats LOANIT as one work. It follows that it must be published as such. If she later decides to market LOANIT in any other configuration (say without 10 programs), the quality of her protection may suffer in that the public record aspect of the registration will be insufficient, due to the lack of a specific match between the marketed and registered versions. In short, registering a multi-program package as one work saves you money and trouble, but you may lose a degree of protection in the event you wish to market parts of the package separately.

For example, if program #18 of LOANIT is infringed, Mary may have an easier time proving it if she has registered #18 separately and made a separate deposit of work from that program. If Mary registered LOANIT as one package, on the other hand, her deposit would probably not contain any of the material from program #18, as it is standard to deposit only the first 25 and last 25 pages of code (see Chapter 10). In other words, the separate registration (and hence separate deposit) of #18 will provide much better proof as to the subject matter of Mary's copyright than will a single deposit for the entire package.

c. Documentation

Documentation which accompanies a program should also be registered using Form

TX.* Indeed, documentation can be registered on the same TX form as your program
if it is published as part of the program
package and at the same time. It is
probably wise, as well as cheaper and
easier, to follow this approach if the
documentation material is published at
the same time as the software it relates
to. If, on the other hand, you think you
might be publishing your documentation
from the beginning as a separate work,
then it must be registered separately.

DEPOSIT NOTE: Unlike deposits for
program and database registrations, which
commonly only involve a portion of the
code, deposits for documentation require
at least one, and sometimes two, complete
copies of the work. This means even if
the documentation is later marketed together or separately with the program,
your public record in the work is maintained without the need for an independent registration.

SIMULTANEOUS PUBLICATION NOTE: We
said above that to register an entire
package on one TX form, the whole thing
must be published at the same time. What
does this really mean? If you get your
disks run off one day and your manuals
from the printer the next week, does this
mean they aren't published at the same
time for copyright purposes? No. As
long as you release your program package
and documentation to the public at the
same time, they are published at the same
time and can be registered together. For
another, and very different, meaning of
the term "simultaneous publication," this
time in the international copyright context, see Chapter 14.

d. Flowcharts

Flowcharts are an unavoidable part of
the computer world. And when we say
flowchart, we do not limit ourselves to
the traditional flowchart (see Type 1,
below), but also refer to all types of
pre-code schematics. For example, programmers use flow charts to design the
logic flow of their work. Information

managers use them to construct databases
and coordinate computer functions at the
user level. Consultants use them to
formulate system designs. Program documentation materials employ them to express core ideas and relationships.

One big question is whether flowcharts
should be registered as part of a program
package or registered separately? And,
if separate registration is the way to
go, what registration form should be
used? As you have probably guessed,
because this section is included under
the "Form TX" subsection of this chapter,
this form is appropriate in many circumstances.

Before we deal with this subject,
however, it is important to say a few
words about the different types of flowcharts. Yes, we know this may not be
fascinating information, but hang on, it
may turn out to be important to you. For
purposes of copyright registration it's
necessary to divide your flow charts into
two broad types.

TYPE 1: Charts which express their
ideas through the use of symbols and the
relationship between symbols.

TYPE 2: Charts which carry their
primary information on text form.

Now, we are ready to review the general
rules for registering flowcharts. Don't
lose patience. We will get back to Type
1 and Type 2 charts in a minute.

Here are the rules:

■ If a flowchart is part of program
documentation and is published with it,
it can be included as part of the package
and registered using a TX form as discussed in F1(b), above. In other words,
no separate registration form and fee is
required.

■ If a flow chart is not part of
program documentation, or is published at
another time than the documentation,
separate registration and a separate fee
is required.

---

* Training films, if separately registered, should be
registered using Form PA. See Section 2 below.

TYPE 1 CHART

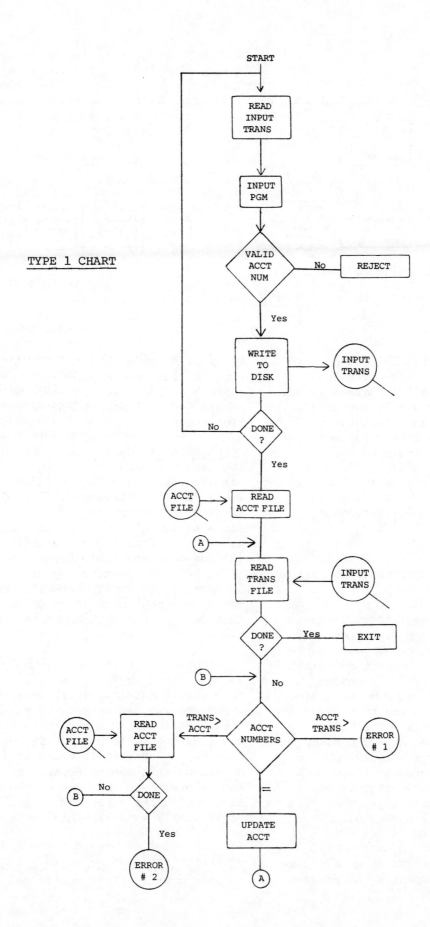

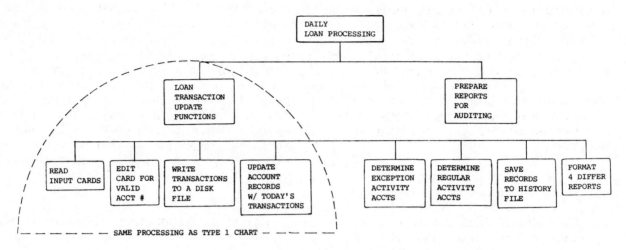

Now, let's assume that for one or more of the reasons set out above, you conclude a separate registration makes sense. What registration form should you use? This is where the distinction between Type 1 and Type 2 flow charts becomes important. A VA form should be used for symbol type charts (Type 1), while a TX form is appropriate for text type charts (Type 2). The VA registration form is discussed in detail below, in Section F(3) of this chapter.

e. Examples of Registrations Using Form TX

EXAMPLE 1: Carl Jones' GOTTCHA computer game is in the form of object code embedded on a chip. It can be copyrighted using Form TX because object code is one of the ways to express a computer program and a computer program is considered by the Copyright Office to be a nondramatic literary work. The fact that the program is embedded on a chip makes no difference, since the chip is only the media on which the program is fixed. The program could be similarly registered with the Form TX if fixed in another type of media (e.g., a tape, diskette, or cassette).

Carl can use the same TX form to register a manual that accompanies the program.

However, remember that if the documentation is published separately, it must be registered separately. Refer to the Appendix for Carl Jones' sample registration forms.

EXAMPLE 2: Carl Jones uses an existing database manager program to create his database, BUGBITS, which lists parts available for Volkwagens. Carl does not register the database manager program, since he doesn't own it. He does, however, use a Form TX to register the resulting data and its database structure (i.e. BUGBITS) produced by his input. See Chapter 10 for the specific requirements relating to the type of deposit that must accompany a database registration.

EXAMPLE 3: Let's now assume Mary Hales' LOANIT package consists of 70 programs, 8 manuals, 70 flowcharts, and two marketing brochures. If she registers each individually, she must fill out and file 150 TX forms.* This would cost $1,500. Whether it is worth it for Mary to expend this amount depends on balancing several factors. One of these is how much profit she expects to make. If she feels LOANIT will earn big bucks, the

---

* This is assuming that the flowcharts are all of the textual or narrative variety. If some of them are of the symbolic type, VA forms would be used.

$1,500 to register each program separately may not loom large, and it does provide a better public record of her work, especially in regard to the programs.* However, if Mary is a little short of cash, isn't sure whether LOANIT will sell well, and plans to market it as one work, she is pretty safe using one TX form to register the whole package, including the documentation.

EXAMPLE 4: BCA Graphics registers QUILTIT, which was done by Kendra Salone as a work for hire, on a TX form. Obviously, they should list themselves as the copyright author, since the work was created by their employee during the normal course of business.

2. Form PA: Works of the Performing Arts

a. Types of works

Copyright registration Form PA is appropriate for all published and unpublished works which involve moving sequential images. Use it to register computer-generated display screens, motion pictures, video or computer games, light shows, and any music, including sound effects, which accompanies such works. This is because sound effects from games, as well as soundtracks from motion pictures, are considered part of the audio-visual work as a whole.

b. Using PA Forms with TX Forms

In the computer software business, it is extremely common to use a PA form in conjunction with a TX form. This is because Form TX registers the computer program itself, while Form PA covers the output screen (i.e., what you see on the monitor when the program is running). Why is it important to register both the program and the output screen? Where video or computer games are involved, the screen display (PacMan, for example) often has great independent value. By separately registering such output, you get added protection against someone writing an entirely new program to produce identical or similar screens.**

c. Examples of Registrations Using Form PA

EXAMPLE 1: Carl Jones' computer game, GOTTCHA, becomes an immediate national hit. As such, it contains several characters the public knows and identifies with. In other words, its output screens have independent economic value. Now, suppose Pauline Pirate, using her own independently-developed program, creates a game, TAG, that contains characters that look much like Carl's. Indications are that, if widely marketed, TAG could seriously cut into GOTTCHA's sales. To gain maximum copyright protection, Carl files a PA form for his output screens, as well as a Form TX for his underlying program. He does this within three months of publication, to qualify for maximum benefits.

ATTRACT AND PLAY MODE NOTE: Video and computer arcade games commonly have two "modes" of operation. One is called the "attract mode." This is when a portion of the game runs by itself to attract the public's attention and encourage play. The other is called the "play mode." This is the sequence of screens displayed during actual play of the game. Although, technically, these are two different expressions of a work, as a practical matter, Carl need only use one PA form to cover both. However, he should

---

* This is assuming that Mary wants such a record. In a few situations, she may wish to deposit as little code as possible, because she plans to license the work narrowly and treat it as a trade secret. In such a situation, Mary would probably make a single registration for the entire package. We discuss the reasons for this approach in Chapter 10, Section D and Chapter 15.

** Some experts feel that output is sufficiently protected by the copyright protection pertaining to the underlying code. Others feel that output should be separately registered for the reasons stated. As with other choices, you will need to balance a fanatic desire to ensure maximum protection with common sense. See Stern Electronics, Inc. v. Kaufman, 669 F.2d 852.

be sure his deposit reflects both forms of the work (see Chapter 10 on deposits).*

EXAMPLE 2: As you may remember from Chapter 2, when we first introduced Mary Hales, her LOANIT loan processing program is accompanied by a training film. This film is considered to be a "work of the performing arts" and can be copyrighted on Form PA. However, it can also be considered documentation, and can therefore be covered by a single TX form as well, assuming LOANIT is registered as a single package. It is normally adequate to register training films as part of a larger TX package, unless the film is published at a different time. The deposit of the entire film, or part of the large package, provides a good public record in case of infringement.

---

* This information may contradict a common belief that two registrations should be submitted for arcade games, one for the attract mode and one for the play mode. While this used to be true, the Copyright Office now discourages the practice. Since your attract mode is merely a specific sequence of your play mode, and they are always published together, one copyright Form PA is adequate, as long as your deposit covers both (Chapter 10) and your notice appears on both.

EXAMPLE 3: BCA Graphics designs a slide program to run a sequence of Kendra Salone's quilt designs at timed intervals for review by potential buyers. As each quilt screen is displayed, an accompanying narration explains more about it. The narration is read from a written script. The entire performance, including the narration, can be registered on Form PA. The script may be, but does not have to be, registered separately on a Form TX. In this situation, it's probably silly to do so, as the script is clearly in support of the slide program. Since it has little or no meaning, except as read along with this demonstration, there is almost no risk of infringement. Thus, BCA Graphics can sensibly register the script along with the slide shows on a single Form PA for audio-visual works.

3. Form VA: Works of Visual Arts

Form VA is used for all published and unpublished pictorial, graphic and sculptural works. In essence, this means all works which are visual stills rather than moving images. Examples common (and not so common) to the computer field include output in graphics form (e.g., a pie chart), whether on screen or paper, computer-generated slides, holographs, still computer simulations of microscopic objects (e.g., DNA molecules) and macroscopic objects (e.g., planets) and other two- and three-dimensional works of fine, graphic and applied arts. Flow charts which express their message primarily through symbols rather than through text-- Type 1 charts, as discussed in Section F1(d)--should be registered using the VA form. Finally, photographs, technical drawings, diagrams and models should also be registered on a VA form.

EXAMPLE 1: Assume Carl Jones draws a picture of the characters in his computer game, GOTTCHA. These pictures will be used in promotional materials and may appear in magazines and perhaps even in a TV ad. If Carl has already copyrighted his output screens on Form PA and his program on Form TX, he is probably adequately protected. However, if he has not already copyrighted his output screen, he should file a Form VA to cover the visual presentation of his characters. Remember, Carl is registering the picture of the characters rather than the media itself (i.e., the screen or paper). As these pictures would very likely be considered to be legally derivative of Carl's original program (see Chapter 4), it may not be logically necessary to register them separately. But, when dealing with very valuable intellectual property rights, it is wise to be on the safe side. This is especially true when dealing with derivative works that involve substantial changes from the original.

EXAMPLE 2: Mary Hales' flowchart in her LOANIT manual is a two-dimensional primarily graphic work where symbols are used to convey the message instead of text. As her chart is part of her program documentation, it is covered by her TX form. However, if this flow chart is published at a different time from her program and has value, she may want to register it separately, using form VA. If the flow chart were primarily textual (i.e., Type 2, as discussed in Section 1(d) above), and did not rely on graphic

symbols to convey information, a separate Form TX would be used.

EXAMPLE 3: BCA Graphics makes a quilt from a design generated by QUILTIT. This quilt is used at trade shows to demonstrate what QUILTIT can do. It may even have economic value if BCA is able to sell the design to a textile company for volume production. BCA would be well-advised to register the quilt pattern using the Form VA.

4. Form SR: Sound Recordings: Records & Tapes

This form is used for phonograph records, tapes, and other "fixed" music or sounds, such as those produced by laser disks. However, if the sound is part of a performing arts display (i.e., moving images), it should be registered on a PA form along with the movie or other audiovisual it accompanies.

EXAMPLE 1: Carl Jones makes a cassette recording of the soundtrack from the cartoon version of GOTTCHA COMIN' & GOIN'. The cartoon is derived from his video game, GOTTCHA. The soundtrack itself is supportive of the cartoon film GOTTCHA COMIN' & GOIN' and would be covered when it was registered on Form PA (audio visual works). However, should the soundtrack be separated from the cartoon and placed on cassette for sale, it is no longer a part of the audiovisual and would now be considered a sound recording. In this situation, it should be registered on Form SR. If the sound is not published separately, however, the copyright registration protection gained as part of the registration on Form VA extends to the separate audio version, and you needn't register it separately.

EXAMPLE 2: As you may remember from Chapter 2, Carl Jones used his computer to generate a musical composition he calls OFFKEY. Carl should register OFFKEY on a Form SR when it is fixed on tape or phonorecord, unless, of course, he is so sure that OFFKEY is terrible and nobody in their right mind would steal it. In this situation, he should put his copyright notice on all copies and save his registration fee.

EXAMPLE 3: BCA Graphics creates a laser disk recording of the sound effects from their laser light show, BLASTIT. They use Form SR to register it. Refer to Example 1, just above, for the reasoning behind this decision.

NOTE: TEXT TO AUDIO: It is common for written documentation to be exactly rendered in an audio version for educational and training purposes. When this is done--in other words, the work appears in a new media--you may want to separately register it on an SR form, if it has value (see Chapter 4).

5. Form SE: Serials, Periodicals, Newsletters, Journals, Magazines

Form SE is used for serialized or logically numbered publications. Each edition of your weekly computer magazine, local newspaper or users' group newsletter should be registered on an SE form. While this registration protects the periodic publication as a whole, individual articles should be separately registered on a Form TX by their copyright owners, if they are owned by someone other than the periodical. This is often the case where a journal only buys one-time use of a particular article or book excerpt.

EXAMPLE 1: The computer users' group Carl Jones belongs to, Byte Me, publishes a monthly newsletter called "Rollin' On," which contains articles on the latest products and tricks of interest to the group. The users' group should register this periodic newsletter each month on Copyright Form SE. The individual articles should also be registered on TX forms by their authors if they still own any rights to them. Thus, if Carl writes an article on GOTTCHA, called "Living in the Space Zone," describing the game in

detail, he should copyright the article in his name on a Form TX. The users' group should then copyright the entire newsletter. Now suppose someone wants to reprint Carl's article. Who do they get permission from, and who do they pay? It depends on the contract between Carl and Byte Me. Often, but by no means always, a writer only grants a periodical one-time use of a particular piece. Other times, the magazine buys the work outright.

EXAMPLE 2: Assume Carl's users' group has purchased only one-time use to his article. This gives them the right to reprint "Living in the Space Zone" in its entirety only if they wish to distribute more copies of the particular edition of "Rollin' On," in which the article appeared. Byte Me could not publish the article in any other form, or sell or license it to anyone else, without Carl's permission. However, if Carl sold Byte Me his article outright, they could reproduce the article or license others to do so as they choose.

NOTE: AUTHORS' CONTRACTUAL AND COPYRIGHT RIGHTS: There are many ways that contracts for selling work to periodicals can be structured. There are even more things you need to know when book length manuscripts are involved. We don't pretend to deal with the rights of journalists or authors here. By far the best work on the subject is Author Law: A Legal Guide For the Working Writer, by Brad Bunnin and Peter Beren (Nolo Press). If you write for pay, buy it.

EXAMPLE 3: BCA Graphics has developed an annual journal of quilt designs. Each year they print a collection of their best designs in a work entitled The Best Quilt Designs of 1985. This yearly journal can be registered using an SE form.

EXAMPLE 4: Carl Jones' users' group decides to publish their newsletter "Rollin' On" on a large national electronic database. They arrange a deal with the database under which monthly editions of the publication will be made accessible to the database's subscribers. Under this arrangement, Byte Me is to receive a royalty each time a subscriber accesses their journal. Byte Me can register the electronic form of "Rollin' On" using an SE form. However, this is probably overkill, as the electronic version is already protected so long as the written version was registered.

6. Form GR/CP: Group of Contributions to Periodicals

This form is designed for works which have been previously published and copyrighted as individual contributions to periodicals and which are now collected into one work. For example, poets often have their individual copyrighted poems published in poetry journals and other types of magazines. At some point, they decide to group such poems together by theme or other organizing principle and publish them as a book. In such a case, they would use the Form GR/CP.

Incidentally, the reason a compilation of independently copyrighted works has value lies in the aesthetics involved in editing and packaging such materials.

The specific rules using a form GR/CP are:

■ All the works must be by the same author, who is an individual (not an employer of hire); and

■ All the works must have been first published as contributions to periodicals within a twelve-month period. This is not a calendar year, but means the publication date of the last piece can't be more than 12 months from the date of the first piece; and

■ Each of the works contained a proper copyright notice when it was first published, and the names on all notices are the same; and

■ One entire periodical in which each work was first published must be deposited; and

■ Each work must be identified on Form GR/CP by the periodical containing it and the date of publication; and

■ The individual works must have been registered on either the TX, VA or PA forms.

Two examples should help to clarify the uses of this form.

EXAMPLE 1: Carl Jones writes monthly articles for his users' group monthly newsletter, "Rollin' On," which is electronically published on a major national on-line data base. Each article contained his proper copyright notice: © Copyright Carl Jones 1986 (or one of the other legal forms of notice). At the end of a year, Carl gathers the 12 articles and publishes them in book form under a separate title. He would use a GR/CP form to register the book. The form could not be used if Carl attempted to combine his articles with those of another author, since this would violate the one-author requirement. The deposit requirement would be met with a printout of each of the 12 articles as originally appearing on screen.

EXAMPLE 2: Carl Jones writes articles for various magazines during the course of two years and then puts them all together in a published work entitled Collected Articles by Carl Jones. This collection (including its new introduction, etc.) cannot be registered by using this form. Why not? Because the articles spanned more than one year. Suppose, however, that the one-year requirement had been met. Then, Carl might use this form to register the book so long as the copyright notice requirement was met in respect to each article. It should be noted that each article could have already been registered on a TX form. If that had been done, Carl might not feel the need to register the collected works unless new material was contained. A lengthy introduction might be reason to do this if it added real value to already copyrighted work.

NOTE: Form GR/CP isn't too widely used for computer-related products because it often doesn't exactly fit people's needs. Although the Copyright Act has a reserved space for a form for "group registration of related works," which certainly would be convenient for a computer system comprised of programs (Form TX), films (Form PA), screens (Form VA) and documentation (Form TX), no action to actually provide this form has been taken. Until Congress addresses the whole computer copyright field (some would say "mess") in detail, we must continue to fit new technology into old law as best we can.

G. Conclusion

At the beginning of this chapter, we suggested that much of the complexity in the registration process arises from the differences in types of registerable materials. Now you know what we meant. Just in case your head is swimming in a murky sea of details, let's summarize the main points relating to copyright registration:

■ Registration is an essential prerequisite to suing infringers;

■ Prompt registration--within three months of publication--affords significant advantages when it comes to recovering damages and attorney fees from infringers;

■ A Form TX is used for programs, accompanying documentation, and textual flow charts. For greatest copyright protection and flexibility in marketing, it's often wise to separately register programs with considerable independent economic value;

■ A Form PA should be used for movie-type works and computer games;

■ A Form VA is used for computer-generated art, graphics, holographs and other visual stills, including symbolic flow charts;

■ A Form SR is used for computer-generated sounds marketed separately from accompanying visual effects;

■ A Form SE is used for periodicals;

■ A Form GR/CP is used for collected works of a single author;

■ It is sometimes wise to register different expressions (e.g., a game program and game screens) of the same work on different forms for maximum protection.

•CHAPTER 9•

Second and Supplementary Registrations (Changes, Mistakes and New Versions)

A. Introduction

As a general rule, only a single copyright registration will be accepted for any version of a work. But, what happens if you:

■ Make mistakes on your registration form;

■ Modify your program after you register it;

■ Add a program to your system;

■ Change any of your manuals, documentation, etc. after original registration;

■ Wish to change the name of the author of your program; or

■ Change your publication date after you register?

Unfortunately, there is no simple set of instructions sufficient to cover all the situations where it is appropriate to change a copyright registration. For an overview of what is involved, however, let's look at the three procedures available to you. Depending on your situation, you can:

■ File a supplemental registration;

■ File a new registration for a previously registered work; or

■ Register the new version or changed portions of your work as a derivative work.

Let's take a closer look at these alternatives. Please read this entire chapter before you make any firm choices.

B. Supplemental Registration

Supplemental copyright registration is available for situations where you register but later discover you either forgot something important, supplied the U.S. Copyright Office with wrong information, or important facts have changed. Generally, this procedure involves a minimum of hassle--that is, a simple form and payment of another copyright registration fee. We only discuss supplemental registration requirements for copyright registrations made after January 1, 1978. If you have a problem with a registration made prior to this date, see a copyright lawyer.

Suppose after you register a copyright you discover you made a mistake or omitted information on one of the standard registration forms (TX, PA, VA, etc.). Because you are entitled to have the court rely on the accuracy of the information on your registration form in the event litigation occurs, it is a good idea to keep the information on your registration form current, and to correct mistakes in all situations where the information in question has possible bearing on your position in any future lawsuit.

Common mistakes that can be corrected by supplemental registration include the birthdate of the author and the spelling of the author's name. A supplemental copyright registration is also appropriate when the author's (or copyright owner's) address changes, and where the title of a program is changed.

1. Birthdate of Author

HAPPY BIRTHDAY DEAR...

A mistake in an author's birthdate can be corrected using a supplemental registration form. However, this may be one type of mistake which is not worth another filing fee. For although facts relevant to the ownership or duration of a copyright should, as a general rule, be kept current and accurate, an author's birthdate is irrelevant to the determination of copyright ownership. Duration, as you doubtless remember from Chapter 5, is based either on the author's life or the date of publication. Still, if you have a passion for accuracy, this may be reason enough to file a supplemental registration if your original registration misstated your birthdate.

2. Misspelled Name of Author

An author's name can be corrected if spelled incorrectly. This common sort of "typo" definitely should be corrected. If there is a later infringement suit, you don't want to have to begin your case by admitting your name was spelled wrong on the registration form. However, the supplemental registration procedure should not be used to change the name of an author where the wrong person was listed. This should be handled by a new copyright registration [see Section D(2) of this chapter].

EXAMPLE: Mary Hales notices that her name was misspelled on the copyright registration certificate she received from the Copyright Office for one of her programs in her LOANIT loan processing package. She checks the copies of the Form TX she sent in and sees that her secretary made the error. Mary should correct this mistake by filing a supplemental registration form. In the unlikely event the error was made by the Copyright Office, Mary can have it corrected without having to file a supplemental registration form. In this situation, a letter will suffice. If Mary marries and takes a new name (Spotteswood, for example), she can either leave her former name on the registration form or change it through the procedure mentioned in Section D(2) below.

3. Change of Address

A supplemental copyright registration can be filed to change a person's address. The principal reason to keep your address current is to allow people who want to use your work to locate you and arrange for permission and compensation. If your work has potential for widespread use, you should definitely keep your address updated. The harder it is to locate you, the more likely it is that your copyright will be infringed. Of course, if you have already licensed all important rights to your work to third parties and have nothing left to sell, you may not want to bother telling the Copyright Office every time you move.

Keeping your address current is not legally required. Should you ever become involved in an infringement suit, the fact that you have moved since your original registration and have not filed a supplemental registration will have no effect.

4. Change in Title of the Work

A supplemental registration form can and should be used if you change the name of a program without changing its content. This can be important, as many program names are important identifying tools. Should you ever wind up in court, you don't want to argue with a copyright infringer about whether the program you claim she stole was PDQ, PRONTO, VITE VITE, or GIDDY-UP.

EXAMPLE 1: Mary Hales sells her LOAN-IT loan processing package both to Big Bank and Small Bank. Small Bank writes to Mary requesting significant revisions in the package that will make LOANIT easier for them to use. Mary decides to make all the revisions requested by Small Bank and market this new version to other small banks under the name LOANIT-SMALL. Big Bank, on the other hand, is very pleased with LOANIT as it is and does not want it changed in any way. As part of

doing the LOANIT-SMALL version, Mary decides to rename her original LOANIT package LOANIT-BIG. This raises a problem, as Mary has already registered this program with the Copyright Office under the name LOANIT. Mary uses a supplemental registration to change the name of LOANIT to LOANIT-BIG. She then registers LOANIT-SMALL as a new work (see Section D, below).

EXAMPLE 2: Kendra Salone, who works for BCA Graphics, makes a number of changes in her QUILTIT program, which is already covered by a copyright registration. BCA Graphics, the copyright owner, decides to call the old version QUILTIT 1.0 and the new version QUILTIT 2.0. BCA Graphics should register QUILTIT 2.0 with a new registration (see Section C). As the original QUILTIT is now being called by the new name QUILTIT 1.0, a supplemental registration form should be filed to reflect this change.

C. When Supplemental Registration Won't Work

There are some types of errors that should not, or cannot, be corrected with a supplemental registration. These include the following:

■ Obvious errors the Copyright Office should have found. This category includes the omission of necessary information, such as your name. It also includes obvious mistakes, such as providing your date of death (presumably prematurely) or an impossible date of publication, such as 1884. Don't worry too much about this. The Copyright Office rarely either makes mistakes in these areas or fails to catch yours. If you do make a gross or silly error such as those we've listed, you can expect either to receive a telephone call from the Copyright Office seeking clarification, or the original registration form will be sent back to you for correction. If these obvious sorts of mistakes do slip by the examiner, however, simply notify the Copyright Office and the mistake will be corrected with no need for a formal supplemental registration or another fee;

■ Changes in copyright ownership by license, inheritance, will or other transfer. There is a separate procedure to accomplish this, which we discuss in detail in Chapter 12;

■ Errors or changes in anything having to do with the content of your work. This category includes such things as errors or changes in the material you deposited. If significant changes are desired, a new copyright registration and deposit will be needed. See Chapters 10 and 11 for information on this process. If you correct a minor bug or make other small code changes, however, there is no necessity to take any corrective action, as your original copyright registration will still provide adequate protection.

■ Errors in copyright notice. These cannot be corrected by supplemental registration. We cover how to correct a defective copyright notice in Chapter 7.

Again we present our three programmers with some examples of situations for which supplemental registration is not appropriate.

EXAMPLE 1: Carl Jones mistakenly fills in the date of death on his copyright registration for GOTTCHA. This is an error the Copyright Office should catch. If the Copyright Office doesn't spot the error, Carl should bring this

error to their attention by letter, keeping a copy in his file. He will receive an acknowledgement from the Copyright Office stating that the correction will be made.

EXAMPLE 2: BCA Graphics omits all the dates on the QUILTIT registration application, leaving them for Kendra Salone to fill in before the form is filed. Kendra, however, is sick that day and the form is mistakenly mailed in by the temporary secretary. These omissions should be caught by the Copyright Office. If they aren't, BCA should simply notify the Copyright Office of the dates by letter.

EXAMPLE 3: Mary Hales and Robert Atkins are joint authors of a work. When they file their joint copyright registration, however, the copy of the work they deposit only has Mary's name on the notice. This is not an error the Copyright Office will catch. Notice errors can be corrected within five years. To do so, Mary and Robert should correct the notice on all copies of their work (see Chapter 7) and make a new registration of their copyright (see Chapters 8 and 11).

EXAMPLE 4: If, in the example above, Mary Hales and Robert Atkins register correctly as joint authors and later sell their work to a third party, they should not file a supplemental registration form. A document recording the transfer can be filed.

SUPPLEMENTAL REGISTRATION PROCEDURE NOTE: If you are interested in filing a supplemental registration, turn to Chapter 11, Section F for instructions.

D. New Registrations for New Versions of Previously Registered Work

We mentioned in the introduction to this chapter that the U.S. Copyright

Office will usually only accept one copyright registration for the same version of a particular work (37 CFR 202). There are two exceptions to this rule:

■ When the same version of a registered unpublished work is later published; and

■ When a substitution of the author's name is desired.

Let's examine these exceptions.

1. Already Registered Unpublished Work

If you have previously registered an unpublished version of your work, the Copyright Act permits you to make a new registration upon publication of the work. The primary purpose for doing this is to establish the publication date as a matter of public record. Registering both unpublished and published versions of the same work has become increasingly common. This is because many programs are widely distributed for market evaluation and testing prior to their actual publication. Although such distribution is commonly done under agreements which purport to preserve the software as a trade secret (discussed in Chapter 15), the copyright laws can also provide unpublished works with supplemental, and in some cases superior, protection.

We saw in Chapter 6 that a copyright notice (absent the publication date) should always be placed on an unpublished work in case an infringement occurs. We have also stressed that valuable additional protections can be obtained if a program is registered prior to infringement and/or before an infringer registers (e.g., presumption of validity, statutory damages and attorney's fees). This principle is as true for unpublished as for published works. In short, it often makes good sense for valuable software to be registered prior to publication and then newly registered when it is published, so that the publication date can be established.

Making a new registration for a previously registered unpublished work is easy. Simply check the box in Section 5 of the copyright registration form (regardless of which form you're using) which states: "This is the first published edition of a work previously registered in unpublished form." See Chapter 11 for specific registration procedures.

2. Changing the Name of the Author

Another acceptable reason for a new registration of an existing version is when your initial registration named the wrong person as author. If this occurs, the true author may make a new registration of the same work.

EXAMPLE: Let's assume QUILTIT was initially registered in Kendra Salone's name, even though Kendra developed QUILT-IT as an employee of BCA Graphics as a work for hire, and they are the actual copyright owners. The mistake is quickly discovered and BCA Graphics newly registers so that their name will be on the copyright registration.

E. New Registration for New Versions

Traditionally, each time a new form, manifestation or version of a particular work was created it was separately registered with the Copyright Office. Thus, when a novel was adopted for stage, screen and sound recording, each adaptation was treated as a new and separate work for copyright notice and registration purposes. The rule of thumb was that a single copyright registration was adequate to protect each new adaptation or version. Usually, there was little problem understanding what constituted a new version. A novel rewritten for the stage clearly qualified, while a novel published in paperback a year after a hard cover appeared did not, and so on.

The single registration per version rule may have been clear in pre-computer days, but no longer. The explosive growth in the number of new software creations and the crushing competitive pressures faced by software publishers who routinely make many changes to existing programs, documentation and packaging, often makes it difficult to tell what is and is not a new version. Rapid changes in hardware capability and the differences among computers have also resulted in software being frequently updated and published in a wide variety of formats. In addition, many programs enter the marketplace before they have been thoroughly tested and debugged. Only if consumer interest is sufficiently strong do successive debugged versions appear. And to further complicate matters, as we saw in Chapter 4, many newly created programs are, in fact, combinations of pre-existing routines. In short, in the software world, it's a vast understatement to say that the line between original works and new versions is often blurred.

How do you cut through this confusion to understand when and how you should register changes in your original work? Or, put another way, when are changes to your software or other computer output qualitatively or quantitatively sufficient to constitute a new version for purposes of a new copyright registration? For example, should you re-register every time you add a few lines of code, update your training manual, or correct a bug? These are good strong questions. Unfortunately, because of the state of the law, our answers are necessarily a little on the weak and wimpy side.

Before we try and provide some answers, there is one point which must be clearly and strongly emphasized. Once you have registered your earlier version, all material contained in that version is protected, regardless of how many new versions are produced. The only question is whether the new material contained in

the new version is worth protecting. Assuming you decide this in the affirmative, the next question is whether the changed version qualifies as a "new version" for purposes of making a new registration.

Guidelines published by the U.S. Copyright Office say that whether something is a "new version" (for registration purposes) depends on the extent of the changes and whether the new version is, in fact, a replacement for the old version. If the changes are minor, or merely correct routine errors, then registration is probably not necessary, and may not be allowed. This is particularly true where the changes are sprinkled here and there and do not make sense standing alone. If, on the other hand, your changes are significant (say you issue a "new release" of your work containing literally hundreds of changes because the old one is out-of-date, or simply not up to speed), then you will want to register the new release as a new version of the original.

REALITY NOTE: In the real world, making a copyright registration can often be one more (albeit minor) administrative pain in the neck. Although a strategy of registering everything possible (including new versions, updates, etc.) gives you maximum legal protection and flexibility, there are clearly many times where changes in an original work of authorship do not need protection. Thus, new material added to an existing work (which is what you would be protecting in your new registration) is often of little or no use without the original material, which is already protected by copyright. Or, even if the new material can stand alone, it may be so obscure as to not create much risk that anyone will infringe it. Accordingly, most people strike some kind of practical balance, registering only when they make large changes which may have independent value, or where the particular program that is changed is so valuable that it merits a maximum defense strategy.

Now let's look at a series of examples where changes in programs or documentation have been made and see whether registration makes sense. In this area particularly, our answers are highly subjective. Change even a few facts in each example and we might well come to a different conclusion. Even with things staying as they are, others might decide to proceed differently. If you have a valuable program and are in any doubt as to your best course of action, see a lawyer (see Chapter 2, Section C).

EXAMPLE 1: Big Bank finds errors in the reports generated by Mary Hales' loan processing program, LOANIT. Mary corrects the errors by changing code in five programs. Only 10 to 20 lines are changed in each program. This is not sufficient change to warrant a copyright registration as a new version. The same result would probably hold if Mary rewrote a few lines of code to reflect changes in the prime rate or the consumer price index.

EXAMPLE 2: Mary Hales reprograms the loan interest algorithms of LOANIT. This amounts to changing about 50% of one of the 70 programs that make up the LOANIT package. However, it entirely changes the way that program works. The changes probably don't qualify the LOANIT package as a whole as a new version. Therefore, if LOANIT was originally registered as one package, it would not be appropriate to register the whole package as a new version. But, if the programs comprising LOANIT were registered separately, then the changed program would constitute a new version of the affected program and could be re-registered. Even if LOANIT was registered as one package, Mary might want to register the changed program if she thought it was a sufficiently valuable to warrant it.

EXAMPLE 3: Mary Hales sells her LOAN-IT package both to Big Bank and Small Bank. Small Bank writes to Mary requesting significant revisions in the package that will make LOANIT easier for them to use. Mary decides to make all the revisions requested by Small Bank and market this new version to small banks under the name LOANIT-SMALL. The changes are prob-

ably major enough for LOANIT-SMALL to be considered a new version of LOANIT. Following the rule of thumb we discussed above, it is usually wise to register a new version of a work to protect the new material it contains, unless that material is of little or no value to potential pirates. In this situation, both versions will continue to be marketed. Therefore, they are two separate works and should both have registration status for the fullest possible protection.

EXAMPLE 4: Kendra Salone, who, as you know, works for BCA Graphics, makes a number of fairly substantial changes in her QUILTIT program, which BCA had already registered in its original version. BCA Graphics, the copyright owner, decides to call the old version QUILTIT 1.0 and the new version QUILTIT 2.0. BCA should register QUILTIT 2.0. As the original QUILTIT is now being called QUILTIT 1.0, a new name, a supplemental registration form should be filed to reflect this change.

HERE- I'M CALLING THE OLD VERSION QUILTIT 1.0 AND THE NEW VERSION QUILTIT 2.0 SO BAC SHOULD REGISTER QUILTIT 2.0 AS THE ORIGINAL QUILTIT IS NOT BEING CALLED QUILTIT 1.0, A NEW GAME.. A SUPPLEMENTAL REGISTRATION FORM SHOULD BE FILED TO REFLECT THIS CHANGE..O.K.?

EXAMPLE 5: Mary Hales adds 10 lines of code and two additional pages to both the training manual and the users' manuals for LOANIT, which she has already registered. These changes are too minor to bother about. They do not constitute a new version of her work as far as copyright law is concerned. If, on the other hand, Mary changes 1,000 lines of code and significantly revises her training manual, she should newly register LOANIT.

EXAMPLE 6: Mary Hales decides that LOANIT-BIG would sell better if it had a multi-bank capability so that the loans of several banks can be processed at once. To do this, Mary writes two additional programs and changes an existing one. She must now decide what to register. She has several choices. The two new programs could be registered separately, using two TX forms. Or, Mary could register the whole new multi-bank program under a new name (perhaps LOANIT-BIGGER). Finally, Mary may decide that the new programs are too minor to worry about and not make a new registration at all, since the original program is already protected.

F. Registering Changes in Existing Works as New Works

What happens when changes to a pre-existing work are themselves able to stand alone as potentially valuable original works of authorship? Should you register them as such, or should you register a new version of the entire program package? The answer depends, at least in part, on what you did in the first place. If you always took a package approach--that is, registered all related program manuals and other documentation published simultaneously on the same TX form, you would probably want to re-register the entire package with the new material and treat it as a new version. However, if you registered all the programs in a package separately and now have added several new programs, it makes sense to follow the same procedure and register each new program on a separate TX form.

EXAMPLE 1: Mary Hales originally registers her LOANIT loan processing programs separately, each on its own TX form. This means that for copyright registration purposes, each is a separate work. Now, assume Mary adds several new programs. She hasn't changed any of the existing programs, since nothing in them was changed or transformed, but has created an original work of authorship. She can either register the new programs as new works or simply protect them with a copyright notice if she concludes that the new programs are not likely to become the subject of intellectual property theft.

EXAMPLE 2: Now assume Mary Hales originally registers LOANIT as a single work, using the TX form for the entire package. How should she register the new programs? In this situation, Mary has several possible choices. She can:

■ Attempt to register the new program as a separate work;

■ Decide to not register because the new material isn't worth anything to a pirate without the rest of LOANIT, which is already protected; or

■ Re-register all of LOANIT as an updated new version.

EXAMPLE 3: Now assume Big Bank creates the new programs. As Mary Hales owns the original LOANIT copyright, the bank obviously cannot copyright a new version of LOANIT without Mary's permission. (They can, however, use it for their own internal use, unless they have signed a contract giving up this right).

If the programs written by Big Bank stand on their own as separate works, Big Bank can file copyright registration forms with the Copyright Office to cover this material.

EXAMPLE 4: Kendra Salone writes a routine that changes QUILTIT, which is owned by BCA Graphics, from a quilt design program to a program to design stained glass windows. Although this involves a number of modifications, the basic QUILTIT program is still more or less intact. Kendra has probably created a derivative work of QUILTIT, which means she doesn't own the stained glass design program unless she has obtained BCA's permission. However, if the new program involves entirely new routines, Kendra could copyright these independently. She could probably then write new code for the entire stained glass design program and register it as her own without infringing BCA's copyright in QUILTIT. If this seems a little hard to follow, it may help to remember your copyright basics—a copyright only protects the expression of an idea, not the idea itself. Thus, an author could probably write three different "How-to" books on the same subject that would be sufficiently different as to not infringe each other's copyright.*

G. Registering New Works with Pre-Existing Material

Many programs and other works contain enough new material to be an original work of authorship even though they incorporate pre-existing material belonging to the author or to someone else. You register this work as you would any other new work, using the forms appropriate to the work and following all the other registration procedures outlined in this book (Chapters 8 - 11). The only difference is that you must identify the work that is pre-existing. Chapter 11 will show you exactly what information needs to be given. Some examples:

EXAMPLE 1: Mary Hales creates a program for processing credit card payments by taking several LOANIT routines and writing a considerable new code relating to credit cards and putting them together to form a credit card payment program. This is a new work (rather than a new version of a pre-existing work) but incorporates material that existed previously. It should be registered separately.

EXAMPLE 2: Mary Hales needs to generate a series of menus on a terminal used for setting up new loan customers. Although Mary writes a new program for use with LOANIT, she decides to borrow the text from certain menus and screens which she created in an earlier program while she worked at Middle Bank. Mary may register her creation as a new work, specifying the menus as pre-existing material. Remember, however, that since Middle Bank owns the copyright (the program was written as a work for hire), Mary will have to obtain Middle Bank's permission to use the menus and screens if she wishes to avoid infringing Middle Bank's copyright.

EXAMPLE 3: Carl Jones wrote a computer game a number of years ago, when he first got a home computer. He registered the code even though he never actually got the program to work. However, he used one of the routines later to set up the characters in his GOTTCHA game. GOTTCHA should be registered as a new work with pre-existing material.

H. Registering Derivative Works

We spent some amount of time in Chapter 4 distinguishing derivative works

---

* This is why it is fairly common for both book publishing and software publishing contracts to contain a clause prohibiting an author from publishing a work on exactly the same subject.

from "original works using pre-existing material." Derivative works should be treated exactly like original works with pre-existing material for registration purposes. Thus, if you own the pre-existing material and your alterations do not have independent value, there is no pressing reason to register. If, however, the derivative work involves a significant new and creative effort, as is often the case, then registration is recommended. If somebody else owns the original work on which your derivative work was based, remember to obtain their permission. Otherwise your registration won't mean a whole lot.

distinguish fact situations which you are likely to encounter, the main point is that you want to obtain protection for your original works of authorship in whatever form it happens to be. The more you think you're onto something hot, the more focused your attention should be on separately registering your work. The less likely your changes are to make millionaires of pirates, the less important such separate protection becomes. In other words, hold on to your common sense when dealing with the principles discussed in this and related chapters.

I. Summary

Let's summarize the material we have just covered.

■ Supplemental registration is used to correct, change or amplify certain information in the initial registration. It is not appropriate to register any substantive changes in the work itself. See Chapter 11, Section F for supplemental registration procedures.

■ A new registration for the same work can be used for a published version of a previously registered unpublished version and for substituting one author's name with another;

■ A new registration is also used to register a new version (updates, major corrections, etc.) of an earlier work, a new work incorporating pre-existing material, and derivative works;

■ It usually does not make sense to register when changes are minor in nature or lack substantial value.

The following is a chart which will help you sort out the various categories of hybrid works and decide when registration is appropriate. Although we have used a number of descriptive phrases to

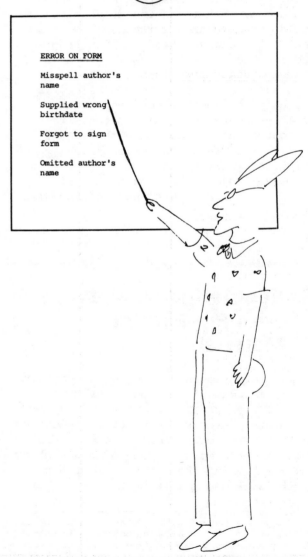

ERROR ON FORM

Misspell author's name

Supplied wrong birthdate

Forgot to sign form

Omitted author's name

CATEGORY	SUPPLEMENTAL REGISTRATION	REGISTER NEW MATERIAL ONLY	NEW REGISTRATION OF ENTIRE WORK	LETTER TO C.O.	OTHER
ERROR ON FORM					
Misspell author's name	X				
Supplied wrong birthdate	X				
Forgot to sign form				Call	
Omitted author's name				X	
Error in copyright notice					See Ch. 7
Author incorrectly listed			X by correct author		
CHANGES SINCE FILING					
Title of work changes	X				
Ownership of copyright changes					See Ch. 12
Owner's address changes	X				
Published version of work registered as unpublished			X		
Minor errors corrected in work itself					do nothing
Major error correction 20% of code changes (either answer is correct, not both)		X	X		
Add a new routine (it depends, see Section F)		X	X		
Create a new version with minor error correction and new code (choose one)		X	X		
HYBRID WORKS					
Use old routines as a part of your work			X See Ch. 11		

CHAPTER 10

Deposit Requirements

A. Introduction

This chapter continues our discussion on registration. In Chapter 8 we covered the ins and outs of choosing the correct registration form. Chapter 9 dealt with when supplementary and new registrations are necessary or desirable. Here we discuss what you should deposit with your copyright registration form in order that your work will receive maximum possible copyright protection.

To register your work with the U.S. Copyright Office, you are required to submit either one or two copies of the work itself. When it comes to the registration of long programs, Copyright Office rules usually allow you to send a portion of the work instead of the whole thing. Deposit requirements are designed to serve two primary functions:

■ To show the Copyright Office that your work is capable of copyright protection (i.e., an original work of authorship); and

■ To serve as an identifier for your work in the event a dispute arises involving your copyright.

Those readers who have worked with deposit requirements for printed materials will probably wonder why we devote an entire chapter to deposit rules. You just send in two copies of the published work with your registration and forget about it. Right? Unfortunately, when it comes to software and computer output, it's not that easy. Here are a few of the areas where questions are commonly asked:

■ Should I deposit the ROM chip which contains my new computer operating system?

■ Do I deposit my entire Encyclopedia Galactica database, which amounts to 4,000 pages when printed out?

■ Can I protect source code as a trade secret and still satisfy the deposit requirements?

It would be easy to list another dozen tough questions, but these should be sufficient to convince you that selecting the appropriate materials for a deposit in connection with your computer-related registration is often problematic.

B. Overview of Deposit Requirements

There are two basic rules for submission of all work for deposit, computer-related or not:

* Each copy of work submitted for deposit must contain a correct notice of copyright (see Chapter 6); and

* Each copy of work submitted for deposit must be the "best version of your work."

However, as noted above, other deposit rules are different when it comes to software. For many software registrations, only a portion of the work, sufficient to identify the work as a whole, need be deposited. Not surprisingly, the Copyright Office refers to this as "identifying material" (see Section D, below). Why will the Copyright Office accept only a portion of your work? Because the goal of the Copyright Office is to determine that you are registering copyrightable material. In this sense, their mandate is very different from that of the Patent Office, which automatically makes a preliminary finding as to whether someone else has already patented the same work.*

---

* Copyright registration (and the accompanying deposit) does not mean the government is certifying you as the true copyright owner, or that your work is original. Your timely registration does mean that your statements in the registration form are presumed correct and that you will be treated as the presumed owner until a contrary showing is made in court (see Chapter 13 for more on this presumption).

Although the Copyright Office may be happy with just a small portion of your software or output, you may not be. This is because the better your deposit identifies your work, the better off you will be in any subsequent copyright litigation. Accordingly, in this chapter, we will not only look at deposit rules for different types of computer-related material, we will discuss a number of specific strategies you may want to adopt to make the best possible deposit, depending on your work and circumstances. First, however, some preliminary words about the very important copyright doctrines known as "rule of doubt" and "special relief."

C. Rule of Doubt and Special Relief

1. Rule of Doubt

The "rule of doubt" is a Copyright Office concept you are are likely to encounter if you register much software, especially object code. Basically, the Copyright Office uses the rule of doubt when it accepts a deposit which it is unable to independently verify as a work of independent authorship. All object code deposits are accepted under the rule of doubt because the Copyright Office can't decipher the ones and zeros.

Exactly what the rule of doubt means from a practical standpoint is uncertain. One thing is clear, however, your work is registered, whether or not the rule is invoked. Some experts believe registration under the rule of doubt may have a bearing on what you have to prove in court should you ever be involved in a copyright infringement case (see Chapter 13). However, as of this writing, there are simply no court interpretations of the rule of doubt. In other words, no one to our knowledge has suffered any negative results from registering object code under the rule of doubt, if you discount all the warnings and throat clearing by their copyright lawyers.

2. Special Relief

Because software is such a new field, many of the traditional Copyright Office rules and procedures are just plain inadequate to deal with it. Fortunately, the Copyright Office recognizes this and has built some flexibility into its procedures. The doctrine they use to do this is called "special relief." Any time you want to make a deposit which is different from the deposit rules established by the Copyright Office, which we discuss in detail below, you must explain what you are depositing and why you can't, or don't wish to, satisfy the regular deposit requirements. The Copyright Office will interpret this letter as a request for special relief, if any is needed. In fact, as we'll see in Chapter 11, it is always a good idea to send along a letter explaining anything unusual about your registration and/or deposit. Only when your registration and deposit are completely straightforward (e.g., you send in one TX form for one program and one users' manual) is it wise to skip such a letter.

There are some types of special relief which are routinely requested for computer-related deposits and which are granted almost as a matter of course. These will be described in detail as they become relevant to our discussion, and we will provide you with the necessary sample letters. The important thing to understand here is that requesting special relief has nothing to do with the rule of doubt. They are independent concepts. In most cases, if the Copyright Office grants special relief, your deposit is good as gold. If, however, you deposit object code or some other product the Copyright Office cannot independently decipher, the registration will proceed, but under the rule of doubt, which, as we said above, may or may not have any negative consequences.

D. Deposit Requirements for Software

1. Generally

The U.S. Copyright Office has provided special requirements for deposits accompanying the registration of computer software. These attempt to cover all types of software in all their many manifestations, including source code (programs in the form written by programmers) and object code (code generated by source codes for direct communication with the computer), and all types of media, including ROM's (Read Only Memories), PROM's (Programmable Read Only Memories), and EPROM'S (Eraseable Programmable Read Only Memories). We will discuss these rules here, but first we have a favor to ask. Please read this entire section through at least once before you even begin to think about making a decision. This material is both overlapping and potentially confusing, and you may well find yourself changing your conclusion as to what you wish to deposit several times.

COMPUTER UNDERSTANDING NOTE: At this point, it is important that you have a basic understanding of how computers work and the various forms of expression associated with computer software and output. We provide you with the basics in Chapter 1. If you are a little hazy on some of these distinctions, such as the difference between object code and source code, return to that chapter for a short review.

2. Program Code Deposit Rules Generally

Under the U.S. Copyright Office regulations [37 CFR 202.70], you do not generally deposit your entire program code (whether source code, object code or both). This is fortunate, both from your standpoint and the Copyright Office's, since programs are often lengthy.

To satisfy the deposit requirement for program code, you must deposit either:

■ The entire program; or

■ If the program is longer than 50 pages, the first and last 25 pages of the program code.

Whether you deposit object code or source code (see Sections 4 & 5 below for which is better), you should deposit a total of 50 pages. In other words, if you deposit object code, you should deposit 50 pages of object code, and not the equivalent of 50 pages of source code translated into object code form. (If you deposit a mixture of source and object code, you will need to ask for special relief.) In other words, no matter how long your program, the maximum amount you have to deposit is 50 pages. A page is not precisely defined, but in practice, computer "sysout" paper of 11" x 14" is the standard used. As an alternative, you may deposit a microfiche of the identifying material. If you do this, deposit the entire program or, if it is longer than 50 pages, microfiche the first and last 25 pages of each program.

EXAMPLE: Mary Hales files 70 TX registration forms for her 70 LOANIT loan package programs. She uses a separate envelope for each registration and deposits the first and last 25 pages of each program along with each registration form. All together, Mary deposits 3,500 pages of code, assuming each program contains at least 50 pages of code. Obviously, if some programs are shorter, her entire deposit would be less than that. Mary would have no reason to send a letter requesting special relief in this situation since, from the Copyright Office's standpoint, each registration is for a single program and each deposit is in the requisite form. However, if Mary did write explaining her deposit and requesting special relief, no harm would be done. The request would just be ignored as irrelevant.

In Chapter 8, when we discussed how to select the proper copyright registration

form, we said that Mary Hales could also register her 70 LOANIT programs on one TX form because, as an integrated set of programs published at the same time, they constitute a single "package." In other words, Mary could register LOANIT as if it were a book and the individual programs were chapters. Again, this can only be done if Mary authored all the programs and the individual programs are units of a larger work and published at the same time as such. If Mary chooses to register LOANIT in this fashion, she should deposit the first 25 pages of program #1 and the last 25 pages of program #70, for a total deposit of 50 pages. Her registration form and deposit should be accompanied by a letter of explanation, which will be treated by the Copyright Office as a request for special relief (see Section C, above). Why? The registration of 70 related programs, either together or separately, is sufficiently unusual to warrant it.

COMMON SENSE NOTE: Requests for special relief are routine and are not something to be avoided. Remember, we're only talking about a brief transmittal letter explaining your deposit. We encourage you to request special relief as a matter of course, unless you're sure you don't need it.

Here is a sample request for special relief which should accompany the registration form and deposit for the entire LOANIT package.

February 3, 198_

Dear Chief Examiner:

Enclosed herein as part of my registration are the first 25 pages of my
source [or object] code for program #1
and the last 25 pages of source [or ob-
ject] code for program #70. All 70 programs are part of one large bank loan
processing package entitled LOANIT. The
enclosed deposit also includes two training manuals and two user manuals, which
were published along with and as part of
the overall package. I authored all the
manuals as well as the programs.

I wish to register the entire package
on one form rather than make separate
registrations. Please grant special relief and accept this deposit.

Sincerely,

Mary Hales

3. Copying Deposits from Copyright Office Files

Before we get into deposit details,
let's spend a moment understanding how
the Copyright Office works. First, as
you probably know, it is located in Washington D.C., so anyone who wants to look
at any records must go there. Second,
direct copying from Copyright Office
files is prohibited by law. More important, it is difficult to do.

It is important to realize that the
Copyright Office stores great masses of
information. Indeed, it normally takes
from one to five days to even get access
to a particular deposit. To look at any
particular deposit, a potential copier
normally needs the registration number or
the exact name of the work and author.
In addition, she will be asked why she
wants to see the particular work. As
part of this process, she must put her
reason in writing and sign it. This
written statement is placed in a file
associated with the copyright deposit in
question and is available to the owner
for examination.

If you suspect that your deposit has
been copied, you may well want to have
the Copyright Office conduct a search of
your file for evidence of such an examination. This can be done by mail. The
Copyright Office charges $10 an hour to
conduct searches. However, unless you
are in Washington D.C., you have very
little choice in the matter. Call the
Copyright Office at (202) 287-8700, tell
them what you want done (in this situation, to search your file to see whether
it has been examined by anyone else) and
ask them what the charge will be. Then,
send this amount and your request to have
your file examined to:

Reference and Bibliography
    Section, LM-450
Copyright Office
Library of Congress
Washington D.C. 20559

When your deposit is retrieved, a
person from the Copyright Office is assigned to the requestor. This employee
is supposed to stay with your deposit at
all times to prevent the requester from
taking notes or copying your deposit in
any way. This means that, as a practical
matter, it's unlikely that your code will
be directly copied from Copyright Office
files. However, it doesn't stop an intelligent pirate from getting a pretty
good overview of your approach.

4. Source Code Deposits: Advantages and Problems

Many people, including the Copyright
Office, recommend that you deposit source
code with your copyright registration.
(If you have any questions about source
code, see Chapter 1). This is because
source code better identifies the nature
of your "original" work of authorship
than does object code.* This can be of

---

* Source code not only is readily understandable by
anyone conversant with the particular programming language, but also is customarily documented with program
comments describing what specific code is intended to
do. The object code form of the program does not contain these comments because they are not reproduced
when the source code is compiled, and thus is not as
good an identifier.

importance should you end up in litigation over your copyright and want the best possible proof of the exact code you have copyrighted. For example, this need commonly occurs in the video game area, where as soon as a game becomes popular, all sorts of "look alike" games are marketed. If you, as the original game author, take infringers to court charging copyright infringement, a source code deposit will make your proof requirement easier to meet.

In addition, source code can be read more easily by the humans staffing the Copyright Office. It is for this reason that the Copyright Office considers source code as the best version of a work, and thus the version which they prefer you deposit.

Despite these excellent reasons why it's a good idea to deposit source code, there are also several important reasons why you may prefer to deposit object code (the ones and zeros which the computer reads). Principal among these are:

■ Your deposit is a matter of public record, and if you deposit source code, it could conceivably be studied by a competitor or pirate, and reproduced in an infringing program; and

■ If you plan to maintain the trade secret status of your source code, there is a danger that you will compromise this status by using the same source code as a registration deposit. You don't have to worry about this problem if you plan to publish your work, because publication of a program in either source code or object code form usually results in the program losing any trade secret status it may have had. However, if you plan to distribute your program on a limited basis and require all users to keep it confidential, you may wish to retain your code as a trade secret, and therefore will want to avoid depositing large chunks of your source code where the public can get access to them. This may lead you to deposit object code or to deposit small pieces of source code and ask for special relief. As we will discuss, this is a

way to minimize any disclosure problems that might develop from depositing source code.

5. Object Code Deposits: Advantages and Problems

As we stated above, you can use object code instead of source code as your registration deposit. Because object code is unreadable by most mortals, a deposit in this form will not likely be examined for ideas and code by a competitor. Also, if you are treating your work as a trade secret, an object code deposit doesn't reveal it. As mentioned above, however, a major problem with depositing object code is that if you ever end up in court, it's a little trickier to demonstrate to the court what you deposited.

All object code deposits necessitate an accompanying request for special relief. If you fail to send a letter of explanation and special relief request with your deposit, the Copyright Office will write you and state that since they cannot read your deposit, and cannot verify that its subject material is copyrightable, you must either send human readable source code or a letter assuring the Copyright Office that your deposit contains copyrightable material (see letter below). Obviously, it makes sense to anticipate this request.

The following letter will get you the special relief you need if you deposit object code.

April 29, 198_

Dear Copyright Examiners:

The enclosed deposit is the object
code form of a computer program of which
I am the author. It is an original work
of authorship. I wish to deposit my object code because my source code contains
valuable trade secrets. Please grant me
special relief.

Proggie Programmer
Author

If you have sent an
object code deposit with-
out a special relief re-
quest, you have received
a letter like the follow-
ing in response:

COPYRIGHT
OFFICE

LIBRARY
OF
CONGRESS

Washington
D.C.
20559

March 14, 1983

Attn: Mr.
  Re: SAFE DEPOSIT BILLING SYSTEM

Dear Mr.

        We are delaying registration of the claim to copyright in
this work because the deposit consists of a printout of the computer
program in object code format.

        Generally, the Copyright Office tries to obtain the best
representation of the authorship that is being registered. Because
printouts in object code format are basically unintelligible to copyright examiners, it is not, therefore, possible for us to examine the
deposit to determine whether there is copyrightable authorship present. Deposit copies of works registered for copyright are available
for inspection by members of the public, but they may not be "copied."

        The Office believes that the best representation of the
authorship in a computer program is a printout of the program in
source code format. Where, however, the applicant is unable or un-
willing to deposit a printout in source code format, we will proceed
with registration under our "rule of doubt," upon receipt of written
assurance from the applicant that the work as deposited in object code
format contains copyrightable authorship.

        Please therefore, forward either a copy of the computer
program consisting of the first and last twenty-five (25) pages in
source code or the letter mentioned above.

        Please do not submit any additional fee at this time.

        In your reply, please return the enclosed carbon referring
to our CONTROL NUMBER 3-070-0253 (A).

                                Sincerely yours,

                                Head, Literary Section
                                Examining Division

                                By:

Enclosures:
  Cir. R7c
  cc: this letter   Copyright Examiner

Your reply should look something like the following:

```
October 10, 198_

Dear Copyright Examiners:

    The deposit accompanying the registra-
tion of PROGRAM #1234555-678 consists of
computer object code.  It is an original
work of authorship of which I am the
author.  I wish to deposit my program in
object code to preserve valuable trade
secrets contained in the source code.
Accordingly, please grant me special
relief.

Sincerely,

Proggie Programmer
Author
```

Once this letter is received, the Copyright Office will register your object code, but will send you a letter cautioning that the registration is being done under the rule of doubt. As we discussed in Section C of this chapter, this means the Copyright Office is unable to independently verify that your deposit is a work of original authorship. The rule of doubt is the Copyright Office's way of warning people that object code deposits might possibly be held deficient later in time. However, our best guess is that if you end up in a copyright infringement suit with an object code deposit, you should benefit from all the legal presumptions and benefits resulting from registration which are discussed in Chapters 3, 8 and 13. Even if this should change, you should have little difficulty establishing your copyright by translating your object code into human readable source code as part of the court procedure.

NOTE: In Subsection 6, just below, we discuss a way you can apply for special relief and deposit what amounts to a teaspoon of source code along with a cup of object code and avoid the rule of doubt entirely.

If you are still confused as to whether to deposit object code, you are not alone. Computer lawyers argue about it daily. The best generalization we can give you is this: if you desire the best possible identifying material for your program, register source code. However, if your desire to maintain your source code as a trade secret outweighs the relatively small risk associated with object code deposits, go with the object code. If you want to ride both horses, follow the deposit procedures discussed directly below.

6. Special Relief for Software Program Deposits

We have already mentioned that you can apply for special relief and make an object deposit under the rule of doubt. Now, let's look at how a special relief request can be used to deposit small amounts of source code in situations where you want to keep as much of your code confidential as possible. Requests for special relief for source code deposits will usually be granted for the following types of program deposits:

■ To allow up to 50% of the standard first and last 25 pages deposit for source code program to be "blacked out." In other words, you deposit 50 pages with only 25 being readable. This obviously helps you to protect source code against infringement, or loss of trade secret status if you decide to deposit it instead of object code;

■ To allow the standard first and last 25 pages of object code (usually the whole program) to be deposited along with any ten consecutive pages of source code. If you ask for this type of special relief, your program is registered without being put under the rule of doubt. In addition, should there be an infringement action, you have at least some source code on file;

■ To allow you to deposit the first and last 10 pages of a source code deposit with nothing "blacked out." This smaller deposit may, depending on the length of the program, or program package, pretty well frustrate pirates and may even allow you to maintain the status of your program as a trade secret. This, of course, has a great deal to do with the length of your program or program package. If, like Mary Hales, you register 70 programs together, 20 pages of source code shouldn't give much, if anything, away.

How to Request Special Relief:

```
July 23, 198_

Dear Chief Examiner:

    Enclosed is my deposit for my regis-
tration for [PROGRAM NAME].  It consists
of [DESCRIBE YOUR DEPOSIT].  I am making
my deposit in this form because I wish to
keep as much of my source code confiden-
tial as possible.  Please grant special
relief and accept this deposit.

Sincerely,

Proggie Programmer
```

E. Deposit Requirements for Documentation

Documentation includes user manuals, training manuals, instruction sheets, textual flowcharts, film, slide shows and all other works which are used to support a program in some way.

Whether you register your documentation separately or include it under your program registration (see Chapter 8), you must deposit two copies of your entire work if it is in written, sound recording or graphic form.* You need only deposit one copy of training or other films.

---
* If your work is unpublished, you need only deposit one copy.

Written documentation can be anything from a two pages stapled together to a bound 500-page book with full color cover. Again, be sure the copies you deposit contain your proper copyright notice.

EXAMPLE 1: Mary Hales publishes her LOANIT package with training manuals and user manuals. She decides to copyright them as part of the package, as they were all published at the same time. Mary should deposit two copies of each manual with her program registration package. She must also explain what she is doing to the Copyright Office, because she is including a number of programs and manuals in one package (see Section C, above).

EXAMPLE : Mary Hales drafts a flow-chart of her LOANIT program, which she publishes separately. The flowchart is primarily textual rather than symbolic in nature [i.e., Type 2 as discussed in Chapter 8(F)(1)(d)] and should thus be registered with a TX form. Mary should submit a separate TX form and provide two copies of the chart. A letter requesting special relief should accompany the submittals. This letter should also explain that the flowchart is more textual in expression than graphic.

SPECIAL RELIEF REMINDER: Once again we wish to emphasize that even though you may not need special relief, it never hurts to enclose a letter explaining your deposit. If the Copyright Office feels you do need special relief, they can probably grant it on the basis of your letter. Remember, a deposit accepted upon a granting of special relief is just as valid as one where no special relief is involved. Special relief should not be confused with the rule of doubt, which the Copyright Office uses when it accepts pure object code instead of source code as a deposit (see Section C, above).

F. Deposit Requirements for Databases and Other Compilations

A database is a collection of pre-existing information arranged in a particular way. Here we are only concerned with databases which are kept or organized by a computer. Computer databases qualify as an original work of authorship for copyright purposes when the method and logic used to organize them is original. The particular compilation need not be sophisticated to be copyrightable. An alphabetical list of all professional downhill skiers under the age of 35 would qualify, as would a list of women of Polish ancestry who live in Boston and oppose nuclear war.

As we mentioned in Chapter 8, to register a database, you must use copyright Form TX. Because databases qualify as a species of software, the general rule is that you should deposit the first and last 25 pages of the database. However, the rules for databases do vary in one important way. When a database is composed of separate and distinct data files, the deposit rule is different. In a multifile structure, the correct deposit should consist of representative portions of each separate data file. A representative portion of a data file consists of one copy of 50 complete data records from each file, or the entire file, whichever is less.

COPYRIGHT NOTICE NOTE: All database deposits should contain a proper copyright notice. See Chapter 6.

Let's review once more:

■ To register a single file database, you only need deposit the first and last 25 pages of the database (i.e., printouts of the data as its stored in the database files);

■ If the database you wish to register has two or more files, deposit each in its entirety, or 50 records from each file, whichever is less. Let's look at some examples:

EXAMPLE 1: As part of her job, Kendra Salone stores all facts she has collected over the years on types of American quilts on a disk file. Printed out, it is 30 pages long. She should deposit all 30 pages if BCA Graphics wishes to register this database. Since the whole file is less than 50 pages, Kendra should include a written explanation to the point that she is only depositing 30 pages because that is the entire work.

EXAMPLE 2: Kendra Salone expands her database to include all quilts of the Western Hemisphere. Now when she prints it out, it is 70 pages in length. She need deposit only the first and last 25 pages, retaining the middle 20 pages. The material she deposits should contain BCA Graphics' correct copyright notice. Even though this is a one-file database of the correct length, and Kendra doesn't believe she need apply for special relief, she would be wise to include a written explanation of what she is doing.

EXAMPLE 3: Kendra Salone continues to expand her database. She now has facts on quilts of the world. A separate file is maintained for the quilts of each country. In printed form, there are five quilt records per page. Remember, since this is a multifile database, Kendra must deposit 50 records from each file. This means she should send in 10 pages per file (10 x 5 = 50). For 20 files, that's 200 pages, for 50 files, 500 pages, and so on. She should be sure her deposit contains her copyright notice. Once again, Kendra should send a letter explaining what she is doing.

REAL WORLD NOTE: Databases tend to remain in one (or a few) computers more often than do application programs, which are often distributed worldwide. For this reason, trade secret law may sometimes be an easier and better way to maintain exclusive rights over your database than would be true with copyright law. Since your deposit will clearly expose the unique way in which you organized your facts to anyone who examines your file, the case for non-registration (and thus non-deposit) may be stronger than with other types of software.

G. Deposit Requirements for Motion Pictures

A motion picture is a fixed sequence of images on film that depicts motion when run on a projector. Training films, films that promote software products, feature films about the wonders of the computer, and video disks which involve the user touching the screen to select images from the disk all qualify as motion pictures. Only one copy of a motion picture, containing a proper copyright notice, is required for a deposit, whether registered separately or as part of a software package. Computer games do not qualify as motion pictures for purposes of the deposit rules. See the following section.

EXAMPLE : Mary Hales deposits one copy of her LOANIT training film, complete with a correct copyright notice, when she registers the film using Form PA. Remember, Mary has the option of registering the film on a TX form as a part of her LOANIT package if she publishes it at the same time. If she does this, she should also deposit one copy.

EXAMPLE 2: Carl Jones makes a video disk version of his GOTTCHA game, which is played by touching the viewing screens and selecting images off the video disk. This is no longer a machine-readable work (i.e., in a form where the machine takes its instructions directly from object code), but rather a sequential series of images selectable by the viewer. As such, it is considered to be a motion picture. Carl should deposit one copy of his video disk, containing his correct copyright notice, along with his PA copyright registration form.

H. Deposit Requirements for Computer Game Screens

The reason a computer game does not qualify as a motion picture is that the computer game is fixed only as a machine-readable program and does not consist of tangible sequential images, as is true with film. Although the output of a computer game program is registered on the same form as motion pictures or other audiovisual works, two copies of the game's screens are required as a deposit.* Although the distinction between computer games and other audiovisual works may seem somewhat arbitrary to you, it is nevertheless real to the Copyright Office.

The Copyright Office has not yet established specific rules for the deposit of computer output screens. However, many developers are registering their screens using Form PA, and these deposits are being accepted. To register your screens, you must, of course, deposit "identifying material." The identifying material requirement isn't difficult to meet. You may deposit two copies of any material, such as a video tape or disk or photograph, which reasonably identifies your work. The more complete your identifying material, the more substantial

---

* If your work is unpublished, you need only deposit one copy.

your protection. In the case of arcade games, you should deposit your "attract" and "play" modes together as part of a single registration in videotape form.

You should include any sound component, either as part of the video tape recording or separately on a cassette. Don't neglect this. The uniqueness of the sound that accompanies game programs has been helpful in establishing ownership of these types of works in several court decisions.

As part of this type of registration, you must also explain your deposit and request special relief.

June 11, 198_

Dear Chief Examiner:

Please find enclosed my deposit consisting of identifying material related to my computer video game [NAME OF GAME]. They consist of [VIDEO TAPE, PHOTOGRAPHS, etc.]. These represent the output screens and accompanying sound from the above-mentioned game. I request you grant special relief and accept this material as a deposit accompanying my PA copyright registration form.

Sincerely

Proggy Programmer

EXAMPLE: Carl Jones makes a video tape of his game screens from GOTTCHA. Several screens from the attract mode of GOTTCHA, which are different than the play mode, are photographed separately. In addition to his PA form, Carl deposits two copies of the video tape, the photographs, and the cassette containing the sound, along with his letter requesting special relief, to the U.S. Copyright Office. All contain a proper copyright notice.

I. Deposit Requirements for Pictorial, Graphic or Sculptural Works

As we saw in Chapter 8, pictorial, graphic or sculptural computer output, such as computer art, slides and symbolic flow charts, fit in this category. For these types of still works, the appropriate deposit is two copies of the work, or photographs or other two-dimensional representations of the work, along with Copyright Form VA. The deposit must depict the actual colors of the work and, of course, must contain the correct copyright notice (see Chapter 6).

EXAMPLE 1: BCA Graphics deposits two copies of Kendra Salone's color photographs of her quilt designs which are on display in the lobby.

EXAMPLE 2: Carl Jones deposits two copies of his design for the blueprints for his program CHIPRACER.

EXAMPLE 3: Mary Hales decides to register certain graphic flowcharts (i.e., communicating primarily through symbols) separately from her LOANIT package. She deposits two copies of the flowchart along with the VA form. She should also include a letter explaining that this flowchart primarily expresses ideas by graphic representation rather than textual material.

J. Deposit Requirements for Sound Recordings and All Other Works

Two copies of sound recordings containing a proper copyright notice must be deposited regardless of whether the recording accompanies an audiovisual work or is registered separately. The deposit should be made in the form of an audiotape, even if the recording was originally released as a phonorecord.

EXAMPLE 1: Carl Jones deposits two copies of his computer-generated musical composition OFFKEY on cassette along with his copyright registration on Form SR.

EXAMPLE 2: Carl Jones deposits two copies of the hit album from the GOTTCHA COMIN' AND GOIN' cartoon film on his SR copyright registration form. This is different than the soundtrack, which was included in the deposit of GOTTCHA COMIN' AND GOIN', along with the PA form.

EXAMPLE 3: Mary Hales makes a slide presentation designed to help market her LOANIT package. She deposits two properly noticed copies of the audio tape, along with identifying material for the slides, her PA form and her transmittal letter/request for special relief.

K. Library of Congress Deposit Requirement

Even if you decide not to register your work, you may still be required to deposit a copy of a published work with the Library of Congress. When you register with the U.S. Copyright Office, your Library of Congress obligations are fulfilled at the same time. It's only if you don't register that you might run afoul of this extra deposit rule. However, this extra deposit requirement is seldom, if ever, enforced.

The important thing to understand is that you need do nothing unless the Register sends you a letter requiring you to deposit your published work for the Library of Congress archives. If you get such a letter, it will tell you how to comply with the deposit requirements and will include a telephone number to which you may direct inquiries.

Your failure to comply with this requirement will in no way affect the validity (or protectability) of your copyright. However, you can be fined if you persist in ignoring the Register's request.

L. Summary

Deposit requirements for registering computer software and output can be concisely summarized as follows:

■ Your deposit must contain a correct copyright notice;

■ Your deposit must accompany a correct registration form;

■ Only one copy of any unpublished work need be deposited;

■ For a program deposit, you can deposit the first and last 25 pages of either source code or object code, or the whole program, if it is less than 50 pages;

■ You can deposit documentation either as part of your software package or separately with a separate TX form;

■ If you copyright a large program package with one copyright form, you only need deposit the first 25 pages of the first program and the last 25 pages of the last program;

■ Deposit source code as first preference if it's important to have the best identifying material on deposit. If you are worried about divulging your code, apply for special relief to deposit blacked out source code or combination object code and source code;

■ Object code is a good deposit choice if you wish to maintain your program as a trade secret, or fear any examination of your work by potential infringers. Object code is accepted as deposit under the rule of doubt. It's not clear that an object code deposit will be given the same protection as a source code deposit in court, but it seems likely that it will be;

■ For a single file database, deposit the entire database or the first and last 25 pages, whichever is less;

■ For a multifile database, deposit either the entire file or 50 records (entities) from each file, whichever is less;

■ Each registration packet should contain a transmittal letter explaining what is being registered and deposited and asking for special relief. If spe- cial relief is granted, your deposit will still be valid. If it is not needed, you have lost nothing.

The following chart summarizes the number of copies which need to be deposited for different types of works.

object code program	1 copy; first & last 25 pages
source code program	1 copy; first & last 25 pages
database input instructions	1 copy; first & last 25 pages
database (output) - single file	1 copy; first & last 25 pages
database (output) - multi file	1 copy; 50 records from each file
documentation - books	2 complete copies
films, training or fiction	1 complete copy
computer game screens	2 copies of identifying material
photographs	2 copies
musical compositions	2 copies
slide presentations	2 copies
flowcharts - textual	2 copies
flowchart - graphic	2 copies

If you are confused by any material in this chapter, have your deposit rejected by the Copyright Office and don't know how to correct it or need advice as to whether a source or object code deposit is best for you, see a knowledgeable attorney.

CHAPTER 11

The Registration Process

A. Introduction

By now, you should have a good handle on which copyright registration form to use and what materials to deposit. If not, a review of the previous three chapters and the sample completed forms in the Appendix is in order. Your next step is to complete your registration form and send the package to the Copyright Office. However, before we journey through the copyright registration forms line by line, let's again review who is entitled to register a copyright.

B. Who Can Register a Copyright?

In previous chapters, we saw that a copyright author is considered to be the "owner" of the copyright. We also saw in Chapter 3 that copyright ownership really consists of a bundle of exclusive rights, all or part of which can be legally transferred to others through licenses and assignments. Finally, we learned that anybody who owns one or more of the exclusive rights which together make up a copyright is considered a copyright owner. In other words, a single work can have a number of copyright owners. Thus, if the exclusive right to publish a popular computer game were divided geographically and licensed to distributors in 18 states, there would be at least 18 copyright owners.

WORK-MADE-FOR-HIRE NOTE: In past chapters we have tended to distinguish between actual authors and persons or entities who are considered the author because of their status as owner of works made for hire. For the purpose of registration, however, they are considered one and the same. That is, an owner of a work made for hire is considered the author of that work.

Who among all of these potential owners is entitled to register a copyright? The answer is, any one of them, so long as another hasn't done the job first. Remember, only one registration per version of a work is allowed. Thus, once a copyright is registered (regardless of who does it), no further registrations can take place, except as we outlined in Chapter 9 when we discussed correcting mistakes, changing information, etc.

As a practical matter, registration is almost always accomplished by a work's author or publisher. The publisher usually has the right to register either as an owner of an exclusive right (the right to publish) or as an authorized agent of the author.

REAL WORLD NOTE: It is common practice in the book publishing business for authors to sign over all copyright rights to their publishers by contract. When this occurs, the publisher usually registers the copyright on its own behalf. Following this same general approach, computer software publishers also obtain copyrights from developers by contract and register on their own behalf if the author has not previously done so. Remember, however, that except for work-made-for-hire situations (see Chapter 3), the author always has the original power to register, and should do so unless

there is a publisher already in the picture who will accomplish this task. It is common for the copyright notice to be in the author's name even though the registration is actually prepared by the publisher's staff.

APPENDIX NOTE: In the Appendix, you will find completed sample registration forms for several different types of programs and computer output. You may wish to refer to them as we proceed.

C. Filling Out Forms TX/VA/PA/SR/SE

Now it's time to put together all we've covered in the last several chapters and complete the job of registration. Because the forms are very similar in format (with the exception of the GR/CP form), we'll go through the TX, PA, VA, SR and SE forms as a group. Significant differences will be indicated as they become relevant.

Space 1: Title

1

TITLE OF THIS WORK ▼
_____

PREVIOUS OR ALTERNATIVE TITLES ▼
_____

PUBLICATION AS A CONTRIBUTION If this work was published as a contribution to a periodical, serial, or collection, give information about the collective work in which the contribution appeared. **Title of Collective Work ▼**
_____

If published in a periodical or serial give: Volume ▼   Number ▼   Issue Date ▼   On Pages ▼

Fill in Title of Your Work

All registration forms have as the first line, "TITLE OF THIS WORK (SERIAL)." This means your work must have a name. Usually this will be a title or heading of some kind. Even if you have decided that all truly great creations should remain nameless, you will need to make an exception if you wish to register your copyright. Your title is used for indexing your work and for reference purposes

when communicating with the Copyright Office.

EXAMPLE 1: Mary Hales registers each program of her LOANIT loan processing package (which contains 70 programs) separately on a separate TX form by giving them semi-descriptive numerical titles. The editing programs are EDIT010, EDIT024, etc.; her report programs are

D-EXCEPTRPT001, M-EXCEPTRPT040, etc.; her loan algorithm routines are RULE78S, AVERBAL, etc. If Mary registered LOANIT as a single package, however, she would simply title the work LOANIT.

EXAMPLE 2: When registering his game program, GOTTCHA, Carl Jones puts "GOTTCHA" on the first line of the TX form. If Carl decides to register his screens separately, he puts "GOTTCHA SCREENS" on the first line of the PA form.

EXAMPLE 3: To register his database on Volkswagen auto parts, Carl puts "BUGBITS DATABASE" on line 1 of a TX form. Because he plans to publish the documentation separately, he registers it on a separate TX form, with the title "BUGBITS USER REFERENCE MANUAL."

TRADEMARK NOTE: Titles are not protected by copyright. However, the law of trademarks will afford an imaginative title excellent protection. We discuss this further in Chapter 15.

Periodicals Only — Fill in Volume, Number, Date

If you are not registering a periodical on Form SE, this blank does not apply to you. If you are, simply fill in the correct volume, number and date of your work.

EXAMPLE 1: Carl Jones' users' group registers the edition of "Rollin' On" he

contributed to by entering " ROLLIN' ON" in the title section and then fills in the second line of that form, as follows:

Volume, 24; Number, 2; Date on Copies, July 1984; Frequency of Publication, Monthly. (See filled-out sample forms in the Appendix at the back of this book.)

Fill in Previous or Alternative Title

Most completed copyright registration forms leave this space blank because they haven't changed the name of the program. However, if your work was registered by a different title in published or unpublished form, or was registered in a different name by someone other than you, the author, you should provide the prior name.

EXAMPLE 1: Mary Hales registered all her LOANIT programs in unpublished form as PROGRAM #1, PROGRAM #2, etc. These names must be put on the previous or

alternative name line when she later registers them as published works with new names.

EXAMPLE 2: BCA Graphics wishes to register substantial revisions Kendra Salone has made in what they now call QUILTIT 1.0. Since QUILTIT 1.0 was first registered as just plain QUILTIT (before BCA filed a supplementary registration in Chapter 9, Section B(4), BCA puts "QUILTIT" on the previous name line. "QUILTIT 1.0" goes on the title line.

Fill in Line C (Depending on Which Form You Use)

Line "c" varies from form to form. Let's examine each variation separately.

■ FORM SE: There is no next line. Space 1 has been completed.

■ FORMS TX AND VA: PUBLICATION AS A CONTRIBUTION: If the work to be registered was part of a collective work or periodical or newspaper (anything that as

a whole could be registered on a form SE), indicate the title of the magazine or periodical and the specific volume, number, date and page that contained your work. Otherwise, leave the section blank.

EXAMPLE: Carl Jones registers the article he wrote for "Rollin' On," a users' group newsletter, on Form TX. He puts the title of his article, "AUTO PARTS DATABASES," on the title line and "ROLLIN' ON," Volume 24, Number 2, July 1984, pages 34 - 39 on the line entitled "Publication as a Contribution."

■ FORMS PA & SR: NATURE OF THE WORK (MATERIAL RECORDED): On these two forms, you must use line "c" to tell something about the work itself. The SR form allows you to check a box, "Musical, Dramatic, Musical-Dramatic, Literary or Other."

EXAMPLE 1: Carl Jones registers his musical composition, OFFKEY, which he generated by computer on Form SR. He checks the box entitled "Musical."

EXAMPLE 2: Mary Hales registers her LOANIT training lecture, which she has published on cassette. She uses Form SR and checks the box "Literary."

EXAMPLE 3: Carl Jones really enjoys making "music" with his computer, but even he has to admit that his last creation, which resembles trains and cars crashing, is not musical, even when that term is stretched as far as well-chewed bubble gum. Carl registers his creation on the SR form and checks the box "Other." He then fills in the blank with "SOUND EFFECTS."

The PA form also has an open line for you to describe your work in a few words. It is important to use the right few words. If the Copyright Office does not understand what you mean, you may have your form returned for a second try. If your description does not describe an audiovisual work, you may be told to start over. As with video adventure games themselves, filling out this blank may look easy, but there are traps and thickets to snare the unwary.

As a general rule:

■ Remember that to use a Form PA, your work must be a performing art or other audiovisual work, as described in Chapter 8, Section F(2);

■ Indicate that the work involves moving images;

■ Indicate any sound which accompanies the work;

■ Do not use the term "computer game" without explanation.

EXAMPLE 1: Mary Hales registers her LOANIT training film on a PA form. She indicates the nature of her work as "TRAINING FILM WITH ACCOMPANYING SOUND TRACK."

EXAMPLE 2: Carl Jones registers the audiovisual parts of his GOTTCHA game on the PA form with the explanation "COMPUTER GAME AUDIO-VISUAL OUTPUT WITH ACCOMPANYING SOUND." He could put "AUDIO-VISUAL WORK WITH SOUND," but he does not want to say just "COMPUTER GAME," because that might be a literary work.

SAUTEED COPYRIGHT   SQUASHED COPYRIGHT   FRESH COPYRIGHT PIE

THE CULINARY COPYRIGHT

Space 2: Author Information

2 **a**

NAME OF AUTHOR ▼

DATES OF BIRTH AND DEATH
Year Born ▼   Year Died ▼

NOTE

Under the law,
the "author" of a
"work made for
hire" is generally
the employer,
not the em-
ployee (see in-
structions). For
any part of this
work that was
"made for hire"
check "Yes" in
the space pro-
vided, give the
employer (or
other person for
whom the work
was prepared)
as "Author" of
that part, and
leave the space
for dates of birth
and death blank.

Was this contribution to the work a
"work made for hire"?
☐ Yes
☐ No

AUTHOR'S NATIONALITY OR DOMICILE
Name of Country
OR { Citizen of ▶
Domiciled in ▶

WAS THIS AUTHOR'S CONTRIBUTION TO
THE WORK
Anonymous?   ☐ Yes ☐ No
Pseudonymous?   ☐ Yes ☐ No

If the answer to either
of these questions is
"Yes," see detailed
instructions

NATURE OF AUTHORSHIP   Briefly describe nature of the material created by this author in which copyright is claimed. ▼

b

NAME OF AUTHOR ▼

DATES OF BIRTH AND DEATH
Year Born ▼   Year Died ▼

Was this contribution to the work a
"work made for hire"?
☐ Yes
☐ No

AUTHOR'S NATIONALITY OR DOMICILE
Name of country
OR { Citizen of ▶
Domiciled in ▶

WAS THIS AUTHOR'S CONTRIBUTION TO
THE WORK
Anonymous?   ☐ Yes ☐ No
Pseudonymous?   ☐ Yes ☐ No

If the answer to either
of these questions is
"Yes," see detailed
instructions.

NATURE OF AUTHORSHIP   Briefly describe nature of the material created by this author in which copyright is claimed. ▼

c

NAME OF AUTHOR ▼

DATES OF BIRTH AND DEATH
Year Born ▼   Year Died ▼

Was this contribution to the work a
"work made for hire"?
☐ Yes
☐ No

AUTHOR'S NATIONALITY OR DOMICILE
Name of Country
OR { Citizen of ▶
Domiciled in ▶

WAS THIS AUTHOR'S CONTRIBUTION TO
THE WORK
Anonymous?   ☐ Yes ☐ No
Pseudonymous?   ☐ Yes ☐ No

If the answer to either
of these questions is
"Yes," see detailed
instructions

NATURE OF AUTHORSHIP   Briefly describe nature of the material created by this author in which copyright is claimed. ▼

These spaces are the same on all copy-right registration forms. Here you must list all the authors. Refer to Chapter 3, Section G if you have any doubt as to who is considered to be an author. Basically, it is either the person or persons who actually created the work or, in the case of a work made for hire, the entity or person commissioning or paying for the work.

MULTIPLE AUTHOR NOTE: Each form has room for up to three authors; if there are more, take an 8 1/2" by 11" piece of typing paper and, following the same general format, include the information requested by the registration form for each. Sometimes it is easy to tell who is a co-author and sometimes it is diffi-cult. For example, if three programmers collaborate on a new computer game, they are all authors and should be described in the spaces provided on the form. Sup-pose, however, that Big Bank is the owner of a large multi-program work made for hire. Before registering it, Big Bank contracts with Mary Hales to create two additional programs as an independent author. Can Big Bank register all the programs as one package when Mary is the author of two of them? The answer is "Yes," if Big Bank lists Mary as a co-author of the entire work.* The answer is "No," if Big Bank wants to restrict Mary's authorship to her two programs. Most likely, Big Bank would register the programs it created independently sepa-rately from the ones it purchased from Mary.

Fill in Name of Author

Put the name of the first, or only, author here. If the work is a work made for hire, put in the commissioning party (often the employer). If the author chooses to remain unknown, you may leave this blank or put in "ANONYMOUS." If the author wishes to use a pseudonym, this is permissible. In this situation, you may either:

■ Put in the pseudonym, identifying it as such; or

■ Put in the pseudonym and the real name, identifying which is which.

---

* Remember, listing someone as an author is not the same thing as saying they own the program. See Chapter 12 for the permutations of copyright owner-ship.

EXAMPLE 1: Mary Hales puts in "MARY HALES" on all her LOANIT program registrations. To register the two programs, she co-authored with Robert Atkins, she puts his name in the the "Next Author" spot [Section (b)].

EXAMPLE 2: BCA Graphics, as Kendra Salone's employer, registers her QUILTIT program, listing "BCA GRAPHICS" on the author line.

EXAMPLE 3: Mary Hales was commissioned by Big Bank to write one report module for their credit card system. There was a written contract and the work qualifies as a work made for hire, as it was part of a larger work. Accordingly, Big Bank puts "BIG BANK" as author of CREDITRPT01.

EXAMPLE 4: Carl Jones does not want to admit to anyone, even his mother, that he authored OFFKEY, so he leaves the author space blank. By doing this, Carl may be cutting some time off the duration of the copyright, since anonymous works are only protected for between 75 and 100 years, while individual works of authorship last for the author's life plus 50 years. See Chapter 5 for a discussion of copyright duration.

Fill in Dates of Birth and Death

This space need only be completed where there is an individual author or authors. Leave it blank if the author is a business entity. Also leave it blank if the work is made for hire or is anonymous or pseudonymous. Assuming you are the author (or publisher, or other copyright owner in a situation where the author is an individual), fill in your (the author's) birthdate. If the author has died, the copyright owner must also fill in the date of death.

EXAMPLE 1: Mary Hales puts 1947 under "Year Born" when she registers her LOANIT package on Form TX.

EXAMPLE 2: Robert Atkins was born in 1960. When Mary registers the two programs Atkins co-authored, she lists his name on the second author birthdate line.

EXAMPLE 3: When BCA Graphics registers QUILTIT, the quilt program authored by Kendra Salone as a work for hire, they do not fill in this blank.

EXAMPLE 4: Carl Jones leaves this space blank on his OFFKEY registration because he doesn't list his name. If he used a pseudonym, he would also leave this line blank.

Work Made for Hire

Next you are asked to check a box if this is a work made for hire. If so, check "Yes." Otherwise, check "No." If you are unsure, re-read Chapter 3, Section G.

Fill in Author's Nationality or Domicile

This blank must be filled in on all program registrations, including works for hire and anonymous and pseudonymous works. Individuals can either give their country of citizenship or the country in which they are living on a more or less

permanent basis (domicile).* Corporations and unincorporated businesses such as partnerships, limited partnerships and

---

* The term domicile has been interpreted in different contexts by virtually thousands of courts. Without going into detail, the term generally refers to the country where you maintain your primary or main residence, with an intent to remain there for the indefinite future. If you have any doubts about your domicile status, see a lawyer.

sole proprietorships should list the country in which their headquarters is located (i.e., the U.S.A. for U.S. corporations).

Fill in Anonymous or Pseudonymous Box

This question asks, "Is the author Remaining Anonymous or Using a Pseudonym?" You can only say "Yes" or "No."

Fill in Nature of Authorship

Of all the boxes on the registration form, this can be the trickiest. What you put in this box will determine whether your registration sails through without incident or whether you are in for another round of correspondence. It is this box which the Copyright Office primarily relies on to determine whether your work is deserving of registration under the copyright laws. Because this description of the nature of your authorship is often compared with what you deposit, putting the wrong words here may raise a question in the copyright examiner's mind as to whether your deposit is adequate. Accordingly, we recommend you pay very close attention to the following material.

Form SE

2 a	NAME OF AUTHOR ▼		DATES OF BIRTH AND DEATH Year Born ▼ Year Died ▼
	Was this contribution to the work a "work made for hire"? ☐ Yes ☐ No	AUTHOR'S NATIONALITY OR DOMICILE Name of Country OR { Citizen of ▶_____ { Domiciled in ▶_____	WAS THIS AUTHOR'S CONTRIBUTION TO THE WORK Anonymous? ☐ Yes ☐ No Pseudonymous? ☐ Yes ☐ No If the answer to either of these questions is "Yes," see detailed instructions
	NATURE OF AUTHORSHIP Briefly describe nature of the material created by this author in which copyright is claimed. ▼ ☐ Collective Work Other:		

* Form SE gives you the option of either checking the box indicating that the work is a collective work, or describing the nature of authorship under "Other." Because the Form SE is used for serial publications, such as newspapers and magazines, you will usually be checking the box. However, if you have added some material or revised the work since it was first published, you may want to describe the new material briefly on the line next to the box marked "Other."

■ All other forms:

The other forms have no box to check. Instead, you must come up with a description of the nature of your authorship which will satisfy the copyright examiners.

MAGIC WORDS NOTE: The Copyright Office maintains a manual for use by its registration form examiners containing specific words and phrases which are, and are not, acceptable to describe the nature of the authorship. The main idea underlying these guidelines is that some descriptions adequately describe a work as something subject to copyright protection while others do not. When we suggest you use some words and phrases and not others, we base our advice on these internal Copyright Office guidelines.

What you put on the nature of authorship line will vary most depending on whether this is:

■ Your first registration for an original work (discussed under "How to Describe Original Works," just below);

OR,

■ A registration for a new version of a previously published work; or a derivative work (discussed below under "How to Describe Derivative Works and New Versions").

How to Describe Original Works

Most computer programs or code being registered on a Form TX can be described using one of the following terms:

Acceptable Terms:

Computer program	Software
Module	Computer software
Text of program	Routine
Program text	Subroutine
Programming text	Program listing
Program listing	Entire program
Program instructions	Entire text
Text of computer game	Entire program code
Wrote program	Entire work

UNACCEPTABLE TERMS: Here is a listing of those terms that will cause the Copyright Office to bounce your registration back for another try:

Unacceptable Terms:

Algorithm	Encrypting
Text of algorithm	Software methodology
Functions	Computer game
System	Analysis
System design	Firmware
Formatting	Logic
Disk	Chip
Printout	EPROM
Cassette	ROM
Programmer	PROM
Language	Mnemonics

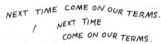

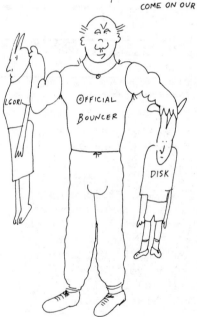

A BUNCH OF UNACCEPTABLE TERMS

If a flowchart or other documentation is included with the program registration (which is only appropriate if all items are published as one unit--see Chapter 8, Section F(1)--you should say "COMPUTER PROGRAM WITH FLOWCHART," "COMPUTER PROGRAM WITH USERS' GUIDE," or "COMPUTER SOFTWARE WITH ACCOMPANYING DOCUMENTATION."

DEPOSIT NOTE: Pick a term that accurately describes your work. If your deposit does not match the descriptive term you choose, you will get a letter asking for clarification and your registration will accordingly be delayed. As we emphatically stressed in Chapter 10, it is a good idea to always explain in writing what you are including in your deposit. Again, this explanation should be consistent with the description you list in blank "f." For example, Mary Hales, our LOANIT loan package author, should write a letter of explanation providing the information the Copyright Office will need to make sense of her deposit and to relate it to her program description.

EXAMPLE 1: Carl Jones registers the object code version of GOTTCHA, his computer game, on a TX form, indicating the nature of authorship as "TEXT OF COMPUTER GAME" or "COMPUTER SOFTWARE." Along with his form and deposit, which consists of the first and last 25 pages of his printed out object code, he encloses a letter explaining the object code is a computer game of copyrightable, original authorship. Carl should not say his program is "firmware" or "object code" (even if he embeds it in a ROM) or a "computer game."

EXAMPLE 2: Mary Hales registers her LOANIT package on one TX form and then registers a flowchart outlining the program separately on another TX form because it is published separately. She indicates it is a "FLOWCHART WITH MAINLY TEXTUAL EXPRESSION" (see Chapter 8, Section F(1)(d) for more on flowcharts). She should include a letter with her deposit explaining that the flowchart is published separately from the program or is unpublished and not part of the published program.

EXAMPLE 3: Carl Jones also registers the screens produced by his GOTTCHA program. He should put "COMPUTER GAME SCREENS AND SOUND" or "COMPUTER GAME OUTPUT SEQUENCES, SIGHT AND SOUND" on line 2f of Form PA.

EXAMPLE 4: Mary Hales registers her LOANIT training lecture on cassette sepa-

rately from the LOANIT loan processing package. She puts "WORDS" on this line of her SR registration form.

EXAMPLE 5: When Mary Hales registers her training film for her LOANIT word processing package, she puts "FILM AND WORDS" on her PA registration form.

EXAMPLE 6: BCA Graphics puts "ARTISTIC DESIGNS" on Form VA when they register the quilt designs generated by QUILT-IT, which Kendra Salone wrote as a work for hire.

EXAMPLE 7: Mary Hales decides to separately register the graphic flowcharts she prepared for LOANIT. To do this, she uses Form VA and puts "GRAPHIC EXPRESSION OF LOGIC FLOW" to describe her work. She also deposits a copy of the flowchart and includes a letter explaining that her flowchart expresses her idea by means of graphic representation and not text.

EXAMPLE 8: When Carl Jones registers his autoparts database, BUGBITS, using a TX registration form, he should say "TEXT OF COMPUTER DATABASE." He must not say merely "compilation" or "facts" or his registration will be rejected.

ABSURDITY NOTE: As arbitrary as it might seem for the Copyright Office to decide in advance which words and phrases will be acceptable and which not (e.g., "database" is acceptable and "compilation" is not), that agency has clearly found it desirable to draw sharp lines as to what language will do the job. Fortunately, if you slip up on this, you will almost always be given additional chances to get it right, as the Copyright Office will return your registration form with a letter telling you to try again, sometimes making helpful suggestions.

How to Describe Derivative Work and New Versions

If you are registering a derivative work or a new version, you have more to consider in explaining your "Nature of Authorship" under Space 20 of your copyright registration form. To be eligible for separate registration, a work based

on a prior work (i.e., derivative works and new versions) must involve enough changes in the prior work to be separately copyrightable. The Copyright Office uses the term "de minimis" to describe works (or changes in existing works) that are not significant enough to warrant a separate copyright registration. This concept applies whether or not the whole work is registered as a derivative work, a new version, or the changes are registered separately, as might be the case if whole new sections of code added to an existing program are able to stand on their own (see Chapter 4).

If the new material you wish to register consists of changes in or revisions to a prior program, you must use very precise language. For example, if you describe the nature of the new material as "editorial revisions," "revised revisions of . . . [NAME OF PROGRAM]," "computer program," "text of program," "programming text," "program listing," "program instructions," "text of computer game," "module," "routine," "subroutine," or "wrote program," your registration should sail through.

However, if you try "error corrections," "debugging," "patching," "features," or "enhancements," you will receive a letter requesting that you either submit a new application with a better statement of authorship, or that you abandon your registration by notifying them that the changes are too minor or "functionally predetermined" to warrant registration as an original work of authorship.

What does functionally predetermined mean? This is when the basic software which is being changed has been specifically designed to accommodate such changes. For example, many operating systems and applications software are deliberately made to easily accept pre-planned changes (patches) which will permit them to compatibly operate with a number of different central processors (i.e., boards or chips). When such patches are made, they are considered as functionally predetermined and ordinarily do not either alter the work or stand by themselves sufficiently to warrant a new registration.

TRANSLATION NOTE: Programs which are significantly adapted or translated to another computer language are usually

considered to be a derivative work and registrable as such (see Chapter 4). In this situation, to correctly describe what is going on in Box 2f, you need to include the name of the language into which the work has been translated. Thus "TRANSLATION TO PASCAL" is deemed sufficient, while "translation" by itself is not. However, if it appears to the Copyright Office that your translation really only enables the pre-existing program to operate on a different machine without the need for a different language, your registration may or may not be approved as a new version, depending on the magnitude of the changes.

For example, if you simply change some of the initial commands to the computer and make a few minor format changes to enable an already registered program to run on different hardware, the Copyright Office will usually consider this to be "de minimis," and thus not registrable. This would also be an example of a functionally pre-defined modification described just above.

===

If you have made significant original changes to a program, make sure the Copyright Office finds out about them in your "Nature of Authorship" statement. For example, if you changed an operations program from BASIC to PASCAL, you would write "TRANSLATION OF BASIC PROGRAM TO PASCAL." However, it is not wise to rely on your "Nature of Authorship" statement alone. Send a letter of explanation as well. In most situations, as we discussed in Chapter 10, you will want to do this anyway, to explain your deposit and request special relief.

===

EXAMPLE 1: Mary Hales issues a new release of her loan processing package, LOANIT, which she originally registered as one package (see Chapter 8). She adds three new programs and modifies four others substantially. In the "Nature of Authorship" box, she should put "ADDITIONAL PROGRAM TEXT AND EXTENSIVELY MODIFIED TEXT."

EXAMPLE 2: Assume now that Mary Hales, who originally registered all other LOANIT programs separately, changes LOANIT substantially as part of a new release. Accordingly, she will register each of the three new programs separately (see the material on how to describe original work, above). When it comes to registering the modified programs, she uses a TX form and describes them as follows: "NEW AND REVISED COMPUTER SOFT-WARE" or "EXTENSIVE REVISIONS TO COMPUTER PROGRAM," or simply, "COMPUTER PROGRAM" or "TEXT OF PROGRAM." She needn't name the programs here since she will have named them earlier in the form. Although the descriptions suggested here may not seem particularly enlightening, they are acceptable because the new claim of copyright is only for the new material.

Fill in Co-Author Information (Box 2)

When a work has co-authors, each author's contribution to the work should be indicated in this space. See our "Multiple Author Note" in Section C of this chapter. Where the work as a whole has been co-authored, simply say so. Where each author contributed to different portions, or made contributions of a different kind, specify these.

EXAMPLE 1: Mary Hales registers all her LOANIT loan processing programs separately. When it comes to the first program, which she wrote with Robert Atkins as a joint effort, the "Nature of Authorship" line should read "CO-AUTHOR OF COMPUTER PROGRAM."

EXAMPLE 2: Let us assume the other LOANIT program Mary Hales and Robert Atkins co-authored was divided between them by subroutines. Because Robert and Mary are registering the overall program as one work, they are registering as co-authors. Mary puts "AUTHOR OF FIVE SUBROUTINES" in her Box 2(f) and Robert puts "AUTHOR OF TEN SUBROUTINES" in his Box 2(f). It would be a good idea to send a letter along with this registration to explain that there are 15 subroutines comprising this one work, and describe specifically which subroutines were authored by which person. If the separate subroutines are able to stand on their own, Mary and Robert could choose to register them as separate original works of authorship instead of co-authored portions of one work.

Space 3: All Relevant Dates

3	YEAR IN WHICH CREATION OF THIS WORK WAS COMPLETED This information must be given ◄ Year in all cases.	DATE AND NATION OF FIRST PUBLICATION OF THIS PARTICULAR WORK Complete this information Month ▶ _____ Day ▶ _____ Year ▶ _____ ONLY if this work has been published. _____ ◄ Nation

On the first line of this section, indicate the year in which the work was completed. This date has nothing to do with publication, but rather, it is the year the work was first fixed in a tangible medium of expression, thus becoming a proper subject for copyright protection.*

---

* This date can be extremely important if you later become locked in a dispute over who created a work first. As we emphasized in Chapter 8, registration of a work gives rise to the presumption that the facts stated in the application are true. Thus, in the event of an infringement suit, your stated date of creation will be presumed true and the other side will have to disprove it.

The next line asks for the publication date. If you are registering an unpublished work, leave this space blank. For published works, give the month, day and year when the work was first widely made available to the public. Chapter 6, Section C contains a complete discussion on what constitutes publication.

You must also list the country or countries in which publication first occurred. Although works are commonly initially published in a single country, international copyright treaties may make it worth your while to simultaneously publish in more than one country. See Chapter 14 on international copyright protection for further discussion of this point.

EXAMPLE 1: Carl Jones completed GOTTCHA in 1984. He and his kids played the game night and day until February 24, 1985, when Carl received a substantial advance from a software publisher as part of signing a contract under which the publisher received the exclusive right to distribute GOTTCHA. The publisher made the first copies generally available for sale on March 18, 1985. Carl should put

"1984" on the completion line and "MARCH 18, 1985" on the publication line.

EXAMPLE 2: Mary Hales created her LOANIT loan processing package over a three-year period, with certain programs being completed in 1983, others in 1984, and still others not until just before publication on May 2, 1985. The programs will have completion dates ranging from 1983 to 1985, but all will have the same publication date, May 2, 1985. If Mary registers LOANIT as one work, the completion date is the date the last program was completed.

Space 4: Copyright Claimants

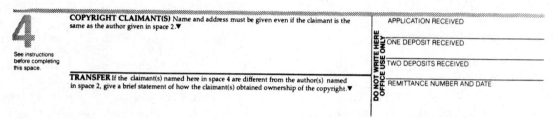

Fill in Name of Author or Owner

This space is used for the name of the author or the name of any person or entity claiming ownership to all of the exclusive rights making up the copyright. As we discussed in Chapter 3, there are really two meanings to the term "copyright owner." One meaning commonly refers to the author of a work (remember, the owner of a work made for hire qualifies as an author) or to any other person or entity who owns all the exclusive copyright rights by virtue of transfers, such as when an author assigns all copyright rights to his or her publisher. The other meaning refers to the owner of one or more of the exclusive rights (e.g., the right to publish, the right to make derivative works, the right to display). On their face, these two meanings of ownership are contradictory. For this reason, the copyright forms use the term "copyright claimant" to describe the author or owner of all rights, and "copyright owner" to describe an owner of one or more (but less than all) copyright rights.

Who, then, should be named as the copyright claimant for the purpose of Space 4?

■ Either the name of the author (which includes the original owner of a work made for hire); or

■ The name of the person who owns all the exclusive rights, if this is not the author.

If, as often happens, a series of transfers has resulted in the ownership of exclusive rights being in more than one person, the author's name remains as the claimant. In other words, the author will always be that claimant, unless somebody else ends up owning all the exclusive copyright rights.

If you are not the author or developer of a work for hire, but think you qualify as a copyright claimant, review Chapter 3 and then go to Chapter 12 and read our discussion about transfers. You may also wish to consult a lawyer if you are still confused. Then, come back to this section and put your name and address in Space 4, assuming you still believe you own all copyright rights and are entitled to do so. Otherwise, the author's name goes on this line.

EXAMPLE 1: In registering her LOANIT loan processing package, Mary Hales puts "MARY HALES, 111 SOFTWARE LANE, SAN FRANCISCO, CA. 00000," because she is the author and has not transferred her copyright.

EXAMPLE 2: Now pretend Carl Jones dies before he registers his computer game, GOTTCHA. (Fortunately, this isn't true, but we need the example.) Belinda Bonner, to whom he left his intellectual property rights by will, accomplishes the registration. Although Carl is the author, Belinda Bonner's name goes in Space 4 as a copyright claimant (through inheritance).

Fill in Transfer Line of Space 4, If Necessary

The other line in Space 4 asks for an explanation of how the claimant obtained copyright ownership if any name other than the author's is put in Space 4. This would usually be by contract, will, or court order. Do not attach the transfer document--merely name or otherwise describe it. Again, see Chapter 12 for a complete discussion of copyright transfers.

EXAMPLE 1: Mary Hales transfers her copyright in her loan processing package, LOANIT, to Big Bank before she registers it. Big Bank can register the work listing Mary as author and themselves as copyright claimant. They enter "BY WRITTEN CONTRACT" on this line in Space 4.

EXAMPLE 2: Now, suppose instead of transferring her entire copyright to Big Bank, Mary retains the exclusive right to

make derivative works. Who is the claimant in this case? Since Mary is the author, and no one else has all the exclusive rights, since Mary retained one of them, Mary should be named as the claimant.

EXAMPLE 3: Finally, suppose Mary wrote LOANIT for Big Bank as a work made for hire? In that case, Big Bank would be both author and claimant.

EXAMPLE 4: Carl Jones' heir, Belinda Bonner, registers GOTTCHA after his death. She lists "BY WILL" on the second line of this space. If Carl left her the program through the device of an intervivos trust, or if he died without a will and she gained ownership by the intestate succession law of her state, she would write "BY INHERITANCE."

Space 5: Any Previous Registration Information

PREVIOUS REGISTRATION Has registration for this work, or for an earlier version of this work, already been made in the Copyright Office?

☐ Yes ☐ No If your answer is "Yes," why is another registration being sought? (Check appropriate box) ▼

☐ This is the first published edition of a work previously registered in unpublished form.

☐ This is the first application submitted by this author as copyright claimant.

☐ This is a changed version of the work, as shown by space 6 on this application.

If your answer is "Yes," give: **Previous Registration Number** ▼   **Year of Registration** ▼

5

If you are hazy on the information covered in Chapter 9 (on registering new versions and derivative works), you will want to review that material before proceeding.

This space asks if the work in question was registered previously, either in its present format or as another version. If this is the first registration, check "No" and go on to Space 6. If you have previously registered this work, or an earlier version of it, you must check the appropriate box to indicate the reason for this registration. There are only three allowable reasons to re-register a previously registered work. The new registration could be because:

■ This is the published version of a work you previously registered as an unpublished work;

■ This is the first registration under the true author's name (previous registration was anonymous or under a pseudonym); or

■ This is a changed version of the previously registered work.

Again, these topics were discussed in detail in Chapter 9. Refer back if you're unsure about the allowable circum-stances or the level of change necessary to support a new registration. No matter which of the reasons you rely on, you must provide the previous registration number and the year the previous registration was made.

NOTE: MAJOR CHANGES: It is common for a programmer to use a small amount of pre-existing code or documentation from a previously registered work as part of a new work. If you face this situation, your best bet is probably to register the new work as an original work of author-ship without worrying about the previous registration. This assumes, of course, that you own the copyright in the earlier material. If someone else owns the copy-right to the pre-existing code, however, you will need to obtain permission from the appropriate copyright owner or face the possibility of a copyright infringe-ment lawsuit.

Space 6: Derivative Work or Compilation Information

If your work is an original one with no pre-existing code, go on to Space 7. This box is only for works which incor-porate pre-existing code and compila-tions. If you struggled with us in our Chapter 4 discussion of the differences between derivative works, original works incorporating pre-existing material and compilations, this section will be easy to handle. If you are still in doubt about these concepts, however, turn back to that chapter and bone up.

There are two lines in Space 6, desig-nated, originally enough, as "a" and "b," as follows:

DERIVATIVE WORK OR COMPILATION Complete both space 6a & 6b for a derivative work; complete only 6b for a compilation.
a. Preexisting Material Identify any preexisting work or works that this work is based on or incorporates. ▼

_____

b. Material Added to This Work Give a brief, general statement of the material that has been added to this work and in which copyright is claimed. ▼

_____

6

See instructions before completing this space

Sections "a" and "b" are to be filled in if your registration is for a deriva-tive work or for any new work containing pre-existing material. Only section "b" is required for a compilation.

Fill in Line a of Space 6

In line "a" you are asked to identify any pre-existing material that the work is based on or incorporates. You should identify the material by one of the fol-lowing phrases:

■ "Work described in Space 5;"

■ "Previous registered routines created by author;"

■ "Previously published routines created by author;"

■ "Previously unregistered computer program;"

■ "Program text."

You do not need to go into detail. Remember, Section "a" is only for works containing pre-existing code.

EXAMPLE 1: Mary Hales enters "PROGRAM DESCRIBED IN SPACE 5" when she registers new versions of her loan processing program, LOANIT, in a situation where she had previously registered LOANIT. Mary enters "PROGRAM IN COBOL" when she registers the PASCAL derivative work of LOAN-IT, which was originally registered in COBOL.

EXAMPLE 2: Carl Jones enters "PROGRAM TEXT FOR HOME COMPUTERS" when registering the handheld computer version of his computer game, GOTTCHA. He enters "AU-THOR'S PREVIOUSLY REGISTERED AUDIOVISUAL WORK" on line "a" of the PA form if he registers the screens for the household version, assuming the handheld version screens are different enough to warrant a separate registration.

Fill in Line b of Space 6

On this line you should describe the new material you add. The way to do this varies somewhat, depending on whether you are registering a compilation (e.g., a combination of subroutines from several different sources in addition to the material which organizes or packages the additions), a derivative work or a new version of an existing work.

Let's look at each:

COMPILATIONS: When registering a compilation, you must briefly describe both the material that has been compiled and any original material added by you. You can say "COMPILATION AND ORIGINAL NEW MATERIAL," or "COMPILATION OF COMPUTER ROUTINES WITH COMMENTARY." Your best bet is to keep it simple, but you do need to indicate that you have added some new material to the compilation.

DERIVATIVE WORK AND NEW VERSIONS: Describing the new material in derivative works and new versions is a bit more complicated. As we mentioned earlier, you should not use words such as "en-hancements," "error corrections," "patches," "features," or "debugging." This is because the Copyright Office tends to rule these types of changes aren't significant enough to warrant another registration. As we saw earlier in this chapter and Chapter 9, this is a gray area. The examples of acceptable terminology given earlier in this chapter should help you.

EXAMPLE 1: Mary Hales registers a new version of her LOANIT loan processing package. She has made a number of sub-stantial changes to improve LOANIT. She enters "REVISED COMPUTER SOFTWARE" in Space 6b. For her PASCAL version of LOANIT, which is viewed by the Copyright Office as being a derivative work, Mary enters "TRANSLATION TO PASCAL." It would also have been acceptable to say, "TRANS-LATION TO ANOTHER COMPUTER LANGUAGE."

EXAMPLE 2: Carl Jones enters "TRANS-LATION TO HANDHELD COMPUTER" when he registers the handheld derivative version of GOTTCHA. Carl should send a letter with his registration, explaining that the handheld GOTTCHA is an original work of authorship involving a substantial rewrite of the original GOTTCHA text. Earlier in this chapter, we discuss the fact that the Copyright Office is likely to reject translations to different ma-chines not involving a fundamental change in the expression itself, as is the case when a program is translated from one computer language to another. To avoid this kind of problem, Carl should avoid the term "translation," without further explanation.

EXAMPLE 3: When Carl Jones registers his film, GOTTCHA COMIN' AND GOIN', a derivative of GOTTCHA, he should describe it as a feature film.

Space 7: Manufacturing Information on TX & SE Forms Only

MANUFACTURERS AND LOCATIONS If this is a published work consisting preponderantly of nondramatic literary material in English, the law may require that the copies be manufactured in the United States or Canada for full protection. If so, the names of the manufacturers who performed certain processes, and the places where these processes were performed **must** be given. See instructions for details.

Names of Manufacturers ▼   Places of Manufacture ▼

PROCEDURE NOTE: We have now reached Space 7. Forms TX and SE request information having to do with publication outside of the U.S. in Spaces 7 & 8. The other forms do not require this information. Just below we will discuss how you handle these spaces on the TX and SE forms only. Then we will proceed as we have before. However, because of the insertion of this additional manufacturing information on the TX and SE forms, Spaces 9, 10 and 11 of the TX and SE forms will be equivalent to Spaces 7, 8 and 9 of the PA, VA, and SR forms.

This section does not apply to software or computer output as such. It does apply to all printed material, including documentation. If you are registering copies of literary works, such as books or printouts of databases which have been manufactured (i.e., printed) outside of the U.S., put the information here. For more information about the copyright effect of printing outside the U.S., see Chapter 14, Section G.

If everything has been printed in the U.S., list the name of the manufacturer, U.S.A.

Space 8: Form TX and SE Only

REPRODUCTION FOR USE OF BLIND OR PHYSICALLY HANDICAPPED INDIVIDUALS A signature on this form at space 10, and a check in one of the boxes here in space 8, constitutes a non-exclusive grant of permission to the Library of Congress to reproduce and distribute solely for the blind and physically handicapped and under the conditions and limitations prescribed by the regulations of the Copyright Office: (1) copies of the work identified in space 1 of this application in Braille (or similar tactile symbols); or (2) phonorecords embodying a fixation of a reading of that work; or (3) both.

a ☐ Copies and Phonorecords   b ☐ Copies Only   c ☐ Phonorecords Only   See instructions

This space is entitled "Reproduction for Use of the Blind or Physically Handicapped Individuals." If you wish to voluntarily grant a free, nonexclusive license that may be terminated on 90 days notice for those persons who are "certi-

fied by competent authorities" as unable to read normal printed material, you may do so by checking the appropriate box. Of course, this does not apply to computer programs or any other machine-readable work, only printed text.

Space 9 (Forms TX & SE) or Space 7 (Forms PA, VA, SR)

DEPOSIT ACCOUNT If the registration fee is to be charged to a Deposit Account established in the Copyright Office, give name and number of Account.

Name ▼   Account Number ▼

CORRESPONDENCE Give name and address to which correspondence about this application should be sent. Name/Address/Apt/City/State/Zip ▼

Be sure to give your daytime phone number ◀

Area Code & Telephone Number ▶

Line 1: Deposit Account Information

This space allows you to pay your registration fee from an account set up

in the Copyright Office. If you wish to do this, money must be deposited in advance, and then drawn down as you file successive registrations. Copyright Office Circular R5 contains the form to be sent to the Copyright Office. You must make an initial deposit of $250 to open your account. If you do, you will receive a deposit account number, which you put in this space. To qualify for a deposit account, you must expect to file at least 12 registrations or other documents requiring a fee in a year's time. Deposit accounts are ideal for software publishers and authors who file a large number of new programs each year. However, if you don't fit this description don't worry about setting up a deposit account, and leave this line blank.

Line 2: Correspondence

Give your name, address and telephone, or that of some other person the Copyright Office should contact in case they have any questions regarding your registration. Provide a person's name, even if the author or copyright owner filing this registration is a corporation. Contact will be made during business hours, so don't give your home phone if you are somewhere else during the day.

Space 10 (Forms TX, SE) or Space 8 (Forms PA, VA, SR)

CERTIFICATION* I, the undersigned, hereby certify that I am the

Check one ▶

☐ author
☐ other copyright claimant
☐ owner of exclusive right(s)
☐ authorized agent of _____

10

of the work identified in this application and that the statements made by me in this application are correct to the best of my knowledge.

Name of author or other copyright claimant, or owner of exclusive right(s) ▲

Typed or printed name and date ▼ If this is a published work, this date must be the same as or later than the date of publication given in space 3.

_____ date ▶ _____

👉 Handwritten signature (X) ▼

This space, entitled "Certification," is for the copyright claimant to sign the registration form. Remember, only certain people are entitled to file a registration (see Section B, above). This space provides a number of alternative boxes to check, depending on who you are:

■ If you are the author, check the author box;

■ If you own a work made for hire either because you employed the programmer or because the program was written under a written work-made-for-hire contract, check the author box. See Chapter 3, Section G for details on work-for-hire rules;

■ If you own all the exclusive copyright rights, check the "other copyright claimant" box;

■ If you only own one or more, but not all, of the exclusive rights, check the "owner of exclusive right(s)" box;

■ If you are the authorized agent, check that box.

After you check the appropriate box, you must legibly print your name and then sign and date the form. If the work is published, the date of your signature may not precede the date of publication shown on the reverse of the form. It may be the same date, however.

Space 11 (Forms TX, SE) or Space 9 (Forms PA, VA, SR)

MAIL CERTIFI-CATE TO	Name ▼		Have you: • Completed all necessary spaces? • Signed your application in space 10? • Enclosed check or money order for $10 payable to *Register of Copyrights*? • Enclosed your deposit material with the application and fee? **MAIL TO:** Register of Copyrights, Library of Congress, Washington, D.C. 20559	11
Certificate will be mailed in window envelope	Number/Street/Apartment Number ▼			
	City/State/ZIP ▼			

Put the return address for your copyright registration certificate here. This is your evidence of registration and should be retained in your copyright file. Be sure to print clearly to insure that the certificate will get to you.

D. Putting It All Together

1. What Should Be Sent to the Copyright Office?

Your copyright registration package should consist of:

■ A Copyright Form: Include the appropriate registration form as discussed in Chapter 8. Remember, copies are not acceptable. It should be filled out according to the instructions in this chapter (you can use the sample completed forms in the Appendix as a further guide). For safety's sake, it's wise to photocopy the form for your own records. In the unlikely event your application gets lost, this will make it easier to trace or resubmit it;

■ Your Deposit: As we discussed in Chapter 10, your deposit will either be a portion of your work (in the case of software) or the whole work (in the case of documentation) and may consist of one or two copies, depending on the rules. See the summary in Chapter 10, Section L for a quick overview of what you should deposit;

■ Transmittal Letter: You will almost always want to write a transmittal letter, as suggested in Chapter 8. The purpose of this is to explain your deposit and to request special relief if you think there is anything unusual or unauthorized about your deposit;

■ Write a Check: Your next step is to write a check for $10 (the registration fee) for each copyright registration, unless you have already established a deposit account, as discussed under Space 9, above;

■ Put Your Application and Deposit in One Envelope: The Copyright Office requires that only one registration form be used per work being registered and that the registration form, associated deposit and any transmittal letter and/or request for special relief be enclosed in a single envelope. For those of you who plan to register a single program and accompanying documentation on one TX form, there is no problem. You simply put the form, one printout of your program code, two copies of your manual or other printed documentation, your transmittal letter (including a request for special relief, if necessary), and a check for $10 in a single envelope and off it goes.

However, the waters become muddier if your work contains a number of programs, or a variety of output screens, or elaborate documentation, or a number of explanatory flow charts or all of the above. How many envelopes and $10 checks do you need? Here is how it works. You need many envelopes (and registration fees) if you are making many registrations, and only one envelope if you are only making one registration. In the case of LOANIT, Mary Hales had 70 programs and a number of documentation items. If she chose to register her documentation along with her programs, but wanted to register each program separately, she would need 70 envelopes (and $10 in each envelope). If she separately registered each piece of documentation as well, she would need that many more envelopes. If, on the other hand, she decided to make one registration for the entire package, she would only send one envelope and one fee. If your documentation is so extensive that no envelope will hold it all, a box is acceptable.

COPYRIGHT OFFICE NOTE: When you send separate envelopes to the Copyright Office, they are processed completely independently of each other. This means that even though separate registrations may be highly interrelated from your standpoint, they are treated as totally unrelated by the Copyright Office. This in no way affects the quality of your protection, since it is the substance of your individual works which you are protecting, not their relationship. Therefore, don't feel the need to inform the Copyright Office of the relationship between separate deposits.

■ Mailing the Envelope: Mail relatively small registrations First Class. However, if you have a number of programs and bulky documentation, First Class or Priority Mail is too expensive. An alternative is to put all the material in the same box and use different postal rates. The documentation qualifies for Fourth Class Book Rate. Your software deposit can go Third Class (if it's not over 16 ounces) and your TX form and transmittal letter go at First Class rates. In short, this allows you to mail your material in one package, with the heaviest material going at the least expensive rate, while the entire package is treated as Third Class Mail and should arrive more quickly. Check with your local postmaster for details. Of course, many of the alternative postal services can also be used. All registrations should be mailed to:

Register of Copyrights
Library of Congress
Washington D.C. 20559

E. Copyright Office Responses to Your Registration

The Copyright Office will respond to your registration application in one of two ways:

1. If there are no flaws in your registration form or deposit, or the flaws are of a nature which can be corrected by the copyright examiner, you will receive a Certificate of Registration in about six weeks. This consists of a copy of your registration form stamped with a copyright registration number and the registration date, and a Certificate of Registration with the Copyright Office seal at the top. Keep it in your file.

2. If there are flaws which appear to be correctible, the Copyright Office will return your registration form and/or deposit for suggested modifications. Most of the possible trouble areas are discussed in detail in this book, and you should have little trouble fixing the defect. Here are the major reasons for rejection of a registration application for software:

■ You forgot to sign the form;

■ You forgot to provide required information, such as nature of authorship;

■ You failed to either meet the deposit requirements or request special relief, as discussed in detail in Chapter 10, Section C;

■ You provided an inadequate description of the work for Copyright Office purposes, as discussed under Space 2 earlier in this chapter;

■ You used separate registration forms to register object code and source code of the same program. Only one registration is allowed for each program, unless you are registering a derivative work or new version (see Chapter 9);

■ You attempted to register a "de minimis" work. As noted in Chapters 3 and 4, it must appear to the Copyright Office that there is a significant amount of original work in what you attempt to register, or they won't accept it. Fortunately, you won't have to guess at what was wrong with your work. The Copyright Office uses a number of form letters to respond to the standard registration flaws. If you manage to make a novel mistake, they will even send you an original letter explaining it to you.

While all of these flaws are potentially correctible, some are more difficult to fix than others. Thus, if you simply used the wrong magic word (see section "f" in the "Nature of Authorship" section of this chapter) to describe your work, you can fix it by using the right one and resubmitting the application. If, however, your description of your work as "minor debugging" was accurate, your work is arguably not qualified for registration. Accordingly, you can either abandon your registration or appeal from that Copyright Office determination. If this becomes an issue, a visit to a knowledgeable copyright attorney is in order (see Chapter 2, Section C).

Assuming you can correct the error, by all means do so. Then, check the letter from the Copyright Office to see whether you need to submit a new fee. Often this isn't necessary. If there is no mention of new fees in the letter, you may want to call the Copyright Office and ask. That number again is (202) 287-8700. Then resubmit your package in one envelope, with or without the new fee enclosed.

3. Occasionally an application falls between the cracks. No system is perfect, although, as these things go, the Copyright Office is pretty good. If you don't receive your certificate or other response within 12 weeks, you should write to the Copyright Office and inquire about your application.

Your letter should include the following:

■ The date of your original application;

■ The form you used, e.g., TX, PA, VA;

■ The name of the work as it appears on the registration form;

■ A brief description of the work;

■ The name of the author;

■ The name of the copyright owner.

F. Form CA — Supplemental Registration

In Chapter 9 we described when a CA form should be used and who could file a Supplemental Copyright Registration. You may wish to refer back to that discussion before we go through the mechanics of filling in Form CA. Keep in mind that one CA form must be filled out for each original registration form you wish to supplement. Thus, if Mary Hales used 70 TX forms to separately register her LOAN-IT programs, she will need to fill out 70 CA forms if she wants to supplement information appearing on each of the 70 originals.

Space A: Basic Instruction

(A) Basic Instructions	**TITLE OF WORK:**	
	REGISTRATION NUMBER OF BASIC REGISTRATION:	**YEAR OF BASIC REGISTRATION:**
	NAME(S) OF AUTHOR(S):	**NAME(S) OF COPYRIGHT CLAIMANT(S):**

In Space A, identify the original registration that you are supplementing. To do this, you must give:

■ The title of the work exactly as you gave it on your original registration form;

■ The registration number;

■ The year your registration was accepted;

■ The authors exactly as they appear on the original registration for; and

■ The copyright claimants exactly as they appear on the original registration form.

©

Even if this information has since changed, you should provide it here exactly as it appears on the earlier registration form. This will allow the Copyright Office to identify the exact form you are supplementing. All this information, including the year your registration was accepted and the registration number, can be taken directly from your earlier registration form and your registration certificate.

EXAMPLE: Mary Hales decides to supplement the registration for her LOANIT package because she wants to put out a second version and rename the first one "LOANIT #1." Despite the fact that the reason Mary is filing is to change the name of her program, she puts the original name, LOANIT, in this space.

Space B: Correction

(B) Correction	**LOCATION AND NATURE OF INCORRECT INFORMATION IN BASIC REGISTRATION:** Line Number . . . . Line Heading or Description . . . .
	INCORRECT INFORMATION AS IT APPEARS IN BASIC REGISTRATION:
	CORRECTED INFORMATION:
	EXPLANATION OF CORRECTION: (Optional)

Before filling in this space, you must decide whether you are making a correction (Space B) or a change or amplification (Space C). Once you do so, fill in either Space B or Space C, not both.

Space B is to be completed if you are correcting an error that was made at the time of the original registration. For example, if you gave the year of your birth as 1947, and you were born in 1957, you would use Space B. In the first section of Space B, simply put the wrong information exactly as it was originally given in Space B.

EXAMPLE: When registering GOTTCHA, Carl Jones incorrectly gave his address as 110 - 11th Street in the space entitled "Correspondence" on both his TX and PA registrations. His correct address is 101 - 11th Street. Carl must fill out two CA forms, one for the TX registration and one for the PA registration.

In the first section of Space B, Carl puts the line number and line heading where the incorrect information is located on the earlier registration. Thus, in the earlier TX form, the incorrect information was found on Line 9 under the heading of "Correspondence." Accordingly, Carl would put:

LOCATION AND NATURE OF INCORRECT INFORMATION IN BASIC REGISTRATION:
Line Number ... *9* ...... Line Heading or Description *CORRESPONDENCE*

Next Carl turns to the second section of Space B:

INCORRECT INFORMATION AS IT APPEARS IN BASIC REGISTRATION:
CARL JONES, 110-11TH STREET

Here Carl puts "CARL JONES, 110-11TH STREET," just as he did in his original application.

The third section of Space B asks for the correct information:

CORRECTED INFORMATION:
CARL JONES, 101-11TH PLACE

Carl puts "CARL JONES 101 - 11TH PLACE."

The fourth section permits you to explain the error if you choose, but it isn't necessary. In the above example, "I goofed" or "Out to lunch" occurs to me, but that isn't likely to help the Copyright Office much, so why bother?

Space C: Amplification

	LOCATION AND NATURE OF INFORMATION IN BASIC REGISTRATION TO BE AMPLIFIED:
© Amplification	Line Number . . . . Line Heading or Description . . . .
	AMPLIFIED INFORMATION:
	EXPLANATION OF AMPLIFIED INFORMATION: (Optional)

If some information has changed (and supplemental registration is the proper way to notify the Copyright Office--refer to Chapter 9), use Space C. This is where you make changes in the title of your work, or your address, or include information you left out on the original form. Remember, if the information you forgot should have been caught by the Copyright Office, send a letter and not a supplemental registration.

EXAMPLE 1: BCA Graphics changes the title of QUILTIT, which Kendra Salone did as a work for hire, to QUILTIT 1.0.

EXAMPLE 2: Mary Hales moves from Los Angeles to New York and wants her address information to be kept up to date so that anyone wanting to contact her to get permission to use her program will be able to do so.

To make this sort of change, first indicate the line and line heading of the line affected by the change or addition.

EXAMPLE 1: BCA Graphics lists Line 1 and "TITLE OF WORK" for their QUILTIT name change.

EXAMPLE 2: Mary Hales puts Line 9 and the heading "CORRESPONDENCE" for her address change. Remember, on some forms the correspondence line would be Line 7.

Next, tell the Copyright Office what the change or addition consists of.

EXAMPLE 1: BCA Graphics fills in this space "CHANGED THE TITLE OF THIS WORK FROM QUILTIT TO QUILTIT 1.0."

EXAMPLE 2: Mary Hales says "ADDRESS CHANGED FROM MARY HALES, 24566 W. COMPUT-ERVINE AVE., LOS ANGELES" to new address: "MARY HALES, 48539 W. 999TH PLACE, NEW YORK, NEW YORK 00000."

Again, you may explain why you are making this change or addition.

Space D: Continuation

<table>
<tr><td>**CONTINUATION OF:** (Check which) ☐ PART B OR ☐ PART C</td><td>**D**
Continuation</td></tr>
</table>

If the information in Space B or Space C exceeds the space allotted, you may continue your explanation or description in this space.

Space E: Deposit Account and Mailing Instructions

<table>
<tr><td>**DEPOSIT ACCOUNT:** If the registration fee is to be charged to a Deposit Account established in the Copyright Office. give name and number of Account:

Name .... Account Number ....

CORRESPONDENCE: Give name and address to which correspondence should be sent:

Name .... Apt. No. ....

Address ....
      (Number and Street,)   (City)   (State)   (ZIP Code)</td><td>**E**
Deposit
Account and
Mailing
Instructions</td></tr>
</table>

This space asks for the same information as line 9 on the original registration for Form TX and SE, and line 7 for Forms PA, VA and SR. Again, if you have a deposit account, you need to give the name and account number. Next, provide the name and address of the person to be contacted regarding this filing. Refer to the registration sections above for more information on completing this space, if necessary.

Space F: Certification

<table>
<tr><td>**CERTIFICATION** ✱ I, the undersigned, hereby certify that I am the: (Check one)

☐ author ☐ other copyright claimant ☐ owner of exclusive right(s) ☐ authorized agent of: ....
                     (Name of author or other copyright clamant or owner of exclusive right(s))
of the work identified in this application and that the statements made by me in this application are correct to the best of my knowledge.

Handwritten signature: (X) ....

Typed or printed name. ....

Date: ....

✱ 17 USC §506(e) FALSE REPRESENTATION—Any person who knowingly makes a false representation of a material fact in the application for copyright registration provided for by section 409. or in any written statement filed in connection with the application. shall be fined not more than $2.500</td><td>**F**
Certification
(Application
must be
signed)</td></tr>
</table>

Here you must indicate your relationship to the work, if you are the author, other copyright claimant, owner of exclusive rights or agent of any of these, and you must sign the form. Again, refer to our discussion under Space 10 of the original registraton form.

Space G: Address for Return of Certificate

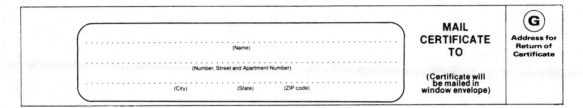

Make sure your address in this space is legible. It will constitute the return address for your Certificate of Supplemental Registration.

G. Filing the CA Form

Send the CA form to the Copyright Office along with a fee of $10. Make your check or money order payable to the Register of Copyrights. No deposit is necessary with a CA form registration. Send form and payment to:

Register of Copyrights
Library of Congress
Washington, D.C. 20559

H. Certificate of Supplemental Registration

You will be issued a separate registration number and certificate for your supplemental registration. It will be linked to your original registration. This means that you, or anyone needing information regarding your registration, will know there is a supplemental registration on file if an inquiry is made regarding the work. The Certificate of Supplemental Registration is a copy of that form, with the number, date and certification stamp on the form. Put it in your file.

I. Expedited Registration

In our discussion of copyright infringement contained in Chapter 13, we noted that an expedited registration procedure is available for those who cannot wait through the eight week period customarily required for processing a registration application. To take advantage of this procedure, you or your attorney must:

■ Write "Special Handling" on the outside of your registration envelope;

■ Enclose an additional $120 registration fee (that makes $130 total);

■ Also request "certified copies" at a cost of $3 each. These will be needed for trial in the event your action goes that far.

•CHAPTER 12•

Transfers of Copyrights: Terminations of Transfers

A. Introduction

In prior chapters we discussed the methods available under United States copyright law for protecting various types of software. We learned, essentially, that copyright "protection" means that the author (or owner of a work made for hire) can prevent others from exercising any of the exclusive copyright rights without permission. Here we look at the ins and outs of granting others permission to use your copyrighted work in exchange for reasonable compensation.

To fully understand what follows, it's important to remember an important point. A copyright is a bundle of separate rights, rather than a single entity. As we mentioned in Chapter 3, a copyright includes the separate rights to:

■ Sell;

■ Display or perform;

■ Make copies; and

■ Make derivative works of an original work of authorship.

Each of these individual rights can be divided in a variety of ways. Here are some examples:

■ A software distribution company can be exclusively licensed to sell (exploit) the right to distribute a particular program in a particular geographical area, while another company can be licensed to do the same thing in another geographical area;

■ An author or other copyright owner can separately license a program to one software company for copying and sale in connection with all personal computers in Europe, and to another software company for similar use in the United States. This is an example of an "exclusive territorial license";

■ An author or owner can exclusively license (grant rights to) one company to sell her software everyplace in the world, for all purposes. This is commonly referred to as "granting" or "licensing world-wide rights";

■ Non-exclusive licenses can be granted to any number of people. For example, using non-exclusive licenses, you can simultaneously license your program for all uses to any number of competing personal computer manufacturers. See Section C, below, for a discussion of non-exclusive licenses.

To summarize, you may transfer your copyright in bits and pieces, transfer all the rights at once, or in almost any way you can think of. Not surprisingly, taking advantage of this sort of flexibility is often at the heart of a successful plan for getting a copyrighted product distributed and sold in the marketplace.

In this chapter we review the different ways you license others to use your work. Then we look at the other legal ways you can transfer copyright rights and compare them to the license process. But, before we do this, let's discuss two types of common transactions involving copyrighted works which do not constitute transfers of copyright ownership as such. These are single copy sales and non-exclusive licenses.

JARGON NOTE: An agreement giving permission and changing ownership is known by several different names, including "contract," "assignment," "grant of right," and just plain "agreement." However, the term most commonly used in the software business is "license." A license is simply a contract which gives someone permission to do or use something. From a software author's point of view, it normally means granting (licensing) a publisher, distributor, manufacturer or business user to exercise some or all of the rights of the copyright owner. In other words, a license is a written agreement or contract incorporating the duration and scope of the permission granted. You can accomplish these things by calling your written agreement a contract or a grant of rights.

B. Single Copy Sales

As we discussed in Chapter 3, if you sell or otherwise transfer an individual copy (or ten, or a thousand) of your program or other work to another person, you do not normally transfer any copyright ownership. An example is selling a book in a bookstore, or a copy of Carl Jones' computer game, GOTTCHA, at Gameland. The sale allows the owner to do as she pleases with the copy she buys. She can tear it, mark it or resell it. However, the purchaser does not have the right to run off ten copies and sell them, since you have not licensed her to do this. Chapter 4, Section J discusses in detail the things an owner of a copy can do with a computer program, such as modify it for her own use and make a back-up copy.

SHRINK-WRAPPED LICENSE NOTE: In the context of single copy sales of software, there is often an attempt to use a so-called "license" for the purpose of restricting rights of the purchaser. If you've bought software over the counter, you will be familiar with the sort of license agreement which is printed on, or enclosed in, the packaging that says something to the effect that if you break the package seal, you have agreed to the terms of the license, which limits your rights to use the software. One common restriction prohibits modifying the software in any way, even for your own use. This sort of provision has not yet been tested in court, but established contract law principles dictate that it probably has no legal effect.*

Another way software publishers have tried to restrict the use of over-the-counter software is to provide an "update" or "warranty" card with the software. If you sign it, you not only qualify for the warranty protection or update service offered, but simultaneously agree to the terms of the "Software Licensing

---

* Louisiana has enacted a software license enforcement act which mandates that a consumer be bound by the specific terms of the manufacturer's license agreement if a software package is opened or used. It remains to be seen if other states will adopt similar laws.

Agreement" included in the package. This sort of agreement is also not likely to be binding in a court of law. This is because the warranty offered is often required by law anyway, and the "updates" are commonly not really updates, but error corrections which, if uncorrected, would justify your requesting a refund, or perhaps even suing the publisher for negligence. In any event, these over-the-counter transactions do not transfer copyright ownership. They merely transfer a copy of the copyrighted work. Any so-called licenses that accompany them are generally designed to restrict rights you already have, not grant more.

C. Non-Exclusive Licenses

A non-exclusive license amounts to the sharing of ownership in a copyright right rather than a transference of ownership. The copyright owner (the licensor) can share a right with (license) as many different people (the licensees) as he wishes. Non-exclusive licensees are given permission to exercise the right in question, but may not prevent the owner from giving others similar rights, unless restrictions in their license contract so provide. In short, a non-exclusive license merely gives the licensee authority to exercise a right, but bestows none of the powers of ownership (e.g., the right to keep others from exercising the right). The only real restriction on the number of non-exclusive licenses a copyright owner can grant is the marketplace itself. If too many people are granted a non-exclusive right to do the same thing, the right isn't worth much.

It's important to understand, however, that just because you grant a non-exclusive right to use one of your bundle of copyright rights, it doesn't mean you give up any of the rest of your bundle of rights. For example, if you grant Game-sell, Gamehype and Gameland a non-exclusive license to sell your hot new comput-er program for identifying and locating lost cats, you do not give them the right

to make derivative works, such as modi-fying the program to find dogs, or any of the other rights which make up a copy-right. You should also realize by now that non-exclusive licenses (like all other licenses) can be restricted in all sorts of ways. Thus, you can grant a non-exclusive license to sell your pro-gram for use on one particular microcom-puter in one country (or county) for a set period of time.

EXAMPLE 1: Mary Hales grants a non-exclusive license to use her loan process-ing package, LOANIT, to Big Bank, Middle Bank and Little Bank. This means they may all use their copy of LOANIT simul-taneously, subject to any restrictions Mary has written into the agreement.

EXAMPLE 2: Mary Hales grants a non-exclusive worldwide license to sell LOAN-IT for use on all computers to Financial Package Sell (FPS) and to Bank Rite Soft-ware. Both companies may sell LOANIT. Mary may grant other non-exclusive rights unless she has agreed not to. In this context, it is common for an author to grant several non-exclusive rights and also agree not to grant more.

EXAMPLE 3: Mary Hales grants a non-exclusive license to FPS to make deriva-tive works based on LOANIT, provided she gets 20% royalties (payment) on the sale of any derivative works they make. By making her grant non-exclusive, Mary retains the right to make LOANIT deriva-tives herself, or to grant the right to anyone or everyone else, as she sees fit.

D. Copyright Transfers: Exclusive Licenses

Now that we have disposed of situa-tions where ownership in a copyright is not transferred but only shared on a restricted basis, let's look at actual transfers of copyright ownership. Assume that Mary Hales granted FPS an exclusive license to make derivative versions of her LOANIT loan processing package. This means that FPS is the only entity authorized to do this. Because this exclusive right is one of the bundle of copyright rights, Mary has, in fact, given up or transferred part of her copyright ownership.

As we mentioned, exclusive licenses always involve an ownership transfer, no matter how limited they may be to time, machine, geography, etc. Thus, even if Mary only licensed FPS the exclusive right to market LOANIT for a two-week period in Rhode Island, for the YumYum Computer, FPS would own part of Mary's copyright. Again, at the risk of beating this particular point to the consistency of tapioca pudding, actual ownership (i.e., exclusive rights) should be distinguished from the shared ownership of a non-exclusive license. As discussed in Section C, above, shared ownership means that the licensee may exercise the specific right granted in the license but has no right to prevent others from doing so. Outright ownership of an exclusive right, however, no matter how limited, involves the right to prevent others from exercising that same right. Let's look at some typical exclusive licenses.

EXAMPLE 1: Carl Jones grants Gameland an exclusive worldwide right to sell his computer game, GOTTCHA, for home computers for three years. This means that during this time period, neither Carl himself, nor anyone else, can legally sell GOTTCHA for home computer use.

EXAMPLE 2: Carl Jones grants Video Ace an exclusive license to sell the video game version of GOTTCHA for video arcades. Since this is not for home computer use, this license does not infringe on the license granted in Example #1.

EXAMPLE 3: Carl Jones grants the Yes Dress Department Store chain the exclusive right to sell the handheld version of GOTTCHA. Carl has the power to do this only if a handheld computer is not considered to be a home computer (see Example #1). This is where the fine print in the license contract comes in. Always be sure you read your license contract carefully.

EXAMPLE 4: Mary Hales grants Bank Rite the exclusive right to make derivative works of her LOANIT program for mainframe computers. She grants the exclusive right to make derivatives for all computers other than mainframes to Financial Package Sell.

EXAMPLE 5: Mary Hales grants FPS an exclusive license to market LOANIT on the West Coast for five years. She grants Tom Fool Systems the exclusive right to market on the East Coast and in Europe.*

EXAMPLE 6: BCA Graphics grants an exclusive license to sell, make copies, make derivatives, perform and display QUILTIT to Quilt Designs of America. This is often called transferring "all rights," since all of the exclusive bundle of copyright rights have been transferred in one license.

COPYRIGHT REGISTRATION NOTE: As in Example #6 above, all of the bundle of rights which make up a copyright are often exclusively licensed to one individual or entity. If this occurs, the copyright itself has been legally transferred or assigned to that person or

---

* Inside the U.S., copyrights are often divided by geography. On the international market, exclusive licenses for software are commonly defined by country (or continent), make of computer, and sometimes language (e.g., all French speaking areas such as France, Martinique, Haiti, and Algeria).

entity and they become the sole copyright owner. This entitles them to refer to themselves as copyright claimant on the registration form (see Chapter 11, Section C). However, if fewer than all of the bundle of copyright rights which make up a copyright are exclusively transferred, or they are all transferred but to different people, the person receiving the rights (the transferee) only qualifies as a copyright owner, not the copyright claimant, for copyright registration purposes. In other words, the original author is the copyright claimant unless all the exclusive rights end up in a single person's (or entity's) hands.

E. Copyright Transfers and Assignments

Here we digress to discuss terminology for a moment. Up to this point, we have used the words "transfer" and "exclusive license" more or less interchangeably. This makes sense because, from a legal standpoint, a transfer and an exclusive license of a copyright right are the same thing. Now, let's introduce a subtle distinction. In intellectual property law circles, the term "exclusive license" tends to be more commonly used when the copyright owner (often, but not always, the author) retains at least some of the bundle of copyright rights or, if none are retained, she has parcelled them out to different entities. This is distinguished from the situation when all exclusive copyright rights are simultaneously granted to one person or entity. If this occurs, it is more common to use either the term "transfer" or another legal term, "assignment."

EXAMPLE: BCA Graphics decides to unload QUILTIT to another company and sells all of its exclusive copyright rights to High Tech Design, Inc. This sale would ordinarily be called a "transfer of copyright" or an "assignment of

all rights." Assume now that BCA decides it wants to get out of the distributing business, but thinks it might want to develop some future spinoffs of QUILTIT (i.e., derivative works). In this situation, it could grant High Tech Design, Inc. the exclusive rights to make copies, market and display QUILTIT, but reserve the exclusive right to prepare derivative works. This sale would commonly be referred to as the grant of an "exclusive license" to the rights in question.

F. Transfer Documents

Let's now examine how copyright ownership can be transferred or licensed. Here are the basics:

■ The copyright transfer must be in writing;

■ The transfer contract must be signed by the owner of the right(s) being transferred.

As we've seen, transfer of copyright ownership normally falls into one of several broad categories. As we discussed above, however, lawyers often use several terms to describe the same basic type of transfer document.

1. Licenses

Exclusive licenses are commonly used in regard to intellectual property rights, such as copyright, patent, trademark or trade secret, because they allow for the granting of permission to use the particular right for a specific time under set conditions and for an established price, which is commonly based on some percentage of either sales, net income or profits. It's important to understand that the word "license" is not a magic term and need never be used as part of a contract to transfer the exclusive ownership of a copyright right. Indeed, it is not uncommon to make exactly the same sort of transfer that is normally called a license without ever using that word. One alternative term in common usage is "grant of rights." Another is "transfer of rights," which we discuss just below.

2. Assignments and Transfers

As we noted in the introduction to this chapter, an assignment or transfer contract is normally used to sell an entire copyright. That is, an assignment or transfer is made without restriction, or, if there are restrictions, they must be enforced through the courts. This is in comparison to a license, where permission to exploit the copyright right is automatically revoked if the terms of the contract are violated or the license expires. (This doesn't mean the courts aren't sometimes necessary here, too.) As with exclusive license transfers, an assignment or transfer must be in writing, and can be written as simply as:

■ I hereby assign (transfer) all rights, title and interest in and to the copyright in LOANIT to Financial Package Sell. Signed: Mary Hales 8/5/85

An assignment may also be made of only one of the bundle of copyright rights:

■ I hereby assign (transfer) the right to make derivative works in the copyrighted work, LOANIT, to Financial Package Sell. Signed: Mary Hales 6/22/84

An assignment (transfer) can be used to divide copyright rights. But, if this occurs, and especially if the assignments are limited in any way, it is more common to call the agreement a license:

■ I hereby assign (license) the right to sell the video game version of GOTTCHA to Video Ace. Signed: Carl Jones 12/9/84

■ I hereby assign (license) the right to sell the home computer version of GOTTCHA to Gameland. Signed: Carl Jones 12/9/84

3. Other Contracts

By now, you should have grasped the point. While the language used to describe copyright transfers falls into several general descriptive categories, these are not necessarily determinative of the substance of the agreement. To know what has been transferred, you must read the contract provisions. The important point to remember is that any transfer of ownership must be in writing, and in order to effect a transfer of ownership, must be exclusive.

If you are contemplating transferring your copyright ownership or purchasing someone else's copyright rights, you need good information as to the ins and outs, as well as the effects, of license and transfer contracts. The best source of this information, complete with sample contracts, is Legal Care For Your Software, by Daniel Remer (Nolo Press).

4. Wills and Trusts

A will is also an effective copyright transfer document. You might inherit a copyright, or part of a copyright. Likewise, you can will a copyright, in whole or in part, to your spouse, children or whomever you please. Copyright rights can also be placed in living (intervivos) or testamentary trusts.*

---

* The entire subject of trusts is far beyond the scope of this book. However, an excellent resource for understanding the basic types of trusts used to leave property outside of probate is Plan Your Estate: Wills, Probate Avoidance, Trusts and Taxes, by Denis Clifford, Nolo Press.

5. Operation of Law

This category refers to all those transfers which occur not because the owner expressly intends them, but because the law says they should. Here are the most common ways copyright ownership is transferred under this category:

■ Intestate succession: This occurs if you die without a will or other estate plan. Your property, including your copyrights, go the way the law of the state of your residence says they do. This is normally first to your spouse and children. If you have neither, to your other relatives;

■ Bankruptcy: Your copyrights are property and can be sold to pay your debts;

■ Divorce: Depending on state law, your spouse may be able to claim a share of your copyright at divorce. In most states, these are called equitable distribution laws. In eight western states, including California, your copyright for a work written during marriage will be considered to be community property, and its value is decided 50-50 with your spouse at divorce.

■ Other court order.

G. The Rights of a Copyright Purchaser or Transferee

When an exclusive copyright right is licensed or transferred, whether in whole or in part the transferee of that right owns it, subject, of course, to any limitations that are part of the transfer or license contract. As the new owner, he may exclude all others from exercising the particular right transferred to him. To accomplish this, he may avail himself of the courts. Persons who become copyright owners through a transfer are entitled to record their ownership inter-ests with the Copyright Office. If they do, they gain valuable legal protection.

EXAMPLE: Carl Jones transfers the right to make copies, sell and display GOTTCHA to Gameland, exclusively. He sells Larry Loafer the right to make derivative works based on GOTTCHA. Who is the copyright owner? The copyright is held by Larry, Gameland and Carl. As far as the Copyright Office is concerned, all are owners of some of the copyright ownership rights, although it's hard to see what Carl really has left. In any case, they are not joint owners because their rights are exclusive of one another.* As no one person or entity owns all the rights, the copyright is still properly listed at the Copyright Office as belonging to Carl as copyright claimant. Similarly, Carl's name will continue on the copyright notice. This is because even though Carl has no rights left, he has not sold all of his rights to one entity. Larry and Gameland may record the ownership interest transferred by Carl with the U.S. Copyright Office. We discuss how to do this, and the resulting advantages, in Section K, below.

Can persons who have become owners by means of a transfer turn around and transfer their new rights? It depends on the terms of the written document (contract) by which they gained their rights. Some documents of transfer permit such transfers, while others do not. Generally, if a transferee receives (purchases) a particular copyright right, or all the bundle of rights to a particular copyright, he can do with them as he pleases. However, if he signs an exclusive license contract with a number of restrictions on use--such as to the type of machine, area, time, etc.--the terms of the license contract will determine whether or not it can be transferred to a third party.

EXAMPLE 1: Carl Jones transfers the exclusive right to sell his computer

_____

* Co-authors are considered to jointly own all of the exclusive rights. Here, on the other hand, the ownership is not considered joint, since the individual rights are separately owned.

game, GOTTCHA, to Gameland under the following terms:

"Carl Jones, copyright owner, hereby grants to Gameland the exclusive right to market the computer game GOTTCHA, worldwide, for a period of two years, unless this right is otherwise terminated as provided herein. Said exclusive right cannot be sold, assigned, licensed or otherwise transferred to any third party." Under this type of contract, the copyright right transferred to Gameland can't be further transferred. In this situation, the contract would also specifically deal with what happens to the copyright if Gameland itself is purchased by another company.

EXAMPLE 2: "Carl Jones hereby transfers all copyright rights in GOTTCHA for the life of the copyright to FPS." Since FPS completely replaces Carl as copyright owner and claimant, they may divide or sell the GOTTCHA copyright in any way they wish.

H. Rights Retained by Copyright Author After Transfer

We have learned that the full bundle of rights contained in a copyright can be transferred, leaving no ownership rights in the original copyright holder. Even though this is true, the copyright author does retain several potentially important ownership benefits even after such a full transfer. These include:

1. Filing Documents: The right to file documents with the Copyright Office regarding the work, including:

■ Supplemental registrations. Certain categories of new information or changes in the information supplied in the original registration may be supplemented by the author, according to the procedures outlined in Chapter 11, Section F, even though the author no longer owns any of the exclusive copyright rights.

■ Notice regarding duration. As you may remember, the duration of a copyright is calculated upon the life of the author (where the author is one or more individuals), and the author is presumed by law to be dead after a certain number of years. This presumption can be corrected by the author if she lives longer than the date in question.

■ Notice regarding the status of a transfer (e.g., terminated or revoked). In the event the author has only transferred ownership of her copyright for a set term, she will want to notify the Copyright Office when the term has expired, so she can expressly reclaim her ownership on the record. Similar notification will be desirable when a transfer is revoked because the transferee did not abide by the terms of his license, or for some other reason.

Your letter to the Copyright Office should say something like the following:

December 12, 198_

Dear Examiner:

My copyright registration #12789, entitled GOTTCHA, was transferred in full to HankyPank, Inc. for a period of five (5) years, commencing on December 11, 198_. This letter is to notify you that the transfer has terminated and I am the sole owner of copyright #12789.

Sincerely,

Carl Jones

---

2. Revocation of transfers or licenses after 35 years. The copyright author or his heirs retain the right to revoke transfer after 35 years. See Section O, below.

3. _Moral Rights_: In some countries outside the U.S., the author automatically retains certain other rights in his work, referred to as "moral rights" (or, "droit moral"). We discuss moral rights in more detail in Chapter 14, on international copyrights.

I. Copyright Transfers and Copyright Duration

The transfer of a copyright, or a portion of one, has no effect on how long a copyright lasts. Most rights are still based on the life of the author plus 50 years, or, in the case of a work for hire, the 75/100-year ownership period. See Chapter 5 for details on copyright duration.

EXAMPLE

Event 1: Carl Jones sells the copyright to his computer game, GOTTCHA, to Larry Loafer.

Event 2: Larry wills his copyright to his son Larry Loafer, Jr.

Event 3: Carl Jones dies.

Event 4: Thirty years later, Larry dies.

Event 5: Larry, Jr. receives a copyright good for 20 more years. Why? Because the copyright was good for the life of the author (Carl) plus 50 years.

J. Recording Copyright Transfers

1. Why Record a Copyright Transfer?

Recording any copyright transfer you receive, whether of the entire copyright or one or more of the bundle of rights, is important for two reasons. First, it helps facilitate the establishment of legal priorities between copyright transferees should the transferor make overlapping or confusing grants. And second, it allows the copyright transferee to take full advantage of the additional benefits provided by registration.*

Here are examples of contexts in which transfers should be recorded:

EXAMPLE 1: Carl Jones transfers the rights to make copies of and sell his computer game, GOTTCHA, under a written contract, to Quickbuck, the new marketing company owned by his buddy, Tom Tootbyte. Since Carl registered GOTTCHA soon after he completed it, Tom need only record the transfer document. Carl will still be listed as the GOTTCHA copyright owner in the copyright notice, as he retained the rights to display the work and to make derivative works.

EXAMPLE 2: As Tom Tootbyte is not prohibited by his contract with Carl from transferring his rights to the GOTTCHA copyright to a third party, he transfers all of his rights to International Package Sell, under a written contract. All IPS need do is record the transfer contract along with the original registration.

EXAMPLE 3: Mary Hales transfers all of her copyright rights to the LOANIT loan processing package to Big Bank soon after she contracts to write the program for them. Big Bank files the original copyright registration listing themselves as the copyright claimant, with Mary as the author. Big Bank is listed as the copyright owner in the notice. Big Bank then sells Small Bank an exclusive right to use the program in Arkansas. Small Bank can record this transfer following the instructions set out later in this chapter.

---

* If the copyright has already been registered, recordation allows the new owner to benefit from the registration the same as the original owner. If the copyright has not already been registered, this must be accomplished before the recordation of transfer can be made.

EXAMPLE 4: On her own time, Kendra Salone writes a new program which creates geometric designs for Christmas wrapping paper. She forgets to register it and several years later assigns the right to market and make copies of the program to BCA Graphics, retaining the right to prepare derivative works for herself. Before BCA can record the transfer of the two exclusive rights with the Copyright Office, they must register the program. They can then record.

2. The Effect of Recordation on Copyright Conflicts

As we mentioned at the beginning of this section, an important reason for recording a copyright transfer is to resolve disputes over conflicting and overlapping rights. Non-exclusive licenses, as well as exclusive licenses, may be recorded. Let's take a closer look at how recordation will help sort out disputes.

What happens, for example, if Carl Jones grants an exclusive license to sell his computer game, GOTTCHA, to Dataland and another identical exclusive license to Gameland? Who's entitled to the exclusive license? Or, what if Carl grants a non-exclusive license to Dataland and then decides to give Gameland an exclusive license? Who prevails?

Fortunately, there are rules for solving these problems, as follows:

■ As between two conflicting exclusive rights, the first one granted is entitled to protection if it is recorded within one month (two months if executed outside the U.S.;

■ If recordation is delayed beyond a month, however, then the first transfer recorded is entitled to protection (even if it was the second one granted), so long as it was received in good faith (without knowledge of the earlier one);

■ A non-exclusive license will prevail (1) over a later granted exclusive license and (2) over an earlier granted exclusive license if the non-exclusive license is granted before the earlier exclusive license is recorded and the person receiving the non-exclusive license had no knowledge of the earlier exclusive license. [17 USC 205] For these rules to operate, however, the non-exclusive license must be in writing and signed by the owner of the rights being licensed.*

Let's look at some examples of how the principles outlined above can be used to resolve conflicts between licenses.

EXAMPLE 1: Mary Hales gives a non-exclusive license for her loan processing package, LOANIT, to Financial Package Sell in 1985. Big Bank then asks for an exclusive on the right to sell LOANIT, and offers Mary big bucks. Somehow, Mary forgets about her earlier non-exclusive license contract to FPS and grants Big Bank exclusive rights. Big Bank then tries to stop FPS from selling LOANIT. They fail and FPS wins the right to keep selling LOANIT. Why? Because FPS legally bought their non-exclusive right first, the license was in writing, and was thus provable in court. Had FPS recorded its non-exclusive license (which it was under no obligation to do), it would have had an even easier time establishing its priority date. Incidentally, Big Bank has a legal action against Mary because she represented the rights sold to them as being exclusive, when in fact they were non-exclusive.

EXAMPLE 2: Now let's change a few facts in this example. This time Mary transfers Financial Package Sell an exclusive license to sell LOANIT in 1985. FPS does not record the transfer. In 1986, Mary transfers the exclusive right to sell LOANIT to Big Bank, who does not know of the earlier transfer. Big Bank

---

* There are no requirements for non-exclusive licenses to be in writing, since they don't transfer ownership. However, if a non-exclusive license is to prevail over a later granted exclusive license, it must be in writing. The moral? As with other legal interactions, a written document is best.

records the transfer in good faith. Big Bank owns the right to sell LOANIT, and FPS is out of luck. Why? As between two conflicting transfers, Big Bank recorded first in good faith. The result would have been different, however, had Big Bank actually known of the earlier transfer. Then, FPS would be entitled to protection. In this case, FPS has a legal action against Mary for selling what she didn't own.

EXAMPLE 3: To continue the previous example, if FPS had received its transfer on May 1, 1985 in the U.S., and recorded it by June 1, 1985, it would have prevailed over Big Bank even had Big Bank gotten a good faith transfer on May 2, 1985 and recorded immediately. Why? Because FPS recorded within the statutory 30-day period, which guarantees full protection.

EXAMPLE 4: FPS receives its transfer on May 1, 1985 and records on December 1, 1985. FPS will prevail over all transfers recorded after December 1, 1985. This includes transfers executed both prior to May 1, 1985 and after.

K. How to Record a Copyright Transfer of a Registered Work

Recording a copyright transfer (or grant of a non-exclusive license) involving a previously registered work is not difficult. Just follow the four-step process set out below:

STEP 1: Send a copy of your written transfer document (or non-exclusive license). This may be a contract, license, grant of rights, assignment, transfer, will, court order or any other written document.

STEP 2: Include the title of the work as given on the original copyright registration and the original copyright registration number. This information can be obtained from the transferor of the right. It is also a good idea to include the original author and copyright registration date, if you can get that information, even though it is not required.

STEP 3: Make a $10 check or money order payable to the Register of Copyrights if the transfer contract is six pages or less. (If there is writing on both sides of a page, it counts as two pages.) Enclose an additional 50 cents for each page over six.

STEP 4: Send all the above to:

Register of Copyrights
Library of Congress
Washington, D.C. 20559

Within six to eight weeks you should receive a Certificate of Recordation from the Copyright Office showing your transfer document (or non-exclusive license) has been recorded.

THE REUNION

L. How to Record a Copyright Transfer of an Unregistered Work

First, review Chapters 8 - 11 on registration before reading this section. There you will find an explanation of how to register a work with the Copyright Office for the first time. Those procedures should be followed, with a few changes. Let's review the proper procedure:

■ Use the correct copyright registration form, depending on your work (e.g., TX, PA, SR). This is exactly the same form you would use if you were registering your work from scratch;

■ Copyright claimant space 4;

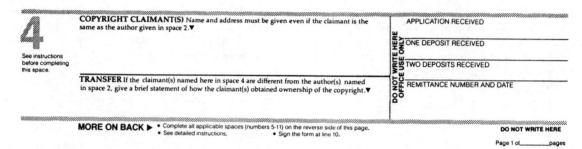

This space only changes from the examples set out in Chapter 11 if you have received a transfer of the complete bundle of rights and own the whole copyright. If you do, this space should not contain the same information as the author section. Instead, it should contain your name and address as the owner by transfer. Explain how you received ownership in a few words, e.g., by written contract, by will, by transfer from author, by transfer from another transferee, etc. Do not attach a copy of the document(s)

of transfer (e.g., contract, license, will);

NOTE: To repeat, if you receive all the bundle of copyright rights by transfer, it means the author space (#2) on the copyright form will be different from "Copyright Claimant's" space. If you do not own all of the rights, the author (or owner of a work made for hire) remains as the copyright claimant.

■ Certification Space

The second change should be made in the section entitled "Certification." This asks you to indicate whether you are an owner of an exclusive right(s) or whether you are the copyright claimant. You are the copyright claimant only if you own the total bundle of rights. If

you own less than all the total copyright, you are a copyright owner.

See Chapter 11, Section E for the description of the Certificate of Copyright you should receive from the Copyright Office after six to eight weeks in addition to your Certificate of Recordation.

M. Other Steps to Protect Your Copyright Transfer

It is possible to receive what is called a Certificate of Acknowledgement from any state or federal judge. This acknowledges your copyright transfer. It is different than the Certificate of Recordation the Copyright Office gives you. The Certificate of Acknowledgement provides prima facie evidence that the copyright transfer was made. This would seem to be valuable until you realize that recordation itself does the same thing.

Nevertheless, if you want a Certificate of Acknowledgement, you get it from any state or federal judge, or justice of the peace. If the transfer occurs outside the U.S., the Certificate can be issued by a diplomat or Consular Office of the U.S. Doing this gives you a little extra protection, at least in theory. If you have an acknowledgement certificate and later there is a court fight over the transfer, the statements in the transfer are presumed true unless successfully rebutted by the other side. If you get this document (most people don't), just keep it for your files. Do not send it to the Copyright Office.

N. Termination of a Copyright Transfer

Transfers of copyrights are sometimes open-ended as far as time is concerned, with provisions providing for automatic termination in the event the terms of the transfer are not met by the transferee. For example, Mary Hales might transfer the right to use her loan processing package, LOANIT, to FPS for the life of the copyright, as long FPS sells 2,000 copies a year. Other types of transfers only last for a finite period of time specified in the transfer document (contract, license, will). This can be anywhere from one day to the life of the copyright.

If some event occurs which you believe terminates a copyright transfer, your first step is to notify the transferee that you claim the rights have reverted to you. The copyright author, the author's heirs or an authorized agent can do this in writing. Be sure to keep a file copy. If more than one author or heir is involved, the rules are a little complicated, and unless you have all appointed the same agent--which can be one of you--you should see a lawyer.

O. Revocation of Copyright Transfer by Author or Author's Heirs

Suppose a transfer gives the transferee the unlimited exclusive right to market a software product for the life of the copyright. This means the author has given up her copyright forever, right? Wrong. Despite the open-ended nature of the transfer, the author can revoke it either 35 years after the date the product is first published by the transferee, or 40 years from the date of transfer, whichever comes first. Thus, if the transfer is made in 1986, and the product is first published 25 years later (e.g., in 2010 A.D.), the author can revoke in 2026 A.D., 40 years after the transfer. If the transfer does not include the right to market, the period of time is a flat 35 years [17 USC 203].

The "right to revoke" rule has one extremely important limitation, however. Unless the revocation is made within five years of the date you become eligible to exercise this right, it is waived. This means you give it up for all legal purposes. Thus, in our example directly above, the author or his heirs would have from 2026 A.D. to 2031 A.D. to exercise his option to revoke. If this is not done in that time, the transfer would continue for the life of the copyright.

It may be helpful to think of this five-year period as a "window." You can go through it to revoke a license only while it's open.

The more practically inclined among you might be wondering why we're discussing this right at all. After all, 2026 A.D. is a long way off, especially when the economic life expectancy of most computer-related products is taken into consideration. The reason is that an author's children or other heirs can inherit this right to revoke. Thus, if an author dies 25 years after making a transfer, his heirs would have the right to revoke between 10 and 15 years later. Or, in other words, this rule could have important consequences should your underlying work prove to have extraordinary longevity.

This longevity factor works against the rule having much impact for most works in the computer field, since 35 years is longer than the valuable life of almost all such products. However, there is one situation where revocation rights can be important, even in the software context. If the owner of the right to prepare derivative works actually produces one, the copyright in that work belongs to that owner the same as would

an original work of authorship. However, once the transfer is revoked, the right to prepare derivative works disappears. Also, the now former owner cannot make derivative works from any derivative works prepared during the period of ownership. For example, suppose Mary transfers all rights in LOANIT to Big Bank. Over the next couple of decades, Big Bank prepares a number of derivative works which improve LOANIT, in keeping with the changes in technology which occur during the same time. If Mary or her heirs later revoke, Big Bank may use its derivative works prepared prior to revocation. But, it cannot make any further derivative works. Thus, to continue improving its loan package, it will need to renegotiate with Mary, who, by virtue of the revocation, has recaptured the right to prepare derivative works.

In order to revoke or terminate a transfer, the copyright owner(s) must be sent proper notice. The notice must be signed by the author, the author's heirs, or an authorized agent. If there is more than one author or more than one heir, the rules are a bit complicated and an attorney should be consulted. In fact, a termination should not be attempted on your own in any event.

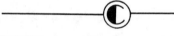

P. Summary

We've covered a lot of technical ground in this chapter. The primary point to remember is that copyrights can be divided up in lots of different ways. The giving of exclusive rights through a license, contract or will involves a transfer of ownership of all or a portion of the copyright, depending on what is transferred. The giving of a non-exclusive right is not a transfer of copyright ownership but rather an agreement to share all or a portion of a copyright. Licenses involving transfers of ownership should be recorded with the U.S. Copyright Office for maximum protection.

Non-exclusive licenses need not be recorded, but may be. No matter how long a transfer might last, by its own terms it is subject to revocation by the author after 35 or 40 years. Such revocation should usually be carried out with the help of an attorney. Remember, the original owner of a work for hire is considered the author for copyright transfer and revocation purposes.

CHAPTER 13

Copyright Infringement and What You Can Do About It

A. Introduction

We have discussed the steps needed to give your work the maximum protection under the copyright laws. Now we explore how these protections are enforced if your rights are violated. This subject is referred to as "copyright infringement."

When a copyright dispute first surfaces, there are normally several self-help steps you can take. These generally amount to telling the infringer, in one way or another, to cut it out. When push comes to shove, however, and an infringer will not pay attention to your "stop" order, there is only one remedy with teeth in it. This is to ask a federal court to order the infringing activity stopped and to award a judgment for damages suffered as a result of the infringement. To understand the overall topic of "copyright infringement," it is therefore essential that you have an overview of how the copyright litigation process works. Because this type of litigation can be procedurally complex, an attorney

skilled in copyright litigation is generally required. Accordingly, this chapter is not intended as a lawyer substitute. Rather, it's our goal to:

■ Give you a general understanding of the subject so you can recognize when infringement has occurred;

■ Suggest several steps you can take on your own which may solve the problem without recourse to courts and lawyers;

■ Inform you what to expect in the event of a court action;

■ Discuss the kinds of defenses to an infringement suit which will be legally sufficient to get the alleged infringer off the hook; and,

■ Let you know what your damage recovery (or payment, if you are the infringer) and other types of court relief are likely to be if you win (or lose) an infringement suit.

Taken together, this information should give you the background necessary to make sensible decisions if you face a copyright infringement lawsuit. It will probably not preclude your use of a lawyer, but should allow you to escape the role of the traditional "client," which is all too often the same as the Latin root for that word--"to hear, to obey." We discuss how to find, hire and deal with a good software lawyer in Chapter 2, Section C.

EDITOR'S NOTE: In the following material we discuss infringement lawsuits primarily from the viewpoint of the person whose material has been pirated (the victim) rather than from the perspective of the pirate. However, if you are on the receiving end of an infringement suit, this information will be at least as essential.

B. What Constitutes Copyright Infringement?

As with other legal terminology, it is easier to define infringement in functional terms than in the abstract. Thus, with several exceptions created by the Copyright Act, infringement occurs whenever one or more of the exclusive rights of a copyright owner is violated by the acts of another. In previous chapters, we emphasized that a copyright is a bundle of separate exclusive rights. These include the exclusive right to sell, market, copy, prepare derivative works from, and display a copyrighted work. The exclusive nature of these rights means that with several exceptions, noted in Section G of this chapter, they cannot be exercised by anybody but the copyright owner, unless the owner's permission is obtained. If they are, the copyright is said to be infringed.

In the software environment, infringement commonly involves copying and marketing programs and/or documentation without permission, as well as the unauthorized creation of derivative works. Sometimes this is out-and-out theft, and the main task is to catch the pirate. Other times, however, the infringement scenario is more complicated. This is the situation:

■ If a program developer carelessly licenses several publishers or manufacturers to do the same, or overlapping, things;

■ A software company issues a program that is fairly similar to, but not an exact copy of, an existing work;

■ A hardware manufacturer thinks it has purchased a particular operating system outright, while the software company which developed it believes it retained some rights.

There are literally hundreds of possible infringement scenarios. Let's look at some examples.

EXAMPLE 1: High Tech., Inc. copies and distributes Carl Jones' computer game, GOTTCHA. They change the name to GET'EM to try and disguise their copying. Carl sees an attract screen from GET'EM while at a local department store and realizes it is exactly like GOTTCHA. Carl's copyright (i.e., his exclusive right to copy, market and display GOTTCHA) has been infringed.

EXAMPLE 2: Mary Hales generates a series of complex menus on a terminal for the purpose of setting up new loan customers. The menus are identical to those she created in another, earlier program while working for Middle Bank as an employee. If Mary fails to obtain permission from Middle Bank (the owner of the copyright in the menus, since Mary created them as a work for hire), Mary is guilty of infringing Middle Bank's exclusive right to make copies.

EXAMPLE 3: Carl Jones' publisher transforms Carl's computer game, GOTTCHA, into a handheld game, a video arcade game and a full-length cartoon show called GOTTCHA COMIN' & GOIN', without first obtaining Carl's permission. Under Carl's contract with his publisher, he has assigned all of his exclusive copyright rights to GOTTCHA to the publisher, except the right to make derivative works. Because the publisher created derivative works without Carl's permission, Carl's copyright has been infringed. However, if the publisher simply marketed GOTTCHA worldwide without consulting Carl, no infringement would occur, because the exclusive rights to distribute and make copies of GOTTCHA belong to the publisher by virtue of the assignment.

EXAMPLE 4: Carl Jones' cartoon, GOTTCHA COMIN' & GOIN', is a hit. Some enterprising person decides to create a t-shirt depicting the GOTTCHA characters. Assuming Carl's permission is not first obtained, this is an infringement of Carl's copyright, or, more specifically, his exclusive right to make derivative works.

EXAMPLE 5: BCA Graphics develops a series of pro-graphics design programs for use in the publishing business. They contract with the Print-It chain of graphic supply stores to publish and distribute their product. BCA then licenses First Quill, a mail order graphics marketing company, to do the same thing. Print-It sues BCA, claiming breach of contract, and First Quill, claiming infringement of their copyright. Who wins? It all depends on the language of the BCA/Print-It contract. If BCA has granted Print-It an exclusive right to publish and distribute the programs, and Print-It recorded their copyright transfer in a timely fashion (see Chapter 12), Print-It should prevail, unless First Quill comes up with a good argument of their own, such as that Print-It was only licensed for retail (not mail order) distribution.

C. Self-Help Remedies for Copyright Infringement

If you suspect your copyright has been infringed, you should discuss your problem with a copyright attorney. A preliminary conference should not be expensive. This is a good idea even if you plan to try to settle or compromise with the infringer without court action. However, whether you see an attorney at this stage or not, there are some preliminary things you can safely do on your own.

Your first step is to make a common sense assessment of who the infringer is, what their motives are, how widespread their infringing conduct is, etc. If you believe your copyright has been infringed by a small software house selling your program without authorization, your problem is very different than if you are dealing either with the hobbyist grapevine or with an international pirate based in Taiwan. Assuming you conclude your particular software pirate is amenable to pressure, here is an approach which may work. First, check to see that your copyright is properly registered (Chapters 8 - 11). Then, send the infringer a "cease and desist letter." This sort of letter serves several functions simultaneously:

■ First, it lets the infringer know that you believe she is infringing your exclusive rights;

■ Second, it dates your discovery of the infringing activity, should more serious action be warranted later. This is important for purposes of the statute of limitations on copyright infringement lawsuits discussed below;

■ Third, it tells the infringer that you have every intention of stopping her piratical actions;

■ Fourth, and perhaps most important, it gives the infringer a chance to explain her conduct and perhaps offer a satisfactory compromise, before you've spent a lot of money initiating a lawsuit. Even though you are sure you are right, it doesn't hurt to listen to the other person's story. In addition, by giving the infringer a chance to respond, you may find out a lot about how she plans to defend a court action.

Here is what is normally covered in a cease and desist letter:

■ Who you are, including your business address and telephone number, or, if you want to protect your privacy, some way to contact you--such as a P.O. Box;

■ The name of your work, date of first publication, and the copyright registration certificate number, if your work is registered;

■ The nature of the activity you believe to be an infringement of your copyright;

■ A demand that the infringer cease and desist from the activity; and

■ A request for a response within a stated period of time.

Your letter can threaten legal action, but you're probably wiser not to at this stage. The spectre of courts and lawyers usually does little but make the other person paranoid and defensive. If you act as if your lawsuit is only hours away, the answer to your letter is likely to come from the infringer's lawyer. Once two lawyers are involved, the chances of any compromise settlement is greatly reduced, as lawyers, by the very nature of their profession, usually get paid more to fight than to compromise. When you draft your letter, remember that you may end up wanting to use it in court. Accordingly, avoid being cute, nasty, tentative or overly dramatic. The following example contains about the right tone and level of information.

WRITING A CEASE AND DESIST LETTER

January 1, 198_

Ms. Oleo Oboe, President
Oboe, Inc.
567 Symphony Drive
Anywhere, USA 11111

Dear Ms. Oboe:

I recently became aware of your manufacture and sale of a computer game called GET'EM. I am the owner of the copyright in a video game entitled GOTTCHA, copyright registration No. 22222222, first published in 198_. I believe that your computer game, GET'EM, is a copy (or a substantial copy) of GOTTCHA. Since I have not authorized you or your company to make or sell copies of GOTTCHA, it follows that you are infringing my copyright by doing so.

This letter is to demand that you and Oboe, Inc. immediately cease and desist from the manufacture and sale of GOTTCHA under the name of GET'EM or any other name. All infringing copies must be destroyed immediately. In addition, I request reasonable compensation for the copies you have already sold.

Please respond to this letter by January 15, 198_ .

Sincerely,

Carl Jones
[ADDRESS]

Cease and desist letters should be sent by certified mail, return receipt requested. If the infringer refuses to accept your letter, arrange to have it delivered personally. This should be accomplished by someone who is not involved in the dispute and who will be available to testify that the letter was received by the party, if that should become necessary.

What you do next depends on the response you receive, as well as the nature of the infringer and the infringing conduct. Reasonable and routine solutions to many infringements include:

■ Payment for profits already made;

- Making the infringement legal through a license under which you are paid an agreed-upon fee (see Chapter 12); and

- Getting the infringer to agree to stop future infringements.

Any compromise settlement should be in writing, signed by all parties. At this point, the help of a lawyer with experience in the area will probably prove to be invaluable. Here is a sample of the way the GET'EM/GOTTCHA dispute might be settled:

Ms. Oleo Oboe, President
Oboe, Inc.
567 Symphony Drive
Anywhere, USA 11111

Dear Ms. Oboe:

This letter embodies the terms and conditions to settle all outstanding disputes between Oboe, Inc. and Carl Jones and to authorize Oboe, Inc. to market the computer program, GOTTCHA. Carl Jones and Oboe, Inc. hereby agree:

1. Oboe, Inc. will pay Carl Jones the sum of $123,000 for copies of GET'EM sold up to the date of our agreement, January 20, 198_.

2. Oboe, Inc. will place the following copyright notice on all copies of GOTTCHA sold from January 20, 198_ until termination of our "Standard Resellers Agreement":

© copyright Carl Jones 1985

3. Oboe, Inc. will execute and be bound by the terms of our Standard Resellers Agreement attached hereto.

4. Carl Jones agrees that this agreement completely settles the matter in dispute between Carl Jones and Oboe, Inc. and releases Oboe, Inc. from any further liability for the sale of GET'EM prior to January 20, 198_.

_____
Carl Jones

_____
Date

_____
Oleo Oboe, President
   Oboe, Inc.

_____
Date

D. Copyright Infringement Lawsuits

Here we review what's involved in filing a civil copyright infringement lawsuit and the remedies you may obtain if you are successful. If you are unable to settle a copyright infringement dispute to your satisfaction, you will need to retain an attorney to file a civil suit on your behalf. Lawsuits for copyright infringement are brought in federal, not state, court. As emphasized earlier, the litigation is complex and should not be attempted without an attorney.

CRIMINAL PROSECUTION NOTE: Willful copyright infringement is a federal crime [17 USC, Section 506]. Accordingly, the United States Attorney General is empowered to prosecute. The problem with a criminal action is that even if successful, you may end up with nothing but the satisfaction that the infringer is being punished. Also, as a practical matter, the resources for investigation and courtroom prosecution of this sort of crime are limited. For reasons having to do with the allocation of available resources (bank robberies and murders of Post Office workers, counterfeiting and dozens of other crimes are given priority), your copyright infringement crime is unlikely to warrant much attention from the federal authorities. For this reason, we do not discuss criminal trials or penalties here.

The most important thing to know is that, in the United States, a civil suit based on a claim of infringement of a U.S. copyright cannot be brought unless and until the copyright has been registered with the U.S. Copyright Office.* This is not the same thing as saying your copyright must be registered prior to the infringing conduct to be able to sue.

---

* If your copyright registration is refused, you may still be able to sue under some circumstances [17 USC 411]. The only other possibility of bringing suit on an unregistered copyright exists if the copyright was originally accomplished both outside the U.S. and in a country which is a member of the Universal Copyright Convention, or has a bilateral copyright treaty with the U.S. (see Chapter 14).

Registration can occur after an infringing act and you can still sue for that infringement. However, as we saw in Chapter 8, if you registered prior to the infringement (or within three months of publication), you are eligible for a higher level of damages, attorney's fees and certain other procedural benefits than if you waited to register.

U.S. copyright registration is accomplished as outlined in Chapters 8 - 11. It normally takes from six to eight weeks. However, if you need to register so that you can sue, there is an accelerated procedure by which registration can be accomplished in about five business days. This involves paying an extra fee and following the procedure set out in Chapter 11, Section I.

E. What You Must Prove in a Copyright Infringement Lawsuit

When a civil copyright infringement action is filed, the person bringing the action (called the "plaintiff") must prove certain facts in order to prevail. This is called the "burden of proof." As we discussed in Chapter 8, registration of your copyright within five years of publication greatly eases this burden. While a detailed discussion of court procedure is beyond the scope of this book, here are the major things the plaintiff must establish to prove infringement:

■ She is the owner of the entire copyright or the particular right that was infringed; and

■ One or more of the copyright rights she owns has been infringed; and

■ The person, partnership or corporation being sued has actually done the infringing act or directly contributed to it (called a "contributory infringer"); and

■ She has been damaged in some way by the infringing action.

To be eligible for statutory damages, as defined in detail in Chapter 8, Section B, and attorney's fees, the person bringing suit (the plaintiff) must also prove her copyright was registered prior to the infringement, or within three months of the work's publication.

Let's look at these proof requirements one at a time:

1. Proof of Copyright Ownership

In Chapter 8, we emphasized that a copyright registration certificate is "prima facie evidence" of the truth of the claimant's ownership if the work is registered within five years of the date of first publication.* What does "prima facie evidence" mean? Simply that the certificate, by itself ("on its face"), will establish the plaintiff's ownership unless the infringer proves otherwise. In short, mere production of the certificate in court operates to shift the burden of proof as to the ownership issue from the plaintiff to the defendant.

What happens if the defendant discredits the registration, or otherwise casts enough doubt on the plaintiff's ownership to require a further proof of ownership by the plaintiff? Depending on the precise questions raised, the plaintiff will then need to present evidence. For example, if the outcome of the case depended on which party developed the work, the proof required might include:

■ Earlier drafts of the work in question;

■ Witnesses who saw earlier drafts of the work;

■ Witnesses who talked with the plaintiff about the work prior to registration; or

_____

* If registration occurs more than five years after the work is first published, the court has discretion (i.e., choice) as to whether the plaintiff should be presumed the copyright owner on the basis of the certificate [17 USC 410].

■ Any other information which would logically help the judge decide the ownership issue.

EXAMPLE 1: Let's go back to Carl Jones' case against Oboe, Inc. for the pirating of GOTTCHA. Assume that at trial Carl produces his registration certificate as evidence of his ownership of the copyright in GOTTCHA. Since he registered within five years of publication, Oboe, Inc. would have the burden of proving Carl is not the owner.

EXAMPLE 2: Assume now that after Carl introduces his copyright certificate, Oboe, Inc. brings in a witness who swears that he saw Oboe's program GET'EM long before GOTTCHA was created, and that Carl had access to Oboe's program. In this situation, Carl's lawyer would want to produce drafts of GOTTCHA that pre-dated registration and, hopefully, the claimed date for GOT'EM's development, witnesses who saw Carl working on the program, witnesses who have information about Oboe's lack of previous effort, etc.

2. Proof Necessary to Establish Copyright Infringement

As a practical matter, most cases of software copyright infringement involve someone making unauthorized copies of somebody else's program, or some part of it. For purposes of illustration, we are going to assume that is the case here. However, the principles we will discuss relative to copying also apply to all the other copyright rights that make up the entire bundle of rights.

To prevail in an infringement lawsuit, the plaintiff must prove that an infringement actually occurred. If someone is caught with an exact copy of a copyrighted work, or is seen copying it, the plaintiff has what is aptly called a "smoking gun." In other words, the infringing villain has been caught "red-handed." Unfortunately, this type of evidence often isn't available. More typically, you spot a program that is very similar to yours and you "know" the person you are suing wrote a little superficial code with the sole motive of trying to disguise her infringement. In this situation, you must then establish that the infringement took place by proving two things:

■ The substantial similarity of the infringing work to your work; and

■ That the claimed infringer had access to your work.

Let's take a closer look at these two infringement criteria.

a. Substantial Similarity

As we mentioned, the best evidence is to produce a "smoking gun" in the hands of the infringer. In the software business, this usually means catching the pirate with a program that is somehow instantly identifiable as being the plaintiff's. Since even the dumbest pirate will probably be smart enough to remove the plaintiff's copyright notice, the wary programmer will bury nonfunctional and idiosyncratic symbols somewhere in the code. The idea is to subtly brand the program so it can easily be identified in the event it is copied by someone else. This is a refinement of the old principle of marking a watch with a little scratch in the lower left hand corner of the back, so as to easily identify it should the need ever arise.

The other way to meet the substantial similarity test is to argue that the codes of the two programs are so similar that the latter logically must have been copied from the former; or, in other words, that such a high degree of similarity could not have occurred by chance. This is usually accomplished by a close examination of the code of both programs to determine the number of statements that are the same and the number that are not. In this situation, it is helpful if the person claiming infringement has her source code on deposit with the Copyright Office. Of course, as we told you in Chapter 10, there are other considerations when deciding what to deposit.

But, the possibility that this type of lawsuit will occur is certainly one argument for depositing at least some source code as "identifying material." Again, if you are confused about this or other deposit rules, see Chapter 10.

How much does a second program have to be like an already copyrighted one for the plaintiff to win in court? When the work is either literary, or consists of source code itself, 87 percent similarity was held to be substantially similar in one case [Midway v. Strohon, 564 F.Supp. 741]. Where audiovisual works are concerned, however, the court tends to take a different approach. Here the court finds substantial similarity where the ordinary observer would regard the aesthetic appeal of the works as the same and tend to overlook disparities unless he set out to detect them [Atari, Inc. v. Amusement World, Inc., 547 F. Supp. 222; Atari, Inc. v. North American Philips, 672 F.2d 607].

b. Access

In addition to proving substantial similarity, a plaintiff trying to establish infringement must also show that the defendant could have had access to the infringed work in order to copy it. This requirement is easy to show if the work is mass-marketed. It may be more difficult if the work has only been accessible to a very few people. Problems can develop, for example, when software which is very narrowly distributed under a license agreement is pirated. In one legal decision, access was established when a marketing firm changed clients and showed a copy of the former client's product to the new clients, resulting in copyright infringement [Synercom Technology, Inc. v. University Computing Company, 462 F.Supp. 1003].

EXAMPLE: Return with us now to the saga of the copyright infringement lawsuit involving GOTTCHA and GET'EM. After establishing ownership of GOTTCHA, Carl Jones' attorney introduces into evidence a GET'EM cartridge and a GOTTCHA cartridge. The judge spends an hour playing the two games. Since GET'EM is almost an exact copy of GOTTCHA, the judge has no trouble deciding that they are so similar that one must have been copied from the other. And since GOTTCHA was available all over the world at the time of the infringement, there is no problem showing that Oboe had access.

DAMAGES NOTE: To recover money as a result of a successful copyright infringement suit, it helps, but isn't always essential, to be able to prove you suffered a monetary loss. We discuss the subject of damages in Section F, below.

F. Remedies For Copyright Infringement

What happens once a plaintiff prevails in a copyright infringement action? The potential remedies include "injunctive relief" (a court order requiring some action or inaction by the defendant), damages (often the profits made by the defendant from the infringement), any other damages the defendant can establish (such as lost business opportunities because of the infringement), statutory damages (if registration was timely) and attorney's fees (also dependent on early registration).

Now let's translate each of these remedies into English. Again, this is not a complete description of all the legal procedures involved, but is designed to give you an overview of the remedies available.

1. Injunctive Relief

An "injunction" is an order from the court telling someone to stop doing some particular activity. In a copyright infringement action, this usually means simply to stop the infringing activity. This is commonly a quick, effective remedy because, under a great number of circumstances, it is possible to get a temporary (preliminary) injunction within several weeks of initiating a lawsuit. This is, of course, long before an actual trial is held to decide if you have won your suit. Such preliminary relief is possible when it appears likely to a federal judge, on the basis of written documentation and usually relatively brief oral agreement, that the plaintiff will win the suit when trial time rolls around. In addition, the judge must find that the plaintiff will suffer "irreparable damage" if the preliminary injunction is not granted. However, this requirement is commonly easy to demonstrate in copyright infringement actions.*

EXAMPLE: Two weeks after Carl Jones learns of Oboe's infringing activity, and after Oboe replies negatively to his suggestions for compromise, Carl's lawyer files suit for copyright infringement. When the suit is filed, he requests a preliminary injunction against Oboe, Inc. to prevent their further sale and manufacture of the GET'EM computer game. He

claims that if Oboe continues selling GET'EM, the market for GOTTCHA will drop so low that Carl will not be able to meet expenses for the coming quarter. The judge makes three decisions to justify granting the preliminary injunction. First, Carl's claim to own the copyright in GOTTCHA is probably correct. Second, GET'EM probably constitutes an infringement of Carl's copyright. Third, Carl will probably suffer irreparable harm from the continued sale and manufacture of GET'EM by Oboe, Inc.

Once an preliminary injunction is granted, it remains in effect pending a further determination at the formal trial. In theory, this will probably be held a year or two later. In fact, the hearing on the preliminary injunction often takes the place of the trial, with the parties fashioning a settlement based on its results. In the software business, waiting a year or two often seems like waiting for the next galactic age. Assuming a full scale trial does occur, however, the same issues are litigated in far more detail. If the plaintiff again prevails, the preliminary injunction will be turned into a permanent one, either including the same terms and orders, or different ones, depending on what the plaintiff proves at trial. If the plaintiff loses, however, the preliminary injunction will be dissolved and the defendant can go back to doing what they were doing before the preliminary injunction was issued.**

2. Money Damages for Copyright Infringement

Damages for copyright infringement generally fall into two categories-- "actual damages" and "statutory damages." Let's look at both.

---

* Irreparable harm is when a party is damaged in some demonstrable way which cannot easily be measured by money. Although the courts commonly award damages for copyright infringement, they also recognize that it is often difficult or impossible to really measure the harm an infringement has caused. Such intangibles as loss of business goodwill when a "competing" infringing product is sold at a substantially lower price, or loss of business opportunities caused by a diminished cash flow, are generally incapable of measurement in monetary terms. Accordingly, the courts are usually willing to rule that the injury threatened by a copyright infringement will, in fact, be irreparable.

** It is not uncommon in these cases for the defendant to countersue the plaintiff on a number of theories, including copyright infringement. These will be tried at the same time as the plaintiff's case. Accordingly, it is possible that the plaintiff will end up owing the defendant money, instead of vice versa.

a. Actual Damages

These are the lost profits and/or other losses which are sustained as a direct result of the copyright infringement. Put another way, actual damages are the amount of money which the plaintiff would have made but for the infringement. Often the copyright owner's actual damages are closely related to the infringer's profits. The theory is that the amount of money that went into the defendant's pocket as a result of the infringement would probably have gone to the copyright owner had no infringement occurred. To qualify for actual damages, the plaintiff must prove in court that they occurred. The plaintiff's word is not enough to accomplish this. Witnesses, ledgers, business records, etc. must be presented to demonstrate how much the defendant made, or, some other way to substantiate plaintiffs loss must be proved. Often it is difficult to prove actual damages.

b. Statutory Damages

These damages are established by law and require no proof of how much the loss was in monetary terms. However, as was discussed above and in Chapter 8 on registration, they are only available if the work has been registered in a timely fashion--that is, within three months of publication or before the infringement occurred. They are awarded at the discretion of the judge and do not depend on having to prove a loss in any specific amount as a result of the infringement. Statutory damages fall within the following range:

■ Between $250 and $10,000 for each copyright infringed;*

■ If ownership is not admitted by the infringer in court and the infringement was not innocent (i.e., the infringer knew they had no legal right to the material, as opposed to incorrectly thinking they had a legal right to use it), the court has the power to increase the amount of damages to $50,000.

---

* Multiple infringing actions involving the same right are not separately counted.

■ However, if the infringer admits the plaintiff's ownership voluntarily, and the infringer is innocent (that is, used the copyrighted material believing he had the right to do so), the judge may award as little as $100.

NOTE ON PLAINTIFF'S CHOICE: Under the law, the plaintiff who is eligible (i.e., registration has occurred in a timely fashion) for both actual and statutory damages must choose which she wants to receive. This choice may be made at any time, up to and during the trial. There is little we can say here about how to make this choice. Your decision will depend primarily on the facts of the particular case. We can, however, make several general points. If you are able to conclusively prove actual damages, you will at least be reasonably certain of receiving that amount. If, on the other hand, you elect to receive statutory damages, which involves leaving the damages amount up to the judge, you necessarily engage in a crapshoot because of the enormous range of statutory damages that the judge has the discretion to award. However, if your proven damages are low but the infringement was willful, and the infringer refused to admit it (i.e., showed bad faith), you might be better off to gamble on the proclivity of the judge to punish willful wrongdoing and choose statutory damages. Let's look at a couple of examples:

EXAMPLE 1: In Carl Jones' suit against Oboe, Inc., assume Carl gets a court order to force Oboe to produce its books. He discovers that Oboe made $123,000 more in the six months it was selling GET'EM than it made in the previous six months. He also discovers that GET'EM was the only new product Oboe marketed in that six-month period, and that 10,000 copies were sold. This evidence tends to show that Oboe made $123,000 as a result of their infringement. In this situation, Carl should be able to get a court judgment for actual damages in the amount of $123,000 from Oboe.

EXAMPLE 2: Now let's change a few facts in our story of Carl and Oboe, Inc.

This time, when Carl examines Oboe's books, they reveal only that they needed a bookkeeper. Carl is left with the feeling that Oboe made big bucks by pirating his program, but he has no solid evidence of how much. The only loss he can absolutely prove is his $20,000 out-of-pocket expense for an ad campaign to warn dealers about the unauthorized GET'EM, and there is no legal authority for the recovery of damages of this type. In addition, assume that Carl can get a former Oboe employee to testify in court that Oboe knowingly copied GOTTCHA. Since Oboe's infringement was willful, and Carl registered within three months after publication, Carl could receive as much as $50,000 in statutory damages if he elects to request them instead of trying to establish actual damages. Here, Carl would probably be wise to choose statutory damages.

3. Destroying the Infringing Software

Another civil remedy for copyright infringement consists of a court "impound and destroy" order. This tells a sheriff or marshal to go to the infringer's place of business (or wherever the infringing material is located) and impound any infringing works. This can happen any time after the trial has begun. If the plaintiff wins, the court will order the sheriff or marshal to destroy or otherwise dispose of any infringing material. But suppose the infringer, who we already know has precious little respect for honest business practices, hides the infringing material? The judge can order him to produce it. If he doesn't, or dishonestly pretends to produce it but continues his piratical practices, the judge can fine him and even send him to jail for contempt of court.

EXAMPLE: Assume Carl Jones wins a preliminary injunction against Oboe, Inc. to stop selling GET'EM. As part of the court order, the judge orders a federal marshal to Oboe's place of business to impound all existing GET'EM cartridges. The marshal stores the GET'EM cartridges until the final decision in the case. When the case is ultimately decided in Carl's favor, the judge orders the cartridges destroyed. It's up to the marshal whether she drives a bulldozer over them or tosses them in an incinerator.

4. Attorney's Fees and Costs

Attorney's fees and other costs of going to court, such as filing fees, can be recovered in some software copyright infringement cases. Again, however, whether you are eligible for such fees and costs depends on your having registered your copyright within three months after publication, or before the infringing action occurred. The cost of bringing an infringement suit can be very high. In some cases, costs and attorney's fees can be as high as $100,000 and more. If for no other reason than this, you should always register a copyright as soon as possible, and in no case later than three months after publication of the work (see Chapter 8, Section B).

EXAMPLE: When Carl sued Oboe, Inc. over their piracy of GOTTCHA, his attorney's fees were $10,0000 and his court costs were $1,500. His fees probably would have been higher if he hadn't won a preliminary injunction. Since Carl registered his copyright before infringement occurred, the court can order that he

183

recover $11,500 in addition to the award of actual or statutory damages.

G. Defenses to a Copyright Infringement Lawsuit

When a person is sued, no matter how awful their alleged piracy, they have a chance to defend themselves. After the copyright owner has presented his case, the defendant can present whatever evidence she feels will help her case. Possible defenses to an infringement action include many general legal defenses which often involve where, when and how the lawsuit was brought, who was sued, etc. We obviously can't cover all of this here. Again, and we can't say this loudly enough, if you find yourself defending an infringement action, please retain a qualified attorney! In this section, we limit ourselves to outlining the several principal defenses which are specific to copyright infringement actions.

1. The Fair Use Defense

The U.S. Copyright Act contains several exceptions to the general rule that copyright rights are exclusive to their owners. These exceptions are generally referred to as "fair use." This concept is also recognized by most other nations and by the international copyright treaties (see Chapter 14). Fair use of a copyrighted work means that if the particular use comes within the legal definition of that term, copyrighted material can be used without the copyright owner's permission, and thus, without compensation. Often, whether a particular exercise of a copyright right is or is not fair use is determined in the context of a copyright infringement case, with the person charged with infringement claiming as a defense, "I didn't infringe your copyright, I only made fair use of it."

Although the U.S. Copyright Act contains several broad categories of what

constitutes fair use, a more specific description is found in the Congressional Committee Report which accompanied the Act as it was being considered by Congress. According to this report, an unauthorized copying of a copyrighted work is considered fair use in the United States if it consists of:

■ Quotations or excerpts in a review or criticism for purposes of illustration or comment;

■ Quotation of a short passage in a scholarly or technical work for illustration or clarification of the author's observation;

■ Use in a parody of some of the content of the work parodied;

■ Summary of an address or article, with brief quotations, in a news report;

■ Reproduction by a library of a portion of a work to replace part of a damaged copy;

■ Reproduction by a teacher or student of a small part of a work to illustrate a lesson;

■ Reproduction of a work in legislative or judicial proceedings or reports;

■ Incidental and fortuitous reproduction, in a newsreel or broadcast, of a work located at the scene of an event being reported.

As you may glean from these examples, fair use is often used to allow the media broad latitude in reporting on items of public interest, even if they are otherwise subject to copyright protection. Fair use is also important to uses involving educational, scientific and political pursuits.

Once a person accused of copyright infringement raises the fair use defense, a court will first look to see if the use is within the general fair use categories established by Congress and set out above. If it is, they will then look at the following factors to decide if the use really is fair use, rather than infringement:

■ The character and purpose of the use. Thus, private and non-profit uses are more likely to be considered fair use than those which are public and/or profit motivated;

■ The nature of the copyrighted work. Thus, legal, scientific and historical works are more often subject to the fair use defense than novels or most commercially-oriented software;

■ The amount and substantiality of the portion of the copyrighted work used in relation to the entire work. Thus, using a small part of a large work is more likely to be considered fair use than if most of the work is used. Similiarly, a part of a work which is somewhat tangential to the whole will qualify as fair use more easily than a portion of core importance; and

■ The effect of the use on the potential market for the copyrighted work, and/or the effect of the use on the value of the copyright work. Thus, if the use actually competes with the copyrighted work (e.g., duplicating a spreadsheet program for an entire accounting class), it may not be fair use. Whereas, if the portion copied serves to promote the interest of the larger work (e.g., using one routine from an accounting package for demonstration purposes), it may be considered fair use.

The courts have not yet gotten around to applying the fair use doctrine to computer software disputes, and thus we can only speculate on the contexts in which this infringement defense might be permitted. We do this in the following examples:

EXAMPLE 1: A software user's group gives classes in video game program writing. At one of the classes, the instructor uses a few lines of code from GOTTCHA to illustrate the code for the attract mode of a video game. This is an educational use of Carl Jones' work and has little or no commercial value. In these circumstances, the impact of the use on the commercial success of GOTTCHA is minimal, and it could even be argued that the use "promotes" GOTTCHA. The instructor has probably made a fair use of Carl's work and does not legally need Carl's permission, although it would be wise to arrange for it if reasonably possible.

EXAMPLE 2: During one of the computer shows where Carl Jones was demonstrating GOTTCHA, a local TV news station which promotes itself as being "in tune with the high tech times" films a screen. They use this film not only in the newscast, but for several weeks afterwards in promotional film clips for the news program. Fair use? Probably "Yes" as to the newscast. Perhaps "No" as to the commercials. Why? Because the newscast is within the scope of what Congress had in mind when it discussed the fair use as promoting public interest and education, but the commercials are primarily intended to attract people to that particular television station's product, the newscast. In this sense, the station is attempting to profit from Carl's work. Could Carl sue? Certainly, but realistically, his best bet is probably to call the situation to the attention of the station and ask for compensation. This could take the form of direct payment or an agreement to provide free promotion or GOTTCHA by specifically identifying it as Carl's product whenever the news promotion is displayed.

EXAMPLE 3: LOANIT was reviewed in Financial Institutions Quarterly, where selected sections of the documentation were printed to illustrate how easy LOANIT is to use and install. Financial Institutions Quarterly does not need Mary's permission, assuming its copy of LOANIT was obtained lawfully and without restrictions.

Congress has specifically authorized two other fair uses which relate to computer programs [17 USC 117]. These allow the lawful owner of software to:

■ Alter it for private use; and

■ Make a back-up (archival) copy for private use.

We discuss this concept in detail in Chapter 4 on derivative works.

2. The Independent Creation Defense

Copyright protection doesn't prevent others from independently developing works based on the same idea. One excellent defense to an infringement suit, therefore, is that the work was not copied but was independently developed. With this type defense, the person sued for infringement tries to prove that he did not copy the copyright owner's work, but that his work is original and that it's only coincidental that the two works are substantially similar. Don't sell this defense short. It has been common throughout history for more than one person to develop similar ideas, inventions, patents, etc. at about the same time. One notable example of this is the simultaneous, but independent, development of calculus by Newton and Leibnitz.

How do you overcome this defense if you have brought an infringement action and are convinced that your program was copied and that the independent creation argument is just another lie by a desperate and unprincipled pirate? The answer is that you have to prove by a preponderance of the evidence that your position is correct. This means you must convince the judge or jury that you more likely than not are the one true owner.

EXAMPLE: After Carl Jones presents his case against Oboe, Inc. at the trial (i.e., shows ownership, substantial similarity, access and damages), Oboe has several employees testify that they had worked on the development of GET'EM and that they had never seen GOTTCHA or even heard of it before Carl sent his cease and desist letter. If this testimony is believed over Carl's evidence, Carl will lose. It would be decided that Oboe had, in fact, independently created GET'EM. Carl would have to prove this wasn't the case by witnesses of his own, as we discussed earlier.

3. The Statute of Limitations Defense

The statute of limitations is exactly that--a limit imposed, by statute, on the time you have to file a lawsuit. For our purposes, the limit is on the amount of time a copyright owner has to file a lawsuit for copyright infringement. A civil action for copyright infringement must be brought within three years from the date the infringing act occurred. Accordingly, the copyright owner may not recover damages for an infringing act which occurred prior to this three-year period, assuming this defense is presented. However, if the infringement began prior to the three-year period, but continued into the three-year period immediately preceding the filing of the lawsuit, a suit may be brought for the later infringement, and resulting damages may be recovered. The hard and fast rule discussed above may be subject to exceptions and presents a number of tricky questions. Thus, if you have any questions about whether the statute of limitations applies to your particular case, you will want to discuss them with a knowledgeable copyright lawyer.

EXAMPLE: Back to Carl and Oboe. Assume Oboe started infringing Carl's GOTTCHA copyright in January of 1981. Carl files his lawsuit in January of 1985. Oboe made the following profits on GET'EM from 1981 to 1985:

1981 to 1982	$75,000
1982 to 1983	125,000
1983 to 1984	150,000
1984 to 1985	150,000

Carl can recover all his profits from Oboe except the $75,000 they made in 1981, since that sum was made more than three years prior to the date he filed his lawsuit.

4. The Invalid Copyright Defense

Here, the defense presented is that the copyright allegedly infringed is not valid and, as a result, the work is in the public domain. Remember that work in the public domain can be used by anyone, for any purpose. Works are commonly categorized as being in the public domain for such reasons as:

■ The work was published without a valid copyright notice and the mistake was not corrected (see Chapters 6 and 7);

■ The work is made up of non-copyrightable material, such as blank forms, nonsense code and material already in the public domain; and

■ The work expresses an idea which can only be expressed in one (or possibly a very limited number) of way(s).

This defense is based on the general principle of copyright law that when there are only a very few ways to express an idea, it's not possible to give anyone copyright protection because doing so would, in effect, give them an exclusive right to the idea itself, something which copyright law does not permit. This issue has not yet been resolved by the courts, although in several recent decisions where it was claimed that operating systems would not be copyrighted because they constituted the only way to operate a particular microcomputer, courts held the operating systems in question to be copyrightable on other grounds.

EXAMPLE: Mary Hales writes a program to calculate the "Rule of 78's" (a complicated rule for figuring out how much prepaid interest to return to a customer in the event a loan is paid off early) and takes all the essential steps to secure full copyright protection. Later, someone else markets a very similar routine. Mary files an infringement action. However, before the case gets to trial,* and regardless of how strong Mary's case is, the court dismisses the suit, holding that there are only two ways to figure

---

* In cases where the parties do not dispute the facts, but only their legal significance, the courts have authority to grant "summary judgment" without the need for a regular trial. This, as well as the preliminary injunctions procedure discussed in Section G above, is a means whereby copyright disputes can be resolved relatively quickly.

the Rule of 78 and that Mary's copyright is invalid.

5. Fair Use Is Legal

In some cases, the alleged infringer is not an infringer, but a legal transferee. For example, the so-called infringer might legitimately claim to have received a license to make a derivative work, and that the work the plaintiff claims to infringe his copyright falls under that license. Another common situation is where conflicting or confusing licenses were granted and the person being sued claims to be the lawful owner of the right in question. It can also occur that a transferee was not restricted in making further transfers, and transferred the copyright to individuals unknown to the original owner. We present many examples of lawful transfers in Chapter 12. If any of these transferees were sued, they would have a good defense, i.e., their use is lawful.

Another common problem area is when someone is issued a license based on their agreement to abide by certain conditions (e.g., that they will spend $50,000 to advertise the software). An argument then develops as to whether the terms of the license have been met and the original owner sends a letter terminating the license and telling the licensee that any further unauthorized activity will be an infringement.

6. Other Defenses

Some of the other possible copyright infringement defenses include such things as:

■ The notion that if the plaintiff is guilty of some serious wrongdoing himself, he cannot complain about others;

■ The notion that since the copyright owner never bothered to assert her rights when she had a chance to before, why should the court allow her to assert them now; and

■ The idea that the copyright owner knows of the defendant's acts and expressly or implicitly consented to them.

Again, we are just giving you an idea of what's involved in a legal battle. Obviously, it can get quite complicated.

H. Conclusion

Although we have covered much potentially confusing material in this chapter, the main points can be concisely summarized.

■ Infringement of a copyright is any use of a work inconsistent with one or more of the exclusive rights making up the copyright;

■ The primary means of enforcement for copyright protection is a federal court civil infringement action. Use of a skilled attorney is strongly advised for all infringement actions;

■ To win an infringement action, the plaintiff must establish:

1. Ownership;

2. That the defendant did the infringement (by showing substantial similarity and access);

3. That some damage was done; and

4. That registration was timely (if statutory damages and attorney's fees are desired);

■ Registration within five years of publication results in presumption of ownership. Registration within three months of publication or before the infringing activity begins qualifies the copyright owner for statutory damages and attorney's fees;

■ Successful infringement actions can result in injunctive relief, actual damages (which are commonly measured by the defendant's profits) and statutory damages (assuming registration is timely). However, the plaintiff must opt between actual damages/profits and statutory damages;

■ Fair use of a copyrighted material is a defense to an infringement action;

■ Fair use occurs when the use is within the contexts recognized by Congress and tends to be for private, non-commercial, educational and public interest ends;

■ As far as copyright law is concerned, copies of computer programs can be made for back-up (archival) purposes and a derivative work can be made for one's own use;

■ Common defenses to infringement actions (in addition to fair use) are independent creation, defective copyright, statute of limitations and legal use;

■ Criminal penalties exist for copyright infringements, but they are rarely pursued.

----------•CHAPTER 14•----------

International Copyright Protection

A. Introduction

Maybe you've thought about marketing your work in England, France or Japan. Or, perhaps you are a Japanese software writer on vacation in Rome, where you spot an Italian program that you think would sell like hotcakes in Kyoto. This sort of scenario would have been unlikely five years ago. Today it is routine. Needless-to-say, this change is not without its problems.

The ease with which software and other computer-related intellectual property is transcending international borders is placing fierce stress on the world's nation-based legal systems. In every country where people deal with software, there is a need for a clear, understandable set of international legal rules to govern intellectual property rights. And, while a number of important steps have been taken towards this end, there are still many problems. In this chapter, we take a close look both at international copyright protection rules and at several potential problem areas you

may face in trying to protect your software on an international basis.

To put international software copyright protection in perspective, it is useful to remember what copyright protection really does. Essentially, it:

■ Allows the owner of a copyright to prevent others from making unauthorized copies of, and alterations to, an original work of authorship, and

■ Establishes rules for the collection of damages and injunctive relief when such copying or alteration does occur.

In preceding chapters we discussed how these goals are achieved in the United States. But, knowing how to copyright software in the U.S. (or Japan, Australia, or Germany) isn't going to help you much if you wake up one day to learn that your video game program, which is protected by a U.S. copyright, has been taken to Italy, copied there by an enterprising

Swiss computer buff, and is being sold throughout Scandinavia by the use of coupons stuffed in Viking Puff cereal boxes. Is this sort of copying legal? What could you have done to anticipate this problem and head it off? What relief is available to you, aside from sabotaging the Viking Puff factory?

And then, suppose that the pirated program is imported back into your country and marketed as the new rage in European video games. How can you prevent this from happening? What are your remedies if it does? To find out the answers to these and similar questions, let's plunge into the sometimes icy waters of international copyright protection and learn the basic rules for protecting your work worldwide.

Fortunately, the international book business has been around for a long time and has influenced most nations of the world to recognize the desirability of having a basic system of copyright protection in force worldwide. To this end, a large number of nations have signed international agreements (called treaties or "conventions") which require each signatory country to provide the same copyright protection and benefits to the nationals and works of the other signing countries as it does to its own nationals and works. In addition, these conventions each establish the steps that must be taken to qualify for such reciprocal treatment, such as placing a c or an "All Rights Reserved" on the work you wish to protect. Finally, they also establish a minimum level of protection that each member country must provide under its copyright laws. This includes a minimum copyright duration period, as well as requiring protection for derivative works.

It is important to understand that each country is also free to provide additional copyright protections or benefits, so long as the opportunity to obtain these is afforded on an equal basis to the nationals of all other countries which have signed the particular copyright convention, and to all works which

are first published in any one of the signing countries.

Let's start with the basics. There are three principal international conventions designed to protect copyrights. They were negotiated at different times, for different purposes, and often overlap as to what they cover. They are: the Universal Copyright Convention (U.C.C.), the Berne Convention and the Buenos Aires Convention. Some nations are signatory members of all three agreements; other nations are members of two; a good number have joined only one; and a few aren't members of any convention. In other words, the conventions not only overlap as to content, but as to membership. For example, Mexico is a member of the Buenos Aires, Berne and Universal Copyright conventions; the United Kingdom and Japan are members of the Berne and Universal Copyright conventions; Uruguay is only a member of the Buenos Aires Convention and Taiwan is not a member of any convention. Of lesser importance are a number of bilateral treaties in force around the world.

Although this attempt at uniformity among nations would appear at first glance to make it fairly easy to understand the international rules for the copyright of software, there is at least one major catch. The conventions do not specify what kinds of software must be provided protection. Until the computer era, this wasn't a big problem. Such works of expression as books, paintings, prints, woodcuts, movies, records and even tape recordings have been around for a long time and virtually all of the signatory nations recognized such items as protectible expressions. Well established publishing industries in all major countries supported this movement and saw to it that rules were enforced. With a few exceptions, such as Taiwan, South Korea and Singapore, where book piracy has never been contained, it has been in everyone's best interest to cooperate. Or, in other words, few, if any, major publishers saw it as being to their long-term advantage to try and avoid the recognition of international copyrights.

Quite to the contrary, huge international trading fairs were established, principally in Frankfurt, but also in London, Mexico City, Bologna, Tokyo and the United States to specifically buy and sell international copyright rights. In short, the publishing industry concluded it was in everyone's best interest to act responsibly.

With the advent of computers, several things occurred to change the relatively pro-copyright recognition system. While most countries had no trouble extending copyright protection to source code as a form of "scientific," "technical" or "intellectual expression," no immediate consensus developed to automatically extend copyright protection to other types of software and computer output. As we've seen throughout this book, computers have spawned a number of gritty questions regarding the protectibility of items like object code, firmware and computer output. Many of these must still be answered on a country-by-country basis. For example, in early 1984, object code and operating systems were considered protectible as literary works in the U.S., but not in Australia, even though the U.S. and Australia are both signatories of the U.C.C.*

In short, while copyright conventions establish a floor for methods and levels of software protection, and most countries tend to protect source code, the law of each country must still be looked to when many types of computer-related work are involved. This is particularly true when it comes to ROM's, EPROM's and other types of firmware.

One reason for this international uncertainty has been the failure of software publishers and hardware manufacturers to communicate with each other and cooperate to establish international standards. Perhaps this is understandable in such a new industry. After all, the microcomputer revolution didn't begin to spawn significant amounts of software

until the late 1970's.** And at first, the new software houses that were springing up all over the world found great rewards in grabbing each other's ideas and marketing them, without paying much attention to copyright ownership. Things moved so fast that computer hackers who copied the occasional disk often didn't stop to think that, as their hobby became a business, they were in danger of becoming large scale international pirates.

More recently, this laissez-faire attitude toward piracy has begun to change, and change fast. Why? Well, with the emergence of a number of good-sized microcomputer-based software companies has come the establishment of international business relationships and friendships. Additionally, major companies with established international business relationships have entered the microcomputer market. Incidentally, much the same thing occurred in the publishing business more than a century ago. Publishers and other people in the software business have quickly learned that while now and then a pirate can make a big killing, the industry as a whole is far better off if all the major players cooperate.

As this trend towards cooperation continues, two things are sure to happen. First, international standards as to exactly what types of software are protected will grow as the software publishing houses in each country pressure their own governments to cooperate. Second, those who continue to play by frontier rules will be caught and punished. In short, there is every reason to think that international protection of software copyrights is improving and will improve more in the near future.

In this chapter, we tell you what protection is available for your computer-related product under the various

---

* In mid 1984, however, an Australian appellate court ruled that such software was, in fact, entitled to copyright protection.

** Prior to this time, only software for larger machines was sold internationally. Since that type of software is usually licensed individually to each user, instead of being sold over the counter, fairly effective protection against piracy was maintained by contract.

copyright conventions. To make the material easy to understand, we do this from a couple of perspectives. First we assume you are a U.S. citizen or permanent resident. Then we assume you are a non-U.S. citizen who, because of an international convention or bilateral treaty, is entitled to protection in the U.S. Finally, this chapter touches on some U.S. export and import rules which might apply to software and related documentation.

B. International Protection for U.S. Citizens and Nationals

1. The Universal Copyright Convention

The United States is not a signatory of the Berne or Buenos Aires conventions. Therefore, the international protection of software written by its citizens and nationals depends on rights granted under the Universal Copyright Convention (U.C.C.) and, in some situations, by bilateral treaties between the U.S. and other nations.

a. National Treatment

As a U.S. citizen or permanent resident, your unpublished or published work is entitled to copyright protection in every country which has signed the U.C.C. The protection you receive is the same as each U.C.C. signatory country affords its own nationals, as long as that protection meets certain U.C.C. minimum standards. This basic reciprocity under the U.C.C. is referred to as "national treatment."

EXAMPLE 1: Suppose Carl Jones, a U.S. citizen, develops HONDABITS in Japan, also a signatory to the U.C.C. Carl would be protected in Japan on the same basis as Japanese nationals. Why? Because Carl is a U.S. citizen and Japan is a signatory to the treaty.

EXAMPLE 2: Assume that Carl develops HONDABITS in Iran, a non-signatory to the U.C.C. The work may enjoy no copyright protection in Iran, but is protected in all U.C.C. countries (including the U.S.) because of Carl's U.S. citizenship.

b. First Publication in U.C.C. Country

Under the U.C.C., if a work is first published in a U.C.C. country, it is also entitled to protection in every other U.C.C. country. This means that an author who is not a national or domiciliary of a U.C.C. country can still obtain full U.C.C. protection by simply first publishing in a signatory nation.

EXAMPLE: Jamal is a national of Iran, which is not a U.C.C. country. If he first published his work in Pakistan, which is a U.C.C. country, Jamal would be protected not only in Pakistan but in the U.S. and every other signatory of the U.C.C.

c. Limitation on Formalities

Although the U.C.C. provisions requiring national treatment and reciprocity among its member nations are extremely helpful, there would be numerous problems if every country had different requirements for every aspect of actually obtaining protection. For example, as we saw in Chapter 6, protection in the U.S. is ultimately dependent upon the proper copyright notice being placed on published copies. Suppose every country differed in respect to such notice requirements? How would you know what to put on your work once it is published?

Fortunately, to solve this problem, the U.C.C. requires that every U.C.C. country accept several uniform minimum copyright standards. For example, when it comes to copyright notice, the notice rules of all member countries are considered satisfied if the specific U.C.C.-approved notice is placed on each copy of the work. What is this notice? The very same one we reviewed in Chapter 6, when we discussed U.S. notice requirements. It consists of: © [YOUR NAME] [DATE OF FIRST PUBLICATION]. Indeed, the U.S. requires this particular notice precisely because it satisfies the U.C.C. minimum formality requirement. Again, this same notice is good in all U.C.C. countries. Just as the U.S. domestic law permits other types of notice, such as the use of the word "copyright" and the abbreviation "copr.," as well as © , other countries also allow variations within their own jurisdictions. Indeed, many, such as the United Kingdom, Germany and France, don't require any copyright notice to be placed on the work at all to maintain its domestic copyright status. However, because of the international U.C.C standard, the overwhelming majority of material published in U.C.C. signatory countries contains the same form of notice: © [YOUR NAME] [DATE OF FIRST PUBLICATION].

UNIVERSAL COPYRIGHT CONVENTION SIGNATORIES

Algeria, Andorra, Argentina, Australia, Austria, The Bahamas, Bangladesh, Barbados, Belgium, Belize, Brazil, Bulgaria, Cameroon, Canada, Chile, Colombia, Costa Rica, Cuba, Czechoslovakia, Denmark, Dominican Republic, Ecuador, El Salvador, Fiji, Finland, France, Federal Republic of Germany (West), Democratic Republic of Germany (East), Ghana, Greece, Guatemala, Guinea, Haiti, Hungary, Iceland, India, Ireland, Israel, Italy, Japan, Kampuchea (Cambodia), Kenya, Laos, Lebanon, Liberia, Liechtenstein, Luxembourg, Malawi, Malta, Mauritius, Mexico, Monaco, Morocco, Netherlands, New Zealand, Nicaragua, Nigeria, Norway, Pakistan, Panama, Paraguay, Peru, Philippines, Poland, Portugal, Senegal, Soviet Union, Spain, Sweden, Switzerland, Tunisia, United Kingdom, Vatican City (Holy See), Venezuela, Yugoslavia, and Zambia.

---

d. Software Protection

Now that you know how to obtain international protection by using the correct copyright notice, let's look at what types of software are protected, as well as the mechanisms by which this is accomplished. As a general matter, every U.C.C. country extends copyright protection to traditional types of expression. This includes literary, artistic and scientific writings, as well as audio-visual and graphic works (see Chapters 3 and 8). As we mentioned earlier, source code, because of its human readable characteristics, was quick to qualify. However, the copyright status of several other types of software, such as firmware (ROM's, EPROM's, etc.), object code, operating systems and computer output, is still uncertain in many parts of the world. If information on any of these forms of software is important to you, check with a lawyer with experience in the international intellectual property arena. As of this writing, the law is simply too uncertain, in too many places, for us to attempt a country-by-country survey.

Assuming now that the software you are concerned about falls within a particular country's definition of copyrightable material. What protection do you receive? Each U.C.C. country must:

■ Offer copyright protection for at least the life of the author plus 25 years; and

■ Offer the author exclusive rights to translate it, with the exception that if a work is imported to another U.C.C. treaty country and not translated within seven years of the work's original publication, the government of that country has the right to make a translation in that country's language, but only under a compulsory licensing system (i.e., the government has to pay the author a fair fee).*

---

* This rule was intended to cover human language translations so that works from other countries could be made available in the translating country in the event the copyright owner became recalcitrant about publishing there. Although there are, as yet, no court decisions to indicate whether this translation rule applies to computer languages, it may not. Why? Because since computer languages are not linked to geography the way human languages are, the reason for the translation rule would not seem to apply.

So much for the basics. In addition to these two required U.C.C. protections, approximately half of the countries listed above have also agreed to protect the author's "economic interests" by international agreement (this means the author's exclusive rights of reproduction and adaptation). The other half have not, although the great majority offer such protection under their own laws.

Why this difference? As it turns out, there was an original U.C.C. held in Geneva in 1952 and another in Paris in 1971. The latter made certain amendments to the Geneva version. Some countries have ratified these amendments, while others have not. The amendments allowed certain exceptions to copyright protection in "developing" countries, but also specified for the first time that each member country should protect an author's "economic interests." As mentioned, most nations do this anyway, under their own laws. However--and now we come to the important part--in those countries which do not adhere to the Paris part of the U.C.C. Convention, or independently provide full protection for an author's "economic interests," you may have trouble protecting object code, since some countries view object code as an adaptation, or derivative of the source code.

COUNTRIES ADHERING TO THE PARIS U.C.C. CONVENTION

Algeria, Australia, Austria, The Bahamas, Bangladesh, Belize, Brazil, Bulgaria, Cameroon, Colombia, Costa Rica, Czechoslovakia, Denmark, Dominican Republic, El Salvador, France, Germany (East and West), Guinea, Hungary, Italy, Japan, Kenya, Mexico, Monaco, Morocco, Norway, Panama, Poland, Portugal, Senegal, Spain, Sweden, Tunisia, United Kingdom, United States, Vatican, and Yugoslavia

---

NOTE: If you are concerned about whether a country that belongs to the U.C.C. but has not ratified the Paris amendments has their own law which protects your particular work, you will have to do some research. Your best bet is probably to contact a lawyer in that country.

In addition to these basic protections offered under the U.C.C. (and under the Paris version of that convention), some countries offer additional benefits if early copyright registration is accomplished. The U.S. is one of these.* Once these additional benefits are made available, however, they apply to all nationals of U.C.C. countries who choose to register their works and to all registered works which were first published in a U.C.C. country.

2. The Berne Convention

The world's first major copyright convention was held in Berne, Switzerland. The resulting agreement has aptly become known as the Berne Convention. We mention this convention after the U.C.C., even though it predates it, because it is less important from the perspective of a U.S.-based software author. Why? Several important nations, the United States and the Soviet Union among them, have not signed the Berne Convention. Since this first section of our discussion is directed primarily to U.S. citizens and permanent residents, you may wonder why we bother with the Berne Convention at all. The answer is simple, and in four parts:

■ By originally publishing her work in a Berne Convention country, such as Canada or Mexico (or by simultaneously publishing in the U.S. and such a country), a U.S. citizen or permanent resident becomes entitled to all the protections allowed under the Berne Convention, without giving up any U.C.C. rights;

---

* Registration with the U.S. Copyright Office provides more extensive benefits than does registration in most other countries which have a registration system. For example, in Japan and Canada, registration provides a means of making your work a public record (and thus may be helpful in case of an infringement action), but does not afford the registrant such additional advantages as the presumption of validity, statutory damages and attorney's fees. Most countries do not provide for registration at all.

■ The Berne Convention offers protection in some countries which are members of Berne, but not of the U.C.C. This means that by qualifying for Berne protection, you can extend the number of countries in which your work will receive basic copyright protection;

■ Even when countries belong to both the U.C.C. and the Berne conventions, the Berne Convention offers several additional protections not available under the U.C.C., such as a longer period of protection;

■ If your work inadvertently escapes your clutches without a proper copyright notice, Berne Convention countries will give it protection, while some U.C.C. countries will not.

COUNTRIES SIGNING THE BERNE CONVENTION

Argentina, Australia, Austria, The Bahamas, Belgium, Benin, Brazil, Bulgaria, Cameroon, Canada, Central Africa Republic, Chad, Chile, Congo, Costa Rica, Cyprus, Czechoslovakia, Denmark, Egypt, Fiji, Finland, France, Gabon, German Democratic Republic, Federal Republic of Germany, Greece, Guinea, Holy See, Hungary, Iceland, India, Ireland, Israel, Italy, Ivory Coast, Japan, Libya, Liechtenstein, Luxembourg, Madagascar, Mali, Malta, Mauritania, Mexico, Monaco, Morocco, Netherlands, New Zealand, Niger, Norway, Pakistan, Philippines, Poland, Portugal, Romania, Rwanda, Senegal, South Africa, Spain, Sri Lanka, Surinam, Sweden, Switzerland, Thailand, Togo, Tunisia, Turkey, United Kindgom, Upper Volta, Uruguay, Venezuela, Yugoslavia, Zaire, Zimbabwe

COUNTRIES SIGNING THE BERNE CONVENTION
BUT NOT THE U.C.C.

Benin, Cameroon, Central Africa Republic, Chad, Congo, Cyprus, Gabon, Ivory Coast, Libya, Madagascar, Mali, Mauritania, Niger, Rwanda, Romania, South Africa, Sri Lanka, Surinam, Thailand, Togo, Turkey, Upper Volta, Uruguay, Zaire, Zimbabwe

---

Thus, by making a simultaneous publication in the U.S. and a Berne Convention country (usually Canada or Mexico), you extend your basic copyright protection to quite a number of additional countries, several of which may become important in the international software marketing business. Simultaneous publication means the publication must be on the same day, under the rules of some Berne Convention countries, and within 30 days of the publication in others. For maximum protection, therefore, it's best to publish the same day. Publication means that you make your work widely available to the public through an established distributor within the country where the publication is occurring.

Most of the major industrialized countries (the U.S. and Soviet Union excepted) in the world belong to the Berne Convention as well as the U.C.C. These countries include the United Kingdom, most of those in western Europe, Japan, and Australia, as well as Canada and Mexico. Therefore, because the Berne Convention bestows extra protection not provided by the U.C.C., a U.S. citizen can increase her copyright protection if she simultaneously or originally publishes in a Berne country.

In a nutshell, Berne member countries agree that a copyright is protected in the following ways:

a. No Formalities

No formalities, such as notice or registration, are required for copyright protection. In other words, despite the notice requirements under the U.C.C., simultaneous publication in a Berne country eliminates the need for such formality as a prerequisite for protection in all Berne countries. What does this mean for works developed by U.S. citizens or permanent residents? If simultaneous publication is made in a Berne country, then nations such as Germany, Canada, Mexico, Japan, the United Kingdom, France and Australia will protect your copyright, even if you inadvertently publish locally without a copyright notice. This means that a copyright could theoretically be lost in the U.S. (see Chapter 6) but remain alive in many other parts of the world.*

---

* This is also true, however, for those many U.C.C. countries which require no local formalities for basic copyright protection.

b. Minimal Protection Laws

Each member country must offer a minimum standard of copyright protection in their own country. This protection must include:

▪ Copyright duration of at least the author's life plus 50 years;

▪ The granting of "moral rights" to the author. Moral rights are generally defined as those rights an author can never transfer to a third party because they are considered an "extension of her being." Briefly, moral rights consist of the right to claim authorship, to disclaim authorship of copies, to prevent or call back distribution under certain conditions, and to object to any distortion, mutilation or other modification of the author's work injurious to her reputation. Moral rights are recognized by some Berne countries regardless of whether publication has occurred in a Berne country. In other words, even if works authored by U.S. citizens are only originally published in the U.S., such authors enjoy "moral rights" in some Berne countries. Consider this a kind of freebe.

▪ Some provision allowing for the "fair" or "free use" of the copyrighted work. This includes material used in quotations for educational purposes, for reporting current events, etc. In the United States, this is called "fair use." We discuss this in some detail in the Chapter 13, Section G(1) on defenses to copyright infringement.

3. The Buenos Aires Convention

The Buenos Aires Convention has little importance to U.S.-based authors because it has been substantially superseded by the U.C.C. There is an exception, however. Several South American countries who signed the Buenos Aires Convention have not signed the U.C.C. These are Bolivia, Hondurus and Uruguay. Therefore, to gain copyright protection in

these countries, it is necessary to comply with the formalities of the Buenos Aires Convention.*. To do this, simply include the words "All Rights Reserved" in the U.C.C. copyright notice. Thus, a copyright notice that would qualify in both U.C.C. and Buenos Aires Convention countries looks like this: © [THE DATE OF PUBLICATION] All Rights Reserved [YOUR NAME].

4. Conflicts Between Conventions

What happens if a country belongs to two or more conventions and treaties and the copyright protections conflict? For example, suppose Carl Jones simultaneously publishes GOTTCHA in Canada and the U.S., and then wants to know what protection he has in France, which belongs to both the Berne and Universal Copyright Conventions. The rule is that Carl is entitled to the most favorable copyright protection. To provide a concrete example, since the minimum duration for copyright protection is life plus 50 years under the Berne Convention, and only life plus 25 years under the U.C.C., Carl's copyright is good for 50 years in France.

Remember, in addition to the minimum protections required by the international conventions, any country is free to extend additional copyright protections (e.g., the U.S. protects copyrights for the life of the author plus 50 years, even though it does not belong to the Berne Convention). If it does so, however, these protections must be made available to the nationals of other countries under the conditions of reciprocity required by both the U.C.C. and Berne conventions.

---

* Because Uruguay is a signatory of the Berne convention, simultaneous publication in a Berne Country would also obtain protection in Uruguay.

5. Protections in Countries Not Covered by Conventions

What about the countries not mentioned under any of the three conventions? Suppose, for example, that you see great potential for your product in the People's Republic of China or Taiwan. In the case of China, South Africa, Thailand and Romania, the U.S. has entered into bilateral treaties (just between the two countries) under which works by U.S. citizens are afforded copyright protection in the country involved.*

Many countries, particularly in Africa, have only become independent in the last several decades and have not yet formally entered into any of the multilateral conventions. However, quite a few of these countries were participants in one or more of the conventions prior to independence. According to the U.S. Copyright Office, many of these countries continue to act as if they were still members. Thus, if you desire copyright

---

* The U.S. also has bilateral treaties with many other countries which are also either Berne or U.C.C. members, or both. Because of the doctrine that the larger conventions control issues they cover, these treaties generally are of little importance, unless they speak to different areas of concern. However, if you have problems with copyright rights in a particular country, an international copyright lawyer should examine all such bilateral treaties, as well as the conventions themselves.

protection in a country not mentioned in this chapter, contact that country's trade representative at their embassy in the U.S. for more information.

Finally, many countries have general reciprocity provisions which afford foreign authors and their works copyright protection if the foreign author's country of origin similarly provides national treatment. It is thus possible for your work to be protected in a country even though your country of origin and the country in which you seek protection do not have any formal treaty relationships.

6. Summary

We have taken a lot of space to explain the different levels of international protection available to U.S. citizens and permanent residents. However, actually securing maximum protection is exceedingly simple and can be summarized in one sentence: Simultaneously publish in the U.S. and a country which is a member of the Berne Convention, such as Canada or Mexico, and put your notice, following this format, on your work upon publication: © Copyright [DATE] [NAME OF COPYRIGHT OWNER], All Rights Reserved. This will result in full copyright protection in all U.C.C. countries, Berne countries, countries with whom the U.S. has bilateral treaties, and in Bolivia and Honduras, who have signed the Buenos Aires Convention but neither of the larger conventions.

NOTE: Inclusion of the word "copyright" after © is not, strictly speaking, necessary to gain international protection, but we recommend it for certainty in the United States, should a printer not print © properly.

C. Protection in the U.S. for Non-U.S. Citizens

We now examine copyright protection in the United States from the point of view of non-U.S. citizens.

1. Protection for Nationals of U.C.C. Countries

If you are a citizen or permanent resident (i.e., national) of a country which is a member of the Universal Copyright Convention, your unpublished or published work is protected under the U.S. copyright laws so long as your published work has the proper notice on it. See Section B(1)(b) above. This is true regardless of where the work was first created or published. Thus, if Mary Hales was a Canadian citizen, she would be entitled to U.S. copyright protection even though she first published LOANIT in China, a non-U.C.C. country.

The protection actually afforded here would be the same as if Mary were a U.S. citizen or permanent resident and properly placed the copyright notice on her published work. However, as we stressed in Chapter 8 and Section B of this chapter, above, Mary may obtain important additional benefits should litigation occur by making a timely registration with the U.S. Copyright Office (within three months of publication or before the infringing activity begins). Under U.S. law, any work protected under a copyright convention, or first published in the U.S., may be registered on a non-discriminatory basis.*

2. The First Publication Rule

If your work is first (or simultaneously) published in any country which is a member of the U.C.C., your U.S. copyright protection is assured. Thus, if Carl is a citizen of Zimbabwe (not a U.C.C. country) and first publishes GOTT-CHA in Australia (a U.C.C. country),

Carl's GOTTCHA copyright is protected in the U.S.

3. Protection for Nationals of Berne Countries

Because the U.S. is not a signatory of the Berne Convention, you cannot obtain U.S. copyright protection solely by being a national of a Berne Convention country or by first publishing in a Berne country. However, if your country is a member of both the Berne Convention and the U.C.C., then your U.C.C. status will protect you in the U.S.

For example, suppose Mary Hales was a citizen of South Africa and first published LOANIT in that country. Because South Africa is a member of the Berne Convention but not of the U.C.C., Mary would not gain any U.S. protection under either convention.** On the other hand, if Mary were a national of Argentina (a member of both conventions), her work would be protected in the U.S. under the U.C.C. Convention.

4. Protection for Nationals of Buenos Aires Countries

All citizens of Buenos Aires countries are entitled to protection in the U.S. if "All Rights Reserved" is placed on their published work. Since most Buenos Aires countries are also members of the U.C.C., this is of little practical importance, except for citizens of Bolivia, Honduras and Uruguay.

D. Checklist for Obtaining Maximum International Copyright Protection

At this point you may be a bit confused. You may even conclude that making

---

* Most other industrial countries do not have a registration or notice system. Instead, virtually all available protections are automatic upon creation of the work. Those countries which do provide a registration procedure, such as Canada and Japan, do not use it in the same way as does the U.S. Registration in these countries is primarily designed to establish the date a work was created should there be a later dispute about whose copyright was first.

** However, Mary might be protected under a bilateral treaty between South Africa and the U.S.

it big in your own country is easier than understanding all of the international rules. Don't give up yet. By asking a few questions and taking a few simple steps, you can cut through a lot of this seeming confusion and preserve rights which later may be worth a lot of money.

Ask yourself these questions:

■ What countries are intended as probable markets? Make a list of every country you think might be interested in your product. In the software world, this will probably surely be West Germany, France, Japan, China, Italy, England, Australia, New Zealand, Spain, Mexico, Canada, Brazil, Sweden, Norway, South Korea, Singapore, Argentina, Taiwan, Venezuela, the Netherlands and a handful of others?

■ Which, if any, conventions do each of these countries belong to?

■ Which, if any, conventions does your country of citizenship or domicile belong to?

■ Have you placed the fullest possible notice on your work (e.g., © Copyright 1986 by Gurusoft All Rights Reserved)?

■ Have you determined if simultaneous publication in one or more countries besides your own will extend your protection to some of these target countries?

■ Do any of your target countries offer additional benefits if you take additional steps locally (such as the necessity to register in the U.S. to qualify for attorney's fees and certain types of damages)? If so, decide if the extra benefits are worth the trouble;

■ Have you located a competent international copyright attorney with whom to consult (see Chapter 2, Section C)?

NOTE: You should conclude that attaining copyright protection is fairly easy for all of these countries except South Korea and Taiwan.

E. Importing Software into the United States

The copyright rights of most foreign authors are protected in the United States. Again, this is because their rights are governed by the agreements their country of domicile has with the United States, such as the U.C.C. As long as the software appears in the U.S. with the proper international notice, i.e., (c) [NAME OF AUTHOR] [DATE], and the work was first published in a U.C.C. country (or by a citizen of that country), no other U.S. formalities must be followed, although registration in the U.S. will provide extra benefits, as discussed in Chapter 8.

But, what about the situation where a U.S. company buys a copyright, or one of the bundle of rights that makes up a copyright, from a non-U.S. author? If that author has not yet registered in the U.S., can the new U.S. owner do so? Yes. And if the non-U.S. author has registered, the new U.S. owner may, and should, record the transfer as we outlined in Chapter 12 on transfers.

F. Exporting Software to Foreign Countries

Interest in international copyright law is not limited to questions having to do with the international sale of rights for publication in another country, although this is the largest area of concern. Software itself is also moving across international boundaries with the speed of a world class hurdler. Of course, this isn't a completely new field. There has been a large international trade in copyrighted literary works for centuries, and a number of rules have developed to govern this trade. These rules are now being applied to software.*

---

* Certain software may be covered by national security restrictions as to the export of technology. Consult the U.S. Customs Service.

The first thing to understand in this area is that rules for importing and exporting works of authorship, including computer programs, are determined by the agreements between the country of domicile (where the copyright owner lives) and the country to which exportation is sought. The second thing you must understand is that the import and export laws of every country differ. Thus, every import-export transaction must be analyzed on a bilateral basis.

For example, suppose that Mary Hales is a U.S. national and wants to directly market her LOANIT package in Mexico by shipping copies from the U.S. To do this, Mary should ask and get answers to the following questions:

■ What are the U.S. restrictions, if any, on exports of software to Mexico?

■ What are the Mexican requirements for import of software into Mexico, if any?

■ Are there any agreements between Mexico and the U.S. which provide guidance on this question?

This kind of analysis must occur in respect to each country to which the import or export of computer-related products is desired. Probably the best place to find the information needed to answer these questions is the Customs or trade office for your country. In the case of U.S, this is the United States Customs Service branch office nearest you.

G. Importing English Language Literacy Works in the U.S.

In an attempt to discourage U.S. publishers of works from having their books "manufactured" in foreign countries, Congress has barred certain categories of works in certain quantities from importation into the U.S. Violation of this rule does not strip the involved work of all copyright protection. However, such

violation can provide a strong defense to an action alleging infringement of the exclusive rights to reproduce and distribute the work [17 USC, Section 602]. In short, you still have your copyright, but large parts of it may be unenforceable.

Now due to expire in 1986, the law, known as the "manufacturing clause" and made part of the Copyright Act [17 USC, Sections 601, 602], applies to all non-dramatic literary works printed in English and authored by U.S. citizens, nationals or domiciliaries. For our purposes, the manufacturing clause covers all printed documentation, but does not cover printouts of the software itself, whether in source code or object code form, since neither is in the English language. Thus, if you are a U.S.-based author and entertain the thought of having your printed English language documentation produced abroad and then imported back into the U.S., read on. The rest of you can proceed to Section H.

The manufacturing processes referred to above include:

■ Printing directly from type;

■ Printing from plates made from type; and

■ Printing from plates made by a lithographic or photo-engraving process [17 USC, Section 601]. To avoid the manufacturing clause importation bar, the type must be set in the United States or Canada and the plates must be made in either country.

There are a number of exceptions to the operation of this clause. Chief among them are:

1. Importation of less than 2,000 copies is allowed; and

2. If the U.S.-based author has in fact been domiciled (i.e., living more or less permanently) outside of the U.S. for a year or more, the law doesn't apply.

In the event you are involved in producing written works abroad, we suggest you consult an attorney for the best way to cope with this law.

H. Preventing Infringing Software from Entering the Country

Suppose one day you are wandering by your neighborhood software store when you spot a program package advertising the enclosed software in terms which could easily apply to your copyrighted work. You buy the program, take it home and quickly realize that you are the victim of a software pirate. A little further checking discloses that the program came from abroad. What can you do?

The law on the subject is relatively clear. Infringing works may not be imported into the U.S. [17 USC, Section 602]. The big question, of course, is what to do about it if it is. As a practical matter, customs officials cannot carefully scrutinize every work of authorship being imported to see whether it does or does not infringe an existing U.S. work. Indeed, even if they had the time, it would be impossible to determine whether a particular imported software infringed any U.S. or U.C.C.-protected copyright. Accordingly, the burden of enforcing the prohibition against infringing works falls squarely on the shoulders of the copyright owner. There are two ways to do this:

1. Recordation with Customs Service: Under the U.S. Customs Act, a copyright owner may record her work with the U.S. Customs Service [19 CFR Part 133 Subpart (D)]. Once this is done, any imports which are either pure copies or are highly similar to yours may be held up until you have a chance to go into court and obtain a court order preventing importation. Unfortunately, the chances of the infringing work being spotted and you being notified are relatively slim. However, the procedure for registering is relatively easy and you have nothing to lose.

2. Initiating an International Trade Commission Complaint: Under the Customs Act, it is possible to seek an order having a work excluded from the U.S. on the ground its importation would be an unfair act or would constitute an unfair method of competition [19 USC, Section 1337]. Copyright infringement meets this test.*

In addition to showing infringement, to get a work excluded you must also prove that:

■ It is produced in another country;

■ It has a tendency to destroy an industry existing in the U.S. (In practice, this qualification is much easier than it looks);

■ The industry being destroyed must be efficiently and economically operated (also almost always found to be the case).

For the most part, any major importation of works that is clearly piratical or which substantially infringes a domestic U.S. work will qualify for exclusion under this law. One well-known example of this happening is when Apple Computers, Inc. prevented the importation of Pineapple Computers in the Apple Computers, Inc. v. Formula International, Inc. [725F.2d 521 (1983)].

To utilize this law, the copyright owner must file a formal complaint with the International Trade Commission. The case is heard by an Administrative Law Judge who is empowered to grant immediate relief and, ultimately, to either ban the works entirely or only a portion. As with infringement cases covered in Chapter 13, it would be unwise to attempt this procedure without the assistance of a skilled attorney. However, if you wish to read more on this subject, an excellent article on the overall proceedings is contained in Protecting Software (Volume 1), published by the Practicing Law Institute (1983).

---

* The customs law also provides a means of barring goods carrying counterfeit or infringing trademarks. See Chapter 15 for more discussion of trademarks.

CHAPTER 15

How Other Protections
Supplement Copyright Law

A. Introduction

Protecting your computer software and output through the use of copyright law has clearly been the primary focus of this book. Yet, it's important to remember there are additional and often complementary means of keeping competitors from unfairly using your intellectual property for their own benefit. Broadly speaking, these practical techniques are based on patent, trade secret, trademark and unfair competition laws. Here we explore the ways in which you can use these legal doctrines to supplement the protection provided by copyright law.

The central points of this chapter can be summed up as follows:

■ The legal methods available to protect your intellectual property often overlap. In other words, you can commonly employ more than one method;

■ Occasionally, however, the simultaneous use of two or more techniques to protect intellectual property is counter productive. That is, one technique precludes another;

■ To thoroughly protect your intellectual property, you should be prepared to use the best possible combination of methods allowable under the law.

This chapter gives you an overview of how patent, trademark, unfair competition and trade secret legal protection doctrines relate to copyright law. An overview, however, is not a substitute for a thorough treatment. Accordingly, we highly recommend Legal Care For Your Software, by Daniel Remer (Nolo Press) for additional information and practical "how to do it" guidance in these other areas of software protection.

Throughout this chapter, we use the term "intellectual property law." Let's define it. Intellectual property refers to any product of the human intellect, such as an idea, invention, expression, unique name, business method, industrial process or chemical formula, which has some value in the marketplace. Among the many computer-related items properly classifiable as intellectual property are computer programs, computer output, hardware inventions (e.g., a new type of disk controller), computer-related names (e.g., Apple, VisiCalc), object code, source code and databases. Put another way, for our purposes intellectual property law is the collection of principles used to determine:

■ Who owns computer-related innovative work;

■ When the owner of this work can keep others from using it without permission; and

■ The various methods by which the owner of computer-related work can best protect her property;

■ The remedies available to an owner of computer-related work when someone seeks to use it without permission.

Let's now review the four main legal devices in addition to copyright law which are useful to protect software and computer output:

■ Trade Secret Law: This body of law is used to protect confidential and valuable business information from being wrongfully obtained or disclosed;

■ Patent Law: In a few circumstances, a statutory 17-year monopoly over the use of an invention will be granted to computer-related intellectual property;

■ Trademark Law: A product or service identifier can be protected under this doctrine.

■ Unfair Competition Law: This legal doctrine prevents businesses from engaging in marketing practices which mislead or deceive the public (e.g., copying a business name).

In the following sections we will examine these areas of the law in more detail.

B. Trade Secret Law

1. Introduction

As we have seen, the copyright laws can provide software developers, publishers and owners excellent legal protection for their work in a number of circumstances. Among the greatest advantages of the copyright mode of protection is the fact that it is recognized nationally and internationally as an effective means to prevent profiting from the work of another without his permission. As you undoubtedly know by now, however, the copyright laws cannot singlehandedly prevent your product from being wrongfully exploited by others. One important reason for this is the fact that copyright law only protects the expression of an idea, and not the idea itself. This means others may be able to profit from your inspiration and hard work by substantially changing the surface appearance of your product and not violate copyright news.

In the software world, this creates particular problems. Why? Because two different codes can produce pretty much the same result or output on the computer. Or, in other words, someone may be able to substantially duplicate your result without actually copying the expression of your idea. For example, suppose Kendra Salone uses BASIC to create her QUILTIT program (original example in Chapter 2, Section A). Now imagine that a COBOL language programmer independently creates another program which produces a similar result but uses a completely different code. The COBOL program would probably be considered an original copyrightable work rather than an infringement of QUILTIT. Why? Because only the underlying concepts of QUILTIT were used. These are not protected by the copyright laws. Yet, in this situation, as in many others, it is the organizational ideas underlying QUILTIT, rather than the form in which such organization is expressed, which are most valuable from a commercial viewpoint.

Fortunately, using trade secret law doctrines, there are several ways to protect the underlying ideas and logic inherent in software at the same time the outward expression of such logic and ideas is being protected by copyright law. In fact, even the "expression" itself can, and probably should, be treated as a trade secret when it comes to "unpublished" software (see Chapter 6, Section D). And sometimes even published software can be protected as a trade secret if publication is limited and takes place under a license requiring strict confidentiality.

As we indicate later in the chapter, whether you qualify for trade secret protection depends in large part on your own actions. Generally, if you rigorously treat your confidential information as a secret, the law will help you to prevent others from wrongfully obtaining or using it. Conversely, information treated as public knowledge will be considered available for public use without protection.

2. Trade Secrets Defined

Broadly defined, trade secret protection means to "protect something of economic value by keeping it a secret." In this context, "something of economic value" means "something" which you know or use that gives you an advantage over others who do not know or use the same "something." This is called a "competitive advantage." The item could be a formula, a scientific or technical design, a process, a procedure or a significant improvement to any one of these. It can also be an idea, an expression of an idea, a machine design or any other secret which gives an economic edge to the holder. Although the item must be novel in some sense (i.e., not generally known by others), it need not be unique or surprising, as is the case with patents (see Section C, below).

"Secret" means that the information is not generally known or available to the public or to others in your trade or business. It doesn't mean that no one else in the world knows, or that you can't tell another living being under any circumstances without risk of losing your protected status. Broadly defined, "secret" does mean that the information has value because a limited and defined group of people has access to it.

Probably the most important thing to remember about trade secret protection is that the more the secret is "out," the more your legal protection is likely to evaporate. This means you must exercise caution in telling anyone about your secret, whether they be your employees, your banker or your spouse. Fortunately, there are specific criteria recognized by most states (trade secret law is a matter of state, not federal, law) which are used to determine whether business secrets have been kept sufficiently confidential to be legally recognized as trade secrets. When deciding a particular case, the state court will examine all of these criteria. Fortunately, in broad outline, trade secret law varies little from state to state and is thus relatively easy to summarize. The usual criteria employed to decide if something is a trade secret in the software contexts are as follows:

■ The extent to which the "secret" is (or is not) already known in the trade. For instance, a new programming technique used by Carl Jones while creating his GOTTCHA program might qualify as a trade secret if it is not in general use in the software programming trade. Conversely, the technique will not be considered a trade secret if it is well known by more than a few other programmers.

■ The extent to which software has a unique logic and coherence. Whether any given software or computer output can qualify as a trade secret will depend in part on whether it is unique. In deciding this question, courts will usually consider whether the program:

1. Has a novel combination of generally known concepts;

2. Offers its developer (or other user) a competitive advantage; and

3. Has a unique application.

In deciding whether this is true, a comparison is often made with similar programs, and the following types of questions are asked. Does the software have superior speed, greater accuracy, greater commercial feasibility, quicker response times to user requests, better interface capabilities, and different error detection techniques, etc.?

■ The extent to which a trade secret is known by a developer's employees. If a program's source code is made available for all employees to view at their pleasure, and without restriction, a court may hold the code was not treated with sufficient confidentiality to qualify as a trade secret. The lesson of this is simple. A software company will do well to only allow its employees to inspect the source code of its programs on a "need to know" basis. To maintain trade secret status, confidentiality and non-disclosure agreements are commonly required of employees.

■ Measures taken by a developer to keep the item secret. Holders of trade secrets are expected to take reasonable "preventative" measures to be sure their secret stays secret. These commonly include:

1. Restricting physical access to the areas where the secret material exists;

2. Posting signs on walls warning employees not to disclose trade secrets;

3. Conducting exit interviews with employees who are leaving employment and advising them of their confidentiality obligations;

4. Denying disgruntled or terminated employees access to the trade secret;

5. Conducting audit trails and trans- action logs regarding the trade secret to document who has viewed the secret, when and for what purpose;

6. Requiring all persons with access to the trade secret to sign non-disclosure

or confidentiality agreements in which they agree to treat the information as a trade secret;

7. Including a notice on all mate- rials that this information is considered a trade secret.

■ The value of the trade secret to others. The more a business competitor would profit by knowing the information in question, the more likely it is that the courts will treat it as a trade se- cret. Conversely, the less useful the information is to others, the less likely it is to be protected.

■ Cost of development. The more a product, idea or information costs to develop, the more likely it is to be considered a trade secret.

■ Time it would take to independently develop. The longer it would take a com- petitor to develop the same or similar information, idea or product on its own, the more likely it is to be considered a trade secret.

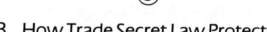

3. How Trade Secret Law Protects Software

Trade secret legal protection works in a relatively straightforward way. During your entire software development phase, from the time the "light bulb" first goes on until you have actually published something, the law of trade secret will afford you protection against the use of your secret information by competitors as long as you keep your work secret and it meets a good number of the criteria spe- cified earlier.

At some point in the process of soft- ware development, a definitive product will emerge. This can be a flowchart, a manual, a lone subroutine or a full- fledged operating program, etc. Whatever it is, once an expression is fixed in a tangible medium, it becomes subject to copyright protection. However, for at least some period of time, such products will also continue to enjoy protection under trade secret laws, so long as they continue to be treated as secrets. This can be particularly important for products which require a number of revisions, changes, beta testing, etc., before they are released to the public. In this context, trade secret status may last for a considerable time, if you maintain it by having all the people who view your work sign a non-disclosure agreement and otherwise continue to treat your work as confidential.

There usually comes a time when you wish to commercially exploit the value of your software. Generally, this occurs when you decide to sell your work for general consumption. At this "publication" stage, you commonly, but not always, must choose between copyright and trade secret protection. If, as is generally true in the microcomputer world, the software is to enjoy relatively wide distribution, copyright law offers you the only realistic way to gain protection. However, if your work will be sold to only a few end-users, it's often possible to maintain some software as a trade secret even after its publication. How this is done is discussed in Section 7, below.

4. How to Legally Protect Trade Secrets

Keeping a secret isn't a whole lot different than establishing it in the first place. In this context, there are two rules to maintaining a trade secret that are more important than all others. First, don't let anyone, whether it be your partner, your banker, your trusted employees or your mother, know your trade secrets unless it is essential. And second, if telling a particular person your secret is essential, require them to sign a non-disclosure agreement. You will find sample trade secret agreements in Legal Care For Your Software, by Daniel Remer (Nolo Press).

Since trade secret protection evaporates as soon as others rightfully learn of the secret, even accidentally, you should go even further to protect yourself, by taking sensible steps to restrict physical access to areas where your secrets are stored and/or worked on. For example, in one case trade secrets were deemed to have been forfeited to the public domain when a company conducted public tours through the area containing the trade secrets in question.

5. Use of Your Trade Secrets by a Competitor

If the kinds of precautions discussed just above are taken and your trade secret is still wrongfully disclosed, you will have a good chance to gain legal redress against the discloser. However, just proving that a wrongful disclosure occurred often doesn't accomplish much. This is because the discloser will commonly not have the means to compensate you for the damage caused by the loss of the trade secret. The real damage, after all, is not the disclosure itself but the fact that the information will then be used by a competitor to make a profit. This brings us to an important issue. What happens if a wrongfully disclosed trade secret is obtained by a competitor? You can take legal action to prevent further use by the competitor and recover damages if appropriate.

6. Trade Secret Protection of Unpublished Works

You should now know that trade secret protection applies to any novel work that gives you a competitive advantage, as long as it is kept secret. This can include the expression of an idea as well as the underlying idea behind its development. If this is true, why isn't trade secret law used to exclusively protect all unpublished software instead of bothering with copyright procedures? There are three reasons:

■ Basic copyright protection is extended to your work automatically, without the necessity of your engaging in any procedures.*

Whether you want it or not, and whether or not you treat your work as a trade secret, you get copyright protection as soon as you fix it in some tangible form. If you treat your unpublished work as a trade secret, you qualify for both types of protection;

■ Trade secret protection only protects secrets as long as they remain secret. If your work is somehow made public and you lose your trade secret, you will want to fall back on copyright protection;

■ Copyright protection is widely available in other developed countries under international treaties, while trade secret protection is very iffy in some parts of the world.

7. Trade Secret and Copyright Protection of Published Works

We have mentioned several times that trade secret status is difficult, and very commonly impossible, to preserve

---

* However, as discussed in Chapter 3 and throughout this book, there are several steps you must take to maintain this protection. The most important of these is to place your copyright notice in your work.

when work is published (i.e., made available to the public through sale, lease and the like). Quite simply, the more people who learn of the trade secret, the less tenable the "secret" label becomes. This means that once work is widely published, trade secret law will no longer help you, and you must rely on copyright protection. Remember, since copyright only protects the expression of an idea, but trade secret protects the underlying idea as well as the expression, you have lost something in the transition from one type of protection to the other. Once it's on the market, anyone can examine your work and, if the underlying idea is good enough, develop their own versions, as long as they don't copy your code or otherwise violate your copyright.

There are two important exceptions to the general rule that publication means loss of trade secret status. As we have mentioned, the first involves software which is distributed on a personalized basis. Software developed for use on mainframes (Mary Hales' LOANIT package is an example) is often provided to the end-user under a marketing scheme which involves one-on-one contact between the end-user and the software developer. For example, Mary or her representatives could personally be involved with each license granted to a bank for use of the LOANIT package. In these situations, the license permitting the use of the software will typically require the end-user to treat the software as confidential. Under this type of "limited publication" program, a good many software licenses can be issued while keeping the program a trade secret. To make sure that confidentiality is maintained, the license contact sometimes requires that the buyer restrict access to the program code to certain key personnel within the buyers company and that these employees all be required to sign non-disclosure agreements.

WARNING! Some people have been tempted to stretch this licensing exception to ridiculous extremes. You have probably seen mass-marketed software with supposed trade secret licensing agreements printed on the packaging. Often, they say something like "By purchasing this software, you agree to treat it as a trade secret." This probably won't work. See footnote in Chapter 12, Section B.

The second exception involves the difference between source code and object code. If you recall, we explained in Chapter 1 that the code which is actually distributed with most programs is the object code (the ones and zeros the machine understands). The source code, on the other hand, typically remains safely behind in the developer's safe.*

The question thus arises as to whether source code can be preserved as a trade secret even though the object code has been published on a mass basis. Legally, the answer is "Yes." So long as the source code can legitimately be said to be a secret, it will be protected against wrongful disclosure and utilization. From a purely practical standpoint, however, the answer is more often "No." Why? Because a sophisticated buyer can reverse engineer your object code to deduce the source code. Obtaining knowledge of a trade secret through the reverse engineering approach is not legally wrongful, and thus no legal protection is available against such a practice. Further, once this is done, the trade secret is destroyed because it is legally "out." As we learned above, once a trade secret is disclosed it is no longer legally protectible. However, from a practical standpoint, keeping source code secret will still prevent many, if not most, users from discovering and utilizing your programmatic logic for competitive purposes.

TRADE SECRET PROTECTION AND COPYRIGHT DEPOSIT RULES: There is one additional potential legal problem you may face should you attempt to maintain trade secret protection on copyrighted works which you register with the Copyright Office. Ironically, this is the deposit requirement which accompanies the copy-

---

* Programs written in BASIC are often an exception to this. Such programs are commonly distributed in source code form.

right registration process. As we saw in Chapter 10, if you deposit a copy of your work with the Register of Copyrights, your deposit is a public record. As you should now know, making your trade secret public is a quick way to blow it. Fortunately, you may well be able to deposit in such a way as not to divulge the trade secret aspects of your work. How can this be done? By making limited disclosure deposits under the Copyright Office doctrine known as "special relief." We discuss this rule and how to take advantage of it in detail in Chapter 10, Section C.

At this stage of software law development we cannot guarantee how the courts will ultimately treat many of the issues raised here. Nevertheless, here are some alternative ways you can attempt to simultaneously protect your software under both trade secret and copyright law. All of these techniques work pretty well for unpublished software and for software published on a limited basis. However, once your software is published, the fact that it can be legally reverse engineered means that a competitor or pirate who wants your material badly enough can probably get it.

■ Place a copyright notice on your work (without a date for unpublished works), but don't register it. If you don't register, you don't deposit. Of course, by not registering you lose potential legal benefits should you become involved in an infringement suit (see Chapter 13). In some circumstances, however, you may conclude this is a good trade-off;

■ Place a copyright notice on your work. Register your copyright, send in your deposit and apply for special relief. This involves asking the Copyright Office to accept a deposit which is altered sufficiently to preclude anybody from deducing your source code by examining it. This sounds like a good strategy, and it may well prove to be one, especially for unpublished work, as it qualifies you for the additional protections associated with copyright registration at the same time that little of your work is disclosed.

■ Place a copyright notice on your work and register it, depositing object code. Object code is probably immune from reverse engineering at the Copyright Office because that office only allows the examination, not the copying, of deposits. In other words, to reverse engineer your object code, a pirate would have to be able to do it in his head while standing in the Copyright Office.

8. The Constitution vs. Software Protection

There is one more point we should mention before we leave trade secret protection. This concerns the potential conflict between trade secret protection doctrines stemming from state law and federal copyright protection law. The supremacy clause of the U.S. Constitution tells us that when there is a state and federal law covering the same thing, federal law rules prevail. Further, the 1976 Copyright Act specifically replaces state laws affording the same or similar copyright protection. How does this apply to protecting your software as a trade secret?

Some legal scholars have argued that because trade secret law and copyright

law are being used to do essentially the same task (i.e., protect ownership rights to intellectual property), only copyright law should be enforced. Other experts, and some courts, disagree with this position. So do we. In our view, the subject matter of the protections are essentially different--copyright only covers a small part of what trade secret covers. The protections are also different in that copyright law protects copying, distributing, performing and making derivative works, while trade secret law protects the use and disclosure of software maintained as a secret. In short, we believe it is wise to use both types of protection, even where they overlap slightly. Certainly this is true for unpublished copyrighted works.

WARNING: Legal questions concerning the issues discussed here are being asked and answered in new ways every day. Especially if your work has great potential value, consult a knowledgeable attorney about your trade secret plans before making a final decision [see Chapter 2(C)].

C. The Role of Patents in Software Protection

1. Introduction

Many of you are probably curious about whether software can be patented. After all, everyone has heard of patents which provide their owners with a statutory 17-year monopoly to make, sell and use the invention covered by the patent. Well, the truth is that while it is possible to indirectly protect software by patent,* the great majority of software does not qualify for patent protection. However, there are some signs that the protection of software by patent will become more important in the future. For this reason, let's review this area briefly.

---

* Software itself is not patentable. However, patents may be granted on inventions which use software in conjunction with a device or machine. We discuss this more later in the chapter.

To qualify for a patent, an invention must be novel and non-obvious at the time of creation [35 U.S.C. Section 102, 103]. The tests for determining novelty and non-obviousness are quite strict. To be novel, an invention ("invention" includes improvements of existing inventions) must be different in some way from previous public conceptions. The term "novel," as used in the patent laws, is therefore different than the "originality" test under the copyright law, which requires that the work be an independent creation.

EXAMPLE: Perhaps it will be easier to grasp this essential point if we think about a vegetable garden. If we go out and buy ten recently published gardening books on growing plump tomatos, all will undoubtedly be protected by copyright, even though the ideas in each are the same. As long as each expresses the "plump tomato" idea differently, there is no copyright infringement. If, however, we then buy ten garden tools, chances are few or none will be protected by patent. This will be true even if several are made with new material or designed in an innovative way. This is because the basic ideas behind shovels, hoes, clippers and rakes have been around so long it's very difficult to come up with one that does the job in a truly novel way.

To qualify as non-obvious, an invention must be relatively unexpected in light of the existing knowledge at the time the invention is made. Or said in reverse, an invention fails the non-obvious test when a person skilled in the prior "art" of the invention (i.e., the general type of technology as it has developed up to the time of the invention) could have said at the time of the invention, "Oh sure, that could be done" or "That exclusively uses ideas we already know about."

2. The Patent Process

The process for obtaining a patent is quite long and difficult. The patent application must be prepared in a certain way which will meet the U.S. Patent and Trademark Office requirements. This involves specialized sentence fragments called "patent claims" (i.e., statements which recite the novel features of your invention and therefore entitle it to protection), a detailed description of your invention, which must be consistent with your patent claim, and a detailed drawing of your invention, all showing how to make and use the invention. It usually takes to between a year and one-half to three years to obtain a patent. Many applications (about 50%) are finally rejected and abandoned.

As mentioned, if a patent is issued, you will be granted the right to exclude others from making, selling or using your invention for 17 years. This means no one can copy your idea or your product, or use it in any way. The protection is all encompassing. Many inventors hire an attorney to help them patent their work. There is also an excellent book on doing your own patent, entitled Patent It Yourself, by David Pressman (Nolo Press).

3. Patents and Software Protection

Traditionally, two reasons were advanced to support the proposition that the overwhelming majority of software was not patentable. First, for a long time, computer programs were considered by the courts to be mathematical algorithms (i.e., a series of mathematical relationships, like differential equations). Mathematical algorithms, in turn, were considered a law of nature, or "pure thought." Patents cannot be granted for a law of nature or mental process because no one can legally have a monopoly over the use of, for instance, "1 + 1 = 2." Thus, software by itself was considered to be nonpatentable. Machines, on the other hand, have always been patentable if they qualify. This dichotomy worked well enough until software began to be built into machines and mechanical processes. Finally, when software was seen to be an essential part of the machine, it too was held to be patentable as part of the patent claim covering the machine. Thus, to take just one example, robots, which are heavily dependent on software, are protected by patents.

Recently, as judicial understanding of computers and software has grown, some courts have been more willing to consider some machine-based programs as inventions worthy of patent protection, even though they really aren't an integral part of a machine or a mechanical process. Thus, patents have been issued for programs which allow the use of scratch pad registers by high-level language programmers [In re Bradley, 600 F.2d 807] and which resolve references in the translations of high-level languages to machine-readable languages [In re Pardo, 684 F.912]. Although in these situations the programs in question governed the internal functioning of a computer, and were thus machine-related, they are not the only programs for which patents have been issued. Thus, a program which translates Russian to English was held patentable because of the way the patent application claimed the program (i.e., as machine-based) and because (as is required in all cases) it was held to be useful, novel and non-obvious, so as to qualify for patent protection [In re Loma, 575 F.2d 872]. In 1983, a patent received by Merrill Lynch for its CMA (Cash Management Account) program was upheld in a preliminary injunction proceeding [Paine Weber v. Merrill Lynch, 564 F.Supp 1358].

From the legal standpoint, it is still unclear whether patent law will be useful to protect most types of software. The instances where patents have been issued to software-related inventions are relatively small compared to the many times patent applications for software have been denied. However, things may be changing for the better as the dividing line between machines and software becomes harder and harder to define.

As mentioned, there is a second important and practical reason why patent protection is often not appropriate for software. This is the tendency of most software to become obsolete within several years. As mentioned, the patent application process is expensive, takes up to three years, and, once granted, the resulting protection only lasts for 17 years. Because of the rapid rate at which computer hardware and software is changing, much software developed for today's market will be out of date by the time a patent could be granted. Also, the test of non-obviousness is probably much too stringent for much of the software produced today. This is because it tends to be firmly based on pre-existing software.

Despite all this, there are some advantages to the patent process should your software qualify. Should you receive a software-based patent, your program and its unique, novel approach cannot be used by others without your permission. In other words, independent creation, which is sufficient to beat a claim that a copyright has been infringed, isn't good enough to defend against a charge of patent infringement. As long as you patent it first, it's yours for 17 years. How many years is your product good for? In the computer world, 3 or 4 years can seem like a lifetime, 17 an eternity.*

4. Where Patent Law Intersects Copyright and Trade Secret Law

In theory there should be little overlap between patent and copyright protec-

---

* We don't want to leave you with the impression that obtaining a patent is the end of your worries. If your product has real value, there are any number of expensive judicial tactics which may be employed by a competitor to either challenge the validity of your patent or uphold patent claims of his own. The term "patent war" is often used to describe the sort of disputes which commonly arise over the ownership of the patents covering any new technology, such as electronics, biotechnology and robotics.

tions, since they protect different types of property rights. Patents protect ideas themselves as they are expressed in machines, articles, processes, "compositions of matter" and new uses of these items. Copyright, on the other hand, only protects the expression of an idea. However, in practice, copyright and patent laws do occasionally overlap. Until recently, for example, there was some doubt as to whether semiconductor circuit designs or "masks" (template designs used to create the circuitry in the chips) were best protected by patent or copyright. Although such designs certainly can be viewed as an expression, they are also quite physical in form. This particular debate was laid to rest by the Semiconductor Chip Protection Act of 1983 which extends copyright protection to "masks," "mask works" and semi-conductor chips created from such masks. See Chapter 3 Section J, item 11.

Also, while a patent is being sought for the particular design of a circuit embedded in a chip, the copyright laws may operate to protect the actual layout of the circuit itself. The point is, it is possible to spread your bets in some instances by applying for a patent and also treating the expression and underlying idea as protectible under copyright and trade secret law respectively. If the patent is granted, copyright protection is no longer relevant. If the patent is denied, however, copyright protection may be applicable.

5. Looking Ahead

As a general rule, patents have not often been utilized for protecting software, due to the demonstrated reluctance of the Patent and Trademark Office to do so and the length and expense of the process involved in getting one. On the other hand, patents have been successfully used to protect inventions falling within the computer hardware category. In addition, much software is now being produced for very specific purposes associated with machines. Although modern military jets and the space shuttle are

obvious examples of "intelligent machines," the common garden variety automobile is increasingly becoming part computer as well. As we mentioned earlier, software may be protected as part of an independently patentable mechanism.

D. How Trademark Law Supplements Copyright Law

1. The Meaning of Trademark

Before we explore how trademark law can be used to protect software, we need to first define exactly what we mean by "trademark law." We only summarize this subject here. For more detailed information, see Legal Care For Your Software, by Daniel Remer (Nolo Press).

In its most literal meaning, a trademark is any word or other symbol which is consistently used to identify or brand products in the marketplace. Examples of trademarks are "Xerox," a word used to identify a line of products stretching from copiers to computers, and the rainbowed apple used to identify Apple computers and related products. Trademarks, therefore, are brand names and/or designs attached to products.

The term "trademark" is also commonly used to describe what the law defines as "service marks." These are marks (words or other symbols) which are attached to services offered in the marketplace. The name "MacDonalds" in connection with the "golden arches" is one example of a service mark. Another example is the emblem used by Blue Cross-Blue Shield for its medical insurance services. Both trademarks and service marks are subject to federal protection and registration under the Lanham Act [15 U.S.C. Secs. 1051-1127].

A third category of business identifier, trade name, is covered by state law. Trade names are the names businesses use to identify themselves as opposed to their products. Sometimes they are the same as a trademark and sometimes they are different.

To understand this better, let's look at one familiar company. The name Apple Computer is both a trade name and a trademark. It is a trademark when used as a proper adjective ("It's an Apple computer") and a trade name when used as a reference to the producer, Apple Computer Corp. The trademark aspect of Apple is protected under the Lanham Act. The trade name aspect is covered under state law. Thus, if a new company called itself "CrabApple Computers," but manufactured and distributed the "Pepperoni Computer," it technically would be in violation of state laws and court decisions protecting trade names because its trade name is too similar to the established "Apple Computers." But it would violate the Lanham Act, which protects trademarks, since Pepperoni couldn't be confused with Apple.

In addition to the laws which specifically protect trademarks, service marks and trade names, federal and state court decisions and statutes also prevent businesses from competing unfairly by:

■ "Misappropriating" the intellectual property of another;

■ Engaging in unfair competition; or

■ "Palming off" their goods.

In practice, these three concepts all mean that one business cannot legally market their goods on the strength of another business' identifying name or symbol. It just isn't fair and leads to the confusion of the public.*

2. Trademark Protection Defined

Why is trademark information important for a software programmer who wants to protect her product from unfair commercial use by others? First, because if you establish a valid trademark, the public will be able to readily identify your product (e.g., IBM, Xerox, MacDonalds). Second, under federal law, a person whose trademark is used by another without permission is entitled to obtain a court order preventing further unauthorized use, to collect actual damages caused by the infringement, and sometimes to collect statutory damages in the event the infringement was willful. In essence, therefore, trademark protection is roughly equivalent to the authority of the courts to prevent a wrongful use of the mark in question and to compensate the owner for the harm done. This is powerful legal protection indeed.

3. Characteristics of a Protectible Trademark

Briefly, your trademark will qualify for legal protection only if it is different in some way and does more than simply describe your product. When deciding if your trademark is a strong one, ask yourself if it is either arbitrary (e.g., "Elephant" Floppy Disks, the partially bitten apple for Apple Computers,

---

* Unfair competition law is another legal phrase you may hear. It is a sort of catchall category which was originally developed under the English common law for the purpose of stopping confusing and misleading business practices. Many, but not all, of these practices are now regulated under state laws and court decisions. Disputes over trade names are generally all governed by unfair competition laws. In the event you end up in a lawyer's hands, one of the points she will consider is whether your dispute possibly involves unfair competition as well as violation of your trademark, service mark or trade name.

as well as the name "Apple" itself), fanciful (e.g., Double Rainbow Ice Cream) or a made-up ("coined") term (e.g., Exxon, Kodak)? Put another way, is your trademark highly distinctive because it is unique either by itself or in the context in which you use it? If so, it will almost surely qualify for the maximum legal protection, provided it is also different from marks on similar goods.

On the other hand, if your mark simply describes your product, such as "Rapid-compute" for a computer, or "Painkiller" for an aspirin, it is said to be descriptive or weak and will probably not qualify for legal protection if someone else uses the same term to describe their product. This is because the courts do not feel that a business should be able to tie up common ways of describing products, businesses or services.

In addition to the strong/weak mark dichotomy, trademarks may be denied protection if they are commonly used to describe an entire type of product. Such trademarks are referred to as "generic." This means they define the type of product generally rather than your specific product line. Thus, "Aspirin" passed from being a strong and protectible trademark to a non-protectible generic name for any type of over-the-counter painkiller using a certain chemical. More recently, the Xerox Corporation has spent millions of dollars asking people not to describe the photocopying process as "xeroxing something." Why? Because the company is afraid its undeniably strong mark will be come generic and therefore be denied its current status as a protectible trademark. Finally, you should know that proper or geographical names (e.g., John O'Donnell, Carol Pladsen, Grant Putnam, Pine Valley) are not protectible by trademark.

EXAMPLE: Carl Jones writes three derivative programs based on his original computer game, GOTTCHA. The first one he calls MAZORK THRILLER; the second one he calls COPS AND ROBBERS; the third one he calls CARL'S COMPUTER GAME. None of these names has been used by anyone else to name a game. MAZORK THRILLER will

probably be considered a strong trademark because of its relative fancifulness. COPS AND ROBBERS may be considered too weak to protect, due to its descriptive nature. CARL'S COMPUTER GAME will fail on two grounds. The first is that proper names are not protectible as trademarks (although they may be protected as tradenames under state law). The second is that the phrase "computer game" is a generic phrase for the entire product line.

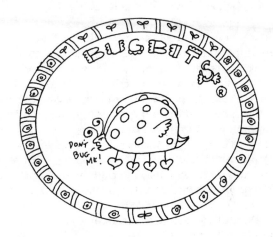

4. How Trademark Law Protects Software

As mentioned in Chapter 3, copyright law does not protect every type of expression. Thus, the title of a work (e.g., GOTTCHA COMIN' AND GOIN') is not protected by copyright. This is where trademarks come in. Trademark protection is available for words, titles, names or other symbols which have been used in connection with a given product or service. Accordingly, trademark law can be used to protect a program's name (e.g., Wordstar, Visicalc). In short, it is the public association with the product name that can be protected under trademark law.

Accordingly, trademark law is commonly used in conjunction with copyright and trade secret law to provide comprehensive protection scheme for the owner of published software. Copyright law protects the object or source code, output, screens and manuals. Trade secret law protects your ideas, business processes, and "know how," and all other valuable information which you treat confidentially, including your programs if you distribute them in ways which keep their secrecy status intact. Trademark law protects your names, titles and other symbols by which you identify and market your business and product.

5. Federal Trademark Law

Federal trademark protection begins when a protectible name or symbol is actually used in connection with goods or services. However, before such a trademark can be registered and receive protection under the Lanham Act, the goods or services must be used:

■ Commercially (i.e., not to a friend or relative for the purpose of satisfying this requirement);

■ With the mark attached;

■ Across state lines.

Although a valid trademark is entitled to protection under the Lanham Act simply by virtue of its first use in interstate commerce, there are additional steps which can be taken to afford the trademark greater protection. The main one is registering it with the U.S. Patent and Trademark Office. However, even before registration, there is something else you should do. Because you must use your trademark in interstate commerce before you can register it, you should indicate your intention that the name or symbol qualify as your trademark. This is done by placing a "T.M." next to the mark. You may have also seen the symbol ® adjacent to trademarks. It stands for "registered trademark." It is only lawful to use ® after all registration formalities have been successfully complied with. There are two registers--the Principal Register and the Supplemental Register. The Principal Register offers the most protection. This includes the statutory presumption that you own the trademark, a means to set the earliest date for use of

the trademark, important benefits in the event litigation becomes necessary, important foreign protection and the opportunity to make the mark "incontestable" after five years on the Principal Register.

If, however, your mark does not qualify for the Principal Register (usually because it is too weak), it may qualify to go on the Supplemental Register, if it has been in actual use for a one-year period. The Supplementary Register provides less protection than the Principal Register, but still allows you to use the R, warning potential infringers that the mark is protected, use the courts under the Lanham Act to prosecute infringement actions, prevent other similar marks from being placed on either register and obtain important protection in foreign countries. Also, once a mark is on the Supplemental Register for five years, it qualifies to be placed on the Prinicipal Register.

Once your mark is placed on either register, you must submit an "affidavit of use" (i.e., that you're still using the mark) after five years to maintain your registration status. Further, to maintain your right to prevent others from using your trademark, you must either continue to use it on a regular basis or have some explanation why not.

6. State Trademark Law

You need not worry about protecting your trademark or service mark under state law if it qualifies for protection under the Lanham Act. This is because federal law controls. However, state protection is useful, even crucial, when there is no federal protection. This is the case with your business name (i.e., trade name), unless it has become associated with your product and hence used as a trademark (as in the case with Xerox Corporation, IBM Corporation and Apple Computer Corporation, among many others). You will also most definitely be interested in state protection for your products if you only do business in one state and thus lack the interstate commerce requirement for federal protection. Unfortunately, state trademark law varies from state to state, and the protection offered is only available on a statewide basis. Accordingly, state law does not offer as wide a protection as the federal trademark law.

The normal process for protecting your trade name under state law is to file a fictitious name statement, or register your name with that state's corporations commissioner. In most states, once your name is on file, other businesses are prevented from filing the same or similar name. Most states also have a registration process under which a trademark or service mark can be registered for maximum protection. Even if a mark is not registered, the law of most states will protect the first user under the unfair competition, misappropriation or palming off theories. A detailed discussion of these state laws is beyond the scope of this book.* If you need more advice in

---

* Also beyond the book's scope is a discussion of such priority-related issues as when a state mark may continue in use in the face of a subsequently registered federal mark, when registration under the Lanham Act precludes use of a competing mark on a local basis, and whether first use of a mark within a state precludes registration of a competing mark under the Lanham Act.

your specific context, we recommend you consult a patent and trademark attorney.

ATTENTION: Xerox, Apple, VisiCalc, IBM, Exxon, Kodak, Elephant and Double Rainbow are registered trademarks.

E. Choosing among Available Software Protection Methods

We have suggested throughout this chapter that choices might be required as to which protection method is most appropriate for your product. This is because one method may involve disclosure, which will preclude the others from applying. The following chart demonstrates the various points at which these decisions must be made. As you can see, in most cases it is possible to enjoy overlapping protections (e.g., in respect to unpublished works of expression), whereas in a few situations, the securing of one form of protection eliminates (for all practical purposes) the enjoyment of another.

PROTECTIONS FOR SOFTWARE UNDER COPYRIGHT
TRADE SECRET & PATENT LAW

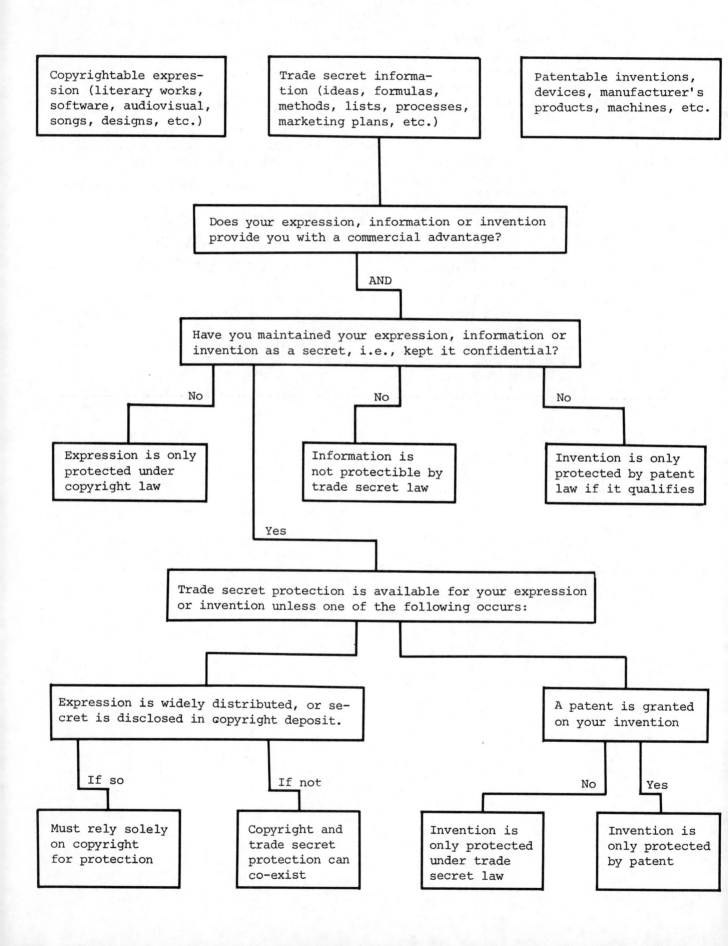

Appendix

SAMPLE COPYRIGHT FORMS

Here we supply you with several sample completed copyright forms. Again, we rely on the same three programmers (and their work) who you have met throughout this book. These samples supplement the specific instructions on how to fill out copyright forms contained in Chapter 11.

A. Single Program Registration (New Published Work—One Author)

Here Mary Hales registers the first program in her LOANIT loan processing package on Copyright Form TX.

FORM TX
UNITED STATES COPYRIGHT OFFICE

REGISTRATION NUMBER

TX   TXU

EFFECTIVE DATE OF REGISTRATION

Month   Day   Year

DO NOT WRITE ABOVE THIS LINE. IF YOU NEED MORE SPACE, USE A SEPARATE CONTINUATION SHEET.

1 TITLE OF THIS WORK ▼

EDIT00]-0]

PREVIOUS OR ALTERNATIVE TITLES ▼

None

PUBLICATION AS A CONTRIBUTION If this work was published as a contribution to a periodical, serial, or collection, give information about the collective work in which the contribution appeared. Title of Collective Work ▼

If published in a periodical or serial give   Volume ▼   Number ▼   Issue Date ▼   On Pages ▼

2 NAME OF AUTHOR ▼

a   Mary T. Hales

Was this contribution to the work a "work made for hire"?
☐ Yes
☒ No

AUTHOR'S NATIONALITY OR DOMICILE
Name of Country
OR { Citizen of ▶ U.S.A.
    Domiciled in ▶

DATES OF BIRTH AND DEATH
Year Born ▼   Year Died ▼
1947

WAS THIS AUTHOR'S CONTRIBUTION TO THE WORK
Anonymous? ☐ Yes ☒ No
Pseudonymous? ☐ Yes ☒ No
If the answer to either of these questions is "Yes," see detailed instructions

NATURE OF AUTHORSHIP Briefly describe nature of the material created by this author in which copyright is claimed. ▼
Test of computer program

NOTE

Under the law, the "author" of a "work made for hire" is generally the employer, not the employee (see instructions). For any part of this work that was "made for hire" check "Yes" in the space provided, give the employer (or other person for whom the work was prepared) as "Author" of that part, and leave the space for dates of birth and death blank.

b   NAME OF AUTHOR ▼

Was this contribution to the work a "work made for hire"?
☐ Yes
☐ No

AUTHOR'S NATIONALITY OR DOMICILE
Name of Country
OR { Citizen of ▶
    Domiciled in ▶

DATES OF BIRTH AND DEATH
Year Born ▼   Year Died ▼

WAS THIS AUTHOR'S CONTRIBUTION TO THE WORK
Anonymous? ☐ Yes ☐ No
Pseudonymous? ☐ Yes ☐ No
If the answer to either of these questions is "Yes," see detailed instructions

NATURE OF AUTHORSHIP Briefly describe nature of the material created by this author in which copyright is claimed. ▼

c   NAME OF AUTHOR ▼

Was this contribution to the work a "work made for hire"?
☐ Yes
☐ No

AUTHOR'S NATIONALITY OR DOMICILE
Name of Country
OR { Citizen of ▶
    Domiciled in ▶

DATES OF BIRTH AND DEATH
Year Born ▼   Year Died ▼

WAS THIS AUTHOR'S CONTRIBUTION TO THE WORK
Anonymous? ☐ Yes ☐ No
Pseudonymous? ☐ Yes ☐ No
If the answer to either of these questions is "Yes," see detailed instructions

NATURE OF AUTHORSHIP Briefly describe nature of the material created by this author in which copyright is claimed. ▼

3 YEAR IN WHICH CREATION OF THIS WORK WAS COMPLETED This information must be given in all cases.
1985 ◀Year

DATE AND NATION OF FIRST PUBLICATION OF THIS PARTICULAR WORK
Complete this information ONLY if this work has been published.
Month ▶ July   Day ▶ 9   Year ▶ 1985
U.S.A. ◀Nation

4 COPYRIGHT CLAIMANT(S) Name and address must be given even if the claimant is the same as the author given in space 2 ▼

Mary T. Hales
222 Program Lane
Miniville, USA 99999

TRANSFER If the claimant(s) named here in space 4 are different from the author(s) named in space 2, give a brief statement of how the claimant(s) obtained ownership of the copyright. ▼

APPLICATION RECEIVED

ONE DEPOSIT RECEIVED

TWO DEPOSITS RECEIVED

REMITTANCE NUMBER AND DATE

DO NOT WRITE HERE
OFFICE USE ONLY

MORE ON BACK ▶ • Complete all applicable spaces (numbers 5-11) on the reverse side of this page.
• See detailed instructions.   • Sign the form at line 10.
DO NOT WRITE HERE
Page 1 of ____ pages

FORM TX

EXAMINED BY

CHECKED BY

☐ CORRESPONDENCE
Yes

☐ DEPOSIT ACCOUNT
FUNDS USED

FOR
COPYRIGHT
OFFICE
USE
ONLY

DO NOT WRITE ABOVE THIS LINE. IF YOU NEED MORE SPACE, USE A SEPARATE CONTINUATION SHEET.

5 PREVIOUS REGISTRATION Has registration for this work, or for an earlier version of this work, already been made in the Copyright Office?
☐ Yes ☒ No If your answer is "Yes," why is another registration being sought? (Check appropriate box) ▼
☐ This is the first published edition of a work previously registered in unpublished form.
☐ This is the first application submitted by this author as copyright claimant.
☐ This is a changed version of the work, as shown by space 6 on this application.
If your answer is "Yes," give: Previous Registration Number ▼   Year of Registration ▼

6 DERIVATIVE WORK OR COMPILATION Complete both space 6a & 6b for a derivative work; complete only 6b for a compilation.
a. Preexisting Material Identify any preexisting work or works that this work is based on or incorporates. ▼
Not Applicable

b. Material Added to This Work Give a brief, general statement of the material that has been added to this work and in which copyright is claimed. ▼
Not Applicable

7 MANUFACTURERS AND LOCATIONS If this is a published work consisting preponderantly of nondramatic literary material in English, the law may require that the copies be manufactured in the United States or Canada for full protection. If so, the names of the manufacturers who performed certain processes, and the places where these processes were performed must be given. See instructions for details.
Names of Manufacturers ▼   Places of Manufacture ▼
Not Applicable

8 REPRODUCTION FOR USE OF BLIND OR PHYSICALLY HANDICAPPED INDIVIDUALS A signature on this form at space 10, and a check in one of the boxes here in space 8, constitutes a non-exclusive grant of permission to the Library of Congress to reproduce and distribute solely for the blind and physically handicapped and under the conditions and limitations prescribed by the regulations of the Copyright Office: (1) copies of the work identified in space 1 of this application in Braille (or similar tactile symbols); or (2) phonorecords embodying a fixation of a reading of that work; or (3) both.
a ☐ Copies and Phonorecords   b ☒ Copies Only   c ☐ Phonorecords Only

9 DEPOSIT ACCOUNT If the registration fee is to be charged to a Deposit Account established in the Copyright Office, give name and number of Account.
Name ▼   Not Applicable   Account Number ▼

CORRESPONDENCE Give name and address to which correspondence about this application should be sent. Name/Address/Apt/City/State/Zip ▼
Mary T. Hales,
222 Program Lane
Miniville, USA 99999
Area Code & Telephone Number ▶ (999) 555-5555

10 CERTIFICATION* I, the undersigned, hereby certify that I am the
Check one ▶
☒ author
☐ other copyright claimant
☐ owner of exclusive right(s)
☐ authorized agent of _____
Name of author or other copyright claimant, or owner of exclusive right(s) ▲

of the work identified in this application and that the statements made by me in this application are correct to the best of my knowledge.

Typed or printed name and date ▼ If this is a published work, this date must be the same as or later than the date of publication given in space 3.
Mary T. Hales   date ▶ August 1, 1985

Handwritten signature (X) ▼
Mary T. Hales

11

MAIL CERTIFI-CATE TO

Certificate will be mailed in window envelope

Name ▼
Mary T. Hales
Number/Street/Apartment Number ▼
222 Program Lane
City/State/ZIP ▼
Miniville USA 99999

Have you:
• Completed all necessary spaces?
• Signed your application in space 10?
• Enclosed check or money order for $10 payable to Register of Copyrights?
• Enclosed your deposit material with the application and fee?
MAIL TO: Register of Copyrights, Library of Congress, Washington, D.C. 20559

*17 U.S.C. § 506(e): Any person who knowingly makes a false representation of a material fact in the application for copyright registration provided for by section 409, or in any written statement filed in connection with the application, shall be fined not more than $2,500.

☆ GPO: 1984—421-278/513

May, 1984—75,000

B. Single Program Registration (Derivative Work)

Now let's look at how Program 39 in the LOANIT package should be registered. This program was derived from an earlier program. Again, Mary uses Form TX to register it.

FORM TX
UNITED STATES COPYRIGHT OFFICE

FORM TX

REGISTRATION NUMBER

TX _____ TXU

EFFECTIVE DATE OF REGISTRATION

Month _____ Day _____ Year _____

FOR COPYRIGHT OFFICE USE ONLY

EXAMINED BY

CHECKED BY

☐ CORRESPONDENCE Yes

☐ DEPOSIT ACCOUNT FUNDS USED

DO NOT WRITE ABOVE THIS LINE. IF YOU NEED MORE SPACE, USE A SEPARATE CONTINUATION SHEET.

1

TITLE OF THIS WORK ▼
LOANP 104-39

PREVIOUS OR ALTERNATIVE TITLES ▼
None

PUBLICATION AS A CONTRIBUTION If this work was published as a contribution to a periodical, serial, or collection, give information about the collective work in which the contribution appeared. **Title of Collective Work ▼**
Not Applicable

If published in a periodical or serial give **Volume ▼** **Number ▼** **Issue Date ▼** **On Pages ▼**

2

NOTE
Under the law, the "author" of a "work made for hire" is generally the employer, not the employee (see instructions). For any part of this work that was "made for hire" check "Yes" in the space provided, give the employer (or other person for whom the work was prepared) as "Author" of that part, and leave the space for dates of birth and death blank.

a
NAME OF AUTHOR ▼
Mary T. Hales

DATES OF BIRTH AND DEATH
Year Born ▼ 1947 **Year Died ▼**

Was this contribution to the work a "work made for hire"?
☐ Yes ☒ No

AUTHOR'S NATIONALITY OR DOMICILE
Name of Country
OR { Citizen of ▶ U.S.A.
     { Domiciled in ▶

WAS THIS AUTHOR'S CONTRIBUTION TO THE WORK
Anonymous? ☐ Yes ☒ No
Pseudonymous? ☐ Yes ☒ No
If the answer to either of these questions is "Yes," see detailed instructions

NATURE OF AUTHORSHIP Briefly describe nature of the material created by this author in which copyright is claimed. ▼
Test of computer program

b
NAME OF AUTHOR ▼

DATES OF BIRTH AND DEATH
Year Born ▼ **Year Died ▼**

Was this contribution to the work a "work made for hire"?
☐ Yes ☐ No

AUTHOR'S NATIONALITY OR DOMICILE
Name of country
OR { Citizen of ▶
     { Domiciled in ▶

WAS THIS AUTHOR'S CONTRIBUTION TO THE WORK
Anonymous? ☐ Yes ☐ No
Pseudonymous? ☐ Yes ☐ No
If the answer to either of these questions is "Yes," see detailed instructions

NATURE OF AUTHORSHIP Briefly describe nature of the material created by this author in which copyright is claimed. ▼

c
NAME OF AUTHOR ▼

DATES OF BIRTH AND DEATH
Year Born ▼ **Year Died ▼**

Was this contribution to the work a "work made for hire"?
☐ Yes ☐ No

AUTHOR'S NATIONALITY OR DOMICILE
Name of country
OR { Citizen of ▶
     { Domiciled in ▶

WAS THIS AUTHOR'S CONTRIBUTION TO THE WORK
Anonymous? ☐ Yes ☐ No
Pseudonymous? ☐ Yes ☐ No
If the answer to either of these questions is "Yes," see detailed instructions

NATURE OF AUTHORSHIP Briefly describe nature of the material created by this author in which copyright is claimed. ▼

3

YEAR IN WHICH CREATION OF THIS WORK WAS COMPLETED This information must be given in all cases.
1985 ◀ Year

DATE AND NATION OF FIRST PUBLICATION OF THIS PARTICULAR WORK Complete this information ONLY if this work has been published.
Month ▶ July Day ▶ 9 Year ▶ 1985
Nation ▶ USA

4

COPYRIGHT CLAIMANT(S) Name and address must be given even if the claimant is the same as the author given in space 2. ▼
Mary T. Hales
222 Program Lane
Miniville, USA 99999

TRANSFER If the claimant(s) named here in space 4 are different from the author(s) named in space 2, give a brief statement of how the claimant(s) obtained ownership of the copyright. ▼
Not Applicable

APPLICATION RECEIVED

ONE DEPOSIT RECEIVED

TWO DEPOSITS RECEIVED

REMITTANCE NUMBER AND DATE

DO NOT WRITE HERE
OFFICE USE ONLY

DO NOT WRITE ABOVE THIS LINE. IF YOU NEED MORE SPACE, USE A SEPARATE CONTINUATION SHEET.

5

PREVIOUS REGISTRATION Has registration for this work, or for an earlier version of this work, already been made in the Copyright Office?
☐ Yes ☒ No If your answer is "Yes," why is another registration being sought? (Check appropriate box) ▼
☐ This is the first published edition of a work previously registered in unpublished form.
☐ This is the first application submitted by this author as copyright claimant.
☐ This is a changed version of the work, as shown by space 6 on this application.

If your answer is "Yes," give: **Previous Registration Number ▼** **Year of Registration ▼**

6

DERIVATIVE WORK OR COMPILATION Complete both space 6a & 6b for a derivative work, complete only 6b for a compilation.
a. **Preexisting Material** Identify any preexisting work or works that this work is based on or incorporates. ▼
Some program text

b. **Material Added to This Work** Give a brief, general statement of the material that has been added to this work and in which copyright is claimed. ▼
Modified earlier text and additional new text

7

MANUFACTURERS AND LOCATIONS If this is a published work consisting preponderantly of nondramatic literary material in English, the law may require that the copies be manufactured in the United States or Canada for full protection. If so, the names of the manufacturers who performed certain processes, and the places where these processes were performed must be given. See instructions for details.
Names of Manufacturers ▼ Not Applicable **Places of Manufacture ▼**

8

REPRODUCTION FOR USE OF BLIND OR PHYSICALLY HANDICAPPED INDIVIDUALS A signature on this form at space 10, and a check in one of the boxes here in space 8, constitutes a non-exclusive grant of permission to the Library of Congress to reproduce and distribute solely for the blind and physically handicapped and under the conditions and limitations prescribed by the regulations of the Copyright Office: (1) copies of the work identified in space 1 of this application in Braille (or similar tactile symbols), or (2) phonorecords embodying a fixation of a reading of that work, or (3) both.
a ☐ Copies and Phonorecords b ☒ Copies Only c ☐ Phonorecords Only

9

DEPOSIT ACCOUNT If the registration fee is to be charged to a Deposit Account established in the Copyright Office, give name and number of Account.
Name ▼ Not Applicable **Account Number ▼**

CORRESPONDENCE Give name and address to which correspondence about this application should be sent. **Name/Address/Apt/City/State/Zip ▼**
Mary T. Hales
222 Program Lane
Miniville, USA 99999
Area Code & Telephone Number ▶ (999) 555-5555

10

CERTIFICATION* I, the undersigned, hereby certify that I am the
Check one ▶
☒ author
☐ other copyright claimant
☐ owner of exclusive right(s)
☐ authorized agent of _____
Name of author or other copyright claimant, or owner of exclusive right(s) ▲
of the work identified in this application and that the statements made by me in this application are correct to the best of my knowledge.

Typed or printed name and date ▼ If this is a published work, this date must be the same as or later than the date of publication given in space 3.
Mary T. Hales date ▶ August 1, 1985

Handwritten signature (X) ▼
Mary T. Hales

11

MAIL CERTIFICATE TO
Certificate will be mailed in window envelope
Name ▼
Mary T. Hales
Number/Street/Apartment Number ▼
222 Program Lane
City/State/ZIP ▼
Miniville, USA 99999

Have you:
• Completed all necessary spaces?
• Signed your application in space 10?
• Enclosed check or money order for $10 payable to Register of Copyrights?
• Enclosed your deposit material with the application and fee?
MAIL TO: Register of Copyrights, Library of Congress, Washington, D.C. 20559

BCA Graphics wishes to register QUILTIT, a computer program developed by Kendra Salone as a work for hire, along with a short operations manual. This work is used by BCA to generate quilt designs in house, and has not been published.

FORM TX

UNITED STATES COPYRIGHT OFFICE

REGISTRATION NUMBER

_____ TX _____ TXU

EFFECTIVE DATE OF REGISTRATION

_____ _____ _____
Month   Day   Year

FORM TX

FOR COPYRIGHT OFFICE USE ONLY

EXAMINED BY

CHECKED BY

☐ CORRESPONDENCE Yes

☐ DEPOSIT ACCOUNT FUNDS USED

DO NOT WRITE ABOVE THIS LINE. IF YOU NEED MORE SPACE, USE A SEPARATE CONTINUATION SHEET.

---

1 **TITLE OF THIS WORK ▼**

QUILTIT

PREVIOUS OR ALTERNATIVE TITLES ▼

None

PUBLICATION AS A CONTRIBUTION If this work was published as a contribution to a periodical, serial, or collection, give information about the collective work in which the contribution appeared. **Title of Collective Work ▼**

Not Applicable

If published in a periodical or serial give: **Volume ▼**   **Number ▼**   **Issue Date ▼**   **On Pages ▼**

---

2 **NAME OF AUTHOR ▼**

a   BCA Graphics

Was this contribution to the work a "work made for hire"?
☒ Yes
☐ No

DATES OF BIRTH AND DEATH
Year Born ▼   Year Died ▼
N.A.

AUTHOR'S NATIONALITY OR DOMICILE
Name of Country
OR { Citizen of ▶ U.S.A.
     Domiciled in ▶

WAS THIS AUTHOR'S CONTRIBUTION TO THE WORK
Anonymous?   ☐ Yes ☒ No
Pseudonymous? ☐ Yes ☒ No
If the answer to either of these questions is "Yes," see detailed instructions.

NOTE
Under the law, the "author" of a "work made for hire" is generally the employer, not the employee (see instructions). For any part of this work that was "made for hire" check "Yes" in the space provided, give the employer (or other person for whom the work was prepared) as "Author" of that part, and leave the space for dates of birth and death blank.

NATURE OF AUTHORSHIP Briefly describe nature of the material created by this author in which copyright is claimed. ▼

Text of program with accompanying documentation

NAME OF AUTHOR ▼

b

Was this contribution to the work a "work made for hire"?
☐ Yes
☐ No

DATES OF BIRTH AND DEATH
Year Born ▼   Year Died ▼

AUTHOR'S NATIONALITY OR DOMICILE
Name of Country
OR { Citizen of ▶
     Domiciled in ▶

WAS THIS AUTHOR'S CONTRIBUTION TO THE WORK
Anonymous?   ☐ Yes ☐ No
Pseudonymous? ☐ Yes ☐ No
If the answer to either of these questions is "Yes," see detailed instructions.

NATURE OF AUTHORSHIP Briefly describe nature of the material created by this author in which copyright is claimed. ▼

NAME OF AUTHOR ▼

c

Was this contribution to the work a "work made for hire"?
☐ Yes
☐ No

DATES OF BIRTH AND DEATH
Year Born ▼   Year Died ▼

AUTHOR'S NATIONALITY OR DOMICILE
Name of Country
OR { Citizen of ▶
     Domiciled in ▶

WAS THIS AUTHOR'S CONTRIBUTION TO THE WORK
Anonymous?   ☐ Yes ☐ No
Pseudonymous? ☐ Yes ☐ No
If the answer to either of these questions is "Yes," see detailed instructions.

NATURE OF AUTHORSHIP Briefly describe nature of the material created by this author in which copyright is claimed. ▼

---

3 **YEAR IN WHICH CREATION OF THIS WORK WAS COMPLETED** This information must be given in all cases.
1984 ◀ Year

DATE AND NATION OF FIRST PUBLICATION OF THIS PARTICULAR WORK
Complete this information Month ▶ _____ Day ▶ _____ Year ▶ _____ ◀ Nation
ONLY if this work has been published.

---

4 **COPYRIGHT CLAIMANT(S)** Name and address must be given even if the claimant is the same as the author given in space 2. ▼

BCA Graphics
Technology Circle
Industrial Circle
Big Town, USA 88888

TRANSFER If the claimant(s) named here in space 4 are different from the author(s) named in space 2, give a brief statement of how the claimant(s) obtained ownership of the copyright. ▼

N.A.

APPLICATION RECEIVED

ONE DEPOSIT RECEIVED

TWO DEPOSITS RECEIVED

REMITTANCE NUMBER AND DATE

DO NOT WRITE HERE OFFICE USE ONLY

MORE ON BACK ▶ • Complete all applicable spaces (numbers 5-11) on the reverse side of this page.
• See detailed instructions.   • Sign the form at line 10.

DO NOT WRITE HERE
Page 1 of _____ pages

DO NOT WRITE ABOVE THIS LINE. IF YOU NEED MORE SPACE, USE A SEPARATE CONTINUATION SHEET.

5 **PREVIOUS REGISTRATION** Has registration for this work, or for an earlier version of this work, already been made in the Copyright Office?
☐ Yes ☒ No If your answer is "Yes," why is another registration being sought? (Check appropriate box) ▼
☐ This is the first published edition of a work previously registered in unpublished form.
☐ This is the first application submitted by this author as copyright claimant.
☐ This is a changed version of the work, as shown by space 6 on this application.
If your answer is "Yes," give: **Previous Registration Number ▼**   **Year of Registration ▼**

6 **DERIVATIVE WORK OR COMPILATION** Complete both space 6a & 6b for a derivative work; complete only 6b for a compilation.
a. **Preexisting Material** Identify any preexisting work or works that this work is based on or incorporates. ▼
N.A.

b. **Material Added to This Work** Give a brief, general statement of the material that has been added to this work and in which copyright is claimed. ▼
N.A.

7 **MANUFACTURERS AND LOCATIONS** If this is a published work consisting preponderantly of nondramatic literary material in English, the law may require that the copies be manufactured in the United States or Canada for full protection. If so, the names of the manufacturers who performed certain processes, and the places where these processes were performed must be given. See instructions for details.
Names of Manufacturers ▼   **Places of Manufacture ▼**
N.A.

8 **REPRODUCTION FOR USE OF BLIND OR PHYSICALLY HANDICAPPED INDIVIDUALS** A signature on this form at space 10, and a check in one of the boxes here in space 8, constitutes a non-exclusive grant of permission to the Library of Congress to reproduce and distribute solely for the blind and physically handicapped and under the conditions and limitations prescribed by the regulations of the Copyright Office: (1) copies of the work identified in space 1 of this application in Braille (or similar tactile symbols); or (2) phonorecords embodying a fixation of a reading of that work; or (3) both.
a ☐ Copies and Phonorecords   b ☐ Copies Only   c ☐ Phonorecords Only

9 **DEPOSIT ACCOUNT** If the registration fee is to be charged to a Deposit Account established in the Copyright Office, give name and number of Account.
Name ▼   **Account Number ▼**
N.A.

CORRESPONDENCE Give name and address to which correspondence about this application should be sent. **Name/Address/Apt/City/State/Zip ▼**
BCA Graphics
Technology Circle
Industrial Circle, Big Town, USA 88888
Area Code & Telephone Number ▶ (777) 555-7777

10 **CERTIFICATION*** I, the undersigned, hereby certify that I am the
Check one ▶
☒ author
☐ other copyright claimant
☐ owner of exclusive right(s)
☐ authorized agent of _____
Name of author or other copyright claimant, or owner of exclusive right(s) ▲

of the work identified in this application and that the statements made by me in this application are correct to the best of my knowledge.

Typed or printed name and date ▼ If this is a published work, this date must be the same as or later than the date of publication given in space 3.
BCA Graphics   date ▶ May 16, 1985

☞ **Handwritten signature (X) ▼**
BCA Graphics

11 **MAIL CERTIFICATE TO**

Name ▼
BCA Graphics

Number/Street/Apartment Number ▼
Technology Circle

City/State/ZIP ▼
Industrial Circle, Big Town, USA 88888

Certificate will be mailed in window envelope

Have you:
• Completed all necessary spaces?
• Signed your application in space 10?
• Enclosed check or money order for $10 payable to Register of Copyrights?
• Enclosed your deposit material with the application and fee?

MAIL TO: Register of Copyrights, Library of Congress, Washington, D.C. 20559

* 17 U.S.C. § 506(e): Any person who knowingly makes a false representation of a material fact in the application for copyright registration provided for by section 409, or in any written statement filed in connection with the application, shall be fined not more than $2,500.

☆ GPO 1984-421-278/513   May 1984—75,000

D. Multi-Package Program Registration

Here is how Mary Hales would register the LOANIT package consisting of 70 programs, 8 manuals, a training film and a brochure on one Copyright Form TX.

224

FORM TX
UNITED STATES COPYRIGHT OFFICE

REGISTRATION NUMBER

_____

TX _____ TXU

EFFECTIVE DATE OF REGISTRATION

Month ____ Day ____ Year ____

DO NOT WRITE ABOVE THIS LINE. IF YOU NEED MORE SPACE, USE A SEPARATE CONTINUATION SHEET.

1 TITLE OF THIS WORK ▼

LOANIT

PREVIOUS OR ALTERNATIVE TITLES ▼

None

PUBLICATION AS A CONTRIBUTION If this work was published as a contribution to a periodical, serial, or collection, give information about the collective work in which the contribution appeared. **Title of Collective Work** ▼

N.A.

If published in a periodical or serial give Volume ▼   Number ▼   Issue Date ▼   On Pages ▼

2 NAME OF AUTHOR ▼

a   Mary T. Hales

DATES OF BIRTH AND DEATH
Year Born ▼ 1947   Year Died ▼

Was this contribution to the work a "work made for hire"?
☐ Yes
☒ No

AUTHOR'S NATIONALITY OR DOMICILE
Name of Country
OR { Citizen of ▶ USA
{ Domiciled in ▶

WAS THIS AUTHOR'S CONTRIBUTION TO THE WORK
Anonymous?   ☐ Yes ☒ No
Pseudonymous? ☐ Yes ☒ No
If the answer to either of these questions is "Yes," see detailed instructions.

NOTE
Under the law, the "author" of a "work made for hire" is generally the employer, not the employee (see instructions). For any part of this work that was "made for hire" check "Yes" in the space provided, give the employer (or other person for whom the work was prepared) as "Author" of that part, and leave the space for dates of birth and death blank.

NATURE OF AUTHORSHIP Briefly describe nature of the material created by this author in which copyright is claimed. ▼
Program texts and associated documentation/Computer instructions and documentation

NAME OF AUTHOR ▼
b

DATES OF BIRTH AND DEATH
Year Born ▼   Year Died ▼

Was this contribution to the work a "work made for hire"?
☐ Yes
☐ No

AUTHOR'S NATIONALITY OR DOMICILE
Name of country
OR { Citizen of ▶
{ Domiciled in ▶

WAS THIS AUTHOR'S CONTRIBUTION TO THE WORK
Anonymous?   ☐ Yes ☐ No
Pseudonymous? ☐ Yes ☐ No
If the answer to either of these questions is "Yes," see detailed instructions.

NATURE OF AUTHORSHIP Briefly describe nature of the material created by this author in which copyright is claimed. ▼

NAME OF AUTHOR ▼
c

DATES OF BIRTH AND DEATH
Year Born ▼   Year Died ▼

Was this contribution to the work a "work made for hire"?
☐ Yes
☐ No

AUTHOR'S NATIONALITY OR DOMICILE
Name of Country
OR { Citizen of ▶
{ Domiciled in ▶

WAS THIS AUTHOR'S CONTRIBUTION TO THE WORK
Anonymous?   ☐ Yes ☐ No
Pseudonymous? ☐ Yes ☐ No
If the answer to either of these questions is "Yes," see detailed instructions.

NATURE OF AUTHORSHIP Briefly describe nature of the material created by this author in which copyright is claimed. ▼

3 YEAR IN WHICH CREATION OF THIS WORK WAS COMPLETED This information must be given in all cases.
1985 ◄ Year

DATE AND NATION OF FIRST PUBLICATION OF THIS PARTICULAR WORK
Complete this information ONLY if this work has been published.
Month ▶ July   Day ▶ 9   Year ▶ 1985   Nation

4 COPYRIGHT CLAIMANT(S) Name and address must be given even if the claimant is the same as the author given in space 2. ▼

Mary T. Hales
222 Program Lane
Miniville, USA 99999

APPLICATION RECEIVED

ONE DEPOSIT RECEIVED

TWO DEPOSITS RECEIVED

REMITTANCE NUMBER AND DATE

DO NOT WRITE HERE
OFFICE USE ONLY

TRANSFER If the claimant(s) named here in space 4 are different from the author(s) named in space 2, give a brief statement of how the claimant(s) obtained ownership of the copyright. ▼
N.A.

DO NOT WRITE ABOVE THIS LINE. IF YOU NEED MORE SPACE, USE A SEPARATE CONTINUATION SHEET.

5 PREVIOUS REGISTRATION Has registration for this work, or for an earlier version of this work, already been made in the Copyright Office?
☐ Yes ☒ No If your answer is "Yes," why is another registration being sought? (Check appropriate box) ▼
☐ This is the first published edition of a work previously registered in unpublished form.
☐ This is the first application submitted by this author as copyright claimant.
☐ This is a changed version of the work, as shown by space 6 on this application.
If your answer is "Yes," give: **Previous Registration Number** ▼   **Year of Registration** ▼

6 DERIVATIVE WORK OR COMPILATION Complete both space 6a & 6b for a derivative work; complete only 6b for a compilation.
a. Preexisting Material Identify any preexisting work or works that this work is based on or incorporates. ▼
N.A.

b. Material Added to This Work Give a brief, general statement of the material that has been added to this work and in which copyright is claimed. ▼
N.A.

7 MANUFACTURERS AND LOCATIONS If this is a published work consisting preponderantly of nondramatic literary material in English, the law may require that the copies be manufactured in the United States or Canada for full protection. If so, the names of the manufacturers who performed certain processes, and the places where these processes were performed must be given. See instructions for details.
Names of Manufacturers ▼   Places of Manufacture ▼
Zorman Printing   U.S.A.

8 REPRODUCTION FOR USE OF BLIND OR PHYSICALLY HANDICAPPED INDIVIDUALS   A signature on this form at space 10, and a check in one of the boxes here in space 8, constitutes a non-exclusive grant of permission to the Library of Congress to reproduce and distribute solely for the blind and physically handicapped and under the conditions and limitations prescribed by the regulations of the Copyright Office: (1) copies of the work identified in space 1 of this application in Braille (or similar tactile symbols); or (2) phonorecords embodying a fixation of a reading of that work; or (3) both.
a ☐ Copies and Phonorecords   b ☒ Copies Only   c ☐ Phonorecords Only

9 DEPOSIT ACCOUNT If the registration fee is to be charged to a Deposit Account established in the Copyright Office, give name and number of Account.
Name ▼   Account Number ▼
N.A.

CORRESPONDENCE Give name and address to which correspondence about this application should be sent.   Name/Address/Apt/City/State/Zip ▼
Mary T. Hales
222 Program Lane
Miniville, USA 99999
Area Code & Telephone Number ▶ (999) 555-5555

10 CERTIFICATION* I, the undersigned, hereby certify that I am the
Check one ▶
☒ author
☐ other copyright claimant
☐ owner of exclusive right(s)
☐ authorized agent of
Name of author or other copyright claimant, or owner of exclusive right(s) ▲

of the work identified in this application and that the statements made by me in this application are correct to the best of my knowledge.

Typed or printed name and date ▼ If this is a published work, this date must be the same as or later than the date of publication given in space 3.
Mary T. Hales   date ▶ August 1, 1985

Handwritten signature (X) ▼
Mary T. Hales

11 MAIL CERTIFICATE TO
Name ▼
Mary T. Hales
Number/Street/Apartment Number ▼
222 Program Lane
City/State/ZIP ▼
Miniville USA 99999

Certificate will be mailed in window envelope

Have you:
• Completed all necessary spaces?
• Signed your application in space 10?
• Enclosed check or money order for $10 payable to: Register of Copyrights?
• Enclosed your deposit material with the application and fee?
MAIL TO: Register of Copyrights, Library of Congress, Washington, D.C. 20559

FOR COPYRIGHT OFFICE USE ONLY

EXAMINED BY _____
CHECKED BY _____
CORRESPONDENCE ☐ Yes
DEPOSIT ACCOUNT FUNDS USED ☐

FORM TX

Here is a registration form for Mary Hales' LOANIT users' manual, registered as a separate work.

FORM TX
UNITED STATES COPYRIGHT OFFICE

REGISTRATION NUMBER

TX _____ TXU

EFFECTIVE DATE OF REGISTRATION

Month _____ Day _____ Year _____

DO NOT WRITE ABOVE THIS LINE. IF YOU NEED MORE SPACE, USE A SEPARATE CONTINUATION SHEET.

1 TITLE OF THIS WORK ▼
LOANIT USER'S MANUAL — Vol I.

PREVIOUS OR ALTERNATIVE TITLES ▼
None

PUBLICATION AS A CONTRIBUTION If this work was published as a contribution to a periodical, serial, or collection, give information about the collective work in which the contribution appeared.   Title of Collective Work ▼
N.A.

If published in a periodical or serial give: Volume ▼   Number ▼   Issue Date ▼   On Pages ▼

2 NAME OF AUTHOR ▼
a   Mary T. Hales

Was this contribution to the work a "work made for hire"?
☐ Yes
☒ No

AUTHOR'S NATIONALITY OR DOMICILE
Name of Country
OR { Citizen of ▶ U.S.A.
{ Domiciled in ▶

DATES OF BIRTH AND DEATH
Year Born ▼   Year Died ▼
1947

WAS THIS AUTHOR'S CONTRIBUTION TO THE WORK
Anonymous?   ☐ Yes ☒ No
Pseudonymous? ☐ Yes ☒ No
If the answer to either of these questions is "Yes," see detailed instructions.

NATURE OF AUTHORSHIP Briefly describe nature of the material created by this author in which copyright is claimed. ▼
Entire text

NOTE
Under the law, the "author" of a "work made for hire" is generally the employer, not the employee (see instructions). For any part of this work that was "made for hire" check "Yes" in the space provided, give the employer (or other person for whom the work was prepared) as "Author" of that part, and leave the space for dates of birth and death blank.

NAME OF AUTHOR ▼
b

Was this contribution to the work a "work made for hire"?
☐ Yes
☐ No

AUTHOR'S NATIONALITY OR DOMICILE
Name of Country
OR { Citizen of ▶
{ Domiciled in ▶

DATES OF BIRTH AND DEATH
Year Born ▼   Year Died ▼

WAS THIS AUTHOR'S CONTRIBUTION TO THE WORK
Anonymous?   ☐ Yes ☐ No
Pseudonymous? ☐ Yes ☐ No

NATURE OF AUTHORSHIP Briefly describe nature of the material created by this author in which copyright is claimed. ▼

NAME OF AUTHOR ▼
c

Was this contribution to the work a "work made for hire"?
☐ Yes
☐ No

AUTHOR'S NATIONALITY OR DOMICILE
Name of Country
OR { Citizen of ▶
{ Domiciled in ▶

DATES OF BIRTH AND DEATH
Year Born ▼   Year Died ▼

WAS THIS AUTHOR'S CONTRIBUTION TO THE WORK
Anonymous?   ☐ Yes ☐ No
Pseudonymous? ☐ Yes ☐ No

NATURE OF AUTHORSHIP Briefly describe nature of the material created by this author in which copyright is claimed. ▼

3 YEAR IN WHICH CREATION OF THIS WORK WAS COMPLETED This information must be given in all cases.
1985 ◀ Year

DATE AND NATION OF FIRST PUBLICATION OF THIS PARTICULAR WORK
Complete this information ONLY if this work has been published.
Month ▶ July   Day ▶ 9   Year ▶ 1985
U.S.A. ◀ Nation

4 COPYRIGHT CLAIMANT(S) Name and address must be given even if the claimant is the same as the author given in space 2. ▼
Mary T. Hales
222 Program Lane
Miniville USA 99999

TRANSFER If the claimant(s) named here in space 4 are different from the author(s) named in space 2, give a brief statement of how the claimant(s) obtained ownership of the copyright. ▼
N.A.

APPLICATION RECEIVED
ONE DEPOSIT RECEIVED
TWO DEPOSITS RECEIVED
REMITTANCE NUMBER AND DATE

DO NOT WRITE HERE
OFFICE USE ONLY

MORE ON BACK ▶ • Complete all applicable spaces (numbers 5-11) on the reverse side of this page.
• See detailed instructions.   • Sign the form at line 10.

DO NOT WRITE HERE
Page 1 of _____ pages

5 See instructions before completing this space.

6

7

8 See instructions.

9 See instructions.

10 Be sure to give your daytime phone number

11

EXAMINED BY

CHECKED BY

CORRESPONDENCE
☐ Yes

DEPOSIT ACCOUNT
☐ FUNDS USED

FOR COPYRIGHT OFFICE USE ONLY

DO NOT WRITE ABOVE THIS LINE. IF YOU NEED MORE SPACE, USE A SEPARATE CONTINUATION SHEET.

PREVIOUS REGISTRATION Has registration for this work, or for an earlier version of this work, already been made in the Copyright Office?
☐ Yes ☒ No If your answer is "Yes," why is another registration being sought? (Check appropriate box) ▼
☐ This is the first published edition of a work previously registered in unpublished form.
☐ This is the first application submitted by this author as copyright claimant.
☐ This is a changed version of the work, as shown by space 6 on this application.
If your answer is "Yes," give: Previous Registration Number ▼   Year of Registration ▼

DERIVATIVE WORK OR COMPILATION Complete both space 6a & 6b for a derivative work; complete only 6b for a compilation.
a. Preexisting Material Identify any preexisting work or works that this work is based on or incorporates. ▼
N.A.

b. Material Added to This Work Give a brief, general statement of the material that has been added to this work and in which copyright is claimed. ▼
N.A.

MANUFACTURERS AND LOCATIONS If this is a published work consisting preponderantly of nondramatic literary material in English, the law may require that the copies be manufactured in the United States or Canada for full protection. If so, the names of the manufacturers who performed certain processes, and the places where these processes were performed must be given. See instructions for details.
Names of Manufacturers ▼   Places of Manufacture ▼
ZORNAN Printers   Miniville, USA

REPRODUCTION FOR USE OF BLIND OR PHYSICALLY HANDICAPPED INDIVIDUALS A signature on this form at space 10, and a check in one of the boxes here in space 8, constitutes a non-exclusive grant of permission to the Library of Congress to reproduce and distribute solely for the blind and physically handicapped and under the conditions and limitations prescribed by the regulations of the Copyright Office: (1) copies of the work identified in space 1 of this application in Braille (or similar tactile symbols), or (2) phonorecords embodying a fixation of a reading of that work, or (3) both.
a ☐ Copies and Phonorecords   b ☒ Copies Only   c ☐ Phonorecords Only

DEPOSIT ACCOUNT If the registration fee is to be charged to a Deposit Account established in the Copyright Office, give name and number of Account.
Name ▼   Account Number ▼
N.A.

CORRESPONDENCE Give name and address to which correspondence about this application should be sent.   Name/Address/Apt/City/State/Zip ▼
Mary T. Hales
222 Program Lane
Miniville, USA 99999
Area Code & Telephone Number ▶ (999) 555-5555

CERTIFICATION* I, the undersigned, hereby certify that I am the
Check one ▶
☒ author
☐ other copyright claimant
☐ owner of exclusive right(s)
☐ authorized agent of _____
Name of author or other copyright claimant, or owner of exclusive right(s) ▲

of the work identified in this application and that the statements made by me in this application are correct to the best of my knowledge.

Typed or printed name and date ▼ If this is a published work, this date must be the same as or later than the date of publication given in space 3.
Mary T. Hales   date ▶ August 1, 1985

✍ Handwritten signature (X) ▼
Mary T. Hales

MAIL CERTIFICATE TO
Certificate will be mailed in window envelope

Name ▼
Mary T. Hales
Number/Street/Apartment Number ▼
222 Program Lane
City/State/ZIP ▼
Miniville, USA 99999

Have you:
• Completed all necessary spaces?
• Signed your application in space 10?
• Enclosed check or money order for $10 payable to Register of Copyrights?
• Enclosed your deposit material with the application form?

MAIL TO: Register of Copyrights, Library of Congress. Washington. D.C. 20559

* 17 U.S.C. § 506(e): Any person who knowingly makes a false representation of a material fact in the application for copyright registration provided for by section 409, or in any written statement filed in connection with the application, shall be fined not more than $2,500.

☆ GPO. 1984—421-278/513

May 1984—75,000

F. A Training Film Registered As a Separate Work

Mary Hales registers her LOANIT training film on Copyright Form PA as a separate work.

FORM PA
UNITED STATES COPYRIGHT OFFICE

REGISTRATION NUMBER

PA   PAU

EFFECTIVE DATE OF REGISTRATION

Month   Day   Year

DO NOT WRITE ABOVE THIS LINE. IF YOU NEED MORE SPACE, USE A SEPARATE CONTINUATION SHEET.

1   **TITLE OF THIS WORK ▼**

LOANIT – A REVOLUTIONARY LOAN PROCESSING SYSTEM

PREVIOUS OR ALTERNATIVE TITLES ▼

None

NATURE OF THIS WORK ▼ See instructions

Training film with accompanying sound

2   **NAME OF AUTHOR ▼**

a   Mary T. Hales

DATES OF BIRTH AND DEATH
Year Born ▼   Year Died ▼
1947

Was this contribution to the work a "work made for hire"?
☐ Yes
☒ No

AUTHOR'S NATIONALITY OR DOMICILE
Name of Country
OR { Citizen of ▶ USA
Domiciled in ▶

WAS THIS AUTHOR'S CONTRIBUTION TO THE WORK
Anonymous? ☐ Yes ☒ No
Pseudonymous? ☐ Yes ☒ No
If the answer to either of these questions is "Yes," see detailed instructions

NATURE OF AUTHORSHIP Briefly describe nature of the material created by this author in which copyright is claimed ▼

Training Film

NOTE
Under the law, the "author" of a "work made for hire" is generally the employer, not the employee (see instructions). For any part of this work that was "made for hire" check "Yes" in the space provided, give the employer (or other person for whom the work was prepared) as "Author" of that part, and leave the space for dates of birth and death blank.

NAME OF AUTHOR ▼

b

DATES OF BIRTH AND DEATH
Year Born ▼   Year Died ▼

Was this contribution to the work a "work made for hire"?
☐ Yes
☐ No

AUTHOR'S NATIONALITY OR DOMICILE
Name of Country
OR { Citizen of ▶
Domiciled in ▶

WAS THIS AUTHOR'S CONTRIBUTION TO THE WORK
Anonymous? ☐ Yes ☐ No
Pseudonymous? ☐ Yes ☐ No

NATURE OF AUTHORSHIP Briefly describe nature of the material created by this author in which copyright is claimed ▼

NAME OF AUTHOR ▼

c

DATES OF BIRTH AND DEATH
Year Born ▼   Year Died ▼

Was this contribution to the work a "work made for hire"?
☐ Yes
☐ No

AUTHOR'S NATIONALITY OR DOMICILE
Name of Country
OR { Citizen of ▶
Domiciled in ▶

WAS THIS AUTHOR'S CONTRIBUTION TO THE WORK
Anonymous? ☐ Yes ☐ No
Pseudonymous? ☐ Yes ☐ No

NATURE OF AUTHORSHIP Briefly describe nature of the material created by this author in which copyright is claimed ▼

3   **YEAR IN WHICH CREATION OF THIS WORK WAS COMPLETED** This information must be given in all cases.
1985 ◀ Year

DATE AND NATION OF FIRST PUBLICATION OF THIS PARTICULAR WORK
Complete this information ONLY if this work has been published.
Month ▶ September   Day ▶ 19   Year ▶ 1985
U.S.A.   ◀ Nation

4   **COPYRIGHT CLAIMANT(S)** Name and address must be given even if the claimant is the same as the author given in space 2 ▼

Mary T. Hales
222 Program Lane
Minivville USA 99999

TRANSFER If the claimant(s) named here in space 4 are different from the author(s) named in space 2, give a brief statement of how the claimant(s) obtained ownership of the copyright ▼

N.A.

See instructions before completing this space.

APPLICATION RECEIVED
ONE DEPOSIT RECEIVED
TWO DEPOSITS RECEIVED
REMITTANCE NUMBER AND DATE

DO NOT WRITE HERE
OFFICE USE ONLY

EXAMINED BY   FORM PA

CHECKED BY

☐ CORRESPONDENCE
Yes

☐ DEPOSIT ACCOUNT
FUNDS USED

FOR COPYRIGHT OFFICE USE ONLY

5

DO NOT WRITE ABOVE THIS LINE. IF YOU NEED MORE SPACE, USE A SEPARATE CONTINUATION SHEET.

PREVIOUS REGISTRATION Has registration for this work, or for an earlier version of this work, already been made in the Copyright Office?
☐ Yes ☒ No If your answer is "Yes," why is another registration being sought? (Check appropriate box) ▼
☐ This is the first published edition of a work previously registered in unpublished form.
☐ This is the first application submitted by this author as copyright claimant.
☐ This is a changed version of the work, as shown by space 6 on this application.
If your answer is "Yes," give: **Previous Registration Number ▼**   **Year of Registration ▼**

6

DERIVATIVE WORK OR COMPILATION Complete both space 6a & 6b for a derivative work; complete only 6b for a compilation.
a. **Preexisting Material** Identify any preexisting work or works that this work is based on or incorporates. ▼

N.A.

b. **Material Added to This Work** Give a brief, general statement of the material that has been added to this work and in which copyright is claimed ▼

N.A.

See instructions before completing this space.

7

DEPOSIT ACCOUNT If the registration fee is to be charged to a Deposit Account established in the Copyright Office, give name and number of Account.
Name ▼   **Account Number ▼**

N.A.

CORRESPONDENCE Give name and address to which correspondence about this application should be sent. Name/Address/Apt/City/State/Zip ▼

Mary T. Hales
222 Program Lane
Minivville USA 99999

Area Code & Telephone Number ▶ (999) 555-5555

Be sure to give your daytime phone ▼ number

8

CERTIFICATION* I, the undersigned, hereby certify that I am the
Check only one ▼
☒ author
☐ other copyright claimant
☐ owner of exclusive right(s)
☐ authorized agent of _____
Name of author or other copyright claimant, or owner of exclusive right(s) ▲

of the work identified in this application and that the statements made by me in this application are correct to the best of my knowledge.

Typed or printed name and date ▼ If this is a published work, this date must be the same as or later than the date of publication given in space 3.

Mary T. Hales   date ▶ December 1, 1985

Handwritten signature (X) ▼

Mary T. Hales

9

MAIL CERTIFICATE TO

Certificate will be mailed in window envelope

Name ▼
Mary T. Hales
Number/Street/Apartment Number ▼
222 Program Lane
City/State/Zip ▼
Minivville USA 99999

Have you:
• Completed all necessary spaces?
• Signed your application in space 8?
• Enclosed check or money order for $10 payable to Register of Copyrights?
• Enclosed your deposit material with the application and fee?

MAIL TO: Register of Copyrights, Library of Congress, Washington, D.C. 20559

Carl Jones registers his GOTTCHA game program on a TX form, as follows:

FORM TX
UNITED STATES COPYRIGHT OFFICE

REGISTRATION NUMBER

TX _____ TXU

EFFECTIVE DATE OF REGISTRATION

Month _____ Day _____ Year _____

DO NOT WRITE ABOVE THIS LINE. IF YOU NEED MORE SPACE, USE A SEPARATE CONTINUATION SHEET.

1 **TITLE OF THIS WORK ▼**
GOTTCHA

PREVIOUS OR ALTERNATIVE TITLES ▼
None

PUBLICATION AS A CONTRIBUTION If this work was published as a contribution to a periodical, serial, or collection, give information about the collective work in which the contribution appeared. **Title of Collective Work ▼**
N.A.

If published in a periodical or serial give: **Volume ▼** **Number ▼** **Issue Date ▼** **On Pages ▼**

2 **NAME OF AUTHOR ▼**
a Carl Jones

DATES OF BIRTH AND DEATH
Year Born ▼ 1959 Year Died ▼

Was this contribution to the work a "work made for hire"?
☐ Yes
☒ No

AUTHOR'S NATIONALITY OR DOMICILE
Name of Country
OR { Citizen of ▶ USA
     Domiciled in ▶

WAS THIS AUTHOR'S CONTRIBUTION TO THE WORK
Anonymous? ☐ Yes ☒ No
Pseudonymous? ☐ Yes ☒ No
If the answer to either of these questions is "Yes," see detailed instructions.

NATURE OF AUTHORSHIP Briefly describe nature of the material created by this author in which copyright is claimed. ▼
Text of program

NAME OF AUTHOR ▼
b

DATES OF BIRTH AND DEATH
Year Born ▼ Year Died ▼

Was this contribution to the work a "work made for hire"?
☐ Yes
☐ No

AUTHOR'S NATIONALITY OR DOMICILE
Name of Country
OR { Citizen of ▶
     Domiciled in ▶

WAS THIS AUTHOR'S CONTRIBUTION TO THE WORK
Anonymous? ☐ Yes ☐ No
Pseudonymous? ☐ Yes ☐ No

NATURE OF AUTHORSHIP Briefly describe nature of the material created by this author in which copyright is claimed. ▼

NAME OF AUTHOR ▼
c

DATES OF BIRTH AND DEATH
Year Born ▼ Year Died ▼

Was this contribution to the work a "work made for hire"?
☐ Yes
☐ No

AUTHOR'S NATIONALITY OR DOMICILE
Name of Country
OR { Citizen of ▶
     Domiciled in ▶

WAS THIS AUTHOR'S CONTRIBUTION TO THE WORK
Anonymous? ☐ Yes ☐ No
Pseudonymous? ☐ Yes ☐ No

NATURE OF AUTHORSHIP Briefly describe nature of the material created by this author in which copyright is claimed. ▼

NOTE
Under the law, the "author" of a "work made for hire" is generally the employer, not the employee (see instructions). For any part of this work that was "made for hire" check "Yes" in the space provided, give the employer (or other person for whom the work was prepared) as "Author" of that part, and leave the space for dates of birth and death blank.

3 **YEAR IN WHICH CREATION OF THIS WORK WAS COMPLETED** This information must be given in all cases.
1985 ◀ Year

DATE AND NATION OF FIRST PUBLICATION OF THIS PARTICULAR WORK Complete this information ONLY if this work has been published.
Month ▶ February Day ▶ 10 Year ▶ 1985
USA ◀ Nation

4 **COPYRIGHT CLAIMANT(S)** Name and address must be given even if the claimant is the same as the author given in space 2.▼
Carl Jones
555 Routine Dr.
Computer Town, USA 22222

TRANSFER If the claimant(s) named here in space 4 are different from the author(s) named in space 2, give a brief statement of how the claimant(s) obtained ownership of the copyright.▼
N.A.

APPLICATION RECEIVED

ONE DEPOSIT RECEIVED

TWO DEPOSITS RECEIVED

REMITTANCE NUMBER AND DATE

DO NOT WRITE HERE
OFFICE USE ONLY
DO NOT WRITE ABOVE THIS LINE

MORE ON BACK ▶ • Complete all applicable spaces (numbers 5-11) on the reverse side of this page.
• See detailed instructions. • Sign the form at line 10.

DO NOT WRITE HERE
Page 1 of _____ pages

FORM TX

FOR COPYRIGHT OFFICE USE ONLY

EXAMINED BY

CHECKED BY

CORRESPONDENCE ☐ Yes

DEPOSIT ACCOUNT FUNDS USED

DO NOT WRITE ABOVE THIS LINE. IF YOU NEED MORE SPACE, USE A SEPARATE CONTINUATION SHEET.

5 **PREVIOUS REGISTRATION** Has registration for this work, or for an earlier version of this work, already been made in the Copyright Office?
☐ Yes ☒ No If your answer is "Yes," why is another registration being sought? (Check appropriate box) ▼
☐ This is the first published edition of a work previously registered in unpublished form.
☐ This is the first application submitted by this author as copyright claimant.
☐ This is a changed version of the work, as shown by space 6 on this application.
If your answer is "Yes," give: **Previous Registration Number ▼** **Year of Registration ▼**

6 **DERIVATIVE WORK OR COMPILATION** Complete both space 6a & 6b for a derivative work; complete only 6b for a compilation.
a. **Preexisting Material** Identify any preexisting work or works that this work is based on or incorporates. ▼
N.A.

b. **Material Added to This Work** Give a brief, general statement of the material that has been added to this work and in which copyright is claimed. ▼
N.A.

7 **MANUFACTURERS AND LOCATIONS** If this is a published work consisting preponderantly of nondramatic literary material in English, the law may require that the copies be manufactured in the United States or Canada for full protection. If so, the names of the manufacturers who performed certain processes, and the places where these processes were performed must be given. See instructions for details.
Names of Manufacturers ▼ **Places of Manufacture ▼**
N.A.

8 **REPRODUCTION FOR USE OF BLIND OR PHYSICALLY HANDICAPPED INDIVIDUALS** A signature on this form at space 10, and a check in one of the boxes here in space 8, constitutes a non-exclusive grant of permission to the Library of Congress to reproduce and distribute solely for the blind and physically handicapped and under the conditions and limitations prescribed by the regulations of the Copyright Office: (1) copies of the work identified in space 1 of this application in Braille (or similar tactile symbols); or (2) phonorecords embodying a fixation of a reading of that work; or (3) both.
a ☐ Copies and Phonorecords b ☒ Copies Only c ☐ Phonorecords Only

9 **DEPOSIT ACCOUNT** If the registration fee is to be charged to a Deposit Account established in the Copyright Office, give name and number of Account.
Name ▼ **Account Number ▼**
N.A.

CORRESPONDENCE Give name and address to which correspondence about this application should be sent. **Name/Address/Apt/City/State/Zip ▼**
Carl Jones
555 Routine Dr.
Computer Town, USA 22222
Area Code & Telephone Number ▶ (888) 555-8888

10 **CERTIFICATION*** I, the undersigned, hereby certify that I am the
Check one ▶ ☒ author
☐ other copyright claimant
☐ owner of exclusive right(s)
☐ authorized agent of
of the work identified in this application and that the statements made by me in this application are correct to the best of my knowledge.

Typed or printed name and date ▼ If this is a published work, this date must be the same as or later than the date of publication given in space 3.
Carl Jones date ▶ February 11, 1985

Handwritten signature (X) ▼
Carl Jones

11 **MAIL CERTIFI-CATE TO**
Name ▼
Carl Jones
Number/Street/Apartment Number ▼
555 Routine Dr.
City/State/ZIP ▼
Computer Town, USA 22222

Certificate will be mailed in window envelope

Have you:
• Completed all necessary spaces?
• Signed your application in space 10?
• Enclosed check or money order for $10 payable to Register of Copyrights?
• Enclosed your deposit material with the application and fee?
MAIL TO: Register of Copyrights, Library of Congress, Washington, D.C. 20559

*17 U.S.C. § 506(e): Any person who knowingly makes a false representation of a material fact in the application for copyright registration provided for by section 409, or in any written statement filed in connection with the application, shall be fined not more than $2,500.

☆ GPO: 1984–421-278/513

May 1984—75,000

H. Computer Game Screens Registration

As noted in the text, it is usually wise to register computer game screens even if you separately register the program. Here is how Carl Jones would register his GOTTCHA game screens using Form PA.

FORM PA
UNITED STATES COPYRIGHT OFFICE

REGISTRATION NUMBER

PA _____ PAU

EFFECTIVE DATE OF REGISTRATION

Month _____ Day _____ Year _____

DO NOT WRITE ABOVE THIS LINE. IF YOU NEED MORE SPACE, USE A SEPARATE CONTINUATION SHEET.

1 TITLE OF THIS WORK ▼

GOTTCHA

PREVIOUS OR ALTERNATIVE TITLES ▼

None

NATURE OF THIS WORK ▼ See instructions

Computer game output screens with accompanying sound

2 NAME OF AUTHOR ▼

a   Carl Jones

DATES OF BIRTH AND DEATH
Year Born ▼ 1959   Year Died ▼

Was this contribution to the work a "work made for hire"?
☐ Yes
☒ No

AUTHOR'S NATIONALITY OR DOMICILE
Name of Country
OR { Citizen of ▶ USA
{ Domiciled in ▶

WAS THIS AUTHOR'S CONTRIBUTION TO THE WORK
Anonymous? ☐ Yes ☒ No
Pseudonymous? ☐ Yes ☒ No
If the answer to either of these questions is "Yes," see detailed instructions.

NATURE OF AUTHORSHIP Briefly describe nature of the material created by this author in which copyright is claimed ▼
Computer game screens

NOTE
Under the law, the "author" of a "work made for hire" is generally the employer, not the employee (see instructions). For any part of this work that was "made for hire" check "Yes" in the space provided, give the employer (or other person for whom the work was prepared) as "Author" of that part, and leave the space for dates of birth and death blank.

NAME OF AUTHOR ▼

b

DATES OF BIRTH AND DEATH
Year Born ▼   Year Died ▼

Was this contribution to the work a "work made for hire"?
☐ Yes
☐ No

AUTHOR'S NATIONALITY OR DOMICILE
Name of Country
OR { Citizen of ▶
{ Domiciled in ▶

WAS THIS AUTHOR'S CONTRIBUTION TO THE WORK
Anonymous? ☐ Yes ☐ No
Pseudonymous? ☐ Yes ☐ No

NATURE OF AUTHORSHIP Briefly describe nature of the material created by this author in which copyright is claimed ▼

NAME OF AUTHOR ▼

c

DATES OF BIRTH AND DEATH
Year Born ▼   Year Died ▼

Was this contribution to the work a "work made for hire"?
☐ Yes
☐ No

AUTHOR'S NATIONALITY OR DOMICILE
Name of Country
OR { Citizen of ▶
{ Domiciled in ▶

WAS THIS AUTHOR'S CONTRIBUTION TO THE WORK
Anonymous? ☐ Yes ☐ No
Pseudonymous? ☐ Yes ☐ No

NATURE OF AUTHORSHIP Briefly describe nature of the material created by this author in which copyright is claimed ▼

3 YEAR IN WHICH CREATION OF THIS WORK WAS COMPLETED This information must be given in all cases.
1985 ◀ Year

DATE AND NATION OF FIRST PUBLICATION OF THIS PARTICULAR WORK Complete this information ONLY if this work has been published.
Month ▶ February Day ▶ 10 Year ▶ 1985
USA ◀ Nation

4 COPYRIGHT CLAIMANT(S) Name and address must be given even if the claimant is the same as the author given in space 2 ▼
Carl Jones
555 Routine Dr.
Computer Town, USA 22222

APPLICATION RECEIVED

ONE DEPOSIT RECEIVED

TWO DEPOSITS RECEIVED

REMITTANCE NUMBER AND DATE

TRANSFER If the claimant(s) named here in space 4 are different from the author(s) named in space 2, give a brief statement of how the claimant(s) obtained ownership of the copyright. ▼
N.A.

DO NOT WRITE HERE
OFFICE USE ONLY

See instructions before completing this space.

EXAMINED BY

CHECKED BY

☐ CORRESPONDENCE Yes

☐ DEPOSIT ACCOUNT FUNDS USED

FOR COPYRIGHT OFFICE USE ONLY

DO NOT WRITE ABOVE THIS LINE. IF YOU NEED MORE SPACE, USE A SEPARATE CONTINUATION SHEET.

5 PREVIOUS REGISTRATION Has registration for this work, or for an earlier version of this work, already been made in the Copyright Office?
☐ Yes ☒ No If your answer is "Yes," why is another registration being sought? (Check appropriate box) ▼
☐ This is the first published edition of a work previously registered in unpublished form.
☐ This is the first application submitted by this author as copyright claimant.
☐ This is a changed version of the work, as shown by space 6 on this application.
If your answer is "Yes," give: Previous Registration Number ▼ Year of Registration ▼

6 DERIVATIVE WORK OR COMPILATION Complete both space 6a & 6b for a derivative work; complete only 6b for a compilation.
a. Preexisting Material Identify any preexisting work or works that this work is based on or incorporates. ▼
N.A.

See instructions before completing this space.

b. Material Added to This Work Give a brief, general statement of the material that has been added to this work and in which copyright is claimed ▼
N.A.

7 DEPOSIT ACCOUNT If the registration fee is to be charged to a Deposit Account established in the Copyright Office, give name and number of Account
Name ▼ Account Number ▼
N.A.

CORRESPONDENCE Give name and address to which correspondence about this application should be sent. Name Address Apt/City/State Zip ▼
Carl Jones
555 Routine Dr.
Computer Town USA 22222
Area Code & Telephone Number ▶ (888) 555-8888

Be sure to give your daytime phone number

8 CERTIFICATION* I, the undersigned, hereby certify that I am the
Check only one ▼
☒ author
☐ other copyright claimant
☐ owner of exclusive right(s)
☐ authorized agent of _____
Name of author or other copyright claimant, or owner of exclusive right(s) ▲

of the work identified in this application and that the statements made by me in this application are correct to the best of my knowledge.

Typed or printed name and date ▼ If this is a published work, this date must be the same as or later than the date of publication given in space 3.
Carl Jones date ▶ February 11, 1985

Handwritten signature (X) ▼
Carl Jones

9 MAIL CERTIFICATE TO

Certificate will be mailed in window envelope

Name ▼
Carl Jones
Number/Street/Apartment Number ▼
555 Routine Dr.
City/State ZIP ▼
Computer Town, USA 22222

Have you:
• Completed all necessary spaces?
• Signed your application in space 8?
• Enclosed check or money order for $10 payable to Register of Copyrights?
• Enclosed your deposit material with the application and fee?
MAIL TO: Register of Copyrights, Library of Congress, Washington, DC 20559

See instructions before completing this space.

I. Cartoon or Animated Film Registration

Carl Jones registers his cartoon, GOTTCHA COMIN' & GOIN' on a motion picture (audiovisual work) Copyright Form PA.

FORM PA
UNITED STATES COPYRIGHT OFFICE

REGISTRATION NUMBER

PA _____ PAU

EFFECTIVE DATE OF REGISTRATION

Month _____ Day _____ Year _____

DO NOT WRITE ABOVE THIS LINE. IF YOU NEED MORE SPACE, USE A SEPARATE CONTINUATION SHEET.

1 TITLE OF THIS WORK ▼

GOTTCHA COMIN' AND GOIN'

PREVIOUS OR ALTERNATIVE TITLES ▼

None

NATURE OF THIS WORK ▼ See instructions

Animated motion picture with accompanying sound

2 NAME OF AUTHOR ▼

a Carl Jones

DATES OF BIRTH AND DEATH
Year Born ▼ 1959   Year Died ▼

Was this contribution to the work a
"work made for hire"?
☐ Yes
☒ No

AUTHOR'S NATIONALITY OR DOMICILE
Name of Country
OR { Citizen of ▶ USA
     Domiciled in ▶

WAS THIS AUTHOR'S CONTRIBUTION TO THE WORK
Anonymous?   ☐ Yes ☒ No
Pseudonymous? ☐ Yes ☒ No
If the answer to either of these questions is "Yes," see detailed instructions.

NATURE OF AUTHORSHIP Briefly describe nature of the material created by this author in which copyright is claimed. ▼
Animated film

NAME OF AUTHOR ▼

b

Was this contribution to the work a
"work made for hire"?
☐ Yes
☐ No

AUTHOR'S NATIONALITY OR DOMICILE
Name of Country
OR { Citizen of ▶
     Domiciled in ▶

WAS THIS AUTHOR'S CONTRIBUTION TO THE WORK
Anonymous?   ☐ Yes ☐ No
Pseudonymous? ☐ Yes ☐ No

DATES OF BIRTH AND DEATH
Year Born ▼   Year Died ▼

NATURE OF AUTHORSHIP Briefly describe nature of the material created by this author in which copyright is claimed. ▼

NAME OF AUTHOR ▼

c

Was this contribution to the work a
"work made for hire"?
☐ Yes
☐ No

AUTHOR'S NATIONALITY OR DOMICILE
Name of Country
OR { Citizen of ▶
     Domiciled in ▶

WAS THIS AUTHOR'S CONTRIBUTION TO THE WORK
Anonymous?   ☐ Yes ☐ No
Pseudonymous? ☐ Yes ☐ No

DATES OF BIRTH AND DEATH
Year Born ▼   Year Died ▼

NATURE OF AUTHORSHIP Briefly describe nature of the material created by this author in which copyright is claimed. ▼

NOTE
Under the law, the "author" of a "work made for hire" is generally the employer, not the employee (see instructions). For any part of this work that was "made for hire" check "Yes" in the space provided, give the employer (or other person for whom the work was prepared) as "Author" of that part, and leave the space for dates of birth and death blank.

3 YEAR IN WHICH CREATION OF THIS WORK WAS COMPLETED This information must be given in all cases.
1985 ◀ Year

DATE AND NATION OF FIRST PUBLICATION OF THIS PARTICULAR WORK Complete this information ONLY if this work has been published.
Month ▶ September Day ▶ 6 Year ▶ 1985
Nation ▶ USA

4 COPYRIGHT CLAIMANT(S) Name and address must be given even if the claimant is the same as the author given in space 2. ▼

Carl Jones
555 Routine Dr.
Computer Town, USA 22222

TRANSFER If the claimant(s) named here in space 4 are different from the author(s) named in space 2, give a brief statement of how the claimant(s) obtained ownership of the copyright. ▼
N.A.

See instructions before completing this space

APPLICATION RECEIVED

ONE DEPOSIT RECEIVED

TWO DEPOSITS RECEIVED

REMITTANCE NUMBER AND DATE

DO NOT WRITE HERE
OFFICE USE ONLY

MORE ON BACK ▶ • Complete all applicable spaces (numbers 5-9) on the reverse side of this page
                    • Sign the form at line 8

DO NOT WRITE HERE
Page 1 of _____ pages

EXAMINED BY

CHECKED BY

CORRESPONDENCE
☐ Yes

DEPOSIT ACCOUNT
FUNDS USED

FORM PA

FOR COPYRIGHT OFFICE USE ONLY

DO NOT WRITE ABOVE THIS LINE. IF YOU NEED MORE SPACE, USE A SEPARATE CONTINUATION SHEET.

5 PREVIOUS REGISTRATION Has registration for this work, or for an earlier version of this work, already been made in the Copyright Office?
☐ Yes ☒ No If your answer is "Yes," why is another registration being sought? (Check appropriate box) ▼
☐ This is the first published edition of a work previously registered in unpublished form.
☐ This is the first application submitted by this author as copyright claimant.
☐ This is a changed version of the work, as shown by space 6 on this application.
If your answer is "Yes," give: Previous Registration Number ▼   Year of Registration ▼

6 DERIVATIVE WORK OR COMPILATION Complete both space 6a & 6b for a derivative work; complete only 6b for a compilation.
a Preexisting Material Identify any preexisting work or works that this work is based on or incorporates. ▼
Based on computer game

b Material Added to This Work Give a brief, general statement of the material that has been added to this work and in which copyright is claimed. ▼
Entire adaptation

See instructions before completing this space.

7 DEPOSIT ACCOUNT If the registration fee is to be charged to a Deposit Account established in the Copyright Office, give name and number of Account.
Name ▼   Account Number ▼
N.A.

CORRESPONDENCE Give name and address to which correspondence about this application should be sent.   Name/Address/Apt/City/State/Zip ▼
Carl Jones
555 Routine Dr.
Computer Town, USA 22222
Area Code & Telephone Number ▶ (888) 555-8888

Be sure to give your daytime phone number.

8 CERTIFICATION* I, the undersigned, hereby certify that I am the
Check only one ▼
☒ author
☐ other copyright claimant
☐ owner of exclusive right(s)
☐ authorized agent of _____
                        Name of author or other copyright claimant, or owner of exclusive right(s) ▲

of the work identified in this application and that the statements made by me in this application are correct to the best of my knowledge.

Typed or printed name and date ▼ If this is a published work, this date must be the same as or later than the date of publication given in space 3.
Carl Jones   date ▶ October 12, 1985

Handwritten signature (X) ▼
Carl Jones

9 MAIL CERTIFICATE TO

Name ▼
Carl Jones
Number/Street/Apartment Number ▼
555 Routine Dr.
City/State/ZIP ▼
Computer Town USA 22222

Certificate will be mailed in window envelope

Have you:
• Completed all necessary spaces?
• Signed your application in space 8?
• Enclosed check or money order for $10 payable to Register of Copyrights?
• Enclosed your deposit material with the application and fee?

MAIL TO: Register of Copyrights, Library of Congress, Washington, D.C. 20559

* 17 U.S.C. § 506(e): Any person who knowingly makes a false representation of a material fact in the application for copyright registration provided for by section 409, or in any written statement filed in connection with the application, shall be fined not more than $2,500.

☆ U.S. GOVERNMENT PRINTING OFFICE 1983: 421-278/508

Nov. 1983—300,000

J. Database Registration

Carl Jones registers his BUGBITS database (a collection of autoparts information) on Copyright Form TX.

FORM TX
UNITED STATES COPYRIGHT OFFICE

REGISTRATION NUMBER

TX   TXU

EFFECTIVE DATE OF REGISTRATION

Month   Day   Year

DO NOT WRITE ABOVE THIS LINE. IF YOU NEED MORE SPACE, USE A SEPARATE CONTINUATION SHEET.

1

TITLE OF THIS WORK ▼

BUGBITS

PREVIOUS OR ALTERNATIVE TITLES ▼

N.A.

PUBLICATION AS A CONTRIBUTION If this work was published as a contribution to a periodical, serial, or collection, give information about the
collective work in which the contribution appeared.   **Title of Collective Work ▼**

N.A.

If published in a periodical or serial give **Volume ▼**   **Number ▼**   **Issue Date ▼**   **On Pages ▼**

2

NAME OF AUTHOR ▼

a   Carl Jones

DATES OF BIRTH AND DEATH
Year Born ▼   Year Died ▼

1959

Was this contribution to the work a
"work made for hire"?
☐ Yes
☒ No

AUTHOR'S NATIONALITY OR DOMICILE
Name of Country
OR { Citizen of ▶ U.S.A.
{ Domiciled in ▶

**WAS THIS AUTHOR'S CONTRIBUTION TO
THE WORK**
Anonymous?   ☐ Yes ☒ No
Pseudonymous? ☐ Yes ☒ No

If the answer to either
of these questions is
"Yes," see detailed
instructions.

NATURE OF AUTHORSHIP Briefly describe nature of the material created by this author in which copyright is claimed. ▼

Database

NOTE

Under the law,
the "author" of a
"work made for
hire" is generally
the employer,
not the em-
ployee (see in-
structions). For
any part of this
work that was
"made for hire"
check "Yes" in
the space pro-
vided, give the
employer (or
other person for
whom the work
was prepared)
as "Author" of
that part, and
leave the space
for dates of birth
and death blank.

NAME OF AUTHOR ▼

b

DATES OF BIRTH AND DEATH
Year Born ▼   Year Died ▼

Was this contribution to the work a
"work made for hire"?
☐ Yes
☐ No

AUTHOR'S NATIONALITY OR DOMICILE
Name of Country
OR { Citizen of ▶
{ Domiciled in ▶

**WAS THIS AUTHOR'S CONTRIBUTION TO
THE WORK**
Anonymous?   ☐ Yes ☐ No
Pseudonymous? ☐ Yes ☐ No

If the answer to either
of these questions is
"Yes," see detailed
instructions.

NATURE OF AUTHORSHIP Briefly describe nature of the material created by this author in which copyright is claimed. ▼

NAME OF AUTHOR ▼

c

DATES OF BIRTH AND DEATH
Year Born ▼   Year Died ▼

Was this contribution to the work a
"work made for hire"?
☐ Yes
☐ No

AUTHOR'S NATIONALITY OR DOMICILE
Name of Country
OR { Citizen of ▶
{ Domiciled in ▶

**WAS THIS AUTHOR'S CONTRIBUTION TO
THE WORK**
Anonymous?   ☐ Yes ☐ No
Pseudonymous? ☐ Yes ☐ No

If the answer to either
of these questions is
"Yes," see detailed
instructions.

NATURE OF AUTHORSHIP Briefly describe nature of the material created by this author in which copyright is claimed. ▼

3

**YEAR IN WHICH CREATION OF THIS
WORK WAS COMPLETED** This information
must be given
◄ Year   in all cases.

1985

DATE AND NATION OF FIRST PUBLICATION OF THIS PARTICULAR WORK
Complete this information Month ▶ August Day ▶ 10 Year ▶ 1985
ONLY if this work
has been published.   USA   ◄ Nation

4

COPYRIGHT CLAIMANT(S) Name and address must be given even if the claimant is the
same as the author given in space 2. ▼

Carl Jones
555 Routine Dr.
Computer Town, USA 22222

TRANSFER If the claimant(s) named here in space 4 are different from the author(s) named
in space 2, give a brief statement of how the claimant(s) obtained ownership of the copyright. ▼

N.A.

APPLICATION RECEIVED

DO NOT WRITE HERE
ONE DEPOSIT RECEIVED
OFFICE USE ONLY
TWO DEPOSITS RECEIVED

REMITTANCE NUMBER AND DATE

MORE ON BACK ▶ • Complete all applicable spaces (numbers 5-11) on the reverse side of this page.   DO NOT WRITE HERE

EXAMINED BY

CHECKED BY

☐ CORRESPONDENCE
Yes

☐ DEPOSIT ACCOUNT
FUNDS USED

FOR
COPYRIGHT
OFFICE
USE
ONLY

FORM TX

DO NOT WRITE ABOVE THIS LINE. IF YOU NEED MORE SPACE, USE A SEPARATE CONTINUATION SHEET.

5

PREVIOUS REGISTRATION Has registration for this work, or for an earlier version of this work, already been made in the Copyright Office?
☐ Yes ☒ No   If your answer is "Yes," why is another registration being sought? (Check appropriate box) ▼
☐ This is the first published edition of a work previously registered in unpublished form.
☐ This is the first application submitted by this author as copyright claimant.
☐ This is a changed version of the work, as shown by space 6 on this application.
If your answer is "Yes," give: **Previous Registration Number ▼**   **Year of Registration ▼**

6

DERIVATIVE WORK OR COMPILATION Complete both space 6a & 6b for a derivative work; complete only 6b for a compilation.
a. **Preexisting Material** Identify any preexisting work or works that this work is based on or incorporates. ▼

None

See instructions
before completing
this space.

b. **Material Added to This Work** Give a brief, general statement of the material that has been added to this work and in which copyright is claimed. ▼

None

7

MANUFACTURERS AND LOCATIONS If this is a published work consisting preponderantly of nondramatic literary material in English, the law may
require that the copies be manufactured in the United States or Canada for full protection. If so, the names of the manufacturers who performed certain
processes, and the places where these processes were performed must be given. See instructions for details.
Names of Manufacturers ▼   **Places of Manufacture ▼**

N.A.

8

REPRODUCTION FOR USE OF BLIND OR PHYSICALLY HANDICAPPED INDIVIDUALS   A signature on this form at space 10, and a
check in one of the boxes here in space 8, constitutes a non-exclusive grant of permission to the Library of Congress to reproduce and distribute solely for the blind
and physically handicapped and under the conditions and limitations prescribed by the regulations of the Copyright Office: (1) copies of the work identified in space
1 of this application in Braille (or similar tactile symbols); or (2) phonorecords embodying a fixation of a reading of that work; or (3) both.

a ☐ Copies and Phonorecords   b ☐ Copies Only   c ☐ Phonorecords Only

See instructions.

9

DEPOSIT ACCOUNT If the registration fee is to be charged to a Deposit Account established in the Copyright Office, give name and number of Account.
Name ▼   **Account Number ▼**

N.A.

CORRESPONDENCE Give name and address to which correspondence about this application should be sent.   **Name/Address/Apt/City/State/Zip ▼**

Carl Jones
555 Routine Dr.
Computer Town, USA 22222

Area Code & Telephone Number ▶ (888) 555-8888

Be sure to
give your
daytime phone
◄ number

10

CERTIFICATION* I, the undersigned, hereby certify that I am the
Check one ▶
☒ author
☐ other copyright claimant
☐ owner of exclusive rights(s)
☐ authorized agent of _____
Name of author or other copyright claimant or owner of exclusive rights(s) ▲

of the work identified in this application and that the statements made
by me in this application are correct to the best of my knowledge.

Typed or printed name and date ▼ If this is a published work, this date must be the same as or later than the date of publication given in space 3.

Carl Jones   date ▶ August 10, 1985

☞ **Handwritten signature (X) ▼**

Carl Jones

11

**MAIL
CERTIFI-
CATE TO**

Name ▼

Carl Jones

Number/Street/Apartment Number ▼

555 Routine Dr.

City/State/ZIP ▼

Computer Town USA 22222

**Certificate
will be
mailed in
window
envelope**

Have you:
• Completed all necessary
spaces?
• Signed your application in space
10?
• Enclosed check or money order
for $10 payable to Register of
Copyrights?
• Enclosed your deposit material
with the application and fee?

MAIL TO: Register of Copyrights,
Library of Congress, Washington,
D.C. 20559

K. Musical Composition Generated by Computer

Here Carl Jones registers OFFKEY, a musical composition generated by computer which is not yet published. He uses Copyright Form SR.

FORM SR
UNITED STATES COPYRIGHT OFFICE

REGISTRATION NUMBER

SR _____ SRU _____

EFFECTIVE DATE OF REGISTRATION

_____ Month _____ Day _____ Year

DO NOT WRITE ABOVE THIS LINE. IF YOU NEED MORE SPACE, USE A SEPARATE CONTINUATION SHEET.

1 TITLE OF THIS WORK ▼
OFFKEY

PREVIOUS OR ALTERNATIVE TITLES ▼
None

NATURE OF MATERIAL RECORDED ▼ See instructions
☒ Musical ☐ Musical-Dramatic
☐ Dramatic ☐ Literary
☐ Other

2 a NAME OF AUTHOR ▼
Carl Jones

Was this contribution to the work a "work made for hire"?
☐ Yes ☒ No

DATES OF BIRTH AND DEATH
Year Born ▼ 1959 Year Died ▼

AUTHOR'S NATIONALITY OR DOMICILE
Name of Country
OR { Citizen of ▶ USA
Domiciled in ▶

WAS THIS AUTHOR'S CONTRIBUTION TO THE WORK
Anonymous? ☐ Yes ☒ No
Pseudonymous? ☐ Yes ☒ No
If the answer to either of these questions is "Yes," see detailed instructions.

NATURE OF AUTHORSHIP Briefly describe nature of the material created by this author in which copyright is claimed ▼
sound recording

NOTE
Under the law, the "author" of a "work made for hire" is generally the employer, not the employee (see instructions). For any part of this work that was "made for hire" check "Yes" in the space provided, give the employer (or other person for whom the work was prepared) as "Author" of that part, and leave the space for dates of birth and death blank.

b NAME OF AUTHOR ▼

Was this contribution to the work a "work made for hire"?
☐ Yes ☐ No

DATES OF BIRTH AND DEATH
Year Born ▼ Year Died ▼

AUTHOR'S NATIONALITY OR DOMICILE
Name of country
OR { Citizen of ▶
Domiciled in ▶

WAS THIS AUTHOR'S CONTRIBUTION TO THE WORK
Anonymous? ☐ Yes ☐ No
Pseudonymous? ☐ Yes ☐ No

NATURE OF AUTHORSHIP Briefly describe nature of the material created by this author in which copyright is claimed ▼

c NAME OF AUTHOR ▼

Was this contribution to the work a "work made for hire"?
☐ Yes ☐ No

DATES OF BIRTH AND DEATH
Year Born ▼ Year Died ▼

AUTHOR'S NATIONALITY OR DOMICILE
Name of Country
OR { Citizen of ▶
Domiciled in ▶

WAS THIS AUTHOR'S CONTRIBUTION TO THE WORK
Anonymous? ☐ Yes ☐ No
Pseudonymous? ☐ Yes ☐ No

NATURE OF AUTHORSHIP Briefly describe nature of the material created by this author in which copyright is claimed ▼

3 YEAR IN WHICH CREATION OF THIS WORK WAS COMPLETED This information must be given in all cases.
1985 ◀ Year

DATE AND NATION OF FIRST PUBLICATION OF THIS PARTICULAR WORK
Complete this information ONLY if this work has been published.
Month ▶ December Day ▶ 26 Year ▶ 1985
Nation ▶ USA

4 COPYRIGHT CLAIMANT(S) Name and address must be given even if the claimant is the same as the author given in space 2. ▼
Carl Jones
555 Routine Dr.
Computer Town USA 22222

TRANSFER If the claimant(s) named here in space 4 are different from the author(s) named in space 2, give a brief statement of how the claimant(s) obtained ownership of the copyright. ▼
N.A.

MORE ON BACK ▶ • Complete all applicable spaces (numbers 5-9) on the reverse side of this page.
• See detailed instructions. • Sign the form at line 8.

DO NOT WRITE HERE
Page 1 of _____ pages

DO NOT WRITE ABOVE THIS LINE. IF YOU NEED MORE SPACE, USE A SEPARATE CONTINUATION SHEET.

PREVIOUS REGISTRATION Has registration for this work, or for an earlier version of this work, already been made in the Copyright Office?
☐ Yes ☒ No If your answer is "Yes," why is another registration being sought? (Check appropriate box) ▼
☐ This is the first published edition of a work previously registered in unpublished form.
☐ This is the first application submitted by this author as copyright claimant.
☐ This is a changed version of the work, as shown by space 6 on this application.
If your answer is "Yes," give: Previous Registration Number ▼
N.A.
Year of Registration ▼

DERIVATIVE WORK OR COMPILATION Complete both space 6a & 6b for a derivative work; complete only 6b for a compilation.
a. Preexisting Material Identify any preexisting work or works that this work is based on or incorporates. ▼
N.A.

b. Material Added to This Work Give a brief, general statement of the material that has been added to this work and in which copyright is claimed. ▼
N.A.

DEPOSIT ACCOUNT If the registration fee is to be charged to a Deposit Account established in the Copyright Office, give name and number of Account.
Name ▼ N.A.
Account Number ▼

CORRESPONDENCE Give name and address to which correspondence about this application should be sent. Name/Address/Apt/City/State/Zip ▼
Carl Jones
555 Routine Dr.
Computer Town USA 22222

Area Code & Telephone Number ▶ (888) 555-8888

CERTIFICATION* I, the undersigned, hereby certify that I am the
Check one ▼
☒ author
☐ other copyright claimant
☐ owner of exclusive right(s)
☐ authorized agent of _____
Name of author or other copyright claimant, or owner of exclusive right(s) ▲

of the work identified in this application and that the statements made by me in this application are correct to the best of my knowledge.

Typed or printed name and date ▼ If this is a published work, this date must be the same as or later than the date of publication given in space 3.
Carl Jones date ▶ January 12, 1986

Handwritten signature (X) ▼
Carl Jones

MAIL CERTIFICATE TO
Name ▼
Carl Jones
Number/Street/Apartment Number ▼
555 Routine Dr.
City/State/ZIP ▼
Computer Town USA 22222

Certificate will be mailed in window envelope

Here you:
• Completed all necessary spaces?
• Signed your application in space 8?
• Enclosed check or money order for $10 payable to Register of Copyrights?
• Enclosed your deposit material with the application and fee?
MAIL TO: Register of Copyrights, Library of Congress, Washington, D.C. 20559

FOR COPYRIGHT OFFICE USE ONLY

EXAMINED BY

CHECKED BY

CORRESPONDENCE
☐ Yes

DEPOSIT ACCOUNT
FUNDS USED

* 17 U.S.C. § 506(e): Any person who knowingly makes a false representation of a material fact in the application for copyright registration provided for by section 409, or in any written statement filed in connection with the application, shall be fined not more than $2,500.
☆ U.S. GOVERNMENT PRINTING OFFICE: 1982-361-278/63

Sept. 1982—210,000

L. Design Generated by Computer

BCA Graphics wishes to copyright a quilt design Kendra Salone generated for them as a work for hire. She uses Copyright Form VA.

FORM VA
UNITED STATES COPYRIGHT OFFICE

REGISTRATION NUMBER

VA VAU

EFFECTIVE DATE OF REGISTRATION:

Month Day Year

DO NOT WRITE ABOVE THIS LINE. IF YOU NEED MORE SPACE, USE A SEPARATE CONTINUATION SHEET.

1 TITLE OF THIS WORK ▼

MAZE OF COLOR

NATURE OF THIS WORK ▼ See instructions

PREVIOUS OR ALTERNATIVE TITLES ▼

PUBLICATION AS A CONTRIBUTION If this work was published as a contribution to a periodical, serial, or collection, give information about the collective work in which the contribution appeared. **Title of Collective Work ▼**

N.A.

If published in a periodical or serial give **Volume ▼** **Number ▼** **Issue Date ▼** **On Pages ▼**

N.A.

2 NAME OF AUTHOR ▼

a BCA Graphics

DATES OF BIRTH AND DEATH
Year Born ▼ Year Died ▼

N.A.

Was this contribution to the work a "work made for hire"?
☒ Yes
☐ No

AUTHOR'S NATIONALITY OR DOMICILE
Name of Country
OR { Citizen of ▶ USA
{ Domiciled in ▶

WAS THIS AUTHOR'S CONTRIBUTION TO THE WORK
Anonymous? ☐ Yes ☒ No
Pseudonymous? ☐ Yes ☒ No
If the answer to either of these questions is "Yes," see detailed instructions

NATURE OF AUTHORSHIP Briefly describe nature of the material created by this author in which copyright is claimed. ▼
Quilt design

NOTE

Under the law, the "author" of a "work made for hire" is generally the employer, not the employee (see instructions). For any part of this work that was "made for hire" check "Yes" in the space provided, give the employer (or other person for whom the work was prepared) as "Author" of that part, and leave the space for dates of birth and death blank.

NAME OF AUTHOR ▼

b

DATES OF BIRTH AND DEATH
Year Born ▼ Year Died ▼

Was this contribution to the work a "work made for hire"?
☐ Yes
☐ No

AUTHOR'S NATIONALITY OR DOMICILE
Name of country
OR { Citizen of ▶
{ Domiciled in ▶

WAS THIS AUTHOR'S CONTRIBUTION TO THE WORK
Anonymous? ☐ Yes ☐ No
Pseudonymous? ☐ Yes ☐ No
If the answer to either of these questions is "Yes," see detailed instructions

NATURE OF AUTHORSHIP Briefly describe nature of the material created by this author in which copyright is claimed. ▼

NAME OF AUTHOR ▼

c

DATES OF BIRTH AND DEATH
Year Born ▼ Year Died ▼

Was this contribution to the work a "work made for hire"?
☐ Yes
☐ No

AUTHOR'S NATIONALITY OR DOMICILE
Name of Country
OR { Citizen of ▶
{ Domiciled in ▶

WAS THIS AUTHOR'S CONTRIBUTION TO THE WORK
Anonymous? ☐ Yes ☐ No
Pseudonymous? ☐ Yes ☐ No
If the answer to either of these questions is "Yes," see detailed instructions

NATURE OF AUTHORSHIP Briefly describe nature of the material created by this author in which copyright is claimed. ▼

3 YEAR IN WHICH CREATION OF THIS WORK WAS COMPLETED This information must be given in all cases. ▼ Year 1985

DATE AND NATION OF FIRST PUBLICATION OF THIS PARTICULAR WORK
Complete this information ONLY if this work has been published. Month ▶ April Day ▶ 21 Year ▶ 1985 Nation ▶ USA

4 COPYRIGHT CLAIMANT(S) Name and address must be given even if the claimant is the same as the author given in space 2. ▼

BCA Graphics
Technology Circle
Industrial Circle
Big Town, USA 88888

APPLICATION RECEIVED

ONE DEPOSIT RECEIVED

TWO DEPOSITS RECEIVED

REMITTANCE NUMBER AND DATE

DO NOT WRITE HERE
OFFICE USE ONLY

TRANSFER If the claimant(s) named here in space 4 are different from the author(s) named in space 2, give a brief statement of how the claimant(s) obtained ownership of the copyright. ▼

N.A.

See instructions before completing this space

DO NOT WRITE ABOVE THIS LINE. IF YOU NEED MORE SPACE, USE A SEPARATE CONTINUATION SHEET.

5 PREVIOUS REGISTRATION Has registration for this work, or for an earlier version of this work, already been made in the Copyright Office?
☐ Yes ☒ No If your answer is "Yes," why is another registration being sought? (Check appropriate box) ▼
☐ This is the first published edition of a work previously registered in unpublished form.
☐ This is the first application submitted by this author as copyright claimant.
☐ This is a changed version of the work, as shown by space 6 on this application.
If your answer is "Yes," give: **Previous Registration Number ▼** **Year of Registration ▼**

FOR COPYRIGHT OFFICE USE ONLY

6 DERIVATIVE WORK OR COMPILATION Complete both space 6a & 6b for a derivative work; complete only 6b for a compilation.
a. **Preexisting Material** Identify any preexisting work or works that this work is based on or incorporates. ▼

N.A.

b. **Material Added to This Work** Give a brief, general statement of the material that has been added to this work and in which copyright is claimed. ▼

N.A.

See instructions before completing this space

7 DEPOSIT ACCOUNT If the registration fee is to be charged to a Deposit Account established in the Copyright Office, give name and number of Account.
Name ▼ Account Number ▼

N.A.

CORRESPONDENCE Give name and address to which correspondence about this application should be sent. Name/Address/Apt/City/State/Zip ▼

BCA Graphics
Technology Circle
Industrial Circle
Big Town, USA 88888

Area Code & Telephone Number ▶ (777) 555-7777

Be sure to give your daytime phone number

8 CERTIFICATION* I, the undersigned, hereby certify that I am the
Check only one ▼
☒ author
☐ other copyright claimant
☐ owner of exclusive right(s)
☐ authorized agent of
Name of author or other copyright claimant, or owner of exclusive right(s) ▲

of the work identified in this application and that the statements made by me in this application are correct to the best of my knowledge.

Typed or printed name and date ▼ If this is a published work, this date must be the same as or later than the date of publication given in space 3.

BCA Graphics date ▶ May 16, 1985

Handwritten signature (X) ▼
BCA Graphics

9 MAIL CERTIFICATE TO

Name ▼
BCA Graphics
Number/Street/Apartment Number ▼
Technology Circle
City/State/ZIP ▼
Industrial Circle, Bigtown, USA 88888

Certificate will be mailed in window envelope

Have you:
• Completed all necessary spaces?
• Signed your application in space 8?
• Enclosed check or money order for $10 payable to Register of Copyrights?
• Enclosed your deposit material with the application and fee?

MAIL TO: Register of Copyrights, Library of Congress, Washington, D.C. 20559

Index

function of, 66
international, 71
for new versions/editions of works, 72
owner's name, error in, 82-83
  requirement of, 69-70
placement of, 72-76
previously copyrighted material, for works containing, 71-72
publication date, error in, 83
  requirement of, 70-71
on published works, 36, 66-67, 69-71
symbol, error in, 82
  requirement of, 69
Universal Copyright Convention, approved by, 71, 193
on unpublished works, 18, 67-68

O

Omission of copyright notice - see also Notice, copyright
correction of, 83-85
innocent infringement due to, 80, 88, 187
owner's name only, 81
publication date only, 82
registration of copyright after, 85, 88
symbol only, 81
on works published 1978 and before 1978, 78
  after 1978, 78-81
Output, computer
databases as, 9-10
defined, 13
dual registering of, with program, 13, 39, 99
Ownership, copyright - see also Rights, copyright
basic rules of, 29-30
in copyright notice, error in, 82, 83
  omission of, 81
  requirement of, 69-70
derivative works, new code in, 47-48
in employment context, 31
when independent developer working for self, 30
  under contract (work made for hire), 31-34
through inheritance, 60-61, 162
intellectual property law for protection of, 203-204
joint, 30

of new works created by using programs owned by others, 48-52
after pre-development transfer, 34
proof of, 88, 178-179
as property, 57, 60
recordation after transfer of, 165-168
for registration purposes, 131-132, 142-143
transferee, rights of, 163-164

P

Package, software
defined, 6, 8
registration of, Form TX for, 95, 132-148
publication requirement for, 96
Patent protection
copyright and trade secret protections, intersecting, 212-213
process for obtaining, 211
qualifications for, 211
for software, appropriateness of, 211-212
Periodical publications
collected works from, Form GR/CP for registering, 103-104
as protectible works, 38
registration of, Form SE for, 102-103, 132-148
Programs, application
copyright notice on, placement of, 72-74
deposit requirements for registering, 119-125
as protectible works, 37
registration of, Form TX for, 95, 132-148
Publication
date in copyright notice, error in, 83
  omission of, 82
  requirement of, 70-71
date of new registration, establishing, 109
defined, 66-67
registration of software package, requirement for, 96
trade secret protection, and loss of, 208
in Universal Copyright Convention country, first, 192, 198
in U.S. and member countries of Berne Convention, simultaneous, 194-195

About the Author

M.J. Salone is a San Francisco, California private attorney who specializes in computer law. She represents a number of companies and individuals developing software for micro and mini computers. Her practice focuses on software protection and contract negotiations. M.J. began working with computers in 1967, when she was a computer science major at the University of Wisconsin. During her career as a systems analyst, she worked with dozens of types of computers in many different contexts. M.J. graduated from law school in 1978, and has since combined her expertise in computers with her legal knowledge. M.J. teaches computer law at Golden Gate University School of Law.

About the Legal Editor

Steve Elias received a law degree from Hastings College of the Law in 1969. He practiced in California, New York and Vermont until 1983, when he decided to make a full-time career of helping non-lawyers understand the law. Steve is the author of Legal Research: How to Find and Understand the Law (Nolo Press) and The International Dictionary of Intellectual Property Law (due to be published by Nolo Press in early 1985). He is also the legal editor for several other Nolo Press books and has authored magazine and newspaper articles on a variety of topics, including several involving the interface between computers and law. In addition, Steve has taught a variety of legal topics in paralegal institutes, and currently teaches legal research in the Nolo Press Saturday Morning Law School.

About the Illustrator

Mari Stein is a freelance illustrator and writer. Her published work has been eclectic, covering a wide range of subjects: humor, whimsy, health education, juvenile, fables and Yoga. This is her fourth collaboration with Nolo Press; she illustrated 29 Reasons Not To Go To Law School, Author Law and Strategies, and Media Law. She works out of a studio in her Pacific Palisades home, where she lives with her dogs and rabbits, cultivates roses, and teaches Yoga.

nolo

self-help law books

How To Form Your Own California Corporation

By attorney Mancuso. Provides you with all the forms, Bylaws, Articles, minutes of meeting, stock certificates and instructions necessary to form your small profit corporation in California. It includes a thorough discussion of the practical and legal aspects of incorporation, including the tax consequences.

California Edition	$21.95
Texas Edition	$21.95
New York Edition	$19.95

The Non-Profit Corporation Handbook

By attorney Mancuso. Includes all the forms, Bylaws, Articles, minutes, and instructions you need to form a non-profit corporation. Step-by-step instructions on how to choose a name, draft Articles and Bylaws, attain favorable tax status. Thorough information on federal tax exemptions which groups outside of California will find particularly useful.

California Edition $21.95

The California Professional Corporation Handbook

By attorneys Mancuso and Honigsberg. In California there are a number of professions which must fulfill special requirements when forming a corporation. Among them are lawyers, dentists, doctors and other health professionals, accountants, certain social workers. This book contains detailed information on the special requirements of every profession and all the forms and instructions necessary to form a professional corporation.

California Edition $24.95

Billpayers' Rights

By attorneys Honigsberg & Warner. Complete information on bankruptcy, student loans, wage attachments, dealing with bill collectors and collection agencies, credit cards, car repossessions, homesteads, child support and much more.

California Edition $10.95

The Partnership Book

By attorneys Clifford & Warner. When two or more people join to start a small business, one of the most basic needs is to establish a solid, legal partnership agreement. This book supplies a number of sample agreements with the information you will need to use them as is or to modify them to fit your needs. Buy-out clauses, unequal sharing of assets, and limited partnerships are all discussed in detail.

National Edition $17.95

Plan Your Estate: Wills, Probate Avoidance, Trusts & Taxes

By attorney Clifford. Comprehensive information on making a will, alternatives to probate, planning to limit inheritance and estate taxes, living trusts, and providing for family and friends. An explanation of the new Calif. statutory will and usable, tear-out forms are included.

California Edition	$15.95
Texas Edition	$14.95

Chapter 13: The Federal Plan to Repay Your Debts

By attorney Kosel. This book allows an individual to develop and carry out a feasible plan to pay his/her debts in whole over a three-year period. Chapter 13 is an alternative to straight bankruptcy and yet it still means the end of creditor harassment, wage attachments and other collection efforts. Comes complete with all necessary forms and worksheets.

National Edition $12.95

Bankruptcy: Do-It-Yourself

By attorney Kosel. Tells you exactly what bankruptcy is all about and how it affects your credit rating, your property and debts, with complete details on property you can keep under the state and federal exempt property rules. Shows you step-by-step how to do it yourself; comes with all necessary forms and instructions.

National Edition $14.95

Legal Care for Your Software

By attorney Remer. Here we show the software programmer how to protect his/ her work through the use of trade secret, trademark, copyright, patent and, most especially, contractual laws and agreements. This book is full of forms and instructions that give programmers the hands-on information they need.
International Edition $24.95

How to Copyright Software

By attorney Salone. Shows the serious programmer or software developer how to protect his or her programs through the legal device of copyright.
International Edition $21.95

Small-Time Operator

By Bernard Kamoroff, C.P.A. Shows you how to start and operate your small business, keep your books, pay your taxes and stay out of trouble. Comes complete with a year's supply of ledgers and worksheets designed especially for small businesses, and contains invaluable information on permits, licenses, financing, loans, insurance, bank accounts, etc. Published by Bell Springs
National Edition $8.95

Start-Up Money: How to Finance Your Small Business

By Michael McKeever. For anyone about to start a business or revamp an existing one, this book shows how to write a business plan, draft a loan package and find sources of small business finance.
National Edition $17.95

The Patent Book

By Attorney Pressman. Complete instructions on how to do a patent search and file a patent in the U.S. Also covers the simple procedure for filing a U.S. patent if a patent has already been granted in another country. Tear-out forms are included.
Pub. date 1/85 $21.95

Dictionary of Intellectual Property Law

By attorney Elias. Provides functional and contextual definitions for the hundreds of law-related words and phrases commonly used in high technology commerce. This book is a "must" for everyone associated with high technology.
Pub. date 2/85 $19.95

FAMILY & FRIENDS_____

How to Do Your Own Divorce

By attorney Charles Sherman. Now in its tenth edition, this is the original "do your own law" book. It contains tear-out copies of all the court forms required for an uncontested dissolution, as well as instructions for certain special forms--military waiver, pauper's oath, lost summons, and publication of summons.
California Edition $12.95
Texas Edition $12.95

The Living Together Kit

By attorneys Ihara and Warner. A legal guide for unmarried couples with information about buying or sharing property, the Marvin decision, paternity statements, medical emergencies and tax consequences. Contains a sample will and Living Together Contract.
National Edition $14.95

California Marriage & Divorce Law

By attorneys Ihara and Warner. This book contains invaluable information for married couples and those considering marriage on community and separate property, names, debts, children, buying a house, etc. Includes sample marriage contracts, a simple will, probate avoidance information and an explanation of gift and inheritance taxes. Discusses "secret marriage" and "common law" marriage.
California Edition $14.95

Sourcebook for Older Americans

By attorney Matthews. The most comprehensive resource tool on the income, rights & benefits of Americans over 55. Includes detailed information on social security, retirement rights, Medicare, Medicaid, supplemental security income, private pensions, age discrimination, as well as a thorough explanation of the new social security legislation.
National Edition $12.95

After the Divorce: How to Modify Alimony, Child Support and Child Custody

By attorney Matthews. Detailed information on how to increase alimony or child support, decrease what you pay, change custody and visitation, oppose modifications by your ex. Comes with all the forms and instructions you need. Sections on joint custody, mediation.
California Edition $14.95

A Legal Guide for Lesbian/ Gay couples

By attorneys Curry and Clifford. Here is a book that deals specifically with legal matters of lesbian and gay couples: raising children (custody, support, living with a lover), buying property together, wills, etc. and comes complete with sample contracts and agreements.
National Edition $14.95

How to Adopt Your Stepchild

By Frank Zagone. Shows you how to prepare all the legal forms; includes information on how to get the consent of the natural parent and how to conduct an "abandonment" proceeding. Discusses appearing in court, making changes in birth certificates.
California Edition $14.95

RULES & TOOLS

The People's Law Review

Edited by Ralph Warner. This is the first compendium of people's law resources ever published. It celebrates the coming of age of the self-help law movement and contains a 50 state catalog of self-help law materials; articles on mediation and the new "non-adversary" mediation centers, information on self-help law programs and centers (for tenants, artists, battered women, the disabled, etc.); articles and interviews by the leaders of the self-help law movement, and articles dealing with many common legal problems which show people "how to do it themselves."
National Edition $8.95

Author Law

By attorney Bunnin and Beren. A comprehensive explanation of the legal rights of authors. Covers contracts with publishers of books and periodicals, with sample contracts provided. Explains the legal responsibilities between co-authors and with agents, and how to do your own copyright. Discusses royalties, negotiations, libel and invasion of privacy. Includes a glossary of publishing terms.
National Edition $14.95

Legal Research: How to Find and Understand the Law

By attorney Elias. A hands-on guide to unraveling the mysteries of the law library. For paralegals, law students, consumer activists, legal secretaries, business and media people. Shows exactly how to find laws relating to specific cases or legal questions, interpret statutes and regulations, find and research cases, understand case citations and Shepardize them.
National Edition $12.95

The Criminal Records Book

By attorney Siegel. Takes you step-by-step through the procedures available to get your records sealed, destroyed or changed. Detailed discussion on your criminal record--what it is, how it can harm you, how to correct inaccuracies, marijuana possession records & juvenile court records.
California Edition $12.95

California Tenants' Handbook

By attorneys Moskovitz, Warner & Sherman. Discusses everything tenants need to know in order to protect themselves: getting deposits returned, breaking a lease, getting repairs made, using Small Claims Court, dealing with an unscrupulous landlord, forming a tenants' organization, etc. Sample Fair-to-Tenants lease and rental agreements.
California Edition $9.95
Texas Edition $6.95

Everybody's Guide to Small Claims Court

By attorney Warner. Guides you step-by-step through the Small Claims procedure, providing practical information on how to evaluate your case, file and serve papers, prepare and present your case, and, most important, how to collect when you win. Separate chapters focus on common situations (landlord-tenant, automobile sales and repair, etc.).
National Edition $9.95
California Edition $9.95

Media Law: A Legal Handbook for the Working Journalist

By attorney Galvin. This is a practical legal guide for the working journalist (TV, radio and print) and those who desire a better understanding of how the law and journalism intersect. It informs you about censorship, libel and invasion of privacy; how to gain access to public records, including using the Freedom of Information Act; entry to public meetings and courtrooms; dealing with gag orders.
National Edition $14.95

How to Change Your Name

By attorneys Loeb and Brown. Changing one's name is a very simple procedure. Using this book, people can file the necessary papers themselves, saving $200 to $300 in attorney's fees. Comes complete with all forms and instructions for the court petition method or the simpler usage method.
California Edition $14.95

Homestead Your House

By attorney Warner. Under the California Homestead Act, you can file a Declaration of Homestead and thus protect your home from being sold to satisfy most debts. This book explains this simple and inexpensive procedure and includes all the forms and instructions. Contains information on exemptions for mobile homes and houseboats.
California Edition $8.95

Your Family Records: How to Preserve Personal, Financial and Legal History

By Pladsen and attorney Clifford. Helps you organize and record all sorts of items that will affect you and your family when death or disability occur, e.g., where to find your will and deed to the house. Includes information about probate avoidance, joint ownership of property, genealogical research, and space is provided for financial & legal records.
National Edition $12.95

Fight Your Ticket

By attorney Brown. A comprehensive manual on how to fight your traffic ticket. Radar, drunk driving, preparing for court, arguing your case to a judge, cross-examining witnesses are all covered.
California Edition $12.95

Marijuana: Your Legal Rights

By attorney Moller. Here is the legal information needed to guarantee constitutional rights and protect privacy and property. Discusses what the laws are, how they differ from state to state, and how legal loopholes can be used against smokers and growers.
National Edition $9.95

Write, Edit & Print

By Donald McCunn. Word processing with personal computers. A complete how-to manual including: evaluation of equipment, 4 fully annotated programs, operating instructions, sample application.
525 pages $24.95

Computer Programming for the Complete Idiot

By Donald McCunn. An introduction to programming your P.C. in BASIC. Hardware & software are explained in everyday language & the last chapter gives information on creating original programs. $6.95

How to Become a United States Citizen

By Sally Abel. Detailed explanation of the naturalization process. Includes step-by-step instructions from filing for naturalization to the final oath of allegiance. Includes study guide on U.S. history & government. Text is written in both English and Spanish.
National Edition $9.95

Landlording

By Leigh Robinson (Express Press). Written for the conscientious landlord or landlady, this comprehensive guide discusses maintenance and repairs, getting good tenants, how to avoid evictions, record keeping and taxes.
National Edition $15.00

The Eviction Book for California

By Leigh Robinson (Express Press). Here are suggestions for preventing evictions and, if that fails, instructions for scrupulous landlords/landladies who want to handle evictions themselves for non-payment of rent, reach of contract, waste, nuisance, unlawful acts or failure to vacate. Forms included.
National Edition $13.50

Murder on the Air

By Ralph Warner & Toni Ihara. An unconventional murder mystery set in Berkeley, California. When a noted environmentalist and anti-nuclear activist is killed at a local radio station, the Berkeley violent crime squad swings into action. James Rivers, an unplugged lawyer, and Sara Tamura, Berkeley's first female murder squad detective, lead the chase. The action is fast, furious & fun. $5.95

29 Reasons Not To Go To Law School

A humorous and irreverent look at the dubious pleasures of going to law school. By attorneys Ihara and Warner, with contributions by fellow lawyers and illustrations by Mari Stein. $6.95

How to Copyright Software

Attorney M.J. Salone

The only book of its kind. Covers the important, trend-setting protections afforded to mass-marketed software by U.S. copyright law. This information will be of particular interest to those concerned with developing protections in their respective countries, as well as to software developers and producers who wish to market their products in the U.S. Designed to be used both by those who know computers well but have little or no legal training, and by lawyers who are strangers to the world of computers.

Approx. 250 pp.   Pub date: 11/84 $21.95

The Patent Book: How to Patent Your Work in the U.S.

Attorney David Pressman

Complete instructions on how to do a patent search and file a patent in the United States. Also covers the simple procedure for filing for a U.S. patent if a patent has already been granted in another country. Tear-out forms are included.

Approx. 175 pp.   Pub. date: 1/85 $21.95

Dictionary of Intellectual Property Law

Attorney Stephen Elias

Provides functional and contextual definitions for the hundreds of law-related words and phrases commonly used in high technology commerce. This book is a necessity for every person associated with high technology pursuits.

Because of the predominant use of English in international intellectual property law dealings, we are primarily interested in proposals to publish the dictionary in bi-lingual editions.

Approx. 275 pp.   Pub. date: 2/85 $19.95

Legal Care for Your Software
International Edition

Attorney Daniel Remer

How to protect software through trade secret, trademark, copyright, patents, contracts and agreements, with a chapter on international applicability of these protections. Contains forms, examples and instructions. Highly recommended by **Byte, Interface Age,** and other major computer magazines. $24.95

Remer writes clearly and with copious amounts of common sense. It's hard to imagine a more useful or less intimidating guide to the legal complexities of protecting software.

Byte Magazine

Write to: Nolo Press
950 Parker St.
Berkeley, CA 94710
U.S.A.
Tel. (415) 549-1976

Order Form

QUANTITY	TITLE	UNIT PRICE	TOTAL

Prices subject to change

☐ Please send me a catalogue of your books

Tax: (California only) 6½% for Bart, Los Angeles, San Mateo & Santa Clara counties; 6% for all others

Name_____

Address_____

_____

☐ I am <u>not</u> on Nolo's mailing list and would like to be. (If you receive the NOLO NEWS you <u>are</u> on the list and need not check the box.)

SUBTOTAL _____

Tax _____

Postage & Handling $1.00

TOTAL _____

Send to:

NOLO PRESS
950 Parker St.
Berkeley, CA 94710
or

NOLO DISTRIBUTING
Box 544
Occidental, CA 95465